Southern Living
Homestyle Cooking

Southern Living®
Homestyle Cooking

Oxmoor House®

©2002 by Oxmoor House, Inc.
Book Division of Southern Progress Corporation
P.O. Box 2463, Birmingham, Alabama 35201

Southern Living® is a federally registered trademark belonging to Southern Living, Inc.

Library of Congress Catalog Number: 2002-141307
ISBN: 0-8487-2519-0
Printed in the United States of America
First Printing 2002

Editor-in-Chief: Nancy Fitzpatrick Wyatt
Executive Editor: Susan Carlisle Payne
Art Director: Cynthia R. Cooper

Southern Living Homestyle Cooking

Editor: Julie Gunter
Copy Chief: Catherine Ritter Scholl
Copy Editor: Donna Baldone
Editorial Assistant: Jane Lorberau Gentry
Photographer: Brit Huckabay
Contributing Photographers: Jim Bathie, Tina Cornett,
William Dickey, Becky Luigart-Stayner,
Charles Walton IV
Photo Stylist: Ashley J. Wyatt
Contributing Photo Stylists: Cindy Manning Barr,
Kay E. Clarke, Buffy Hargett
Director, Test Kitchens: Elizabeth Tyler Luckett
Assistant Director, Test Kitchens: Julie Christopher
Recipe Editor: Gayle Hays Sadler
Test Kitchens Staff: Jennifer A. Cofield; Gretchen P. Feldtman, R. D.;
David Gallent; Ana Price Kelly; Kathleen Royal Phillips; Jan A. Smith
Publishing Systems Administrator: Rick Tucker
Director, Production and Distribution: Phillip Lee
Books Production Manager: Theresa L. Beste
Production Assistant: Faye Porter Bonner

Contributors:
Designer: Rita Yerby
Indexer: Mary Ann Laurens
Editorial Intern: McCharen Pratt
Nutrition Editor: Carolyn Land, R.D., L.D.

To order additional publications, call 1-205-445-6560.

For more books to enrich your life, visit
oxmoorhouse.com

Cover: Fudge Pecan Ripple Layer Cake (p. 172)
Back Cover, clockwise from top right: Salsa Eggs (p. 138); Southwestern Casserole (p. 64); Streusel Shortcake (p. 386);
Grilled Apple and Cheese Sandwiches (p. 292) and Brunswick Stew (p. 311); Chicken Salad (p. 289);
Hearty Mint Juleps (p. 106) and Cheese Straws (p. 87); Fried Okra (p. 20); Family Dinner (p. 365); Apple-Walnut Cake (p. 169);
Country-Fried Steak with Cream Gravy (p. 210); Mashed Potatoes with Shallots, Goat Cheese, and Herbs (p. 342);
Summer Squash and Cherry Tomatoes in Basil Butter (p. 49)

Contents

A Homestyle Welcome

*W*e Southerners take great pride in our colorful culinary heritage. Down-home goodness combined with gracious hospitality creates a cuisine that is rich and abiding. So how is Southern homestyle cooking best described? Perhaps it's a plate piled high with crispy fried chicken for Sunday dinner, or the aroma of freshly baked chocolate chip cookies, or cornbread sizzling in a cast-iron skillet, or just a tall glass of tea. All of these images evoke memories of food we grew up with, and they nurture the cook within.

We invite you to experience firsthand, *Southern Living® Homestyle Cooking,* a treasury of family-style comfort food, guaranteed to enhance mealtime around the table. You'll find authentic Southern-style recipes from Fried Green Tomatoes to Peach Cobbler in our "Taste of the South" chapter. You wouldn't believe the staff controversy over choosing 10 favorite Southern foods to feature. Some folks really took it to heart when we had to forego barbecue, shrimp, and sweet potatoes.

Elsewhere in the book you'll find Quick & Easy recipes, Healthy Homestyle favorites, and menus for busy weeknights as well as casual entertaining. A little something for everyone—every day of the week.

Southern homestyle cooking summons you to take your time with a meal and enjoy the company. Social occasions such as church picnics, barbecues, fish fries, showers, and teas all revolve around plenty of good food and gracious, easy entertaining. We invite you to try the recipes on the following pages and to celebrate the down-home goodness and legacy of the Southern table.

The Editors

Taste of the South

Fried Green Tomatoes,
page 21

Fried

When Southerners speak of their fondness for fried catfish, opinions abound on how to cook it and what goes with it.

Fish Tips

■ Remove excess moisture from fish before dredging.

■ Keep 1 hand clean for dredging and the other hand available for frying.

■ Use a Dutch oven or deep cast-iron skillet to keep the hot oil from popping out.

■ Don't overcrowd the skillet; fry in batches 2 fillets at a time. Bring remaining oil back to the proper temperature before frying the next batch.

■ Remove fish from skillet with a wide, slotted, curved spoon.

■ To keep fried fish warm, place on a wire rack with an aluminum foil-lined pan underneath; place in a 250° oven. For a crisp texture, do not cover fillets.

■ If you purchase frozen fillets, place them in a colander with a pan underneath, and thaw in the refrigerator overnight; otherwise, keep them in the coldest part of your refrigerator, and use within 2 days.

*W*hen it comes to the Southern delicacy of fried catfish, the very words evoke a flood of personal memories for our Foods staff. In searching for the perfect fried catfish recipe, we tried a variety of techniques. The more we sampled, the more we realized that it's hard to beat what you grew up eating.

When we whipped up our Classic Fried Catfish recipe, it didn't stay on the table long. We relished it hot from the skillet and even continued munching at room temperature. What made it so popular? The cornmeal offered a crunchy texture without a greasy taste.

Enhance these crisp fillets with your favorite side dishes. And as for condiments, Ed Scott, a retired catfish farmer from Mississippi says, "The No. 1 item for catfish is hot sauce." For us, though, a dab of ketchup and tartar sauce and a squeeze of lemon were also high on the list.

Catfish

◀ Classic Fried Catfish

Our Test Kitchens found 4- to 6-ounce, thin-cut fillets easy to manage in the skillet, and they curl up when cooked, giving great eye appeal.

¾ cup yellow cornmeal
¼ cup all-purpose flour
2 teaspoons salt
1 teaspoon ground red pepper
¼ teaspoon garlic powder
6 (4- to 6-ounce) farm-raised
    catfish fillets
¼ teaspoon salt
Vegetable oil

COMBINE first 5 ingredients in a large shallow dish. Sprinkle fish with ¼ teaspoon salt; dredge in cornmeal mixture, coating evenly.

POUR oil to a depth of 1½ inches into a deep cast-iron skillet; heat to 350°. Fry fish, in batches, 5 to 6 minutes or until golden; drain on paper towels. Yield: 6 servings.

Farm-Raised Fish

Farm-raised catfish is growing in reputation, thanks to aquaculture, the practice of farming fish in a controlled environment. The catfish are raised in freshwater, where they eat grain and feed from the surface of the water. This controlled environment, in contrast to a natural lake, yields catfish with a mild flavor and desirable firm texture that are harvested year-round. As a result, chefs and home cooks alike are inspired to look at catfish with fresh ideas in mind.

Here are some favorite side dishes to enhance the crispy fillets.

Tartar Sauce

1 cup mayonnaise
1 tablespoon dill pickle relish
1 tablespoon chopped pimiento-
    stuffed olives
1 tablespoon capers
1 tablespoon grated shallots
1 tablespoon lemon juice
⅛ to ¼ teaspoon hot sauce

STIR together all ingredients. Cover and chill sauce 2 hours. Yield: 1¼ cups.

Coleslaw

2 cups mayonnaise
¼ cup sugar
¼ cup Dijon mustard
¼ cup cider vinegar
1½ to 2 tablespoons celery seeds
1 teaspoon salt
⅛ teaspoon pepper
1 medium cabbage, shredded
2 carrots, grated
1 green bell pepper, diced
2 tablespoons grated onion

STIR together first 7 ingredients in a large bowl; add cabbage and remaining ingredients, tossing gently.

COVER and chill 3 to 4 hours; serve with a slotted spoon. Yield: 12 servings.

LaJuan Coward
Jasper, Texas

Hush Puppies

Bacon drippings add extra flavor to these Hush Puppies.

1½ cups self-rising white
    cornmeal
½ cup all-purpose flour
½ teaspoon baking powder
1 small onion, diced (optional)*
1½ teaspoons sugar
1 cup plus 2 tablespoons
    buttermilk
1 tablespoon bacon drippings
Vegetable oil

COMBINE first 5 ingredients in a large bowl; make a well in center of mixture.

ADD buttermilk and bacon drippings to dry ingredients, stirring just until dry ingredients are moistened.

POUR oil to a depth of 2 inches into a large Dutch oven; heat oil to 350°.

DROP batter by tablespoonfuls into oil, and fry in batches 3 minutes on each side or until golden. Drain on paper towels. Yield: 2 dozen.

*NOTE: ½ teaspoon onion powder may be substituted for onion.

Corn

Just-picked corn and its many possibilities, such as Tee's Corn Pudding (below), are sweet reminders to us to savor the summer months.

*S*erve golden sweet corn pudding the next time you're looking for a side dish that offers old-fashioned Southern appeal. The most delicious corn pudding relies on the ripest corn, so don't be tempted to buy it out of season. Corn's peak season falls between May and September. Take your cue to purchase corn when it appears at your local farmers market.

Look for corn with bright green husks and golden brown silk. The kernels should be small and in straight, evenly spaced rows with no signs of mold or decay. To check for ripeness, puncture a kernel with your thumbnail. If a milky liquid spurts out, it's ready for eating. Purists insist that corn is best eaten as soon as it's picked.

Often described as the most immediate of vegetables, corn has a high sugar content that converts to starch quickly after harvest, making a less flavorful, starchier vegetable the longer it's not used. But if you don't have the luxury of enjoying it straight from the field, wrap the ears, unhusked, in moist paper towels, and place in a zip-top plastic bag; refrigerate up to 2 days.

Pudding

◄ Tee's Corn Pudding

Aah...corn pudding. That creamy sweet custard of eggs, milk, and sugar that envelops fresh corn—a sign that summer is in full swing.

¼ cup sugar
3 tablespoons all-purpose flour
2 teaspoons baking powder
1½ teaspoons salt
6 large eggs
2 cups whipping cream
½ cup butter or margarine, melted
6 cups fresh corn kernels (about 12 ears)*

COMBINE first 4 ingredients.

WHISK together eggs, whipping cream, and butter. Gradually add sugar mixture, whisking until smooth; stir in corn. Pour mixture into a lightly greased 13- x 9-inch baking dish.

BAKE at 350° for 45 minutes or until golden brown and set. Let stand 5 minutes. Yield: 8 servings.

*6 cups frozen whole kernel corn or canned shoepeg corn, drained, may be substituted.

NOTE: For testing purposes only, we used "Silver Queen" corn.

Southwestern Corn Pudding

STIR 1 (4.5-ounce) can drained chopped green chiles and ¼ teaspoon ground cumin in with eggs in the recipe above.

Take your cue to purchase corn when it appears at your local farmers market.

Creamed Corn

¼ cup butter or margarine
2½ cups fresh corn kernels
½ cup milk
1 tablespoon cornstarch
1 tablespoon sugar
½ teaspoon salt

MELT butter in a large skillet over medium heat; stir in corn kernels and milk. Sprinkle with cornstarch, sugar, and salt; stir well.

BRING mixture to a boil, stirring constantly. Reduce heat, and simmer, stirring constantly, 10 to 12 minutes. Serve hot. Yield: 4 servings.

Dori Sanders
Dori Sanders' Country Cooking
(Algonquin Books of Chapel Hill)

Buttermilk Fried Corn

3 cups fresh corn kernels
2¼ cups buttermilk
1 cup all-purpose flour
1 cup cornmeal
1 teaspoon salt
1½ teaspoons pepper
Corn oil

STIR together corn and buttermilk; let stand 30 minutes. Drain.

COMBINE flour and next 3 ingredients in a large heavy-duty zip-top plastic bag. Add corn to flour mixture, a small amount at a time, and shake bag to coat.

POUR oil to a depth of 1 inch in a Dutch oven; heat to 375°. Fry corn, in small batches, 2 minutes or until golden. Drain on paper towels. Serve immediately. Yield: 3 cups.

Fresh Corn

Some experts say yellow corn has a fuller flavor than white corn, but "Silver Queen," a popular white variety, wins the affection of many Southerners. There are other hybrids of sweet corn such as "Silver King" and "Supersweet" on farm stands. The most important factor is to buy local corn for optimum freshness and to eat it ASAP.

Black-Eyed Peas

You might call them soul mates—the humble, nutritious black-eyed pea and the savory quick bread made from corn. On a chilly day, a steaming bowl of peas served with a wedge of fresh-from-the-oven cornbread is simple Southern goodness.

Both foods are inexpensive standbys that have evolved with the times. Cooks use them in inventive dishes; black-eyed peas show up in salads and fritters, and cornbread dotted with herbs is used to stuff everything.

Peas come fresh, frozen, dried, and canned—take your pick. We prefer fresh or dried, which require up to an hour of cooking time. In a pinch, however, canned black-eyed peas doctored with chopped country ham or smoked sausage make a respectable 10-minute substitute.

Cornbread mixes vary in the color of cornmeal used (white is traditional), in flavor, and in texture. Cornbread can be a sturdy, savory round with a rich butter-milk twang or sweet and crumbly with a cakelike texture. Both the humble, hearty peas and crisp bread from a skillet make a great addition to almost any meal.

& Cornbread

Peas and cornbread are like old friends who never tire of each other.

◄ Hearty Black-Eyed Peas

1 (16-ounce) package dried
    black-eyed peas
4 cups water
1 medium onion, chopped
½ teaspoon pepper
¾ teaspoon salt
1 (1-pound) ham steak, cut into
    ½-inch cubes, or
    1 ham hock
4 whole jalapeño peppers
    (optional)

BRING first 6 ingredients and, if desired, jalapeños to a boil in a Dutch oven; cover, reduce heat, and simmer 1 hour or until peas are tender. Yield: 8 servings.

Here are a few of our favorite good ol' crispy Southern cornbread recipes.

Buttermilk Cornbread

2 tablespoons vegetable oil or
    shortening
1 cup yellow or white cornmeal
1 tablespoon all-purpose flour
1½ teaspoons baking powder
¼ teaspoon baking soda
¼ teaspoon salt
1 cup buttermilk
1 large egg

HEAT oil in an 8-inch cast-iron skillet or muffin pans in a 450° oven 5 minutes.

COMBINE cornmeal and next 4 ingredients in a medium bowl; make a well in center of mixture.

STIR together buttermilk and egg; add to dry ingredients, stirring just until moistened. Pour into hot skillet.

BAKE at 450° for 20 minutes or until golden. Yield: 6 to 8 servings.

Mary Lynn Hanily
Tuscaloosa, Alabama

Hot-Water Cornbread

2 cups white cornmeal
¼ teaspoon baking powder
1¼ teaspoons salt
1 teaspoon sugar
¼ cup half-and-half
1 tablespoon vegetable oil
1 to 2 cups boiling water
Vegetable oil
Softened butter

COMBINE first 4 ingredients in a bowl; stir in half-and-half and 1 tablespoon oil. Gradually add boiling water, stirring until batter is the consistency of grits.

POUR oil to a depth of ½ inch into a large heavy skillet; place over medium-high heat. Scoop batter into a ¼-cup measure; drop into hot oil, and fry in batches 3 minutes on each side or until golden. Drain on paper towels. Serve with softened butter. Yield: 1 dozen.

NOTE: The amount of boiling water needed varies depending on the type of cornmeal used. Stone-ground (coarsely ground) cornmeal requires more liquid.

Corn Sticks

2 jalapeño peppers, seeded
    and chopped
2 garlic cloves, minced
⅓ cup vegetable oil
½ cup yellow cornmeal
½ cup all-purpose flour
2 teaspoons baking powder
¾ teaspoon salt
1 tablespoon sugar
1 large egg, lightly beaten
½ cup milk

COOK jalapeño peppers and garlic in oil in a saucepan over medium heat, stirring constantly, until tender; set aside.

COMBINE cornmeal and next 4 ingredients; add jalapeño pepper mixture, egg, and milk, stirring until smooth.

COAT a cast-iron breadstick or corn stick pan with cooking spray; heat in a 425° oven 3 minutes or until hot. Remove pan from oven; spoon batter into pan. Bake at 425° for 15 to 20 minutes or until lightly browned. Yield: 8 breadsticks or 6 corn sticks.

Fried

Crispy fried chicken is simple food that goes to the heart of what's good about the South.

Frying Matters

■ When frying chicken, we prefer to use a cast-iron skillet, because it maintains a consistent temperature.

■ Fry in batches; too many pieces crowd the skillet, lower the oil temperature, and increase grease absorption.

■ How you prepare chicken before frying affects the end result. If you have a little lead time, try the first recipe (opposite page) that soaks chicken 8 hours in a salt water solution. This technique, called brining, produces the juiciest fried chicken around. The quicker recipe that follows it forgoes the soaking step in favor of a dip in a milk and egg mixture before breading.

■ And what to fry it in? Vegetable oil is a good, all-purpose frying oil. Some recipes add bacon grease for old-fashioned flavor, while some use shortening, an old secret Southerners say produces extra crispy results.

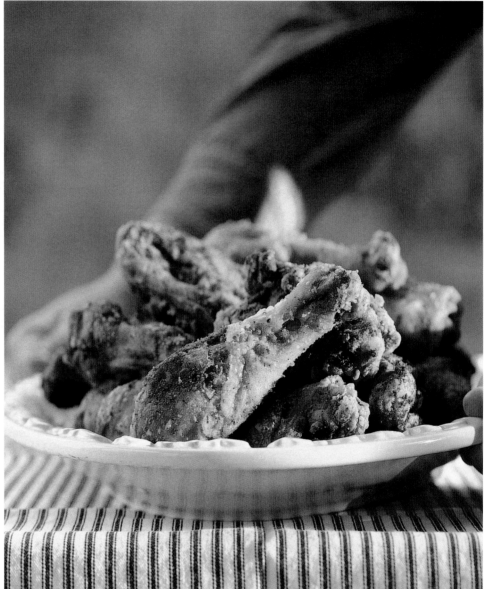

*S*alt, pepper, flour, and a skillet of hot grease turn plain poultry into crispy paradise. It's the simple things in life that give us the greatest pleasure. And fried chicken is an eating experience that lingers. It appears on the menu at most Southern picnics and on Grandma's table for Sunday dinner. How you eat it is almost as important as how you cook it. It's a delicious hands-on activity— all you need are a pile of napkins and a big appetite. And please leave the skin on—it's perhaps the best part of all.

Chicken

◄ Our Best Southern Fried Chicken

3 quarts water
1 tablespoon salt
1 (2½-pound) whole chicken, cut up
1 teaspoon salt
1 teaspoon pepper
1 cup all-purpose flour
2 cups vegetable oil
¼ cup bacon drippings

COMBINE 3 quarts water and 1 tablespoon salt in a large bowl; add chicken. Cover and chill 8 hours.

Drain chicken; rinse with cold water, and pat dry. Combine 1 teaspoon salt and pepper; sprinkle half of mixture over chicken.

COMBINE remaining salt and pepper mixture and flour in a large heavy-duty zip-top plastic bag. Place 2 pieces of chicken in bag; seal. Shake to coat. Remove chicken; repeat procedure with remaining chicken, 2 pieces at a time.

COMBINE oil and bacon drippings in a 12-inch cast-iron skillet or chicken fryer; heat to 360°. Add chicken, a few pieces at a time, skin side down. Cover and cook 6 minutes; uncover and cook 9 minutes.

TURN pieces; cover and cook 6 minutes. Uncover and cook 5 to 9 minutes, turning pieces during the last 3 minutes for even browning, if necessary. Drain on paper towels; keep warm. Yield: 4 servings.

NOTE: For best results, keep the oil temperature between 300° to 325°. Substitute 2 cups buttermilk for the saltwater solution, if desired.

Picnic Fried Chicken

2 (2-pound) whole chickens, cut up
2 cups milk
1 large egg
2 cups all-purpose flour
2 tablespoons salt
2 teaspoons pepper
3 cups shortening
2 teaspoons salt

RINSE chicken with cold water; pat dry, and set aside.

WHISK together milk and egg in a bowl. Combine flour, 2 tablespoons salt, and pepper in a heavy-duty zip-top plastic bag.

DIP 2 chicken pieces in milk mixture. Place in plastic bag; seal and shake to coat. Remove chicken; repeat procedure with remaining pieces.

MELT shortening in a Dutch oven over medium heat; heat to 350°. Fry chicken, in batches, 10 minutes on each side or until done and golden brown. Drain on paper towels. Sprinkle evenly with 2 teaspoons salt. Yield: 6 servings.

Fried Right

Don't let times and temperatures discourage you. Get the oil sizzling hot, but not smoking. Ease no more than 4 large, floured pieces into hot oil at a time. Fry until cooked through, evenly browned and crisp, using tongs to turn. You may need to test a wing for doneness (one of the perks of being the cook).

Stuffed Eggs

Stuffed Eggs seem the perfect match for picnic fried chicken. These eggs are like those Grandma used to make—guaranteed to go fast at a family reunion.

6 large hard-cooked eggs
¼ cup mayonnaise
1½ tablespoons sweet pickle relish
1 teaspoon prepared mustard
⅛ teaspoon salt
Dash of pepper
Paprika
6 pimiento-stuffed olives, halved

SLICE eggs in half lengthwise, and carefully remove yolks. Mash yolks with mayonnaise. Add relish and next 3 ingredients; stir well.

SPOON or pipe yolk mixture into egg whites. Sprinkle with paprika, and top each with an olive half. Yield: 6 servings.

Peach

Peach Pointers

■ A deep gold or yellow skin and a strong, perfumy aroma are the signs of a ripe peach. Underripe peaches are hard and have a green tinge.

■ Try not to squeeze a peach to check ripeness; that bruises the flesh.

■ Peaches are an easy fruit to store. Simply display them in a bowl on your kitchen table; check for ripeness daily.

■ For the fullest flavor, serve ripe peaches at room temperature.

■ Peaches typically fall into 2 categories: clingstone, where the flesh clings to the pit; and freestone, where the pit easily pulls away from the flesh. Distinguishing between them is hard without cutting them open.

*S*outhern summers bring ripe, juicy peaches to roadside stands, farmers markets, and the kitchen table. And while there is nothing more American than apple pie, there is nothing more Southern than peach cobbler—topped with ice cream, of course.

Cobbler is casual food. Some desserts, like this peach-laden delight, just have a way of making guests feel right at home.

No question about it, fruit cobblers fall into the comfort food category. They're just a bit more rustic than other desserts.

The best peach dishes start with top-quality fruit. Look for peaches with a creamy to gold undercolor; better yet, smell them instead. Scent is the best indicator of ripeness. If a peach smells like a peach, you've got a keeper. And when cooking, it will help to remember that 4 medium peaches equals 2 cups of slices.

Cobbler

◄ Peach Cobbler

8 cups sliced fresh peaches
    (about 5 pounds peaches)
2 cups sugar
¼ cup all-purpose flour
½ teaspoon ground nutmeg
1 teaspoon vanilla extract
⅓ cup butter or margarine
Pastry for double-crust
    9-inch pie (at right)

COMBINE first 4 ingredients in a Dutch oven; set aside until syrup forms. Bring peach mixture to a boil; reduce heat to low, and cook 10 minutes or until tender. Remove from heat; add vanilla and butter, stirring until butter melts.

ROLL half of pastry to ⅛-inch thickness on a lightly floured surface; cut into a 9-inch square. Spoon half of peaches into a lightly buttered 9-inch square pan; top with pastry square.

BAKE at 475° for 12 minutes or until lightly browned. Spoon remaining peaches over baked pastry square.

ROLL remaining pastry to ⅛-inch thickness, and cut into 1-inch strips; arrange in lattice design over peaches. Bake 15 to 18 more minutes or until browned.

SPOON cobbler into serving bowls, and top each with ice cream, if desired. Yield: 8 servings.

Double-Crust Pastry

2 cups all-purpose flour
1 teaspoon salt
⅔ cup plus 2 tablespoons
    shortening
4 to 5 tablespoons ice water

COMBINE flour and salt; cut in shortening with a pastry blender until mixture is crumbly. Sprinkle ice water, 1 tablespoon at a time, evenly over surface; stir with a fork until dry ingredients are moistened. Shape into a ball; chill until ready to use. Roll and fit pastry into pan as recipe directs. Yield: 8 servings.

Peach Crisp

4 cups sliced fresh or frozen
    peaches
¾ cup sugar, divided
½ teaspoon ground cinnamon
1 cup all-purpose flour
½ cup butter or margarine

TOSS peaches, ⅓ cup sugar, and cinnamon in a large bowl; spoon into a lightly greased 8-inch square baking dish or a 9-inch deep-dish pieplate, and set aside.

COMBINE flour and remaining sugar; cut in butter with a pastry blender until mixture is crumbly. Sprinkle on top of peaches. Bake at 375° for 35 to 40 minutes. Yield: 6 to 8 servings.

Betty Mitchell
Little Rock, Arkansas

Peach Jam

3 pounds fresh peaches
1 (1¾-ounce) package
    powdered pectin
2 tablespoons lemon juice
5 cups sugar
½ teaspoon whole allspice

PEEL, pit, and coarsely mash peaches to measure 4 cups. Combine peaches, pectin, and lemon juice in a Dutch oven; bring to a boil over high heat, stirring constantly. Stir in sugar and allspice; return to a boil, and cook, stirring constantly, 1 minute. Remove from heat; skim off foam.

QUICKLY ladle hot mixture into hot sterilized jars, filling to ¼ inch from top. Remove air bubbles; wipe jar rims. Cover at once with metal lids, and screw on bands. Process in boiling-water bath 5 minutes. Yield: 6 half pints.

Azine G. Rush
Monroe, Louisiana

Grits

Some folks call pearly grits the "potatoes of the South."

This Grain Has Grit

■ Instant, quick, and regular grits have the germ removed, giving them a long shelf life. Stone-ground grits contain the oily germ, requiring storage in either the refrigerator or freezer.

■ Scholars argue that grits were America's first food. Based on the fact that the Powhatan Indians (of the Tidewater area of Virginia) served the earliest Virginia settlers a hot substance made from ground corn, they just might be right. In any case, grits certainly have been a part of Southern cooking for centuries.

*T*hrough the years grits have been the workhorse of the Southern table. Enlisted to fill plates when more expensive ingredients were scarce, grits also acted as a foundation for flavorful items such as gravy, hash, and eggs. In the past decade or so, grits have experienced a renaissance. Chefs are incorporating them into high-style dishes of all kinds. Yet some folks outside the South still wonder just what grits are.

Commercially produced grits are made from ground, degerminated, dried white or yellow corn kernels that have been soaked in a solution of water and lye. The only grits for purists are produced by the old-fashioned method of stone grinding with a water-turned stone. These grits retain a natural texture and rich flavor.

Most folks enjoy grits made with more than just water, salt, and pepper. We're showcasing traditional Creamy Grits and topping them with either Tomato Gravy or pairing them with Country Ham and Redeye Gravy for an authentic and delicious Deep South twist.

◀ Creamy Grits

2 cups milk
2 cups water
1 to 1½ teaspoons salt
1 cup uncooked regular grits
1 cup whipping cream
¼ cup butter or margarine
1 to 2 teaspoons freshly ground
    pepper

BRING first 3 ingredients to a boil in a large saucepan; gradually stir in grits. Reduce heat; simmer, stirring occasionally, 30 to 40 minutes or until thickened.

STIR in whipping cream, butter, and pepper; simmer, stirring occasionally, 5 minutes. Yield: 6 servings.

NOTE: For thinner grits, stir in more milk. To lighten, use 1% milk, fat-free half-and-half for cream, and reduce butter to 2 tablespoons.

Pair Creamy Grits
with either of these
gravies.

Country Ham With Redeye Gravy

2 cups hot strong brewed coffee
¼ cup firmly packed light
    brown sugar
1 pound center-cut country
    ham slices

STIR together coffee and sugar.

COOK ham in a large cast-iron skillet over medium heat 5 minutes on each side or until browned. Remove ham; reserve drippings in skillet.

ADD coffee mixture to skillet, stirring to loosen particles from bottom; bring to a boil. Boil, stirring occasionally, until reduced by half (about 15 minutes). Serve with ham. Yield: 6 servings.

Tomato Gravy

2 tablespoons butter or
    margarine
2 tablespoons minced shallots
    or onion
1 (14½-ounce) can diced
    tomatoes, undrained
½ cup whipping cream
1 teaspoon chicken bouillon
    granules
½ teaspoon sugar
¼ teaspoon pepper

MELT butter in a large skillet over medium heat; add shallots, and sauté until tender. Stir in tomatoes; bring to a boil. Reduce heat, and simmer, stirring constantly, 2 to 3 minutes.

STIR in whipping cream and remaining ingredients; simmer, stirring often, 3 minutes or until mixture is thickened. Yield: 2 cups.

Garlic-Cheese Grits

4 cups water
1 teaspoon salt
2 garlic cloves, pressed
1 cup uncooked regular grits
1 (12-ounce) block sharp
    Cheddar cheese, shredded
½ cup butter or margarine
1 teaspoon seasoned pepper
1 teaspoon Worcestershire
    sauce
¼ teaspoon hot sauce
3 large eggs, lightly beaten
Paprika

BRING first 3 ingredients to a boil in a large saucepan; gradually stir in grits. Return to a boil; reduce heat, and simmer, stirring occasionally, 15 minutes or until thickened.

ADD Cheddar cheese and next 4 ingredients, stirring until cheese melts. Remove from heat; let stand 10 minutes.

STIR in eggs, and pour into a lightly greased 11- x 7-inch baking dish. Sprinkle with paprika.

BAKE at 350° for 1 hour or until set. Yield: 8 to 10 servings.

Carolyn Flournoy
Shreveport, Louisiana

Fried Okra &

Fried okra connoisseurs are like pound cake lovers—they all have favorite recipes for the beloved morsels.

bacon, reserving 2 tablespoons drippings in skillet. Crumble bacon.

DREDGE okra in flour. Sauté onion in reserved drippings until tender. Add okra; cook, stirring occasionally, 5 minutes.

STIR in tomato and sugar; cook over low heat, stirring occasionally, 6 to 8 minutes. Stir in salt and pepper. Sprinkle with bacon. Serve over rice, if desired. Yield: 4 servings.

Karen Raborn
Covington, Louisiana

▲ Fried Okra

Clearly, okra fans all have their favorite recipe. If bacon drippings aren't used, try adding them. We did and made a great dish even better.

1 pound fresh okra
2 cups buttermilk
1 cup self-rising cornmeal
1 cup self-rising flour
1 teaspoon salt
¼ teaspoon ground red pepper
Vegetable oil
¼ cup bacon drippings

CUT off and discard tip and stem ends from okra; cut okra into ½-inch-thick slices. Stir into buttermilk; cover and chill 45 minutes.

COMBINE cornmeal and next 3 ingredients in a bowl. Remove okra from buttermilk with a slotted spoon; discard buttermilk. Dredge okra, in batches, in cornmeal mixture.

POUR oil to a depth of 2 inches into a Dutch oven or cast-iron skillet; add bacon drippings, and heat to 375°. Fry okra, in batches, 4 minutes or until golden; drain on paper towels. Yield: 4 servings.

Okra and Tomatoes

"Panfried" in bacon drippings, okra mingles with tomatoes in this home-style side dish.

4 bacon slices
1 pound sliced fresh okra
2 tablespoons all-purpose flour
1 large onion, chopped
4 plum tomatoes, seeded and chopped
2 teaspoons sugar
½ teaspoon salt
½ teaspoon pepper

COOK bacon in a large skillet over medium heat until crisp; drain

Pickled Okra

2 pounds small fresh okra
9 small fresh or dried hot peppers
9 garlic cloves
3 tablespoons dill seeds
4 cups white vinegar (5% acidity)
4 cups water
½ cup salt
¼ cup sugar

PACK okra into 9 hot jars, filling to ½ inch from top; place 1 hot pepper, 1 garlic clove, and 1 teaspoon dill seeds in each jar.

BRING vinegar and remaining 3 ingredients to a boil. Pour over okra, filling to ½ inch from top. Remove air bubbles; wipe jar rims. Cover at once with metal lids; screw on bands.

PROCESS in boiling-water bath 10 minutes. Yield: 9 pint jars.

Louise Osborne
Lexington, Kentucky

Fried Green Tomatoes

Who can resist these crumb-coated tangy tomatoes fresh from a sizzling skillet?

▲ Fried Green Tomatoes

⅔ cup white cornmeal
¼ teaspoon salt
¼ teaspoon pepper
3 large green tomatoes, sliced
1 large egg, beaten
¼ cup plus 2 tablespoons
    vegetable oil or olive oil

COMBINE first 3 ingredients in a small bowl; stir well. Dip tomato slices in beaten egg; dredge in cornmeal mixture, coating well on both sides.

HEAT 2 tablespoons oil in a large skillet over medium-high heat until hot. Add 1 layer of coated tomato slices, and fry 3 to 5 minutes or until browned, turning once. Remove tomato slices from skillet. Drain; set fried tomato slices aside, and keep warm. Repeat procedure twice with remaining oil and tomato slices. Serve immediately. Yield: 6 servings.

Fried Green Tomato Cheeseburgers

½ cup mayonnaise
1 garlic clove, pressed
1½ pounds lean ground beef
½ pound ground pork sausage
½ cup Italian-seasoned
    breadcrumbs
2 large eggs
3 tablespoons white wine
    Worcestershire sauce
1 teaspoon fennel seeds,
    crushed
3 green tomatoes, cut into
    ¼-inch-thick slices
½ teaspoon salt
¼ teaspoon pepper
1 cup yellow cornmeal
2 to 4 tablespoons vegetable
    oil
8 kaiser rolls, split
Lettuce leaves
8 slices sharp Cheddar cheese
Purple onion slices
Garnish: pimiento-stuffed olives

COMBINE mayonnaise and garlic; cover and chill.

COMBINE ground beef and next 5 ingredients; shape into 8 patties. Cover and chill.

SPRINKLE tomato slices with salt and pepper; let stand 5 minutes. Dredge in cornmeal.

COOK tomato slices in oil in a large skillet over medium heat until golden brown on each side. Drain on paper towels, and keep warm.

PLACE patties in a grill basket coated with cooking spray. Grill, covered with grill lid, over medium-high heat (350° to 400°) 4 to 5 minutes on each side or until done.

SPRAY cut sides of rolls with cooking spray; place rolls, cut side down, on rack, and grill until lightly browned.

PLACE a lettuce leaf on bottom half of each roll; place a patty on lettuce, and top each patty with a cheese slice, green tomatoes, purple onion slices, mayonnaise mixture, and top half of bun. Garnish, if desired. Yield: 8 servings.

Turnip

True Southerners would walk a country mile for a bowl of greens.

The Goodness of Greens

■ In the Old South, greens were part of daily meals and believed to be very good for you. Today, we still praise them for their health benefits. So we carve out time to simmer a pot of greens to tender perfection.

■ It's the flavor of smoked meat that cooks with the greens that makes them taste so good. Streak-of-lean (salt pork) and bacon are good choices.

■ Pepper Sauce (recipe on facing page) adds a splash of spunk to a pot of greens. Some folks are fond of salt, pepper, and sugar or lemon juice for seasoning a mess o' greens.

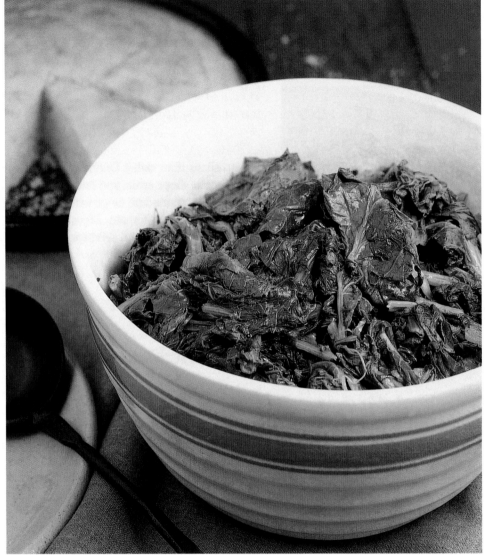

The South is known for its good cooks and good food. We take pride in preserving our traditional recipes. If you want to taste serious Southern cooking, then sample some greens. Some recipes are so simple and good that little has been done to them over the years to improve the flavor. Turnip greens are a prime example. Most Southerners have been bred to want their greens seasoned with ham hock and little else.

And the bonus that comes with cooking greens is reheating the "potlikker," pouring it over a piece of cornbread, and eating it with a spoon. Now that's some real Southern eating.

Greens

◂Turnip Greens

2 quarts water
2 teaspoons salt
1 ham hock
6 pounds fresh turnip greens,
    trimmed and rinsed
½ cup sugar (optional)
1 tablespoon hot sauce

COMBINE first 3 ingredients in a stockpot; bring to a boil. Cover, reduce heat, and simmer 20 minutes.

ADD greens, a few at a time, to stockpot; add sugar, if desired, and hot sauce. Cover and cook over medium heat 40 minutes or to desired doneness; discard ham hock. Yield: 8 servings.

NOTE: You can substitute 3 (10-ounce) packages frozen turnip greens, thawed, for fresh.

Turnip Greens With Turnips

2 (1-pound) packages prewashed
    fresh turnip greens
2 turnips
¼ pound salt pork (streak of
    lean), smoked pork
    shoulder, or bacon
1 quart water
1 tablespoon bacon drippings
½ teaspoon sugar
Pepper Sauce (optional)

REMOVE and discard stems and discolored spots from greens. Peel and coarsely chop turnips; set aside. Wash greens thoroughly; drain and tear into 2-inch pieces.

BRING salt pork and 1 quart water to a boil in a Dutch oven. Cover, reduce heat, and cook 45 minutes to 1 hour or until liquid is reduced by half and meat is tender. Add greens, bacon drippings, and sugar; cook, without stirring, 30 minutes or until greens are tender.

ADD turnips; cover, reduce heat, and simmer 30 minutes or until turnips are tender. Serve with Pepper Sauce, if desired. Yield: 4 to 6 servings.

Turnip Greens Stew

Frozen seasoning blend is a mixture of diced onion, red and green bell peppers, and celery.

2 cups chopped cooked ham
1 tablespoon vegetable oil
3 cups chicken broth
2 (16-ounce) packages frozen
    chopped turnip greens
1 (16-ounce) package frozen
    seasoning blend (see Note)
1 teaspoon sugar
1 teaspoon seasoned pepper

SAUTÉ chopped ham in hot oil in a Dutch oven over medium-high heat 5 minutes or until lightly browned. Add chicken broth and remaining ingredients; bring greens mixture to a boil. Cover, reduce heat to low, and simmer, stirring occasionally, 25 minutes. Yield: 6 to 8 servings.

For testing purposes only, we used McKenzie's Seasoning Blend.

Pepper Sauce

¾ cup cider or white wine
    vinegar
10 long fresh green chile
    peppers, washed and
    trimmed*

BRING vinegar to a boil in a saucepan.

PACK peppers tightly into a hot 12-ounce jar. Cover with boiling vinegar. Cover at once with metal lid, and screw on band. Store at room temperature up to 2 weeks. Yield: 1 (12-ounce) jar.

*Banana peppers, jalapeño, or other hot peppers may be substituted.

NOTE: For an 8-ounce jar, use 6 peppers and ½ cup vinegar.

Pecan

Orange Pecans

1 cup sugar
1/3 cup orange juice
1 teaspoon cream of tartar
2 1/4 cups pecan halves, toasted
1/2 teaspoon grated orange rind

COMBINE first 3 ingredients in a large heavy saucepan. Cook over low heat, stirring constantly, until sugar dissolves and mixture boils. Cover and cook 2 minutes to wash down sugar crystals. Uncover and cook, without stirring, until mixture reaches soft ball stage (236°).

REMOVE from heat; beat with a wooden spoon until mixture begins to thicken. Stir in pecans and orange rind. Working rapidly, drop by rounded teaspoonfuls onto wax paper. Cool. Yield: 2 dozen.

Dining with Southern Elegance
Terrebonne Association for Family and Community Education
Houma, Louisiana

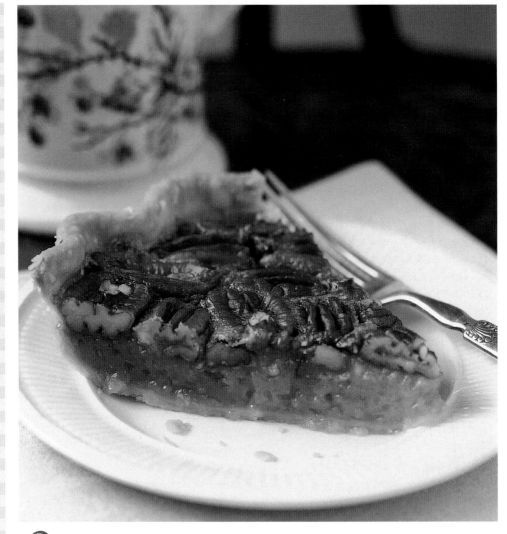

*O*f the many kinds of nut pies that appear on Southern tables, pecan is probably the most often served. No other dessert quite measures up to the richness of Southern pecan pie.

Southerners can make almost any dessert better simply by adding pecans. In fact, we're famous for pecan pies. But don't stop there with fall's bountiful harvest. Try our Pecan Pie Bars and Pecan Tassies, too.

When stocking up on pecans for the holiday baking season, try to find the freshest nuts possible. Nuts in the shell resist aging much longer than those that have been shelled. It's important to store pecans properly, too. Left in the shell, pecans stay fresh about 6 months. Shelled pecans will keep 9 months if refrigerated, and up to 2 years frozen.

Pie

◄ Pecan Pie

½ cup butter or margarine,
    melted
1 cup sugar
1 cup light corn syrup
4 large eggs, beaten
1 teaspoon vanilla extract
¼ teaspoon salt
½ (15-ounce) package
    refrigerated piecrusts
1⅓ cups pecan halves or
    1¼ cups chopped pecans

COMBINE first 3 ingredients; cook over low heat, stirring constantly, until sugar dissolves. Cool slightly. Add eggs, vanilla, and salt to mixture; stir well.

FIT piecrust into a 9-inch pieplate according to package directions. Fold edges under, and crimp.

POUR filling into unbaked pastry shell, and top with pecan halves. Bake at 325° for 55 minutes or until set. Serve warm or cold. Yield: 8 servings.

RUM PECAN PIE: Prepare recipe as directed above, adding 3 tablespoons dark rum with the eggs; stir well.

Pecan Pie Bars

2 cups all-purpose flour
½ cup sugar
⅛ teaspoon salt
¾ cup butter or margarine,
    cut up
1 cup firmly packed light brown
    sugar
1 cup light corn syrup
½ cup butter or margarine
4 large eggs, lightly beaten
2½ cups finely chopped
    pecans
1 teaspoon vanilla extract

COMBINE flour, sugar, and salt in a large bowl; cut in ¾ cup butter thoroughly with a pastry blender until mixture resembles very fine crumbs. Press mixture evenly into a greased 13- x 9-inch pan, using a piece of plastic wrap to press crumb mixture firmly in pan. Bake at 350° for 17 to 20 minutes or until lightly browned.

COMBINE brown sugar, corn syrup, and ½ cup butter in a saucepan; bring to a boil over medium heat, stirring gently. Remove from heat.

STIR one-fourth of hot mixture into beaten eggs; add to remaining hot mixture. Stir in pecans and vanilla. Pour filling over crust.

BAKE at 350° for 34 to 35 minutes or until set. Cool completely in pan on a wire rack. Cut into bars. Yield: 16 large bars.

Pecan Tassies

½ cup butter or margarine,
    softened
1 (3-ounce) package cream
    cheese, softened
1 cup all-purpose flour
1½ cups firmly packed light
    brown sugar
2 tablespoons butter or
    margarine, melted
2 large eggs, lightly beaten
1 teaspoon vanilla extract
⅔ cup chopped pecans

BEAT softened butter and cream cheese at medium speed with an electric mixer until creamy. Gradually add flour, beating well. Cover and chill 2 hours.

SHAPE dough into 30 (1-inch) balls; press balls into lightly greased miniature (1¾-inch) muffin pans. Set aside.

COMBINE brown sugar and next 3 ingredients; stir well. Stir in pecans. Spoon 1 tablespoon pecan mixture into each pastry shell.

BAKE at 350° for 25 minutes. Remove from pans immediately, and cool completely on wire racks. Yield: 2½ dozen.

Brenda Owen
Recipes on Parade
Calloway County Band Boosters
Murray, Kentucky

Ham &

Ham &

Salty ham and flaky biscuits are about as Southern as it gets.

Hamming It Up

Here are some different hams defined.

■ **Bone-in ham:** This ham has the entire bone intact. It's available whole, butt end, or shank end only.

■ **Boneless ham:** This ham has the entire bone removed, and the ham is rolled or packed in a casing.

■ **Country ham:** Ham prepared with a dry-rub cure. Most country hams are very dry and salty and require soaking before cooking. They're often named for the city in which they're processed. Smithfield ham is one of the most popular types.

■ **Dry-cured ham:** The ham's surface is rubbed with a mixture of salt, sugar, nitrites, and seasonings, and then air-dried.

■ **Smoked ham:** Ham that's been hung in a smokehouse after the curing process in order to take on the smoky flavor of the wood used.

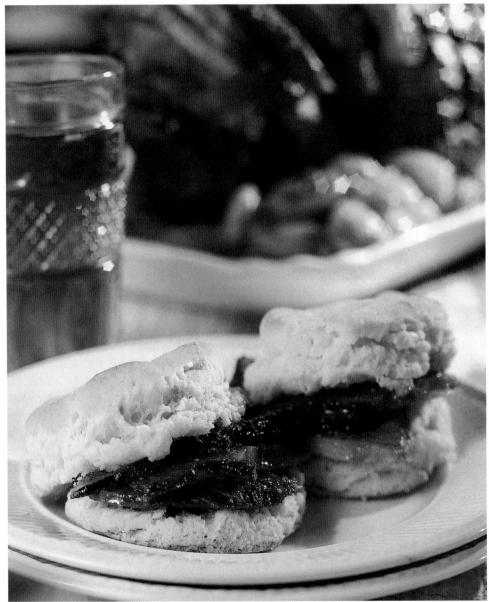

*M*any folks across the South serve country ham when a crowd gathers for a special occasion, whether it's for breakfast, brunch, or lunch. This full-flavored meat makes a hearty entrée, and often provides leftovers for other recipes.

Nothing beats a hot, fluffy buttermilk biscuit stuffed with slivers of juicy ham for a good old-fashioned Southern breakfast. Just remember, biscuits are at their best when freshly baked.

Biscuits

◄ Harvest Ham

1 (15-pound) uncooked
    country ham
2 tablespoons whole cloves
½ cup firmly packed dark
    brown sugar
½ cup honey mustard
½ cup honey
1 teaspoon ground ginger
2 cups apple juice
1 cup pineapple juice
1 cup Madeira
2 cups dried apricot halves
1 cup golden raisins

PLACE ham in a very large container; cover with water, and soak at least 24 hours. Pour off water. Scrub ham with warm water, using a stiff brush, and rinse well.

REMOVE skin, leaving a ¼-inch layer of fat. Score fat in a diamond design, using a sharp knife. Stud with whole cloves. Place ham in a large roasting pan.

COMBINE brown sugar, mustard, honey, and ginger. Coat exposed portion of ham evenly with mustard mixture. Pour apple juice and pineapple juice into roasting pan. Cover and bake at 350° for 2 hours. Add Madeira, apricot halves, and raisins to pan. Cover and bake 1½ more hours or until a meat thermometer inserted into thickest part of ham registers 142°. To serve, slice ham across the grain into very thin slices. Yield: 26 servings.

Stacy Taylor Layton
Beyond Cotton Country
The Junior League of Morgan County
Decatur, Alabama

Here are two of the best biscuits
that ham will ever meet.

Elsie's Biscuits

3 cups all-purpose flour
2 tablespoons baking powder
1 teaspoon salt
½ cup butter or margarine
½ cup milk
½ cup buttermilk
⅓ cup sour cream
⅛ teaspoon sugar
⅛ teaspoon vanilla extract

COMBINE first 3 ingredients; cut in butter with a pastry blender until mixture is crumbly.

COMBINE milk and remaining 4 ingredients; add to dry ingredients, stirring just until dry ingredients are moistened.

TURN dough out onto a lightly floured surface; knead 3 or 4 times. Roll to ½-inch thickness; cut with a 1½-inch round cutter, and place on a lightly greased baking sheet.

BAKE at 450° for 7 to 9 minutes. Yield: about 3 dozen.

Laurey Masterton
Asheville, North Carolina

NOTE: Rolled dough may be cut with a 2½-inch round cutter; bake at 450° for 10 to 12 minutes. Yield: 1 dozen.

Sweet Potato Biscuits

4 cups all-purpose flour
2 tablespoons baking powder
2 teaspoons salt
1 cup butter or margarine
1 cup cooked mashed sweet
    potato
¾ to 1 cup buttermilk

COMBINE first 3 ingredients. Cut in butter with a pastry blender until crumbly.

STIR together sweet potato and buttermilk; add to dry ingredients, stirring just until moistened.

TURN dough out onto a lightly floured surface, and knead 3 to 4 times. Pat or roll to ½-inch thickness. Cut dough with a 3-inch round cutter, and place biscuits on a lightly greased baking sheet.

BAKE at 425° for 10 to 15 minutes or until biscuits are golden. Yield: 14 biscuits.

A Salty Situation

One of the trademarks of country ham is its saltiness. To remove some of the salt and to restore moisture to the ham, soak the ham at least 24 hours or up to 3 days, changing water every 12 hours.

*Summer Squash and Cherry Tomatoes
in Basil Butter, page 49*

Quick & Easy Homestyle

*T*ime is as precious to us as

ever these days, particularly

family time around the table.

In this chapter, we offer you dozens

of recipes that can

be ready in roughly 30 minutes.

Spiced Holiday Pecans MAKE AHEAD PARTY FOOD

Hot sauce and red pepper dictate how spicy these snacking nuts are. Bake them ahead and cool; they'll stay fresh up to 5 days in a cookie tin.

Nuts to You
Almonds, cashews, or unsalted peanuts taste great coated and baked in these spices, too. Pass out little gift bags of nuts as party favors.

3 tablespoons butter or margarine, melted	1 teaspoon salt
½ teaspoon ground red pepper	3 tablespoons Worcestershire sauce
½ teaspoon ground cinnamon	Dash of hot sauce
	4 cups pecan halves

STIR together first 6 ingredients. Add pecans; toss gently until coated. Place in an ungreased 15- x 10-inch jellyroll pan.

BAKE at 300° for 25 to 28 minutes, stirring twice. Allow to cool completely. Store pecans in an airtight container. Yield: 4 cups.

Ione Morris
We're Cooking Up Something New: 50 Years of Music, History, and Food
Wichita Falls Symphony League
Wichita Falls, Texas

Cheese Quesadillas PARTY FOOD

Get a head start prepping this popular appetizer by mixing up the cheese filling up to a day ahead; store it in the refrigerator. Use a pizza cutter to cut these crispy flats in half or into little wedges for a party crowd.

Double Duty
The cheese quesadilla filling is also yummy spooned over a piping hot baked potato or as the inside of a grilled cheese sandwich.

4 cups (16 ounces) shredded Monterey Jack cheese	2 tablespoons minced fresh cilantro
4 pickled jalapeño peppers, finely chopped	1 teaspoon ground cumin
2 green onions, chopped	2 tablespoons butter or margarine, softened
	8 (7-inch) flour tortillas

COMBINE first 5 ingredients; stir well. Set aside.

SPREAD butter evenly on 1 side of each tortilla. Spoon cheese mixture evenly over unbuttered side of 4 tortillas; top with remaining 4 tortillas, buttered side up.

COOK quesadillas, 1 at a time, in a large skillet over medium-high heat 2 minutes on each side or until lightly browned. To serve, cut tortillas in half. Yield: 8 servings.

Sue Ann Graves
A Place Called Hope
The Junior Auxiliary of Hope, Arkansas

Sausage and Cheese Tartlets PARTY FOOD

Your guests will devour these zesty tartlets. Ranch dressing is the secret flavoring agent that makes these mouthfuls so memorable.

1   pound mild ground pork sausage
1¼ cups (5 ounces) shredded
    Monterey Jack cheese
1¼ cups (5 ounces) shredded sharp
    Cheddar cheese
1   (8-ounce) bottle Ranch-style
    dressing

1   (4¼-ounce) can chopped ripe
    olives, drained
1   teaspoon ground red pepper
5   (2.1-ounce) packages frozen mini
    phyllo shells

COOK sausage in a large skillet, stirring until it crumbles and is no longer pink; drain. Combine sausage and next 5 ingredients in a large bowl.

FILL each shell with a heaping teaspoonful of sausage mixture, and place on ungreased baking sheets. Bake at 350° for 8 to 10 minutes or until cheese melts. Serve warm. Yield: about 6 dozen.

Creating A Stir
The Fayette County Medical Auxiliary
Lexington, Kentucky

Buying Time
Fill and freeze these unbaked tartlets in their original tray. The tray slips neatly into a large zip-top plastic bag. When you're ready to bake the frozen tartlets, transfer them to ungreased baking sheets and add 2 to 3 minutes to the original baking time.

Summer Iced Tea MAKE AHEAD

Stir up a pitcher of this Southern sipper spiked with citrus. Serve it on the front porch to cut the heat of summer, or pour it to enjoy with supper anytime of year.

6   tea bags
4   cups boiling water
1½ cups sugar
1   (6-ounce) can frozen lemonade
    concentrate, thawed

1   (6-ounce) can frozen orange juice
    concentrate, thawed
10 cups water
1   cup pineapple juice

STEEP tea bags in boiling water 5 minutes; discard tea bags. Combine steeped tea, sugar, and remaining ingredients in a 1-gallon pitcher. Serve over ice. Yield: 1 gallon.

Simple Pleasures: From Our Table to Yours
Arab Mothers' Club
Arab, Alabama

Tea Tip
To keep iced tea from being diluted, freeze some of the tea itself in plastic ice cube trays; you can even add a mint leaf to each cube. Then when ready to serve, just pop the frozen tea cubes into each glass.

Lime Sherbet and Mint Punch

Mint Anytime
Mint is an easy herb to grow. In fact, it will take over your garden if you let it. You can also find plastic packs of fresh mint in the produce department year-round.

There's a subtle mint flavor in this punch. If you're a fan of fresh mint, toss a few more leaves into the sugar mixture. For the limeade, we diluted a can of frozen limeade concentrate.

1 cup water
½ cup sugar
4 fresh mint leaves, coarsely chopped

2 cups limeade
1 quart lime sherbet, softened
Garnish: fresh mint sprigs

COMBINE first 3 ingredients in a small saucepan. Bring to a boil; reduce heat, and simmer, uncovered, 10 minutes. Remove and discard mint leaves. Cover and chill.

COMBINE sugar mixture and limeade in a medium bowl; stir well. Add sherbet, and mix well. Serve immediately. Garnish, if desired. Yield: 6 cups.

Margo Davis
Recipes from a New England Green
Middlebury Congregational Church
Middlebury, Connecticut

Sweet Potato Biscuits

Biscuit Bonanza
You can make these 20-minute biscuits whatever size you'd like. For parties, smaller 1½- to 2-inch biscuits are ideal; then you can tuck in slivers of meat and pile them on a platter as hearty appetizers. For breakfast, we recommend cutting larger 2½-inch biscuits as we did in the photograph shown at right.

Four ingredients, a biscuit cutter, and a baking sheet produce these tender, puffed rounds. Turkey, ham, or pork taste great tucked inside.

⅓ cup cold butter or margarine, cut into pieces
2½ cups biscuit mix

1 cup canned mashed sweet potato
½ cup milk

CUT butter into biscuit mix with a pastry blender until mixture is crumbly. Combine sweet potato and milk; add to biscuit mix, stirring with a fork just until dry ingredients are moistened.

TURN dough out onto a lightly floured surface; knead 4 or 5 times. Pat or roll dough to ¾-inch thickness; cut with a 2-inch round biscuit cutter. Place biscuits on a large ungreased baking sheet. Bake at 450° for 10 to 12 minutes or until golden. Yield: 22 biscuits.

Rosemary Anderson
Stepping Back to Old Butler
Butler Ruritan Club
Butler, Tennessee

Sweet Potato Biscuits

Easy Cheddar Biscuits WEEKNIGHT FAVORITE

Cheese Chat

Keep a cup or two of shredded cheese in a zip-top bag in the refrigerator—one less job to do when a recipe calls for shredded cheese. If you spray your grater with cooking spray before shredding cheese, it makes cleanup easy.

Bake up a batch of these little Cheddar biscuits in minutes. They'll go with just about any dinner menu.

1½ cups all-purpose flour
1 tablespoon baking powder
1 tablespoon sugar
½ teaspoon salt

1 cup (4 ounces) shredded sharp
   Cheddar cheese
⅓ cup shortening
½ cup milk

PROCESS first 4 ingredients in a food processor until blended. Add cheese and shortening; pulse 4 or 5 times or until mixture is crumbly. Add milk, and pulse just until mixture forms a dough.

TURN dough out onto a lightly floured surface; shape into a ball. Pat dough to ½-inch thickness. Cut with a 2-inch round biscuit cutter. Place biscuits on an ungreased baking sheet. Bake at 425° for 10 minutes or until golden. Yield: 15 biscuits.

Laura C. Robelen
What's Cooking in Delaware
American Red Cross in Delaware
Wilmington, Delaware

Pecan Mini-Muffins PARTY FOOD

Petit Pans

Find inexpensive mini muffin pans at large grocery stores on the aisle where other kitchenware is sold. For a recipe such as this one with a large yield, baking runs smoothly if you have 2 pans.

These muffins taste like pecan tassies but are easier to prepare because there's no separate crust.

1 cup firmly packed light brown
   sugar
½ cup butter or margarine, melted
2 large eggs

1 teaspoon vanilla extract
1 cup chopped pecans
½ cup all-purpose flour

COMBINE first 4 ingredients in a bowl, beating with a wire whisk until smooth. Stir in pecans and flour. Spoon batter into miniature (1¾-inch) muffin pans coated with cooking spray, filling to within ⅛ inch from top. Bake at 375° for 12 minutes or until lightly browned. Cool in pans on wire racks 1 minute. Remove from pans; cool completely on wire racks. Yield: 40 muffins.

Caroline Rippee
First Baptist Church Centennial Cookbook
First Baptist Church
Cushing, Oklahoma

Apple Pizzas

Shape these novel breakfast pizzas from refrigerated biscuits. Piled with melted cheese, apples, and a sprinkling of cinnamon sugar, these quick bites take only minutes to make.

½ cup firmly packed light brown
    sugar
2 tablespoons all-purpose flour
1 teaspoon ground cinnamon
1 (17.3-ounce) can refrigerated
    biscuits (contains 8 biscuits)

1 cup (4 ounces) shredded Cheddar
    cheese
2 small cooking apples, peeled,
    cored, and sliced
¼ cup butter or margarine

COMBINE first 3 ingredients in a small bowl; stir well.

ROLL biscuits into 4-inch circles, and place on a lightly greased baking sheet. Sprinkle shredded cheese evenly over circles, leaving ¼-inch borders. Arrange apple slices over cheese. Sprinkle cinnamon mixture over apples, and dot with butter. Bake at 350° for 18 to 20 minutes. Yield: 8 pizzas.

Kim Love
Seasonings
The 20th Century Club Juniors of Park Ridge, Illinois

Apple Appeal
Usher in autumn with these little sugar-topped apple pizzas. Use your favorite crisp apple or try one of these: Fuji, Jonagold, Braeburn, Mutsu, or Arkansas black.

Beignets ONE POT

Frozen rolls provide a quick start for these New Orleans pastries. Whether serving beignets for breakfast or as a late-night dessert, be liberal when dusting with powdered sugar—and don't forget the café au lait!

1 (16-ounce) package frozen rolls,
    thawed (we tested with Rich's)

Vegetable oil
Powdered sugar

FLATTEN and stretch each roll slightly.

POUR oil to a depth of 2 inches into a Dutch oven; heat to 375°. Fry beignets, 4 at a time, in hot oil 1 to 2 minutes or until golden, turning often. Drain on paper towels. Sprinkle with powdered sugar; serve immediately. Yield: 21 beignets.

Debbie and Lucille Landry
Nun Better: Tastes and Tales from Around a Cajun Table
St. Cecilia School
Broussard, Louisiana

Beignet Bliss
A generous dusting of sugar deems these doughnuts dessert. But savory beignets, minus the sugar, are nice split and stuffed with chicken salad or crabmeat. "Beignet" comes from the French term for fritter.

Easy Peanut Butter Cookies KID FRIENDLY

Kiss Choices

You'll find a small variety of chocolate kisses on the candy aisle. There's a swirled version and a nutty version. Mix 'em up and use a few of each in this simple recipe.

These cookies are good with or without chocolate kisses—either way you have a winner.

1 (14-ounce) can sweetened
   condensed milk
¾ cup creamy peanut butter
2 cups biscuit mix (we tested with
   Bisquick)

1 teaspoon vanilla extract
Sugar
66 milk chocolate kisses, unwrapped
   (optional)

COMBINE condensed milk and peanut butter in a large mixing bowl. Beat at medium speed with an electric mixer until blended. Add biscuit mix and vanilla; beat well.

SHAPE mixture into 1-inch balls; roll in sugar. Place 2 inches apart on ungreased baking sheets. Dip a fork in sugar; flatten cookies in a crisscross design. Bake at 375° for 6 to 7 minutes. After removing from oven, immediately press a chocolate kiss in center of each cookie, if desired. Remove cookies to wire racks to cool completely. Yield: 5½ dozen.

Mike Stillwell
Praise the Lord and Pass the Gravy
Stanley United Methodist Church
Stanley, Virginia

Easy Peanut Butter Cookies

Lemon Crispies MAKE AHEAD

No need to squeeze fresh lemons for these cookies. Lemon pudding mix packs the tart punch in this recipe.

¾ cup shortening
1 cup sugar
3 large eggs
2 cups all-purpose flour

¾ teaspoon baking soda
⅛ teaspoon salt
2 (3.4-ounce) packages lemon instant pudding mix

BEAT shortening at medium speed with an electric mixer until creamy. Gradually add sugar, beating well. Add eggs, 1 at a time, beating well after each addition.

COMBINE flour and remaining 3 ingredients; gradually add to shortening mixture, beating well. Drop dough by rounded teaspoonfuls onto lightly greased baking sheets. Bake at 375° for 8 to 9 minutes or until cookies are lightly browned. Cool 1 minute on baking sheets; remove to wire racks to cool completely. Yield: 5½ dozen.

Janette Tower
A Taste of Greene
Playground Committee
Greene, Iowa

Lemon Lazy
It pays to keep a few packages of instant pudding on the shelf. This easy cookie recipe is delicious proof. Crumble some of these crisp treats over your favorite vanilla ice cream.

Quick Chocolate Mousse MAKE AHEAD

You won't find another luscious two-ingredient dessert like this—homemade, yet ultra easy. For added flavor, stir 1 to 2 teaspoons coffee liqueur, orange liqueur, or vanilla extract into the melted chocolate mixture.

5 ounces dark chocolate, chopped
   (we tested with Perugina by Nestle)

1¼ cups whipping cream

COMBINE chocolate and whipping cream in a heavy saucepan. Cook over medium-low heat, stirring constantly, until chocolate melts and mixture is smooth. Remove from heat, and cool completely. Cover and chill at least 8 hours.

JUST before serving, beat chocolate mixture at medium-high speed with an electric mixer until mixture thickens to desired consistency. Spoon into individual dessert dishes. Yield: 6 servings.

Made in the Shade
The Junior League of Greater Fort Lauderdale, Florida

Mousse Matters
This rich mousse doesn't need a garnish. Chill it overnight; then beat it, and simply spoon it into serving dishes. Look for good quality dark chocolate on the candy or baking aisle of your supermarket.

Angel Toast   ONE PAN

This yummy dessert will remind you of cinnamon toast like mom used to make.

Dessert Decisions
This unusual and decadent dessert lends itself to lots of options. Try chocolate ice cream and pound cake slices for variety.

8 (1-inch-thick) slices angel food cake
¾ cup butter, melted
1 cup firmly packed light brown
    sugar

½ gallon coffee ice cream

BRUSH cake slices on both sides with butter; sprinkle both sides with sugar.
PLACE cake slices on a lightly greased baking sheet. Broil 5½ inches from heat 1 to 2 minutes on each side or until cake is toasted and sugar is bubbly. Let stand 2 to 3 minutes. Top each cake slice with a scoop of ice cream, and serve immediately. Yield: 8 servings.

Kathy Jones
A Fare to Remember
Dublin Service League
Dublin, Georgia

Quick and Easy Torte   MAKE AHEAD

Purchase a pound cake and dress it up with a simple, satiny chocolate-sour cream frosting.

Torte in No Time
You may have on hand the ingredients for this showy, make-ahead dessert.

1 (10.75-ounce) loaf pound cake
1 cup (6 ounces) semisweet
    chocolate morsels

1 teaspoon instant coffee granules
1 teaspoon hot water
1 (8-ounce) container sour cream

SLICE pound cake horizontally into 5 layers; set aside.
PLACE chocolate morsels in top of a double boiler; bring water to a boil. Reduce heat to low; cook until chocolate melts. Remove from heat.
COMBINE coffee granules and water, stirring until granules dissolve. Stir coffee mixture and sour cream into melted chocolate. Spread chocolate mixture between layers and on top and sides of cake. Cover and chill thoroughly. Yield: 10 servings.

Barbara Shapiro
Perfect for Every Occasion
P.E.O. Sisterhood, Chapter BQ
Longwood, Florida

Blueberry Icebox Pie MAKE AHEAD

Blueberries make a nice variation from the traditional lemon icebox pie. This recipe makes 2 pies—one to keep and one to give away.

2 (14-ounce) cans sweetened
    condensed milk
⅔ cup fresh lemon juice
1 teaspoon vanilla extract
1 teaspoon almond extract

1 (12-ounce) container frozen
    whipped topping, thawed
1 (15½-ounce) can blueberries in
    syrup, drained
2 (6-ounce) graham cracker crusts

COMBINE first 4 ingredients in a large bowl; stir well. Fold in whipped topping. Gently fold in blueberries. Spoon mixture evenly into crusts. Cover and chill at least 3 hours. Yield: 2 (9-inch) pies.

Robbie Boshart
The Fruit of the Spirit
Sumrall United Methodist Women's Circle
Sumrall, Mississippi

Pie Plans
Canned blueberries mean you can make this pie year-round. Make it ahead and chill it, tightly covered, up to 3 days, or freeze it and serve it partially thawed.

Cookie Dough Cheesecake PARTY FOOD

Refrigerated cookie dough becomes the crust and topping for this clever cheesecake that you cut into squares.

2 (18-ounce) packages
    refrigerated sliceable
    chocolate chip cookie dough
2 (8-ounce) packages cream cheese,
    softened

½ cup sugar
2 large eggs
1 teaspoon vanilla extract

CUT 1 roll of cookie dough into 24 slices; arrange slices in bottom of a lightly greased 13- x 9- inch pan. Press slices together with fingers, covering bottom of pan to edges. Set pan aside.

BEAT cream cheese at medium speed with an electric mixer until creamy; gradually add sugar, beating well. Add eggs, 1 at a time, beating well after each addition. Add vanilla; beat well. Pour mixture into prepared pan.

CUT remaining roll of cookie dough into 24 slices; arrange slices over cream cheese mixture. Bake at 350° for 45 minutes. Cool in pan on a wire rack. Cut into squares. Yield: 15 servings.

Debra Metzger
A Pawsitively Purrfect Cookbook
The Hope for Animals Sanctuary of Rhode Island
Slatersville, Rhode Island

Pan Plus
This cheesecake is baked in a large pan rather than the typical round springform pan. This way, you can serve more guests with one recipe.

Sloppy Joe

Sloppy Joes WEEKNIGHT FAVORITE

As fast as you can brown beef in a skillet, you'll have this familiar sandwich favorite ready for toasted buns.

1 pound ground chuck
1 medium onion, chopped
½ cup ketchup
3 tablespoons sweet pickle relish
1 tablespoon light brown sugar

1 tablespoon prepared mustard
¼ teaspoon salt
¼ teaspoon pepper
5 hamburger buns, toasted

BROWN ground chuck and onion in a large nonstick skillet, stirring until meat crumbles; drain. Stir in ketchup and next 5 ingredients. Bring to a boil; cover, reduce heat, and simmer 5 minutes, stirring occasionally. Spoon meat mixture over bottom halves of buns; top with remaining halves. Yield: 5 servings.

Nena Moon
Bread from the Brook
The Church at Brook Hills
Birmingham, Alabama

Sloppy Options

If you like your Sloppy Joes on the sweet side, add another tablespoon of brown sugar. If you want a spicy sandwich, use hot ketchup. For a tangy sandwich, spread a little extra mustard on the bun.

Taco Casserole WEEKNIGHT FAVORITE

This Mexican main dish is chock-full of beef, beans, cheese, and chips. Just add a salad or slaw and some rice to the plate.

1 pound ground chuck
½ cup chopped onion
1 (1¼-ounce) envelope taco
    seasoning mix
1 (15½-ounce) can chili hot beans,
    undrained

1 (8-ounce) can tomato sauce
2 cups (8 ounces) shredded Colby
    cheese
1 (9-ounce) package nacho cheese-
    flavored tortilla chips, crushed

BROWN ground chuck and onion in a large skillet, stirring until beef crumbles and onion is tender; drain.
RETURN meat mixture to skillet; stir in taco seasoning, chili beans, and tomato sauce. Layer half each of meat mixture, shredded cheese, and tortilla chips in a lightly greased 13- x 9-inch baking dish. Repeat procedure with remaining meat mixture, shredded cheese, and tortilla chips.
BAKE, uncovered, at 350° for 25 minutes or until thoroughly heated. Yield: 6 servings.

Cindy Skuce
Food for the Soul
Campground Church Ladies
Fosterville, Tennessee

Seasoning Secret

Taco seasoning can perk up just about any ground beef dish. Try sprinkling a tablespoon into beef-vegetable soup, chili, or mix some into ground beef for hamburger patties.

Beef and Bean Enchiladas WEEKNIGHT FAVORITE

Enchilada Intrigue

The difference between an enchilada and a burrito is that an enchilada is rolled up, smothered in sauce, and baked. A burrito is rolled up and eaten out-of-hand.

Once you've filled and rolled one tortilla and placed it in the dish to bake, the rest will go quickly. Then you can leave it to bake unattended while you enjoy a margarita.

1½ pounds ground chuck	3 (10-ounce) cans enchilada sauce
1 medium onion, chopped	Vegetable oil
1 (16-ounce) can refried beans	12 (6-inch) corn tortillas
1 teaspoon salt	3 cups (12 ounces) shredded
⅛ teaspoon garlic powder	Cheddar cheese, divided

BROWN ground chuck and onion in a large skillet, stirring until meat crumbles; drain. Return meat mixture to skillet. Add beans, salt, and garlic powder; cook over medium heat, stirring constantly, until thoroughly heated. Set aside.

PLACE enchilada sauce in a saucepan. Cook over medium heat until thoroughly heated. Pour 1 cup sauce into a lightly greased 13- x 9-inch baking dish; set dish and remaining sauce aside.

POUR vegetable oil to a depth of ½ inch into a large heavy skillet. Fry tortillas, 1 at a time, in hot oil over medium heat 3 to 5 seconds on each side or just until softened. Brush tortillas lightly on each side with 1 cup sauce. Spoon ⅓ cup bean mixture down center of each tortilla; sprinkle each with 1 tablespoon cheese. Roll up tortillas; place seam side down in prepared dish. Pour remaining sauce evenly over tortillas; sprinkle with remaining cheese. Bake at 350° for 15 minutes or until cheese melts and enchiladas are thoroughly heated. Yield: 6 servings.

Dorothy Harrison
Recipes on Parade
Calloway County Band Boosters
Murray, Kentucky

Pork Chops Supreme WEEKNIGHT FAVORITE

New Picture of Pork

Boneless center-cut loin chops are a far cry from the shoe leather pork chops of decades past. These thick chops taste best when first browned and then slowly simmered in a little liquid.

Skillet-seared chops smothered in sweet prunes and onion, left alone to simmer until perfect tenderness—aah, an easy dinner.

6 (1-inch-thick) boneless center-cut loin pork chops	14 pitted dried prunes
½ teaspoon salt	3 small onions, thinly sliced
½ teaspoon pepper	½ cup water
2 teaspoons vegetable oil	2 tablespoons light brown sugar
	2 tablespoons cider vinegar

SPRINKLE pork chops with salt and pepper. Cook pork chops in hot oil in a large skillet over medium-high heat 5 minutes on each side or until browned. Drain.

ADD prunes and remaining ingredients to skillet. Cover, reduce heat to medium, and simmer 30 minutes or until meat is tender. Yield: 6 servings.

Ginger Schlipf
Blue Stocking Club Forget-Me-Not Recipes
Blue Stocking Club
Bristol, Tennessee

20-Minute Chicken Parmesan   WEEKNIGHT FAVORITE

Served atop a plateful of pasta, this saucy Chicken Parmesan makes a hearty entrée.

4 skinned and boned chicken
    breast halves
1 large egg, lightly beaten
½ cup Italian-seasoned breadcrumbs
2 tablespoons butter or
    margarine, melted

1¾ cups spaghetti sauce
½ cup (2 ounces) shredded
    mozzarella cheese
1 tablespoon grated Parmesan
    cheese
¼ cup chopped fresh parsley

PLACE chicken between 2 sheets of heavy-duty plastic wrap; flatten to ¼-inch thickness, using a meat mallet or rolling pin. Dip chicken in egg, and dredge in breadcrumbs.

COOK chicken in butter in a large skillet over medium-high heat until browned on both sides. Spoon spaghetti sauce over chicken; bring to a boil. Cover, reduce heat, and simmer 10 minutes.

SPRINKLE with cheeses and parsley; cover and simmer 5 minutes or until cheeses melt. Yield: 4 servings.

Nancy Applegate
Recipes of Love
Alpha Delta Pi, Jackson Area Alumnae Association
Brandon, Mississippi

Recipe Pointers
If you're going to serve this chicken over pasta, put the pasta water on to boil first thing; then coat and cook the chicken. Dress up store-bought spaghetti sauce by adding a shake of dried oregano or basil or a clove of crushed garlic.

Chicken à la King   WEEKNIGHT FAVORITE

This creamy Chicken à la King recipe gives you a comfort food supper in about 20 minutes.

1 (10-ounce) package frozen puff
    pastry shells
½ cup chopped green bell
    pepper
2 tablespoons butter or margarine,
    melted

1 (10¾-ounce) can cream of chicken
    soup, undiluted
½ cup milk
2 cups chopped cooked chicken
1 (2-ounce) jar diced pimiento,
    drained

BAKE pastry shells according to package directions.

MEANWHILE, sauté green pepper in butter in a large skillet until tender. Add soup and milk; stir until smooth. Stir in chicken and pimiento. Cook over medium-high heat, stirring constantly, until heated. Spoon chicken mixture into pastry shells. Yield: 4 to 6 servings.

Simply the Best . . . Recipes by Design
Columbus Area Visitors Center
Columbus, Indiana

Quick Chicken
It takes 3 to 4 skinless, boneless chicken breast halves to yield 2 cups chopped meat. Cook chicken by placing breast halves in a greased baking dish. Drizzle with olive oil, salt and pepper. Bake at 350° for 20 to 25 minutes; cool and chop chicken.

Shrimp Manale   ONE PAN

Serve these simply broiled shrimp with lots of crusty French bread. You'll need it to soak up the glorious garlic-butter sauce.

3 pounds unpeeled, medium-size
   fresh shrimp
1 cup butter, melted

½ cup dry white wine
6 garlic cloves, crushed

PLACE shrimp in broiler pan. Combine butter, wine, and garlic; pour over shrimp. Broil 5 inches from heat 21 minutes or until shrimp turn pink. Yield: 6 servings.

Gina Banister
Texas Sampler
The Junior League of Richardson, Texas

Crush Course

Crush garlic easily by smashing it under the flat side of a chef's knife. The peel will slip right off, and the garlic juices will be released when it hits the hot butter.

Salsa-Sauced Fish   ONE DISH

Here's your chance to sport your favorite salsa, whether it's homemade or store-bought, spicy or mild. Spoon it over these flaky fillets for an easy supper.

1½ pounds orange roughy fillets
½ cup salsa
2 tablespoons mayonnaise

2 tablespoons honey
2 tablespoons prepared mustard

CUT fish into 6 portions; place in an ungreased 13- x 9-inch baking dish. Bake, uncovered, at 450° for 6 to 7 minutes or until fish flakes easily when tested with a fork. Drain well.

COMBINE salsa and next 3 ingredients; spoon evenly over fish. Bake, uncovered, 2 to 3 minutes or until thoroughly heated. Remove fish to individual serving plates; spoon sauce over fish. Yield: 6 servings.

Carol DeLoach
Treasured Gems
Hiddenite Center Family
Hiddenite, North Carolina

Fish Talk

You can substitute any mild-flavored fish, such as flounder or tilapia, for orange roughy in this recipe.

Black-Eyed Pea Salad   MAKE AHEAD

Toss black-eyed peas and some fresh produce with creamy salad dressing and put it aside to chill.

2 (15½-ounce) cans black-eyed peas,   1 medium tomato, chopped
    rinsed and drained   1 medium onion, chopped
1 ripe avocado, peeled and chopped   ½ cup Catalina salad dressing

COMBINE all ingredients in a large bowl; toss well. Cover and chill 8 hours. Yield: 6 servings.

Janie Ingram
Home Cookin'
Volunteer Services Council for Abilene State School
Abilene, Texas

Spinach, Basil, and Pine Nut Salad   WEEKNIGHT FAVORITE

Fresh basil leaves add to the greens in this aromatic spinach salad.

6 cups loosely packed torn fresh   ½ cup olive oil
    spinach   4 ounces cooked ham, cut into very
2 cups loosely packed torn fresh   thin strips
    basil   1 cup freshly grated Parmesan
½ cup pine nuts   cheese
3 garlic cloves, minced

COMBINE spinach and basil in a salad bowl; toss gently.
COOK pine nuts and garlic in oil in a large skillet over medium-high heat, stirring constantly, just until pine nuts begin to brown. Add ham; cook 1 minute, stirring constantly. Immediately pour pine nut mixture over spinach mixture; sprinkle with cheese. Toss gently, and serve immediately. Yield: 4 servings.

Back Home Again
The Junior League of Indianapolis, Indiana

Picking Avocado
Pick a black-skinned avocado for this recipe. (We think they have the best flavor.) You'll know an avocado's ripe when you gently press it and it yields to the pressure of your finger.

Buying Time
To save prep time for this simple salad, use the refrigerated shredded Parmesan cheese that's now available in the supermarket dairy case.

Zesty Tomato Treats

This super simple recipe tastes just like a BLT without the bread.

6 medium tomatoes
12 lettuce leaves
½ cup mayonnaise

½ cup sour cream
2 tablespoons finely chopped onion
6 bacon slices, cooked and crumbled

SLICE both ends off tomatoes, and cut tomatoes in half horizontally. Arrange lettuce leaves on a serving platter and top each with a tomato half.

COMBINE mayonnaise, sour cream, and onion in a small bowl. Spoon mayonnaise mixture evenly over each tomato half, and sprinkle with bacon. Yield: 12 servings.

More Enchanted Eating from the West Shore
Friends of the Symphony
Muskegon, Michigan

Simple Salad

This tomato salad is easy and so good on busy summer days. It presents several options for you—red or yellow tomatoes, and iceberg or green leaf lettuce just to name two.

Barbecue Slaw MAKE AHEAD

Move over ordinary coleslaw—this easy barbecue-flavored variation made with ketchup is sure to become a favorite in your family.

⅓ cup sugar
⅓ cup ketchup
⅓ cup white vinegar

11 cups shredded cabbage (about 1 medium cabbage)

COMBINE first 3 ingredients in a small saucepan; bring to a boil, stirring until sugar dissolves. Pour hot vinegar mixture over cabbage; toss well. Cover and chill at least 3 hours. Yield: 8 servings.

Nothin' Finer
Chapel Hill Service League
Chapel Hill, North Carolina

Slaw Sleuth

When you're in need of a shortcut, pick up 2 bags of coleslaw mix in the grocery produce section instead of shredding cabbage. Want a spicier slaw? Try a hot ketchup.

Quick Baked Beans ONE PAN

Pork and beans get a quick makeover with a few basic flavor-boosting ingredients.

1 (31-ounce) can pork and beans
⅓ cup ketchup
2 to 3 tablespoons brown sugar

1 tablespoon dried minced onion
½ teaspoon salt
½ teaspoon dry mustard

COMBINE all ingredients in a medium saucepan, stirring well. Bring to a boil; reduce heat, and simmer 10 minutes, stirring occasionally. Yield: 4 servings.

Dorinda Miller
Candlelight and Wisteria
Lee-Scott Academy
Auburn, Alabama

Sweet-Tangy Options

You can use light or dark brown sugar in these beans. Dark brown sugar has a more intense flavor. If you don't have dry mustard on hand, just squirt a little "ballpark" mustard in its place.

Quick Hoppin' John

Quick Hoppin' John   ONE PAN

This good-luck peas and rice dish is the ideal accompaniment with pork or ham, and not just on New Year's Day, but year-round.

3 bacon slices, chopped
½ cup chopped celery
⅓ cup chopped onion
1 cup water
1 (15-ounce) can black-eyed peas,
　　undrained

1 cup uncooked quick long-grain rice
2 tablespoons chopped fresh parsley
½ teaspoon dried thyme
Garnish: celery leaves

COOK bacon in a large saucepan until crisp, stirring often. Add celery and onion; cook, stirring constantly, until vegetables are tender.

STIR in water and peas; bring to a boil. Cover, reduce heat, and simmer 5 minutes. Stir in rice, parsley, and thyme. Remove from heat; cover and let stand 5 minutes or until liquid is absorbed and rice is tender. Garnish, if desired. Yield: 2 to 4 servings.

Celebrating Our Mothers' Kitchens
National Council of Negro Women
Washington, DC

Bacon Shortcut
Typically, Hoppin' John includes ham. This flavorful, fast version uses bacon. If you're really in a rush, buy precooked bacon and skip the first step. Then just sauté chopped celery and onion in 1 teaspoon of vegetable oil.

Broccoli Bake

Dotted with bits of smoky bacon, cheesy Broccoli Bake is a fresh alternative to the typical broccoli-rice casserole.

1½ pounds fresh broccoli
5 large eggs, lightly beaten
1 cup cottage cheese
2 tablespoons all-purpose flour

½ teaspoon salt
4 bacon slices, cooked and crumbled
½ cup (2 ounces) shredded Cheddar
    cheese

REMOVE and discard broccoli leaves and tough ends of stalks; cut into florets. Arrange broccoli in a steamer basket over boiling water. Cover and steam 3 minutes or until crisp-tender.

PLACE broccoli in a lightly greased 11- x 7-inch baking dish. Combine eggs and next 4 ingredients, stirring well; pour over broccoli. Bake at 350° for 20 minutes. Sprinkle evenly with Cheddar cheese. Bake 5 more minutes. Let stand 5 minutes before serving. Yield: 6 servings.

Nancy Rumbaugh
Lake Murray Presbyterian Preschool Cookbook
Lake Murray Presbyterian Preschool Parents Organization
Chapin, South Carolina

Pineapple Casserole

We couldn't decide whether we liked this best as a sweet and crunchy side dish or with a scoop of ice cream for a warm dessert. You decide.

1 (8-ounce) can pineapple chunks,
    undrained
1 (8-ounce) can crushed pineapple,
    undrained
⅓ cup all-purpose flour
⅓ cup sugar

2 cups (8 ounces) shredded Cheddar
    cheese
1½ cups round buttery cracker
    crumbs (about 35 crackers)
½ cup butter or margarine, melted

COMBINE first 5 ingredients, stirring well. Spoon mixture into a greased 13- x 9-inch pan or baking dish. Combine cracker crumbs and butter, stirring well. Sprinkle crumbs over casserole. Bake, uncovered, at 350° for 30 minutes. Yield: 8 servings.

Judy Johnson
Carolinas Heritage
47th National Square Dance Convention
Charlotte, North Carolina

Rice-Cheese Casserole WEEKNIGHT FAVORITE

This recipe tastes grand with a full 16 ounces of cheese, but we found it almost as delicious with half that amount. Either way, this dish is a nice accompaniment with any simple meat or poultry entrée, or any Mexican main dish.

2 cups cooked rice
1 (8-ounce) container sour cream
1 (4.5-ounce) can chopped green
    chiles, undrained

2 to 4 cups (8 to 16 ounces)
    shredded Monterey Jack cheese

COMBINE first 3 ingredients in a large bowl. Spoon half of rice mixture into a lightly greased 11- x 7-inch baking dish. Cover with half of cheese. Spoon remaining half of rice mixture over cheese, and sprinkle with remaining cheese. Bake, uncovered, at 350° for 25 minutes. Yield: 8 to 10 servings.

Paige Swiggart
Somethin's Cookin' with Married Young Adults
Houston's First Baptist Church
Houston, Texas

Quick Rice Tip
In a rush? Use boil-in-bag rice for this recipe. You can even cook it a day ahead and keep it chilled until time to assemble the casserole. A spicy option for this dish is to use Pepper Jack cheese that has flecks of red pepper in it.

Summer Squash and Cherry Tomatoes in Basil Butter

Pictured on page 28

If you have Basil Butter to spare or are inspired to make a double batch, try slathering it on corn on the cob or a baked potato.

1 pound yellow squash, thinly sliced
8 ounces cherry tomatoes, halved

⅔ cup Basil Butter, divided

SAUTÉ squash and tomato in 2 tablespoons Basil Butter in a large skillet over medium-high heat 10 minutes or until squash is tender. Serve with remaining Basil Butter. Yield: 6 servings.

Basil Butter

3 garlic cloves, minced
1 shallot, minced
¾ cup tightly packed fresh basil
    leaves

½ cup butter or margarine, softened
Freshly ground pepper to taste

PROCESS all ingredients in a food processor until smooth, stopping once to scrape down sides. Cover and chill until ready to use. Yield: ⅔ cup.

Dining by Fireflies: Unexpected Pleasures of the New South
The Junior League of Charlotte, North Carolina

Buying Time
Slice yellow squash and halve the tiny tomatoes; then seal in separate zip-top bags. Refrigerate up to 1 day before sautéing for this side dish.

Southwestern Casserole, page 64

Healthy Homestyle Cooking

Good Southern homestyle cooking doesn't mean food has to be deep-fried or overcooked. Fill your plate with these healthy recipes that also fit the bill as simple comfort food.

Mexican Shrimp Cocktail PARTY FOOD

This south-of-the-border shrimp cocktail entertains tangy flavors, an array of textures, and bright colors.

2 pounds unpeeled, large fresh shrimp
6 cups water
2 to 3 tablespoons fresh lime juice
3 garlic cloves, pressed
¼ teaspoon salt
½ teaspoon pepper
1 cup ketchup
½ cup fresh lime juice
¼ cup minced sweet onion
½ to 1 teaspoon hot sauce
½ cup chopped tomato
½ cup chopped fresh cilantro
Avocado slices, lime wedges, saltine crackers (optional)

PEEL shrimp, and devein, if desired.

BRING 6 cups water and next 4 ingredients to a boil in a large saucepan; add shrimp. Cook 2 to 3 minutes or just until shrimp turn pink. Drain shrimp, reserving ½ cup liquid.

STIR together reserved liquid, ketchup, and next 3 ingredients. Stir in shrimp, tomato, and cilantro. Cover and chill. If desired, serve with avocado slices, lime wedges, and saltine crackers. Yield: 6 servings.

Elisa Levy
Tallahassee, Florida

Per serving: Calories 172 (11% from fat); Fat 2.1g (sat 0.4g, mono 0.3g, poly 0.8g); Protein 21.8g; Carb 17.8g; Fiber 1.2g; Chol 154mg; Iron 3.2mg; Sodium 795mg; Calc 76mg

Veggie Roll-Up QUICK & EASY

This calcium-rich roll-up will tone your bones and teeth.

2 tablespoons reduced-fat cream cheese
2 teaspoons light mayonnaise
⅛ teaspoon dill seeds
⅛ teaspoon dried parsley flakes
Dash of garlic powder
Dash of dried basil
1 small carrot, diced
1 small celery rib, diced
1 (7½-inch) flour tortilla

STIR together first 6 ingredients. Stir in carrot and celery. Spread on 1 side of tortilla. Roll up, and wrap in plastic wrap; chill. Unwrap and slice. Yield: 1 roll-up.

Shaylee Erdelbrock
Castle Rock, Washington

Per roll-up: Calories 292 (37% from fat); Fat 12g (sat 4.5g, mono 2.9g, poly 0.7g); Protein 9g; Carb 38g; Fiber 2.8g; Chol 20mg; Iron 1.8mg; Sodium 492mg; Calc 173mg

Sweet-and-Sour Meatballs PARTY FOOD

Put these saucy appetizer meatballs on a buffet line in a chafing dish to keep them warm. Guests will enjoy the sweet-tangy pairing.

¾ pound extra-lean ground beef
¾ pound ground turkey
1 small onion, minced
¼ cup egg substitute
½ cup Italian-seasoned breadcrumbs
¾ cup ketchup

⅓ cup white vinegar
¼ cup low-sodium Worcestershire sauce
3 tablespoons sugar
2 teaspoons dry mustard

COMBINE first 5 ingredients; shape mixture into 1-inch balls.

BROWN meatballs, in batches, in a large nonstick skillet over medium-high heat. Remove meatballs from skillet, and wipe skillet clean. Stir together ketchup and remaining 4 ingredients in skillet; bring to a boil.

ADD meatballs; reduce heat, and simmer 5 minutes or until meatballs are no longer pink. Yield: 3½ dozen.

Sharon Anderson
Franklin, Tennessee

Per meatball: Calories 43 (33% from fat); Fat 1.5g (sat 0.5g, mono 0.6g, poly 0.2g); Protein 3.5g; Carb 3.5g; Fiber 0.1g; Chol 9mg; Iron 0.4mg; Sodium 95mg; Calc 6mg

Make-Ahead Meatballs

Meatballs may be thoroughly cooked without sauce and frozen. Thaw and reheat with sauce.

Mint Tea QUICK & EASY   WEEKNIGHT FAVORITE

Tea Tips
The longer you steep tea, the stronger it will taste. So keep track of the 12 minutes for this recipe. For variety, use herb-flavored tea bags.

This sweet summer sipper keeps calories and fat low while providing lots of vitamin C.

4 cups water
8 regular-size tea bags
5 fresh mint sprigs
½ cup sugar
1 (46-ounce) can pineapple juice

1 (6-ounce) can frozen lemonade
   concentrate, thawed and
   undiluted
4 cups cold water

BRING 4 cups water to a boil in a large saucepan. Add tea bags, mint sprigs, and sugar; remove from heat. Cover and steep 12 minutes. Remove and discard tea bags and mint sprigs, squeezing tea bags gently. Add pineapple juice and lemonade concentrate, stirring until blended. Stir in cold water. Serve over ice. Yield: 16 (1-cup) servings.

Today's Traditional: Jewish Cooking with a Lighter Touch
Congregation Beth Shalom
Carmichael, California

Per serving: Calories 90 (0% from fat); Fat 0.1g (sat 0.0g, mono 0.0g, poly 0.0g); Protein 0.3g; Carb 22.7g; Fiber 0.0g; Chol 0mg; Iron 0.1mg; Sodium 3mg; Calc 0.8mg

Get-Up-and-Go Shake QUICK & EASY

Soy Solution
Soy milk has numerous health benefits for women and men. You can find it in vanilla, chocolate, and coffee flavors.

Here's a quick breakfast-in-a-blender idea for rushed weekdays.

2 cups low-fat soy milk or fat-free
   milk (we tested with White Wave
   Silk Plain Soymilk)
1 (8-ounce) container vanilla
   low-fat yogurt

½ cup frozen apple juice concentrate,
   thawed
4 large peaches, diced and frozen
   (about 2 cups)
½ teaspoon vanilla extract

PROCESS all ingredients in a blender until smooth, stopping to scrape down sides. Yield: about 5 cups.

Per cup: Calories 161 (8% from fat); Fat 1.5g (sat 0.3g, mono 0.2g, poly 0.5g); Protein 4.2g; Carb 34.1g; Fiber 1.5g; Chol 3mg; Iron 0.4mg; Sodium 75mg; Calc 91mg

DOUBLE STRAWBERRY SHAKE: *Substitute strawberry yogurt for vanilla yogurt and 2 cups frozen strawberries for 4 large peaches.*

English Muffin French Toast MAKE AHEAD

Serve this crispy French toast with fresh fruit for a satisfying start to the day.

1 cup egg substitute
1 cup fat-free milk
1 teaspoon vanilla extract
6 English muffins, split
Vegetable cooking spray

Chopped kiwifruit, blueberries,
   nectarines, strawberries
   (optional)
Garnish: fresh mint sprigs

STIR together egg substitute, milk, and vanilla. Place in a gallon-size zip-top plastic bag; add English muffins. Seal and chill 8 hours, turning occasionally. Remove muffins from bag, discarding remaining liquid.

COOK English muffins, in batches, in a large skillet coated with cooking spray, over medium-high heat 2 to 3 minutes on each side or until muffins are golden. Serve with light pancake syrup and, if desired, kiwifruit, blueberries, nectarines, and strawberries. Garnish, if desired. Yield: 6 servings.

Per serving: Calories 326 (8% from fat); Fat 3g (sat 0.7g, mono 0.4g, poly 0.2g); Protein 15.2g; Carb 60g; Fiber 2.3g; Chol 5mg; Iron 3mg; Sodium 468mg; Calc 309mg

Plan Ahead
Soak these muffins overnight in a light custard. Then most of your breakfast work is done.

Breakfast-Stuffed Potatoes MAKE AHEAD

These miniature stuffed potatoes are just the right size to pop in your mouth for breakfast. They're loaded with bacon, cheese, and broccoli.

6 (4-ounce) Yukon gold potatoes
¼ cup fat-free half-and-half
4 ounces fat-free cream cheese,
   softened
2 tablespoons grated Parmesan cheese
¼ teaspoon garlic salt
¼ teaspoon freshly ground pepper

4 turkey bacon slices, diced
½ small sweet onion, chopped
½ (10-ounce) package frozen
   chopped broccoli, thawed and
   drained
¼ cup (1 ounce) reduced-fat
   shredded Cheddar cheese

BAKE potatoes at 400° for 35 to 40 minutes or until tender; cool slightly.

CUT potatoes in half crosswise; gently scoop out pulp, leaving a ¼-inch-thick shell and reserving pulp. Stand potato shells, cut side up, in miniature muffin pan cups.

STIR together reserved pulp, half-and-half, and next 4 ingredients.

COOK bacon in a nonstick skillet over medium-high heat 2 to 3 minutes or until browned. Add onion and broccoli; sauté 4 to 5 minutes or until tender. Stir into potato mixture.

STUFF mixture evenly into potato shells. Sprinkle with Cheddar cheese.

BAKE stuffed potatoes at 350° for 15 minutes. Yield: 6 servings.

Per serving: Calories 239 (30% from fat); Fat 7.9g (sat 3.1g, mono 2.7g, poly 1.4g); Protein 15g; Carb 24.4g; Fiber 2.5g; Chol 36mg; Iron 1.1mg; Sodium 840mg; Calc 211mg

Buying Time
This is a great make-ahead recipe. Bake and scoop out potatoes, cook the bacon, and prepare the filling up to a day ahead. Then just stuff and bake potato halves while the coffee's brewing the next morning.

Cheddar Cheese Loaf `WEEKNIGHT FAVORITE`

Savor a slice of this Cheddar loaf with a bowl of soup or a salad.

3¾ cups reduced-fat biscuit mix
¾ cup (3 ounces) reduced-fat
    shredded sharp Cheddar cheese
1½ cups fat-free milk

¼ cup egg substitute
⅛ to ¼ teaspoon ground red pepper
Vegetable cooking spray

COMBINE biscuit mix and cheese. Add milk, egg substitute, and pepper, stirring 2 minutes or until blended. Spoon into a 9- x 5-inch loafpan coated with cooking spray.
    BAKE at 350° for 45 minutes. Yield: 1 loaf.

Marsha Tennant
Falmouth, Virginia

Per serving: Calories 157 (20% from fat); Fat 3.5g (sat 0.5g, mono 2g, poly 1g); Protein 6g; Carb 27g; Fiber 0.9g; Chol 2mg; Iron 1.3mg; Sodium 534mg; Calc 122mg

Cheese Toast

Make cheese toast using thin slices of this light loaf. Slice and toast in toaster. Or, go over the top and add an extra sliver of cheese to each slice and run it under the broiler. Serve cheese toast with a green salad.

Corn Sticks `QUICK & EASY`

Corn muffin batter gets transformed into sticks, ready for the oven in 10 minutes.

1 cup all-purpose flour
1 cup yellow cornmeal
1 tablespoon baking powder
1 teaspoon salt
1 (11-ounce) can sweet whole kernel
    corn, drained
2 tablespoons minced red bell pepper

¼ teaspoon ground red pepper
¾ cup 1% low-fat milk
½ cup egg substitute
2 egg whites
1 tablespoon vegetable oil
Vegetable cooking spray

COMBINE first 7 ingredients; make a well in center. Stir together milk and next 3 ingredients. Add to flour mixture, stirring just until moistened.
    HEAT cast-iron corn stick pans in a 450° oven 5 minutes or until hot. Remove pans from oven, and coat with cooking spray. Spoon batter into hot pans.
    BAKE at 450° for 15 minutes. Remove from pans immediately; cool slightly on wire racks. Yield: 20 sticks.

Rachel Taylor
Wadley, Alabama

Per breadstick: Calories 76 (11% from fat); Fat 0.9g (sat 0.1g, mono 0.4g, poly 0.2g); Protein 2.7g; Carb 14g; Fiber 0.6g; Chol 0mg; Iron 0.8mg; Sodium 252mg; Calc 55mg

Collecting Cast Iron

Cast-iron cookware is a must in any homestyle kitchen. Look for cast-iron corn stick pans at yard sales; they most likely will be well-seasoned from years of use.

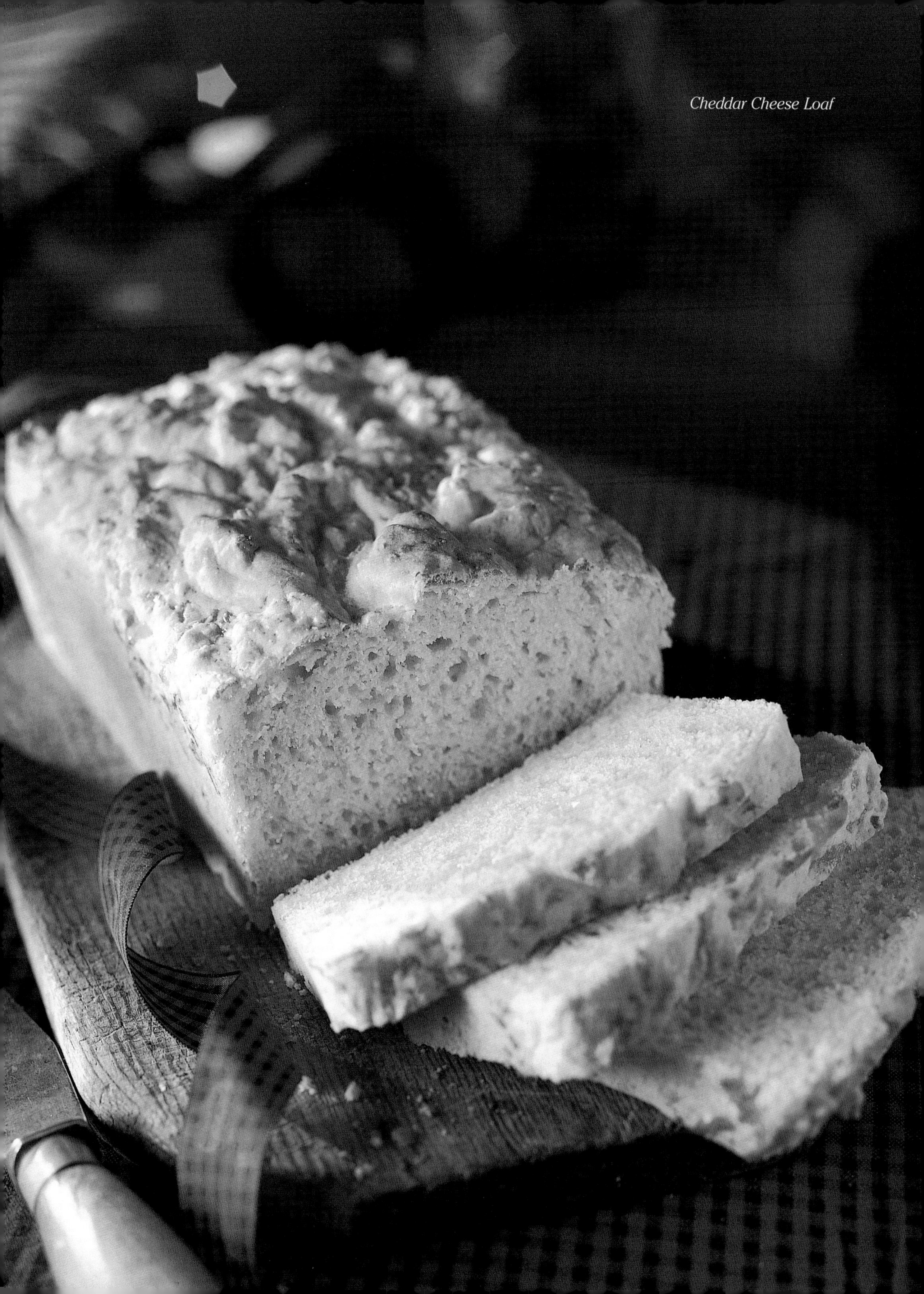
Cheddar Cheese Loaf

Oatmeal-Honey Bread

Loafing Around

If you don't own a 7½- x 3-inch loafpan, you can use a larger loafpan for this bread; the bread just won't fill the pan as full and will be a flatter loaf. It might bake a little quicker, too.

Slice and enjoy this golden loaf laced with honey for breakfast, lunch, or dinner.

1 (¼-ounce) envelope active dry yeast
1 teaspoon sugar
½ cup warm water (105° to 115°)
1 cup plain nonfat yogurt
1 cup quick-cooking oats
3 tablespoons honey

1 teaspoon salt
¼ teaspoon baking soda
2⅓ cups all-purpose flour
2 tablespoons all-purpose flour, divided
Vegetable cooking spray
1 tablespoon honey

COMBINE first 3 ingredients in a 1-cup liquid measuring cup; let stand 5 minutes.

COOK yogurt over medium heat until warm. Combine warm yogurt, oats, and next 3 ingredients in a large mixing bowl; beat at medium speed with an electric mixer until blended.

ADD yeast mixture to oat mixture; mix until blended. Gradually stir in enough flour to make a soft dough.

SPRINKLE 1 tablespoon flour over work surface. Turn dough out onto floured surface; knead until smooth and elastic (about 5 minutes). Place in a bowl coated with cooking spray, turning to coat top. Cover and let rise in a warm place (85°), free from drafts, 45 minutes or until doubled in bulk.

PUNCH dough down. Sprinkle remaining 1 tablespoon flour over work surface. Turn dough out onto floured surface, and knead lightly 4 or 5 times; roll into a 12- x 5-inch rectangle.

ROLL up dough, starting at short side, pressing to eliminate air pockets; pinch ends to seal. Place dough, seam side down, in a 7½- x 3-inch loafpan coated with cooking spray.

COVER and let rise in a warm place, free from drafts, 30 minutes or until doubled in bulk. Bake at 400° for 15 minutes. Reduce heat to 350°; bake 20 minutes or until loaf sounds hollow when tapped. Remove from pan immediately; brush with 1 tablespoon honey, and cool on a wire rack. Yield: 12 (½-inch-thick slice) servings.

A Slice of Paradise
The Hospital Service League of Naples Community Hospital
Naples, Florida

Per serving: Calories 155 (5% from fat); Fat 0.8g (sat 0.1g, mono 0.2g, poly 0.3g); Protein 5.1g; Carb 31.9g; Fiber 1.5g; Chol 0mg; Iron 1.6mg; Sodium 237mg; Calc 33mg

Heart-Healthy Chocolate Cupcakes

KID FRIENDLY   QUICK & EASY

Yes, even gooey rich chocolate desserts can be transformed into light fare. These cupcakes will satisfy kids of all ages. Pack 'em for a picnic or in lunchboxes.

1½ cups all-purpose flour	⅓ cup water
1 teaspoon baking soda	3 tablespoons vegetable oil
½ teaspoon salt	1 tablespoon white vinegar
½ cup sugar	1 teaspoon vanilla extract
¼ cup unsweetened cocoa	1 teaspoon powdered sugar
½ cup unsweetened orange juice	

COMBINE first 5 ingredients in a medium bowl; make a well in center of mixture. Combine orange juice and next 4 ingredients; add to dry ingredients, stirring just until dry ingredients are moistened.

SPOON batter into paper-lined muffin pans, filling two-thirds full. Bake at 375° for 12 to 14 minutes or until a wooden pick inserted in center comes out clean. Remove from pans immediately, and cool on a wire rack. Sprinkle powdered sugar evenly over cooled cupcakes. Yield: 1 dozen.

Sister Marguerite Charette
Not by Bread Alone
Catholic Committee on Scouting and Camp Fire for the Diocese of
Lake Charles, Louisiana

Per Cupcake: Calories 134 (26% from fat); Fat 3.8 g (sat 0.4g, mono 2.1g, poly 1.1g) Carb 22.6 g; Fiber 1.0g; Protein 2.2g; Iron 1.0g; Chol 0mg; Sodium 204mg; Calc 6mg

Cool Cocoa
You can store cocoa in its original container in a cool, dry place, such as the pantry, up to 2 years.

Blue Ribbon Angel Food Cake

This feathery light cake is great alone or with fresh berries.

1½ cups sifted cake flour	1 teaspoon vanilla extract
12 egg whites	¼ teaspoon almond extract
1¼ teaspoons cream of tartar	1⅓ cups sugar
¼ teaspoon salt	

SIFT flour 4 times, and set aside.

BEAT egg whites and next 4 ingredients at high speed with an electric mixer until soft peaks form (about 5 minutes). Gradually add sugar, ⅓ cup at a time, beating until blended after each addition. Fold in flour. Pour batter into an ungreased 10-inch tube pan.

BAKE at 375° for 35 minutes. Invert pan onto a wire rack, and let stand 1 hour or until cake is completely cool. Run a knife around cake to loosen edges. Yield: 16 servings.

Carrie E. Treichel
Johnson City, Tennessee

Per serving: Calories 111 (1% from fat); Fat 0.1g (sat 0.0g, mono 0.0g, poly 0.0g); Protein 3.3g; Carb 24g; Fiber 0g; Chol 0mg; Iron 0.7mg; Sodium 78mg; Calc 3mg

"Eggstra" Idea
Angel food cake is one of those naturally light, airy desserts, thanks to the power of egg white. You will, however, have 12 egg yolks available after making the cake. We suggest whipping up a nice omelet for brunch and sharing it, of course.

Sour Cream Pound Cake with Raspberry Sauce PARTY FOOD

You'd never guess this moist, sugary snow-capped cake is light. The two-ingredient sauce adds brilliant color to each dessert plate, but the cake's just as good sans sauce, too.

Vegetable cooking spray
All-purpose flour
1 (18.25-ounce) package reduced-fat yellow cake mix
½ cup sugar
1 (8-ounce) container fat-free sour cream

1 cup egg substitute
¾ cup applesauce
1 teaspoon almond or vanilla extract
Raspberry Sauce
Garnishes: powdered sugar, fresh mint sprigs

COAT a 12-cup Bundt pan with cooking spray, and sprinkle with flour, shaking to coat pan.

BEAT cake mix and next 5 ingredients at medium speed with an electric mixer 4 minutes. Spoon into pan.

BAKE at 325° for 45 minutes or until a wooden pick inserted in center comes out clean. Cool in pan on a wire rack 10 minutes. Remove from pan; cool completely on wire rack. Serve with Raspberry Sauce; garnish, if desired. Yield: 16 servings.

Raspberry Sauce

4 (10-ounce) packages frozen raspberries, thawed

4 teaspoons sugar

PROCESS both ingredients in a blender until smooth. Pour through a wire-mesh strainer, discarding seeds. Chill 1 hour. Yield: 3 cups.

Catherine Lawler
Baton Rouge, Louisiana

Per slice with 3 tablespoons sauce: Calories 262 (6% from fat); Fat 1.9g (sat 0.5g, mono 1.0g, poly 0.3g); Protein 4.4g; Carb 57.4g; Fiber 3.7g; Chol 1mg; Iron 1.3mg; Sodium 238mg; Calc 84mg

Cutting Cake Corners

A package of cake mix assures you of minimal mixing time for this recipe. And applesauce and sour cream stand in for creamy butter to give the cake a tender texture.

*Sour Cream Pound Cake with
Raspberry Sauce*

Breaded Chicken Drumsticks KID FRIENDLY

Dark-Meat Delicious

Dark meats, such as drumsticks, are juicier due to the higher fat content. But don't dismay, most of the fat's in the skin, which you remove before baking.

A colorful blend of spices coats these drumsticks that bake in the oven to crispy perfection.

½ cup fine, dry breadcrumbs
   (store-bought)
2 teaspoons onion powder
2 teaspoons curry powder
½ teaspoon dry mustard
¼ teaspoon salt
¼ teaspoon garlic powder

¼ teaspoon paprika
¼ to ½ teaspoon ground red pepper
12 chicken drumsticks, skinned
   (3 pounds)
¼ cup skim milk
Vegetable cooking spray
Garnish: fresh parsley sprigs

COMBINE first 8 ingredients in a shallow dish.

DIP chicken in milk; coat with crumb mixture, and place in a 13- x 9-inch baking dish coated with cooking spray. Coat chicken with cooking spray.

BAKE at 375° for 1 hour or until done. Garnish, if desired. Yield: 6 servings.

Nora Henshaw
Okemah, Oklahoma

Per serving: Calories 226 (24% from fat); Fat 5.8g (sat 1.5g, mono 1.9g, poly 1.4g); Protein 32.9g; Carb 57g; Fiber 0.6g; Chol 117mg; Iron 2.4mg; Sodium 314mg; Calc 57mg

Honey-Baked Chicken WEEKNIGHT FAVORITE

Browning the Bird

A spritz of cooking spray and a sprinkling of paprika helps to brown this bird.

Honey and lite soy sauce glaze this bird in delicious golden color.

¼ cup honey
¼ cup lite soy sauce
⅓ cup minced onion
2 tablespoons grated fresh ginger

2 garlic cloves, minced
1 (3-pound) whole chicken, skinned
Vegetable cooking spray
2 teaspoons paprika

COMBINE first 5 ingredients in a large heavy-duty zip-top plastic bag; add chicken. Seal and chill 1 hour, turning occasionally.

COAT a rack in a roasting pan with cooking spray.

REMOVE chicken from marinade, and place breast side up on rack. Pour marinade over chicken. Tuck wings under.

BAKE, covered with aluminum foil, at 375° for 45 minutes. Uncover; coat chicken with cooking spray, and sprinkle with paprika. Bake, uncovered, 45 more minutes or until a meat thermometer inserted into chicken thigh registers 180°, basting occasionally. Remove from oven, and let stand 15 minutes. Transfer to a serving dish. Yield: 6 servings.

Mary Frances Lanning
The Woodlands, Texas

Per serving: Calories 211 (28% from fat); Fat 6.6g (sat 1.9g, mono 2.5g, poly 1.5g); Protein 23.3g; Carb 14.1g; Fiber 0.4g; Chol 67mg; Iron 1.1mg; Sodium 477mg; Calc 18mg

Curried Chicken Salad MAKE AHEAD

Chicken salad is such satisfying comfort food. This version is not only low cal, but it gets a little crunch from toasted nuts, color from green grapes, and great flavor from a key ingredient: mango chutney.

2¼ cups cubed cooked chicken
    (skinned before cooking and
    cooked without salt)
2 cups seedless green grapes, halved
¾ cup thinly sliced green onions
¼ cup chopped walnuts, toasted

¼ cup light mayonnaise
¼ cup plain nonfat yogurt
1 teaspoon curry powder
5 green leaf lettuce leaves
5 tablespoons mango chutney

COMBINE first 7 ingredients in a large bowl, tossing well. Cover and chill at least 2 hours.
SPOON 1 cup chicken mixture onto each individual lettuce-lined salad plate. Top each serving with 1 tablespoon mango chutney. Yield: 5 servings.

Shug Lockett
River Road Recipes III: A Healthy Collection
The Junior League of Baton Rouge, Louisiana

Per serving: Calories 283 (38% from fat); Fat 12.1g (sat 1.7g, mono 1.4g, poly 3.5g); Protein 21.7g; Carb 23.1g; Fiber 2.2g; Chol 58mg; Iron 1.6mg; Sodium 309mg; Calc 47mg

Curry Comments

Curry powder keeps sodium to a minimum because it replaces salt in this familiar main-dish salad. It's widely used in Middle Eastern cuisines and gives a hint of yellow color.

Chicken-Rice Casserole WEEKNIGHT FAVORITE

Casseroles are a family cook's best friends—they're easy to prepare and are universally popular. This classic chicken and rice combo cuts calories while keeping taste intact.

½ cup chopped celery
¼ cup chopped onion
2 garlic cloves, minced
Vegetable cooking spray
1 (8-ounce) package sliced fresh
    mushrooms
1 cup uncooked regular rice
1 (10¾-ounce) can reduced-sodium,
    reduced-fat cream of
    mushroom soup, undiluted

1 cup water
1 (8-ounce) can sliced water
    chestnuts, drained
3 tablespoons chopped fresh parsley
¼ cup dry sherry (optional)
6 skinned bone-in chicken breast
    halves
½ teaspoon salt
½ teaspoon pepper

SAUTÉ first 3 ingredients in a large nonstick skillet coated with vegetable cooking spray over medium heat 5 minutes or until tender. Add mushrooms, and sauté 2 minutes. Stir in rice, next 4 ingredients, and, if desired, sherry; spoon into a lightly greased 13- x 9-inch baking dish. Top with chicken. Sprinkle chicken with salt and pepper.
BAKE, covered, at 350° for 1 hour or until chicken is done. Yield: 6 servings.

Per serving: Calories 300 (9% from fat); Fat 2.9g (sat 0.9g, mono 0.4g, poly 0.5g); Protein 29.7g; Carb 36.8g; Fiber 2.4g; Chol 67mg; Iron 8.9mg; Sodium 476mg; Calc 75mg

Simple Servings

In this casserole, chicken breast halves are left intact to cook atop a bed of saucy mushroom rice, designating 6 hearty servings.

Southwestern Casserole   SUPPER CLUB

Pictured on page 50

Pictured on page 50

Soup or Sauce?

Cream of chicken and mushroom soups become the sauce for this comfort casserole. When you prepare a recipe with multiple canned items, open cans all at once to make preparation move along more smoothly.

Here's a great chicken casserole for the whole family or for supper club. A handful of canned goods and tortilla chips mixed with chicken and cheese make it convenience food at its finest.

1 onion, chopped
1 green bell pepper, chopped
1 jalapeño pepper, seeded and
    chopped
2 garlic cloves, minced
2 to 3 teaspoons chili powder
1 teaspoon dried oregano
Vegetable cooking spray
1 (10¾-ounce) can reduced-sodium,
    reduced-fat cream of
    mushroom soup, undiluted

1 (10¾-ounce) can reduced-sodium,
    reduced-fat cream of chicken
    soup, undiluted
1 (10-ounce) can diced tomatoes and
    green chiles, undrained
2¼ cups chopped cooked chicken
2 cups crumbled baked tortilla chips
5 tablespoons chopped fresh
    cilantro, divided
1 cup (4 ounces) shredded
    reduced-fat Cheddar cheese

SAUTÉ first 6 ingredients in a large nonstick skillet coated with vegetable cooking spray over medium heat 8 minutes. Stir in mushroom soup, next 4 ingredients, and 4 tablespoons cilantro; spoon into a lightly greased 13- x 9-inch baking dish.

BAKE, covered, at 350° for 30 minutes or until bubbly.

TOSS remaining 1 tablespoon cilantro with cheese. Uncover casserole; sprinkle with cheese mixture. Bake 3 minutes. Yield: 8 servings.

Georgana Dettman
Wiemar, Texas

Per serving: Calories 239 (25% from fat); Fat 6.4g (sat 3.0g, mono 0.6g, poly 0.8g); Protein 18.0g; Carb 26.1g; Fiber 2.8g; Chol 47mg; Iron 1.0mg; Sodium 704mg; Calc 180mg

An Apple-a-Day Pork Chops   WEEKNIGHT FAVORITE

Pork and Apple Pairing

Pork and apples are a classic combination. You can use any type of crisp eating apple in this skillet recipe; we just happen to be partial to the flavor of Red Delicious.

Simple ingredients create lightly sweet and tangy flavor in these homestyle chops that cook quickly in a hot skillet.

6 (4- to 6-ounce) boneless pork loin
    chops
Vegetable cooking spray
1 to 1½ tablespoons fresh or dried
    rosemary
½ to ¾ teaspoon salt
½ to ¾ teaspoon freshly ground pepper
1 medium-size Red Delicious apple,
    peeled and chopped

½ cup golden raisins
½ cup currants
2 teaspoons olive oil
¾ cup Marsala wine or apple cider
Garnishes: fresh rosemary sprig and
    apple slices

COAT both sides of pork chops evenly with cooking spray. Combine rosemary, salt, and pepper. Rub mixture evenly on both sides of pork; set aside.

COOK apple, raisins, and currants in hot oil in a large skillet over medium-high heat, stirring often, 5 minutes. Add ¼ cup wine, stirring constantly, until most of liquid is evaporated. Add remaining wine, and cook 15 minutes or until mixture is thickened.

COOK pork chops in a large skillet coated with cooking spray over medium-high heat 5 minutes on each side or until done. Top with apple mixture. Garnish, if desired. Yield: 6 servings.

Mary Grace Ellis
Delmar, Maryland

Per serving: Calories 286 (34% from fat); Fat 10.9g (sat 3.3g, mono 5g, poly 1.1g); Protein 24.5g; Carb 23g; Fiber 1.4g; Chol 68mg; Iron 1.9mg; Sodium 276mg; Calc 38mg

Oven-Fried Pork Chops   WEEKNIGHT FAVORITE

Now here's an easy dish. Just dip the pork chops in an egg white mixture, dredge them in seasoned breadcrumbs, and relax while they bake.

4 (6-ounce) lean center-cut
   pork loin chops
1 egg white
2 tablespoons unsweetened
   pineapple juice
1 tablespoon lite soy sauce

¼ teaspoon ground ginger
¼ teaspoon paprika
⅛ teaspoon garlic powder
⅓ cup Italian-seasoned breadcrumbs
Vegetable cooking spray

TRIM fat from pork chops. Combine egg white and next 5 ingredients in a shallow bowl, and whisk gently. Dip pork chops in egg mixture, and dredge in breadcrumbs.

PLACE chops on a rack in a roasting pan coated with cooking spray. Bake at 350° for 25 minutes; turn and bake 25 more minutes or until pork chops are done. Yield: 4 servings.

Libby Siskron
Traditions
First United Methodist Church/United Methodist Women
Tallassee, Alabama

Per serving: Calories 204 (28% from fat); Fat 6.1g (sat 1.9g, mono 2.5g, poly 0.6g); Protein 26.9g; Carb 8.3g; Fiber 0.4g; Chol 70mg; Iron 1.5mg; Sodium 381mg; Calc 39mg

Oven-Fried Fashion
These chops cook long and slow in a moderate oven for juicy, tender, and crispy results. Dipping the chops in egg white batter helps the breadcrumbs adhere for baking.

Honey-Grilled Tenderloins GRILL LOVERS

Butterfly Basics
Cutting a piece of meat down the center and unfolding it to open it flat (butterfly-ing) allows the meat to cook quickly and evenly.

Let outdoor grilling become a culinary obsession. Your kitchen will stay cool and clean, and you'll stay lean. Grilling adds wonderful flavor and color without adding fat and calories.

2 (¾-pound) pork tenderloins
¼ cup lite soy sauce
5 garlic cloves, minced
½ teaspoon ground ginger

2 tablespoons brown sugar
3 tablespoons honey
2 teaspoons dark sesame oil

MAKE a lengthwise cut down center of each tenderloin to within ¼ inch of opposite side; press to open.

COMBINE soy sauce, garlic, and ginger in a shallow dish; add tenderloins. Cover or seal, and chill 3 hours, turning occasionally.

STIR together brown sugar, honey, and oil.

GRILL tenderloins, covered with grill lid, over medium-high heat (350° to 400°) 20 minutes or until a meat thermometer inserted into thickest portion registers 160°, turning occasionally and basting with honey mixture. Yield: 6 servings.

Tammy Goff
Norfolk, Virginia

Per serving: Calories 139 (20.9% from fat); Fat 4.3g (sat 1.2g, mono 1.9g, poly 0.9g); Protein 24.8g; Carb 12.1g; Fiber 0g; Chol 74mg; Iron 1.8mg; Sodium 408mg; Calc 20mg

Low-Fat Spaghetti Casserole WEEKNIGHT FAVORITE

Time to Toss
Baking this spaghetti dish gives you time to toss a salad and pre-pare garlic bread.

Sausage adds some sass to this spaghetti casserole. It's the familiar thick and tasty tomato sauce spooned over pasta and topped with cheese, only it's baked.

7 ounces uncooked spaghetti
⅓ cup grated Parmesan cheese
2 egg whites, lightly beaten
1 tablespoon margarine
1 (8-ounce) container nonfat cottage cheese
1 pound low-fat ground pork sausage
½ cup chopped onion
¼ cup chopped green bell pepper

1 garlic clove, minced
1 (14½-ounce) can no-salt-added stewed tomatoes
1 (6-ounce) can no-salt-added tomato paste
1 teaspoon sugar
1 teaspoon dried oregano
½ cup (2 ounces) shredded reduced-fat mozzarella cheese

COOK spaghetti according to package directions, omitting salt; drain. Toss spaghetti with Parmesan cheese, egg whites, and margarine. Place in a lightly greased 8-inch square baking dish. Spread cottage cheese over spaghetti mixture.

COOK sausage and next 3 ingredients in a large nonstick skillet over medium heat, stirring until sausage crumbles and is no longer pink. Drain and pat with paper towels. Wipe drippings from skillet with a paper towel. Return sausage mixture to skillet; stir in stewed tomatoes and next 3 ingredients.

COOK over medium heat until thoroughly heated. Spoon over cottage cheese.

BAKE at 350° for 25 minutes. Sprinkle with mozzarella cheese before serving. Yield: 6 servings.

Karen C. Christiansen
Little Rock, Arkansas

Per serving: Calories 417 (31% from fat); Fat 13.7g (sat 5.1g, mono 1.0g, poly 0.4g); Protein 28.6g; Carb 41.2g; Fiber 4.3g; Chol 58mg; Iron 3.9mg; Sodium 814mg; Calc 215mg

Jerk Steak Tacos GRILL LOVERS

Soft tacos are basically small fajitas without the sizzle of the skillet. Instead, the marinated steak for these tortillas hits the grill and gets filled with smoky goodness.

4 green onions, coarsely chopped	2 tablespoons lime juice
1 garlic clove	1 to 1½ pounds flank steak
1 jalapeño pepper, seeded	1 bunch green onions
1 tablespoon ground allspice	4 large tomatoes
1 teaspoon dried thyme	Vegetable cooking spray
½ teaspoon ground nutmeg	¼ teaspoon salt
½ teaspoon ground red pepper	8 (8-inch) flour tortillas, warmed

PROCESS first 8 ingredients in a blender or food processor until smooth, stopping to scrape down sides. Spread seasoning mixture evenly over steak; cover and chill 8 hours.

GRILL steak, covered with grill lid, over medium-high heat (350° to 400°) 6 to 7 minutes on each side or to desired degree of doneness. Let stand 10 minutes; cut into thin slices.

COAT 1 bunch green onions and tomatoes evenly with cooking spray; sprinkle with salt.

GRILL, covered, over medium-high heat 10 to 15 minutes, turning occasionally. Coarsely chop vegetables. Serve with steak in warm tortillas. Yield: 8 servings.

Judy Carter
Winchester, Tennessee

Per serving: Calories 232 (26% from fat); Fat 6.6g (sat 2g, mono 1.8g, poly 0.3g); Protein 16g; Carb 29g; Fiber 2.5g; Chol 29mg; Iron 3.2mg; Sodium 399mg; Calc 89mg

Genuine Jerk

For several centuries, Jamaicans have enjoyed the spicy flavor of jerked meat. The culinary term "jerk" comes from this Caribbean style of food preparation in which a dry seasoning blend is rubbed on meats meant for the grill. The blend usually contains chiles, onion, garlic, thyme, and a blend of earthy spices.

Oven-Fried Catfish QUICK & EASY

Hot Sauce Savvy

Hot sauce soaks these fillets with fiery flavor so you won't miss the fact that they aren't fried. There are multiple hot sauces available. Keep in mind that hot sauces are made from different peppers; jalapeño is milder than cayenne; habanero is hotter than cayenne. When in doubt, check the sauce label.

Now you can enjoy Southern fried fish guilt free. This version's from the oven with a crisp cornmeal crust and a kick of hot sauce from the marinade.

6 (4-ounce) catfish fillets	1 to 1½ cups yellow cornmeal
¾ teaspoon salt	Vegetable cooking spray
1 (2-ounce) bottle hot sauce	Tartar Sauce

SPRINKLE fish with salt; place in a heavy-duty zip-top plastic bag. Add hot sauce; seal and chill 2 hours, turning occasionally.

REMOVE fish from marinade; dredge in cornmeal. Place fish on a baking sheet coated with cooking spray.

BAKE at 425° for 10 minutes or until fish flakes with a fork. Broil 3 inches from heat 4 minutes or until lightly browned. Serve with Tartar Sauce. Yield: 6 servings.

Per serving: Calories 209 (15% from fat); Fat 3.2g (sat 0.8g, mono 1.0g, poly 1.0g); Protein 20.4g; Carb 22g; Fiber 0.6g; Chol 66mg; Iron 1.3mg; Sodium 379mg; Calc 16mg

Tartar Sauce

1 cup light mayonnaise	1 tablespoon capers
1 tablespoon dill pickle relish	1 tablespoon grated shallots
1 tablespoon chopped pimiento-stuffed olives	1 tablespoon lemon juice
	⅛ to ¼ teaspoon hot sauce

STIR together all ingredients. Cover and chill 2 hours. Yield: 1¼ cups.

Per tablespoon: Calories 42 (86% from fat); Fat 4.0g (sat 0.6g, mono 0.1g, poly 0.0g); Protein 0.1g; Carb 1.4g; Fiber 0.1g; Chol 4mg; Iron 0.1mg; Sodium 132mg; Calc 2mg

Cheesy Spinach Lasagna SUPPER CLUB

Cheese and spinach provide the filling for this ultimate Italian comfort food gone healthy.

9 uncooked lasagna noodles
2 cups (8 ounces) shredded part-skim
    mozzarella cheese, divided
1 (16-ounce) container fat-free
    ricotta cheese
1 (10-ounce) package frozen chopped
    spinach, thawed and well drained
½ cup grated Parmesan cheese

1 teaspoon dried Italian seasoning
½ teaspoon garlic powder
¼ teaspoon salt
1 (3-ounce) package Canadian bacon,
    chopped
½ small onion, diced
Vegetable cooking spray
1 (26-ounce) jar low-fat pasta sauce

COOK pasta according to package directions; set aside.

STIR together 1½ cups mozzarella cheese, ricotta cheese, and next 5 ingredients.

SAUTÉ chopped Canadian bacon and diced onion in a skillet coated with cooking spray over medium heat 5 to 6 minutes or until onion is tender. Stir into cheese mixture.

SPREAD ½ cup pasta sauce in an 11- x 7-inch baking dish coated with cooking spray. Layer with 3 noodles and ½ cup pasta sauce; top with half of cheese mixture. Repeat layers once, ending with remaining cheese mixture. Top with remaining 3 noodles and remaining pasta sauce.

BAKE at 350° for 30 minutes. Sprinkle with remaining ½ cup mozzarella cheese; bake 5 more minutes or until cheese melts. Let stand 5 minutes. Yield: 8 servings.

Shannon Gaudin
Shreveport, Louisiana

Per serving: Calories 295 (22% from fat); Fat 7.3g (sat 4.3g, mono 2.2g, poly 0.5g); Protein 24g; Carb 33g; Fiber 3.6g; Chol 42mg; Iron 2.9mg; Sodium 799mg; Calc 504mg

NOTE: Freeze individual portions as desired. To reheat, bake, covered, at 300° for 1 hour.

Less is More
To reduce sodium and enjoy a meatless entrée, omit Canadian bacon and salt in this recipe.

Quick 3-Cheese Pizza

Quick 3-Cheese Pizza   WEEKNIGHT FAVORITE

One-Dish Delight

When your whole meal's in one dish, it's more economical. Meat also goes farther when stretched with vegetables. And cleanup's a snap.

No time for menu planning? Try this one-dish meal in a pizza, complete with healthy veggies and ready in under 45 minutes.

1 (10-ounce) can refrigerated pizza crust
Vegetable cooking spray
1 large red bell pepper, cut into thin strips
½ (8-ounce) package sliced fresh mushrooms
1 teaspoon olive oil
4 plum tomatoes, sliced
½ (10-ounce) package fresh spinach, torn

½ (14-ounce) can artichoke hearts, drained and coarsely chopped
3 ounces goat cheese, crumbled
1 cup (4 ounces) shredded reduced-fat mozzarella cheese
2 tablespoons shredded Parmesan cheese
1 teaspoon dried Italian seasoning
½ (10-ounce) package Canadian bacon, cut into thin strips

UNROLL pizza dough, and press into a 15- x 10-inch jellyroll pan coated with cooking spray.

BAKE at 425° for 5 to 7 minutes.

SAUTÉ bell pepper and mushrooms in hot oil in a large nonstick skillet over medium-high heat 5 to 7 minutes or until tender.

SPRINKLE bell pepper mixture, tomato, and remaining 7 ingredients over pizza crust.

BAKE at 425° for 6 to 10 minutes or until cheese melts. Let stand 5 minutes before serving. Yield: 4 servings.

Per serving: Calories 417 (34% from fat), Fat 15.6g (sat 7.5g, mono 4.3g, poly 0.8g), Protein 26.4g, Carb 43.0g, Fiber 3.1g, Chol 55mg, Iron 4.5mg, Sodium 1329mg, Calc 382mg

Avocado Citrus Salad   QUICK & EASY

For a complete meal, top this tangy salad with grilled chicken strips or canned albacore tuna.

3 tablespoons cider vinegar
2 tablespoons vegetable oil
1 tablespoon sugar
¼ teaspoon salt
8 cups torn salad greens
2 oranges, peeled and sectioned
1 large grapefruit, peeled and
    sectioned

1 pear, peeled and thinly sliced
2 ripe avocados, peeled and sliced
1 cup seedless green grapes
2 tablespoons chopped walnuts,
    toasted (optional)

WHISK together first 4 ingredients.

PLACE greens in a large bowl. Add orange sections and next 4 ingredients. Drizzle with dressing, tossing gently to coat. Sprinkle with walnuts, if desired. Serve immediately. Yield: 6 servings.

Ellie Wells
Lakeland, Florida

Per serving: Calories 355 (35% from fat); Fat 14g (sat 2g, mono 7.6g, poly 3g); Protein 4g; Carb 34g; Fiber 11g; Chol 0mg; Iron 1.5mg; Sodium 109mg; Calc 71mg

Buying Time
Peel and section the citrus for this salad, store in zip-top bags in the refrigerator, and whisk together the dressing up to a day ahead; then salad making becomes a breeze.

Creamy Cucumber Salad   MAKE AHEAD

Serve this simple cucumber salad with grilled chicken or a hamburger at a picnic.

¼ cup nonfat yogurt
1 teaspoon olive oil
½ teaspoon lemon juice
½ teaspoon minced fresh mint

¾ teaspoon salt
¼ teaspoon sugar
⅛ teaspoon pepper
2 cucumbers

STIR together first 7 ingredients until well blended.

PEEL, seed, and slice cucumbers. Add to yogurt mixture, tossing to coat. Cover and chill, stirring occasionally, at least 2 hours. Yield: 4 servings.

Charlotte Bryant
Greensburg, Kentucky

Per serving: Calories 35 (33% from fat); Fat 1.3g (sat 0.2g, mono 0.8g, poly 0.2g); Protein 1.7g; Carb 5g; Fiber 1.2g; Chol 0mg; Iron 0.4mg; Sodium 306mg; Calc 46mg

Cool as a Cucumber
Cucumbers are year-round food. They'll stay fresh in the refrigerator veggie drawer, uncut, up to 10 days. It's easy to select this produce in its prime—just look for cucumber with smooth, unblemished skin, a firm feel, and no soft spots.

White Bean-and-Tuna Salad QUICK & EASY

Stuff a whole wheat pita with this refreshing salad for a new way to enjoy tuna and beans.

On Beans
Cannellini beans are white Italian kidney beans. You'll often see them adding substance to salads and soups. If you can't find them, substitute great Northern beans.

2 tablespoons lemon juice
1 tablespoon olive oil
¼ teaspoon salt
½ teaspoon freshly ground pepper
½ teaspoon dried oregano
1 (20-ounce) can cannellini beans, rinsed and drained

1 (6½-ounce) can solid white tuna in spring water, drained and flaked
4 green onions, thinly sliced
2 tablespoons chopped fresh parsley
Lettuce leaves

STIR together first 5 ingredients. Add beans, tuna, and green onions, tossing gently to coat. Sprinkle with parsley, and serve over lettuce. Yield: about 3 servings.

Anna T. Rucker
Norfolk, Virginia

Per serving: Calories 261 (22% from fat); Fat 6.3g (sat 1.1g, mono 3.8g, poly 1.1g); Protein 23g; Carb 30g; Fiber 5.5g; Chol 17mg; Iron 3.7mg; Sodium 711mg; Calc 113mg

Vegetable Slaw MAKE AHEAD ONE BOWL

Never has slaw been so colorful and crunchy. This side dish has a surprising addition of bright bits of broccoli and cauliflower.

Slaw Decisions
There are several ways to yield 3 cups shredded cabbage for this recipe. You can shred it from a head of cabbage using a box grater or a shredding disk of a food processor. Or you can buy a bag of shredded slaw mix at the grocery.

¼ cup light mayonnaise
¼ cup light sour cream
1 tablespoon white vinegar
1 teaspoon salt
¼ teaspoon pepper
3 cups shredded cabbage

1 cup fresh broccoli florets, chopped
1 cup fresh cauliflower florets, chopped
2 cups seeded, diced plum tomato
½ cup chopped purple onion

STIR together first 5 ingredients in a large bowl. Add cabbage and remaining ingredients, tossing well; cover and chill 2 hours. Yield: 6 servings.

Janice Dellinger Whisenhunt
Goldsboro, North Carolina

Per serving: Calories 79 (46% from fat); Fat 4.4g (sat 1.1g, mono 0.1g, poly 0.2g); Protein 2.2g; Carb 9.4g; Fiber 2.5g; Chol 7mg; Iron 0.7mg; Sodium 532mg; Calc 45mg

Ranch-Style Beans   ONE PAN

Chili powder and spicy tomatoes spruce up these long-simmering cowboy beans.

1 (1-pound) package dried pinto beans	1 tablespoon chili powder
8 cups water	¾ teaspoon salt
1 cup diced onion	½ teaspoon dry mustard
1 small green bell pepper, diced	¼ teaspoon pepper
1 garlic clove, minced	1 (10-ounce) can diced tomatoes and
2 tablespoons Worcestershire sauce	green chiles

PLACE beans in a Dutch oven; add water 2 inches above beans. Bring to a boil. Boil 1 minute; cover, remove from heat, and let stand 1 hour. Drain.

BRING beans and 8 cups water to a boil in Dutch oven. Cover, reduce heat, and simmer 1 hour or until beans are tender. Add onion and next 7 ingredients; simmer 30 minutes. Add tomatoes; simmer 30 minutes. Yield: 7 cups.

Mary Jayne Allen
Chattanooga, Tennessee

Per serving: Calories 235 (4% from fat); Fat 1.2g (sat 0.2g, mono 0.2g, poly 0.4g); Protein 13.4g; Carb 44.9g; Fiber 14.5g; Chol 0mg; Iron 4.7mg; Sodium 474mg; Calc 96 mg

Cooking Dried Beans
Step one in this recipe rehydrates dried beans by the "quick soak" method. It heats the beans quickly and then allows time for them to soften in the hot water before cooking continues. No more soaking beans overnight with this recipe.

Tomato-Stuffed Yellow Squash

WEEKNIGHT FAVORITE

Shapely yellow squash make ideal serving shells for this summery herbed tomato stuffing.

3 medium-size yellow squash	2 tablespoons chopped fresh oregano
¼ cup chopped onion	¼ teaspoon salt
3 garlic cloves, minced	¼ teaspoon freshly ground pepper
2 teaspoons olive oil	⅓ cup fine, dry breadcrumbs
3 plum tomatoes, peeled, seeded,	1½ tablespoons shredded Parmesan
and diced	cheese

COOK squash in a saucepan in boiling water to cover 5 minutes or until tender; drain. Plunge into ice water to stop the cooking process; drain. Cut squash in half lengthwise; carefully scoop out seeds, and discard. Set shells aside.

SAUTÉ onion and garlic in hot oil in a saucepan 5 minutes or until tender. Stir in tomato and next 3 ingredients; cook over medium heat just until thoroughly heated. Stir in breadcrumbs; spoon mixture into squash shells. Sprinkle with cheese, and place on a baking sheet.

BAKE, covered, at 375° for 25 minutes or until heated. Yield: 6 servings.

Per serving: Calories 77 (28% from fat); Fat 2.5g (sat 0.6g, mono 1.4g, poly 0.3g); Protein 2.9g; Carb 11.2g; Fiber 2.7g; Chol 1mg; Iron 0.9mg; Sodium 181mg; Calc 67mg

Squash Shortcut
Boiling tenderizes the squash and makes it easier to halve them and scoop out the seeds. And it gives you a headstart on cooking.

Thyme-Scented Green Beans with Smoked Almonds   QUICK & EASY

Ingredient Options

You can substitute 1 tablespoon chopped fresh thyme for the dried thyme. Also, 1 tablespoon chopped toasted almonds may be substituted for the smoked almonds.

A sprinkling of smoked almonds adds an extra burst of flavor to these basic beans. Find smoked almonds in the snack section of the supermarket.

1 pound fresh green beans, trimmed	¼ teaspoon salt
1 tablespoon light butter	¼ teaspoon pepper
1 teaspoon dried thyme	1 tablespoon chopped smoked almonds

ARRANGE green beans in a steamer basket over boiling water. Cover and steam 6 minutes or until crisp-tender.

MELT butter in a large skillet over medium heat. Stir in green beans, thyme, salt, and pepper; cook until thoroughly heated. Sprinkle beans with almonds. Yield: 4 servings.

Beth Royals
Richmond, Virginia

Per serving: Calories 76 (44% from fat); Fat 3.7g (sat 2g, mono 0.5g, poly 1g); Protein 3.1g; Carb 10g; Fiber 3g; Chol 5mg; Iron 3.5mg; Sodium 196mg; Calc 80mg

Oven-Roasted Sweet Potatoes and Onions   ONE PAN

On Roasting

Roasting vegetables at a high temperature with just a tiny bit of oil brings out their natural sweetness. It's a simple, healthy cooking method that you can apply to just about any vegetable. Just be sure to cut pieces the same size so they'll cook evenly.

Toss and roast sweet potatoes and onions with a little oil and seasoning, and you've got a side dish fit for chicken, pork, or turkey.

4 medium-size sweet potatoes (about 2¼ pounds)	¼ teaspoon salt
2 medium-size sweet onions	Vegetable cooking spray
1 tablespoon olive oil	
½ teaspoon garlic pepper seasoning (we tested with Lawry's Garlic Pepper Blend)	

PEEL sweet potatoes, and cut each into 2-inch pieces. Cut onions into 1-inch pieces.

TOSS together sweet potato, onion, oil, and seasonings in a 15- x 10-inch jellyroll pan coated with cooking spray.

BAKE at 425° for 35 minutes or until tender, stirring occasionally. Yield: 6 servings.

Joy Howell
Anniston, Alabama

Per serving: Calories 190 (11% from fat); Fat 2.5g (sat 0.4g, mono 1.7g, poly 0.3g); Protein 3.1g; Carb 40.0g; Fiber 5.2g; Chol 0mg; Iron 0.8mg; Sodium 113mg; Calc 50mg

Smoky Mashed Potato Bake   SUPPER CLUB

Some fattening side dishes may seem impossible to lighten, but not these mashed pota-
toes. A little bit of smoky cheese and chipotle peppers (smoked jalapeños) make these
potatoes dynamite delicious.

3 garlic cloves, minced
1 teaspoon olive oil
Vegetable cooking spray
3½ pounds new potatoes, cut into
    1-inch pieces
¾ cup (3 ounces) shredded smoked
    Gouda cheese, divided

1 cup fat-free half-and-half
2 to 3 chipotle peppers in adobo
    sauce, minced
½ cup light margarine
½ (8-ounce) package fat-free cream
    cheese, softened
¼ teaspoon salt

SAUTÉ garlic in hot oil in a small skillet coated with cooking spray over medium-high heat 2 to 3 minutes or until tender. Set aside.

COOK potatoes in a Dutch oven in boiling water to cover 25 to 30 minutes or until tender; drain.

MASH potatoes in a large bowl. Stir in garlic, ¼ cup Gouda cheese, half-and-half, and remaining 4 ingredients until blended. Spoon mixture into a 13- x 9-inch baking dish coated with cooking spray. Sprinkle evenly with remaining ½ cup Gouda cheese.

BAKE at 350° for 30 minutes or until thoroughly heated. Yield: 10 servings.

Michelle Zacharia
Omaha, Nebraska

Per ½ cup: Calories 245 (32% from fat); Fat 8.8g (sat 1.6g, mono 1g, poly 0.2);
Protein 7.3g; Carb 32g; Fiber 2.9g; Chol 12mg; Iron 2.1mg; Sodium 369mg; Calc 152mg

Potato Peels

Leave the peeling on the new potatoes for this casserole. It'll save you time, and the peel will add bits of rustic red color to the dish.

Low-Fat Corn and Potato Chowder

ONE PAN

Perfect for a chilly autumn day, this chowder's ready in about 20 minutes.

1½ cups peeled, cubed baking potato
¾ cup chopped onion
½ cup chopped celery
½ cup chopped carrot
1 cup water
½ teaspoon salt
½ teaspoon dried parsley flakes

1 teaspoon chicken bouillon granules
¼ teaspoon ground white pepper
1 (15¼-ounce) can whole kernel corn, undrained
2½ cups 2% low-fat milk
1 cup instant potato flakes

COMBINE first 6 ingredients in a medium saucepan. Bring to a boil; reduce heat, and simmer, uncovered, 15 minutes or until vegetables are tender, stirring occasionally. Stir in parsley flakes and next 4 ingredients. Cook over low heat until thoroughly heated (do not boil). Stir in potato flakes. Serve immediately. Yield: 7½ cups.

A Slice of Paradise
The Hospital Service League of Naples Community Hospital
Naples, Florida

Per 1½ cups: Calories 202 (15% from fat); Fat 3.3g (sat 1.5g, mono 0.7g, poly 0.2g); Protein 7.5g; Carb 35.9g; Fiber 3.8g; Chol 9mg; Iron 0.9mg; Sodium 726mg; Calc 167mg

Vegetable Stew MEATLESS MAIN

This stew makes a filling meal. Add a little shredded cheese to each serving so you'll get plenty of protein, and cornbread's a good idea, too.

2 poblano peppers
1 onion, chopped
2 teaspoons olive oil
1 medium butternut squash, peeled and cut into ½-inch cubes
2 garlic cloves, minced
1 (16-ounce) package frozen butter peas

3 (14½-ounce) cans low-sodium fat-free chicken broth
1½ teaspoons grated fresh ginger
¼ teaspoon ground red pepper
1 (14½-ounce) can diced tomatoes, undrained
½ teaspoon salt
½ cup chopped fresh cilantro

BROIL peppers on an aluminum foil-lined baking sheet 5 inches from heat about 5 minutes on each side or until peppers look blistered.

PLACE peppers in a zip-top plastic bag; seal bag, and let peppers stand 10 minutes to loosen skins. Peel peppers; remove and discard seeds. Chop peppers, and set aside.

SAUTÉ onion in hot oil in a Dutch oven over medium-high heat until tender. Add squash and garlic; cook, stirring often, 15 minutes or until squash begins to soften.

PROCESS half of squash mixture in a food processor or blender until smooth, stopping to scrape down sides. Return to Dutch oven.

ADD chopped pepper, peas, and next 5 ingredients; cook over medium heat 15 minutes or until squash is tender. Stir in cilantro; remove from heat. Yield: 8 servings.

Per cup: Calories 156 (10% from fat); Fat 1.7g (sat 0.3g, mono 0.9g, poly 0.2g); Protein 7.1g; Carb 28.2g; Fiber 2.8g; Chol 0mg; Iron 2.5mg; Sodium 243mg; Calc 70mg

Full-of-Veggies Chili ONE POT

Two kinds of beans, zucchini, and corn will fill your stockpot with flavor and make dinner for a crowd.

1 large sweet onion, diced
1 large green bell pepper, diced
2 garlic cloves, minced
2 tablespoons vegetable oil
1 (12-ounce) package ground beef substitute
1 large zucchini, diced
1 (11-ounce) can whole kernel corn, undrained
2 (15-ounce) cans no-salt-added tomato sauce

2 (10-ounce) cans diced tomato and green chiles, undrained
1 (15-ounce) can black beans, rinsed and drained
1 (15-ounce) can pinto beans, rinsed and drained
1 teaspoon sugar
1 (1¾-ounce) envelope Texas-style chili seasoning mix

SAUTÉ first 3 ingredients in hot oil in a large stockpot over medium-high heat 5 minutes or until tender. Stir in beef substitute and remaining ingredients. Bring to a boil; reduce heat. Simmer, uncovered, stirring often, 20 minutes. Yield: about 4 quarts.

Pam Echeverria
Tucson, Arizona

Per cup: Calories 128 (14% from fat); Fat 2g (sat 0.4g, mono 0.6g, poly 1g); Protein 16g; Carb 19g; Fiber 3g; Chol 0mg; Iron 1.6mg; Sodium 547mg; Calc 44mg

Chili Reserves

Since this chili yields 1 gallon, you can make it go a long way. Package it in freezer-proof containers and freeze up to 3 months. Thaw containers in refrigerator; then reheat chili over medium heat in a saucepan or in the microwave.

New Year's Day Soup ONE PAN

Spinach Sleuth

Use this soup to sneak some spinach into your family's diet. The tomato-based blend is so full of smoky ham and peas, they won't even notice the greens.

This soup certainly has all the good-luck ingredients you need—spinach and black-eyed peas. It's also packed with vitamins to help you stay healthy in the New Year.

1 cup diced smoked lean ham
2 celery ribs, chopped
1 medium onion, chopped
2 carrots, chopped
2 garlic cloves, minced
2 (15-ounce) cans black-eyed peas, undrained
2 (14½-ounce) cans low-sodium fat-free chicken broth
2 (14½-ounce) cans no-salt-added stewed tomatoes, undrained
1 (14½-ounce) can no-salt-added diced tomatoes, undrained
1 (8-ounce) can tomato sauce
1½ cups chopped fresh spinach
½ cup chopped fresh parsley
½ teaspoon pepper
Garnish: chopped fresh spinach

SAUTÉ first 5 ingredients over medium heat in a Dutch oven until vegetables are tender.
STIR in black-eyed peas and next 4 ingredients; bring mixture to a boil. Cover, reduce heat, and simmer 1 hour and 30 minutes. Stir in 1½ cups spinach, parsley, and pepper. Garnish, if desired. Yield: 10 cups.

Chris Schrang
Cumming, Georgia

Per cup: Calories 126 (5% from fat); Fat 0.8g (sat 0.2g, mono 0.3g, poly 0.1g); Protein 9.9g; Carb 22.7g; Fiber 6.0g; Chol 6mg; Iron 3.1mg; Sodium 984mg; Calc 88mg

Appetizers, Snacks & Beverages

Hearty Mint Juleps, page 106
Cheese Straws, page 87

BLT Dip QUICK & EASY

Variations on a Theme

For a spicier version, use salsa in place of the tomatoes. For a lighter version, use light mayonnaise, fat-free sour cream, and turkey bacon.

If you're a BLT fan, you'll delight in this dip—it includes everything but the lettuce! Or enjoy it over lettuce as a chunky salad dressing.

1 cup mayonnaise
1 (8-ounce) container sour cream

1 pound bacon, cooked and crumbled
2 large tomatoes, chopped

COMBINE mayonnaise and sour cream in a medium bowl, stirring well with a wire whisk; stir in bacon and tomato. Serve immediately with melba toast rounds. Yield: 4 cups.

Savour St. Louis
Barnes-Jewish Hospital Auxiliary Plaza Chapter
St. Louis, Missouri

Coyote Caviar MAKE AHEAD PARTY FOOD

Choosing Chips

This is one of those dips that goes with just about any type of chip for dipping.

For this crowd pleaser, sprinkle a colorful marinated black bean dip over a bed of cream cheese, and then top it with a ring of chopped egg and green onions.

1 (15-ounce) can black beans, rinsed and drained
1 (4¼-ounce) can chopped ripe olives
1 (4.5-ounce) can chopped green chiles, undrained
1 small onion, finely chopped
1 garlic clove, minced
¼ cup chopped fresh cilantro
2 tablespoons vegetable oil
2 tablespoons lime juice
2 teaspoons chili powder

1 teaspoon black pepper
¼ teaspoon salt
¼ teaspoon dried crushed red pepper
¼ teaspoon ground cumin
1 (8-ounce) package cream cheese, softened
2 hard-cooked eggs, peeled and chopped
2 green onions, chopped

STIR together first 13 ingredients in a bowl. Cover and chill at least 2 hours.

TO SERVE, spread softened cream cheese on a round serving platter. Spoon bean mixture over cream cheese. Sprinkle egg around edge of bean mixture. Sprinkle green onions over bean mixture. Serve with tortilla chips. Yield: 12 appetizer servings.

Patti Hunter
Southern Elegance: A Second Course
The Junior League of Gaston County
Gastonia, North Carolina

Blue Chip White Salsa MAKE AHEAD

Cilantro lovers will fancy this salsa mixed with 1½ cups of the pungent herb. The salsa is also good as an accompaniment with grilled fish.

1 cup mayonnaise
1 (8-ounce) container sour cream
¼ cup fresh lime juice
4 garlic cloves, minced
1½ cups finely chopped fresh cilantro

1 (4¼-ounce) can chopped ripe olives
1½ cups chopped green onions
½ teaspoon hot sauce
⅛ teaspoon salt
⅛ teaspoon pepper

COMBINE mayonnaise and sour cream in a medium bowl, stirring well with a wire whisk; stir in lime juice and remaining ingredients. Cover and chill at least 6 hours; serve salsa with blue corn chips. Yield: 4 cups.

Simply Divine
Second-Ponce de Leon Baptist Church
Atlanta, Georgia

Fresh Flavor
Fresh lime juice really makes a flavor difference in a simple salsa recipe. To yield ¼ cup for this recipe, you'll need 2 limes. Just roll them on the countertop; then cut in half and squeeze.

Guacamole PARTY FOOD   QUICK & EASY

Everyone needs a simple guacamole recipe for those really ripe avocados. Here it is, with a little kick from jalapeño pepper and chopped tomato for color.

1 cup chopped tomato
3 ripe avocados, peeled and mashed
¼ cup finely chopped onion

1 jalapeño pepper, chopped
1 tablespoon lemon juice
1 teaspoon salt

RESERVE 1 tablespoon chopped tomato for garnish; place remaining chopped tomato in a medium bowl. Add avocado and remaining 4 ingredients; stir well. Sprinkle with reserved tomato. Serve with tortilla chips. Yield: 4 cups.

Kay Bauer
Angel Food
St. Vincent de Paul School
Salt Lake City, Utah

Turn Up the Heat
For maximum heat from a jalapeño, chop the pepper, seeds and all. The fiery oils are in the seeds and ribs.

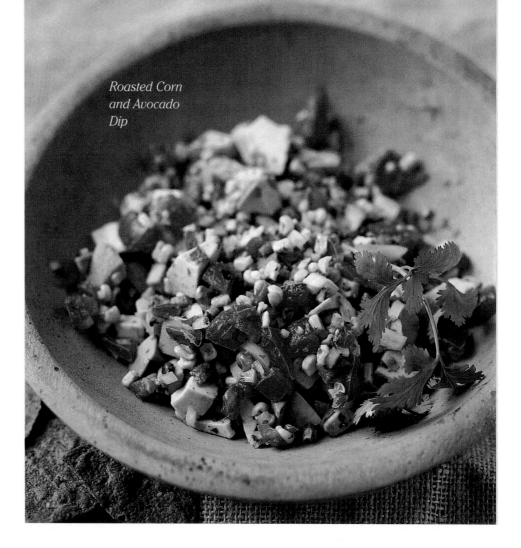

Roasted Corn and Avocado Dip

Roasted Corn and Avocado Dip

MAKE AHEAD

Caramelized Corn

Roasted corn throws a tasteful curve into this colorful dip. It takes only minutes of high-temperature roasting to bring out corn's natural caramelized sweetness. If you use fresh corn, just cut 1 cup's worth of kernels off the cob (about 2 ears).

A little chopping and stirring create a sassy multicolored do-ahead dip. Serve this fancy guacamole with a variety of chip colors for fun.

1 cup fresh or frozen whole kernel corn, thawed and patted dry
2 teaspoons olive oil
2 ripe avocados, peeled and chopped
¾ cup seeded, diced tomato
3 tablespoons lime juice
3 tablespoons chopped fresh cilantro

2 tablespoons minced onion
2 small canned jalapeño peppers, seeded and diced
2 garlic cloves, minced
½ teaspoon salt
¼ teaspoon ground cumin

COMBINE corn and oil in a shallow pan. Bake at 475° for 15 minutes or until corn is lightly browned, stirring occasionally. Cool.

COMBINE corn, chopped avocado, and remaining ingredients, stirring well. Cover and chill at least 8 hours before serving. Serve with tortilla chips. Yield: 2¾ cups.

Charlie Ward
Pepper Lovers Club Cookbook, Volume I
Pepper Lovers Club of Virginia Beach, Virginia

Cheesy Almond Spread   QUICK & EASY   PARTY FOOD

Bubbly hot cheese dip always goes over well at parties. This nutty Swiss recipe is no exception.

1 (8-ounce) package cream cheese, softened
1½ cups (6 ounces) shredded Swiss cheese
⅓ cup sliced almonds
⅓ cup mayonnaise or salad dressing
2 green onions, chopped
¼ teaspoon ground nutmeg
⅛ teaspoon pepper
Garnish: toasted almond slices

COMBINE first 7 ingredients, stirring well. Spread mixture into a 9-inch pieplate. Bake, uncovered, at 350° for 15 minutes or until heated. Garnish, if desired. Serve with crackers. Yield: 2 cups.

Judy Cross
Party Pleasers
GFWC Philomathic Club
Duncan, Oklahoma

Toasting Almonds

Toast almonds first, once your oven's preheated to bake the cheese spread. Spread them on a small baking pan and bake 5 to 10 minutes, stirring once or twice.

Hot Spinach Dip   PARTY FOOD

Chili powder and cumin are key spices in this twist on traditional spinach dip which will delight a hungry crowd. Halve the recipe if you're serving just a few.

2 (10-ounce) packages frozen chopped spinach, thawed
2 (8-ounce) packages cream cheese, softened
2 cups (8 ounces) shredded Monterey Jack cheese
1 cup freshly grated Parmesan cheese
1 small onion, chopped
1 (14-ounce) can artichoke hearts, drained and chopped
2 (10-ounce) cans diced tomatoes and green chiles, drained
2 teaspoons ground cumin
2 teaspoons chili powder
1 teaspoon garlic powder

DRAIN spinach; press between layers of paper towels to remove excess moisture.
COMBINE spinach, cream cheese, and remaining ingredients, stirring well. Spoon mixture into a greased 2½-quart baking dish. Bake, uncovered, at 350° for 30 minutes or until bubbly. Serve with melba toast rounds or corn chips. Yield: 8 cups.

Debbie Robinson
Blessings
First Presbyterian Church
Pine Bluff, Arkansas

Dip Tips

If you're one who likes a saucy, runny dip, don't drain the diced tomatoes and green chiles for this recipe. This dip is great with toasted baguette slices, assorted crackers, tortilla chips, or thin breadsticks.

Orange Hummus

Hummus has become a universally applauded dip. You'll find it on many restaurant menus and in small plastic tubs in large grocery stores in the deli/cheese area.

Southerners love to break bread together and enjoy the gift of gab. Dipping pita chips in hummus, the popular Middle Eastern favorite, provides the perfect opportunity.

2 (15-ounce) cans chick-peas, drained
⅓ cup orange juice
¼ cup tahini (sesame seed paste)
¼ cup olive oil
4 garlic cloves, crushed
1 tablespoon cider vinegar
1 teaspoon soy sauce
1½ teaspoons salt

¼ teaspoon ground cumin
¼ teaspoon ground coriander
¼ teaspoon ground ginger
¼ teaspoon dry mustard
¼ teaspoon ground turmeric
¼ teaspoon paprika
4 green onions, sliced

PROCESS first 14 ingredients in a food processor until smooth, stopping once to scrape down sides. Stir in green onions. Serve with pita chips. Yield: 3 cups.

Music, Menus & Magnolias
Charleston Symphony Orchestra League
Charleston, South Carolina

Vidalia Onion-Cheese Dip PARTY FOOD

Sweet Vidalias

Vidalia, Georgia, has the perfect soil for growing these sweet onions which are harvested, bagged, and sent across the South and beyond. If you can't find Vidalias, look for Walla Walla or Texas sweet onions instead.

This recipe really toots the horn of the beloved Southern Vidalia onion. It's sloppy, cheesy, gooey, and great with chips.

3 large Vidalia onions or other sweet onions, coarsely chopped
2 tablespoons unsalted butter or margarine, melted
2 cups (8 ounces) shredded sharp Cheddar cheese

1 cup mayonnaise
½ teaspoon hot sauce
1 garlic clove, minced

COOK onion in butter in a large skillet over medium-high heat, stirring constantly, until tender.

COMBINE onion, cheese, mayonnaise, hot sauce, and garlic; stir well. Pour into a lightly buttered 1½-quart casserole. Bake, uncovered, at 375° for 20 to 25 minutes or until bubbly and golden. Serve dip with tortilla chips or assorted crackers. Yield: 4 cups.

Come On In!
The Junior League of Jackson, Mississippi

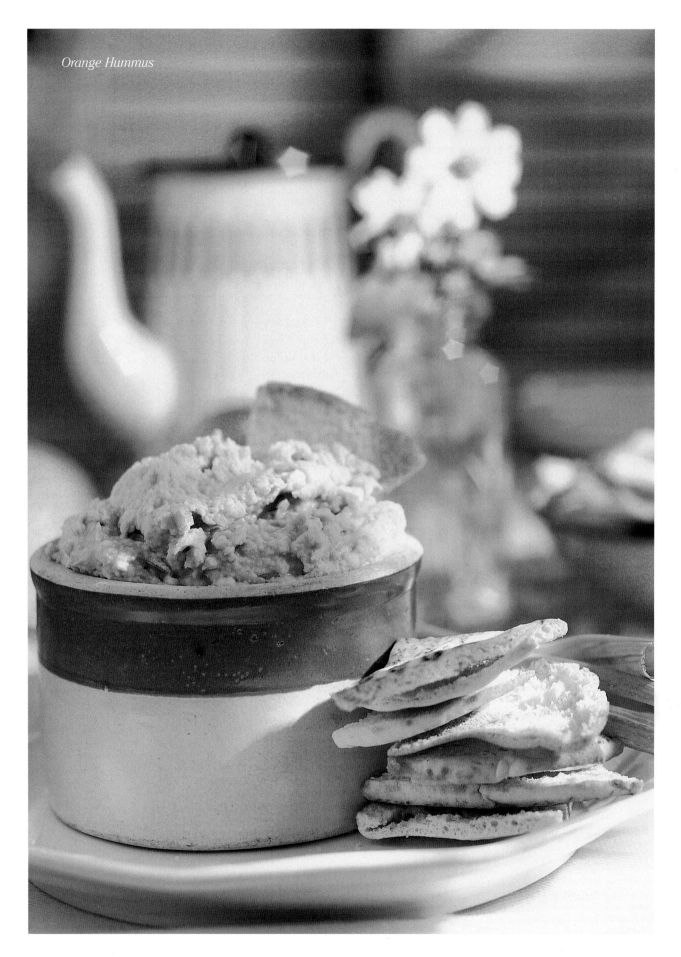

Orange Hummus

Crostini al Pomodoro PARTY FOOD

Toasting the Tomato

Pomodoro is Italian for tomato. In Italy, tomato-topped toasts (crostini) are a common and revered appetizer. Salting tomatoes draws out moisture, so when spooned over crostini, the toasts won't become soggy.

American Southerners and Italians share a love for juicy summer tomatoes. Here, the essence of summertime is enjoyed atop thin toasts.

8 plum tomatoes, diced	⅛ teaspoon freshly ground pepper
1 teaspoon salt	¼ cup olive oil
2 garlic cloves, minced	24 (¼-inch-thick) slices Italian bread,
2 tablespoons chopped fresh basil	toasted or grilled
2 tablespoons chopped fresh Italian parsley	

COMBINE tomato and salt; stir well. Place mixture in a wire-mesh strainer; drain 30 minutes. Combine tomato, garlic, and next 4 ingredients in a medium bowl; stir gently. Serve tomato mixture over toasts. Yield: 8 appetizer servings.

Elizabeth Mueller
The Educated Palate: The Hamlin School Cookbook
The Hamlin School
San Francisco, California

Hot Chili Peanuts

A Salty Situation

If you have unsalted dry-roasted peanuts in your pantry and prefer to use them instead of salted peanuts, simply add 1 to 2 tablespoons of salt instead of the ½ teaspoon called for in this recipe.

If peanuts are your thing, you'll love this spicy recipe. It makes enough to serve at several parties with enough left over to give away in gift bags.

9 cups salted dry-roasted peanuts (about 2½ pounds)	2 tablespoons ground red pepper
¼ cup plus 2 tablespoons butter or margarine, melted	1 tablespoon plus ½ teaspoon chili powder
	½ teaspoon salt

SPREAD peanuts in a single layer in an ungreased 15- x 10-inch jellyroll pan. Combine butter and remaining 3 ingredients; stir well. Pour butter mixture over peanuts; toss gently. Bake at 350° for 15 minutes, stirring often. Yield: 9 cups.

Karen Kohut
Tri-State Center for the Arts Celebrity Cookbook
Tri-State Center for the Arts
Pine Plains, New York

Cheese Straws MAKE AHEAD PARTY FOOD

Pictured on page 79

Cheddar cheese straws could be comparable to an old friend you look forward to seeing at a party. And when you serve 'em, the plate's always cleaned quickly.

4 cups (16 ounces) finely shredded sharp Cheddar cheese	2 cups all-purpose flour
½ cup butter or margarine, softened	1 teaspoon salt
	⅛ teaspoon ground red pepper

LET shredded cheese stand at room temperature 1 hour.

COMBINE cheese and butter in a large mixing bowl; beat at medium speed with an electric mixer until blended.

COMBINE flour, salt, and pepper; add to cheese mixture, beating until dough is no longer crumbly.

ROLL dough to about ¼-inch thickness on an unfloured surface. Cut into ½- x 3-inch straws. Place 1 inch apart on greased baking sheets. Bake at 350° for 14 to 15 minutes or until lightly browned. Cool on wire racks. Yield: 11 dozen.

Janci Cahoon
1840 - 1990 Sesquicentennial Cookbook
Group #4 Christian Women's Fellowship of Bethany
Christian Church
Arapahoe, North Carolina

Cookie Gun Fun
For a shapely variation, press dough through a cookie gun fitted with a 1½- x ⅛-inch disk, making long strips of dough 2 inches apart on greased baking sheets. Cut dough crosswise into 3-inch strips. Bake at 350° for 13 to 14 minutes or until lightly browned. Cool on wire racks. Yield: 7½ dozen.

Cayenne-Ginger Wafers MAKE AHEAD PARTY FOOD

White Cheddar and spicy candied ginger turn these cheese straw cousins into a dressed up appetizer.

1 cup (4 ounces) shredded white Cheddar cheese	¼ teaspoon ground red pepper
½ cup butter, softened	1 cup all-purpose flour
1 teaspoon salt	1 tablespoon finely chopped crystallized ginger

BEAT first 4 ingredients at medium speed with an electric mixer until creamy; add flour, and mix thoroughly. Shape dough into a ball. Wrap in plastic wrap, and chill 30 minutes.

SHAPE dough into 30 balls. Place 1 piece of ginger in center of each ball; place 2 inches apart on ungreased baking sheets, and flatten slightly with palm of hand. Bake at 350° for 15 minutes or until golden. Remove to wire racks to cool. Yield: 2½ dozen.

The Cook's Canvas
St. John's Museum of Art
Wilmington, North Carolina

Candied Ginger
Crystallized, or candied, ginger comes in a jar and is located in the spice section on the baking aisle of most grocery stores. It has a spicy, sweet taste and a little goes a long way in baked goods. If you use too much, it takes on a soapy taste.

Bleu Cheese Ball MAKE AHEAD   PARTY FOOD

Cheese Ball Finesse

What makes a cheese ball come together easily is giving the cheeses ample time to soften before blending with other ingredients. And for this cheese ball, we suggest toasting the pecans if you have time.

The belle of this ball is the whole package of crumbled blue cheese that's mixed with black olives and cream cheese and then rolled in crunchy pecans.

1 (8-ounce) package cream cheese, softened
1 (4-ounce) container crumbled blue cheese

½ cup chopped ripe olives
1 teaspoon Worcestershire sauce
1 cup finely chopped pecans

COMBINE first 4 ingredients in a bowl, stirring until blended. Shape into a ball, using wet hands; roll in pecans. Cover and chill thoroughly. Yield: 8 to 10 servings.

Gator Championship Recipes
Florida Goal-Liners
McIntosh, Florida

Almond-Bacon-Cheese Crostini

PARTY FOOD

Baguettes

A baguette is a long, narrow crusty loaf. You usually can find them individually sacked in the bakery section of large grocery stores. Use a serrated bread knife for easy slicing.

Bacon, cheese, and almonds are loaded onto little toasts and baked until oozing—be ready to serve them hot from the oven.

1 French baguette
4 bacon slices, cooked and crumbled
1 cup (4 ounces) shredded Monterey Jack cheese
⅓ cup mayonnaise

¼ cup sliced almonds, toasted
1 green onion, chopped
¼ teaspoon salt
Garnish: toasted sliced almonds

SLICE baguette into 36 (¼-inch-thick) slices. Arrange slices on an ungreased baking sheet; bake at 400° for 6 minutes or until golden.

COMBINE bacon and next 5 ingredients in a small bowl; stir well. Spread cheese mixture on slices; bake at 400° for 5 minutes or until cheese melts. Garnish, if desired. Serve immediately. Yield: 3 dozen.

The Dining Car
The Service League of Denison, Texas

Stuffed Mushrooms QUICK & EASY   PARTY FOOD

For a flavor-teaser, substitute ground turkey sausage or mild or hot Italian sausage for the pork sausage.

36 fresh mushroom caps
1 pound ground pork sausage

1 (8-ounce) package cream cheese,
     softened

CLEAN mushroom caps with damp paper towels; set aside.

BROWN sausage in a large skillet, stirring until it crumbles; drain well. Place sausage in a medium bowl; add cream cheese, and stir well. Spoon sausage mixture evenly into mushroom caps. Place mushrooms on an ungreased baking sheet. Bake, uncovered, at 350° for 10 minutes. Broil 5½ inches from heat 3 minutes or until lightly browned. Serve immediately. Yield: 3 dozen.

Janette Garland
Recipes on Parade
Calloway County Band Boosters
Murray, Kentucky

'Shroom School
Mushrooms are like sponges; that's why when cleaning them, you don't want to soak them in water. The best method is to wipe them with damp paper towels or a mushroom brush.

Parmesan-Coated Brie   MAKE AHEAD   PARTY FOOD

Enhance a round of Brie with this coating of Parmesan cheese and Italian breadcrumbs. It's cooked to a golden crunch which warms the cheese inside perfectly for spreading over French bread or crackers.

1 large egg, lightly beaten
1 tablespoon water
½ cup Italian-seasoned breadcrumbs
¼ cup freshly grated Parmesan cheese

1 (15-ounce) round Brie with herbs
¼ cup vegetable oil
Garnish: fresh rosemary sprigs

COMBINE egg and water in a shallow dish; set aside. Combine breadcrumbs and Parmesan cheese in a shallow dish. Dip Brie in egg mixture, turning to coat all sides. Dredge in breadcrumb mixture, turning to coat all sides. Repeat procedure. Chill at least 1 hour for coating to set.

HEAT oil in a small skillet over medium heat. Cook Brie in hot oil 2 minutes on each side or until golden. Garnish, if desired. Serve with sliced French bread or crackers. Yield: 10 to 12 appetizer servings.

Southern . . . On Occasion
The Junior League of Cobb-Marietta
Marietta, Georgia

Oui, Brie
Brie is a creamy, soft French cheese that's sold in rounds and often packaged in wooden crates. Brie coated and baked in pastry is a popular appetizer. This quick skillet version has a Parmesan-breadcrumb coating instead of pastry.

Cherry Tomato and
Gruyère Tarts

Cherry Tomato and Gruyère Tarts

MEATLESS MAIN   PARTY FOOD

These appetizer (or light lunch) tarts are addictive. They have a flaky, crisp pastry bottom, juicy tomato slices, herbs, and rich cheese.

1½ cups all-purpose flour
1½ tablespoons unsalted butter
⅛ teaspoon salt
5 to 7 tablespoons ice water
2 tablespoons Dijon mustard
6 ounces Gruyère cheese, thinly
    sliced
30 cherry tomatoes, sliced

1½ tablespoons fresh or 1½ teaspoons
    dried thyme
Salt to taste
Freshly ground pepper to taste
¾ cup (3 ounces) shredded Gruyère
    cheese
2 tablespoons olive oil
Garnish: fresh thyme

PULSE flour, butter, and ⅛ teaspoon salt in a food processor 12 times or until mixture is crumbly. Add 5 tablespoons water; process just until dough begins to leave sides of bowl and forms a ball, gradually adding remaining 2 tablespoons water, if necessary, for dough to form ball.

DIVIDE dough in half; shape each portion into a ball. Cover and chill 20 minutes.

ROLL each portion of dough to ⅛-inch thickness on a lightly floured surface. Cut pastry into 12 rounds, using a 4½-inch cutter. Place rounds on 2 ungreased 15- x 10-inch jellyroll pans. Crimp edges, if desired.

SPREAD rounds evenly with Dijon mustard; top with cheese slices, tomato, thyme, salt, and pepper. Sprinkle rounds with shredded cheese; drizzle with oil. Bake at 425° for 15 minutes or until pastry is golden. Garnish, if desired. Serve immediately. Yield: 1 dozen.

Herbal Harvest Collection
Herb Society of America, South Texas Unit
Houston, Texas

On Gruyère

Gruyère is a nutty Swiss hard cheese prized for eating out-of-hand and for cooking.

Baked Jalapeños PARTY FOOD

Boiling peppers tames the heat in this recipe. Even sensitive taste buds will love these stuffed peppers after the 10-minute boiling time. For hot pepper lovers, boil only 5 minutes.

25 medium jalapeño peppers
1 (8-ounce) package cream cheese, softened
3 cups (12 ounces) shredded Cheddar cheese

1½ teaspoons Worcestershire sauce
4 bacon slices, cooked and crumbled

CUT jalapeño peppers in half lengthwise; remove seeds.

COOK peppers in boiling water 5 to 10 minutes. Drain well.

COMBINE cream cheese, Cheddar cheese, and Worcestershire sauce; stir well. Place 1 heaping teaspoon cheese mixture in each pepper half; sprinkle with bacon. Place on a baking sheet. Bake at 400° for 5 minutes or until cheese is melted. Yield: 50 appetizers.

Saint Louis Days, Saint Louis Nights
The Junior League of St. Louis, Missouri

Fried Cheese with Italian Sauce

MAKE AHEAD   PARTY FOOD

Now you can make this restaurant favorite at home. The freezing time helps keep the cheese from leaking out of its golden fried shell.

2 (8-ounce) packages part-skim mozzarella cheese, cut into 1-inch cubes
3 large eggs, lightly beaten
½ cup all-purpose flour
¾ cup Italian-seasoned breadcrumbs
1 garlic clove, minced
1 teaspoon vegetable oil

1 (28-ounce) can whole tomatoes, undrained and chopped
1 teaspoon dried oregano
½ teaspoon sugar
¼ teaspoon salt
¼ teaspoon dried basil
Vegetable oil

DIP cheese in beaten egg. Dredge in flour. Dip coated cheese in beaten egg again; dredge in breadcrumbs, pressing firmly so that crumbs adhere. Place cheese on a wax paper-lined baking sheet, and freeze at least 1 hour.

COOK garlic in 1 teaspoon oil in a large skillet over medium-high heat, stirring constantly, until tender. Add tomatoes and next 4 ingredients. Bring to a boil, reduce heat, and simmer, uncovered, 45 minutes or until thickened, stirring occasionally. Set aside, and keep warm.

POUR oil to a depth of 1½ inches into a Dutch oven; heat to 375°. Fry cheese until golden. Drain on paper towels. Serve immediately with tomato sauce. Yield: 20 appetizers.

Mary Hules
Sharing Our Feast
Holy Apostles Episcopal Church
Memphis, Tennessee

Cold Smoked Salmon Soufflé

MAKE AHEAD   PARTY FOOD

Cream cheese and sour cream spiked with Madeira and fresh dill create a heavenly base to lace with smoked salmon. Cream cheese and gelatin make this mold a little denser than a traditional soufflé and perfect for spreading on bagel chips or Belgian endive.

2 envelopes unflavored gelatin
¼ cup Madeira
½ cup chopped purple onion
3 shallots, chopped
1 (16-ounce) container sour cream
2 (8-ounce) packages cream cheese, softened
2 tablespoons grated lemon rind

½ cup minced fresh dill
1 teaspoon salt
½ teaspoon ground white pepper
1 pound thinly sliced smoked salmon, finely chopped
Garnishes: fresh dill sprigs, grated lemon rind

SPRINKLE gelatin over Madeira in a small microwave-safe bowl; stir and let stand 1 minute. Microwave at HIGH 15 seconds; stir until gelatin dissolves. Set aside.

PROCESS onion and shallots in a food processor until very finely chopped, stopping once to scrape down sides. Add sour cream, cream cheese, lemon rind, dill, salt, pepper, and reserved gelatin mixture; process until well blended, stopping to scrape down sides. Transfer mixture to a large bowl; fold in salmon.

POUR salmon mixture into a lightly oiled 8-cup mold lined with plastic wrap. Cover and chill 4 hours or until firm.

ABOUT 30 minutes before serving, invert mold onto a platter, and peel away plastic wrap. Garnish, if desired. Serve with bagel chips, pumpernickel squares, or Belgian endive. Yield: 7½ cups (about 30 appetizer servings).

Lore M. Dodge
De Nuestra Mesa: Our Food, Wine, and Tradition
New Hope Charities, Inc.
West Palm Beach, Florida

Gel Power
Dissolving unflavored gelatin is a two-step process. First you need to soften it in liquid; then you heat it to dissolve it. And then it's ready to be stirred into remaining ingredients to do its firming work.

That Junior League Pesto Mold `MAKE AHEAD`

Cooking Mold Options

If you don't own a mold for cooking, you can use any 6-cup round bowl for this recipe. To check the size of a bowl, just pour water in the bowl to almost full; then measure that amount of water.

The title of this recipe hints that it's the talk of the party whenever it's served, and we understand why. Not only does it taste exceptional, but it's easy to make ahead. And it unmolds to make a stately presentation with ribbons of pretty green pesto layered between cream cheese whipped with butter.

2 (8-ounce) packages cream cheese, softened
1 pound unsalted butter, softened
¼ cup pine nuts, toasted
2 or 3 garlic cloves
1 cup tightly packed fresh spinach leaves, stems removed
1 cup tightly packed fresh basil, stems removed

½ cup fresh parsley, stems removed
½ teaspoon salt
½ cup olive oil
3 cups freshly grated Parmesan cheese (about ¾ pound)
3 tablespoons butter, softened
Garnish: fresh parsley sprigs

BEAT cream cheese and 1 pound butter at medium speed with an electric mixer until smooth; set aside. Process pine nuts, garlic, spinach, basil, parsley, and salt in a large food processor until smooth, stopping once to scrape down sides. Gradually pour olive oil through food chute with processor running; process until well blended. Add Parmesan cheese and 3 tablespoons butter; process just until blended.

LINE a 6-cup mold with an 18-inch piece of cheesecloth or heavy-duty plastic wrap, smoothing any wrinkles. Place one-fourth of cream cheese mixture in an even layer in prepared mold; top with one-fourth of pesto mixture. Repeat layers three times, using remaining cream cheese and pesto mixtures. Fold cheesecloth or plastic wrap over top, and pack down lightly. Chill at least 8 hours.

ABOUT 30 minutes before serving, unfold cheesecloth or plastic wrap, and invert mold onto a serving platter. Carefully peel away cheesecloth or plastic wrap. Garnish platter, if desired. Serve mold with water crackers or thinly sliced baguettes. Yield: 24 to 30 appetizer servings.

Gracious Gator Cooks
The Junior League of Gainesville, Florida

Artichoke Cheesecake `MAKE AHEAD` `PARTY FOOD`

Feta Fête

Feta cheese comes in several flavor varieties. We liked feta with herbs for this cheesecake. Chilling cheesecakes uncovered prevents condensation from forming on the top.

Thinly slice this savory appetizer cheesecake; it's quite rich. Each slice shows pretty pieces of pepper, artichokes, and herbs.

¼ cup fine, dry breadcrumbs (store-bought)
¼ cup grated Parmesan cheese
2 tablespoons dried Italian seasoning
2 (8-ounce) packages cream cheese, softened
1 cup crumbled feta cheese
3 large eggs
1 (8-ounce) container sour cream
1 (14-ounce) can artichoke hearts, drained and chopped

¾ cup chopped sweet red pepper
¾ cup chopped green pepper
¾ cup chopped green onions (including ½-inch green tops)
1 large garlic clove, pressed
1 teaspoon dried tarragon
1 teaspoon dried basil
Garnish: fresh tarragon

GENEROUSLY butter a 9-inch springform pan. Combine first 3 ingredients; coat bottom of pan with breadcrumb mixture, and set aside remaining mixture.

PROCESS cream cheese in a food processor bowl until smooth, stopping to scrape down sides. Add feta cheese, eggs, and sour cream. Process until smooth, stopping to scrape down sides. Add chopped artichoke and next 6 ingredients to processor bowl. Stir well. Pour mixture into prepared pan.

BAKE, uncovered, at 375° for 45 to 50 minutes or until golden. Cool completely in pan on a wire rack. Chill at least 2 hours.

CAREFULLY remove sides of springform pan. Pat reserved breadcrumb mixture on sides of cheesecake. Garnish, if desired. Serve with toast points or assorted crackers. Yield: one 9-inch cheesecake (16 appetizer servings).

Ambrosia
The Junior Auxiliary of Vicksburg, Mississippi

Artichoke Cheesecake

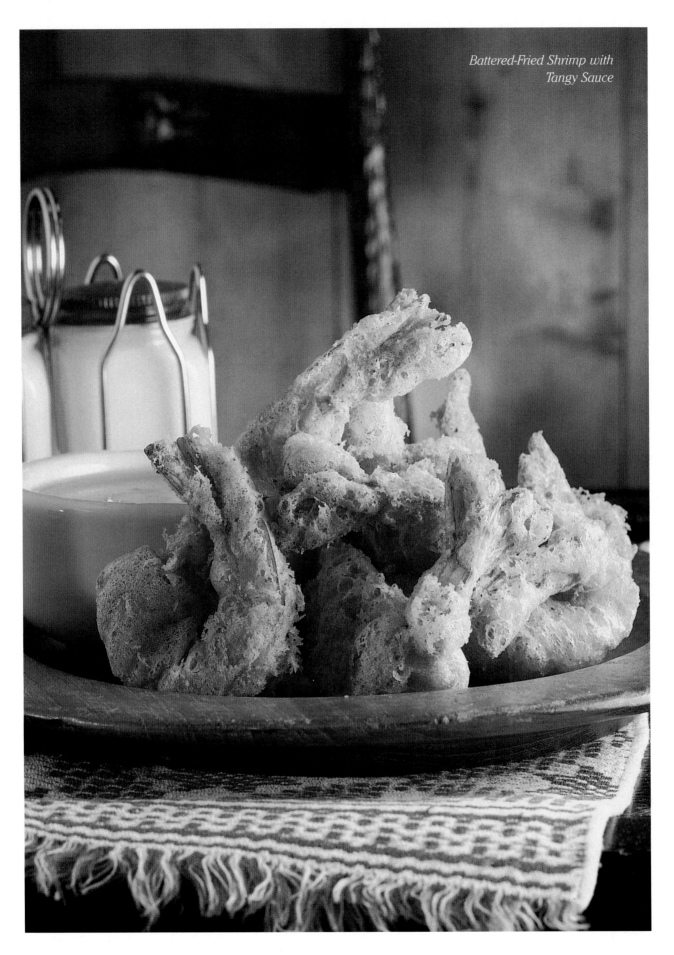

Battered-Fried Shrimp with
Tangy Sauce

Battered-Fried Shrimp with Tangy Sauce PARTY FOOD

Crispy fried shrimp with tails fanned out are a Southern delicacy. Here they're dunked in a spicy orange marmalade sauce.

2 pounds unpeeled, large fresh shrimp
½ teaspoon garlic powder
1 (12-ounce) jar orange marmalade
3 tablespoons lemon juice
2 tablespoons orange juice
1½ to 2 tablespoons prepared horseradish
1½ teaspoons Dijon mustard

1½ cups all-purpose flour
1 tablespoon baking powder
1 teaspoon salt
1 teaspoon paprika
½ cup vegetable oil
1 cup cold water
Additional vegetable oil

PEEL, devein, and butterfly shrimp, leaving tails intact. Sprinkle butterflied shrimp lightly with garlic powder. Cover and chill thoroughly.

PROCESS orange marmalade, lemon juice, orange juice, horseradish, and mustard in a blender until smooth, stopping to scrape down sides. Set sauce aside.

COMBINE flour, baking powder, salt, and paprika in a large bowl; stir well. Gradually add ½ cup oil, stirring until mixture leaves sides of bowl and forms a ball. Gradually add water, stirring until blended. (Batter will be very thick.)

DIP several shrimp into batter. Fry shrimp, a few at a time, in deep hot oil (360°) 2 or 3 minutes or until golden. Remove shrimp with a slotted spoon, and drain on paper towels.

PLACE shrimp on a large baking sheet; keep warm in a 200° oven. Repeat procedure with remaining shrimp and batter. Serve shrimp with reserved sauce. Yield: 4 servings.

Stirring Performances
The Junior League of Winston-Salem, North Carolina

Shrimp Talk

These shrimp are coated with a thick batter, giving you an extra crispy mouthful. If you want the recipe to serve more, buy medium shrimp instead of large, and fry these smaller shrimp a minute less.

Mini Crab Cakes with Salsa Mayonnaise

Crab and Salsa

Chilling crab cake ingredients before shaping and cooking them helps the final results stay shapely. Picante sauce and salsa are similar. In fact, if you have a jar of salsa on hand, use it in the mayonnaise recipe.

The Salsa Mayonnaise that tops these little crab cakes is culinary creativity at its best. For a wonderful entrée, just make the patties larger.

3 tablespoons butter
¾ cup finely chopped onion
⅓ cup finely chopped celery
1 jalapeño pepper, seeded and minced
3 large eggs, beaten
¼ cup sour cream
1 pound fresh lump crabmeat, drained
1½ cups Italian-seasoned
    breadcrumbs

1 cup (4 ounces) shredded Monterey
    Jack cheese with jalapeño pepper
½ cup diced roasted red pepper
½ cup chopped fresh cilantro
2 tablespoons vegetable oil
Salsa Mayonnaise

MELT butter in a large skillet over medium heat. Add onion, celery, and jalapeño; cook, stirring constantly, 5 minutes or just until tender. Transfer to a large bowl; cool.

ADD eggs and sour cream to onion mixture. Gently stir in crabmeat and next 4 ingredients. Cover and chill 1 hour. Shape crab mixture into 36 (1½-inch-wide) patties.

HEAT 1 teaspoon oil in a large skillet over medium heat; add 6 patties to skillet. Cook 4 minutes on each side or until golden. Set aside, and keep warm. Repeat procedure with remaining oil and patties. Serve crab cakes with Salsa Mayonnaise. Yield: 3 dozen.

Salsa Mayonnaise

1 cup mayonnaise
½ cup sour cream

½ cup picante sauce

COMBINE all ingredients in a small bowl; stir well. Cover and chill. Yield: 2 cups.

Taste of the Territory, The Flair and Flavor of Oklahoma
The Service League of Bartlesville, Oklahoma

Tuscan Grilled Chicken Bites   GRILL LOVERS

Universal Grill

Grilling meats for simple suppers is a way of life in Tuscany, the farming region of Italy. It's true in much of the U.S., too. This marinated chicken takes on robust flavor once it hits the grill. The final dish, all tossed together, makes a great pizza topping, too.

This versatile dish is great served in the Tuscan style as an antipasto platter or otherwise spooned into pita pockets.

¾ cup vegetable oil
¾ cup chili oil
¾ cup red wine vinegar
½ cup soy sauce
¼ cup white wine Worcestershire
    sauce
1 tablespoon sweet red pepper flakes
1 tablespoon dried Italian seasoning
4 garlic cloves, minced

3 bay leaves
8 skinned and boned chicken breast
    halves (about 3½ pounds)
2 (14-ounce) cans artichoke hearts,
    drained and quartered
1 cup oil-packed dried tomatoes,
    drained and chopped
1 bunch green onions, chopped
Pepper Vinegar Dressing

COMBINE first 9 ingredients in a large bowl; add chicken. Cover and marinate in refrigerator 8 hours. Remove chicken from marinade, discarding marinade.

GRILL chicken, covered with grill lid, over medium-high heat (350° to 400°) 9 to 10 minutes on each side or until chicken is done. Cool; cut into 2-inch pieces. Combine chicken, artichoke hearts, and remaining ingredients; toss gently. Yield: 8 to 10 servings.

Pepper Vinegar Dressing

¼ cup hot pepper-infused vinegar
½ cup vegetable oil
1 teaspoon Creole seasoning

1 teaspoon salt-free herb-and-spice blend
1 teaspoon salt

COMBINE all ingredients in a jar. Cover tightly, and shake vigorously. Yield: ¾ cup.

Susan Mitchell
The Art of Cooking
The Muscle Shoals District Service League
Sheffield, Alabama

Honey Chicken Wings PARTY FOOD

There's something fun about nibbling away on spicy chicken wings. Kids love 'em; guys love 'em. They're a guaranteed hit with any party crowd.

16 chicken wings (about 3½ pounds)
1 cup honey
½ cup ketchup
½ cup soy sauce

2 teaspoons vegetable oil
¼ teaspoon pepper
2 large garlic cloves, minced

CUT off and discard wing tips; cut wings in half at joint. Place wings, skin side down, in a single layer in a lightly greased 15- x 10-inch jellyroll pan.

COMBINE honey and remaining 5 ingredients, stirring well. Pour honey mixture over chicken. Turn chicken, skin side up, brushing with honey mixture to coat.

BAKE, uncovered, at 375° for 1 hour or until done, basting every 15 minutes. Yield: 8 appetizer servings.

Eva Buckler
Tasty Treasures
Immanuel Lutheran Church Ladies Aid
Leland, Michigan

Make-Ahead Option

Once you get the wings and the honey marinade in the pan, you can marinate the wings in the refrigerator up to an hour before baking.

Cajun Grilled Tenderloin with Mustard-Horseradish Cream PARTY FOOD

Tenderloin Talk
Beef tenderloin is perfect party food. Once you've grilled it, it can "rest" under foil on a platter up to an hour before serving. You can also serve this tenderloin as an entrée for 8. Just leave the buns and arugula off the menu and add some mashed potatoes.

We chose to turn this luxurious entrée into an appetizer by thinly slicing the tenderloin and serving it on cocktail buns.

1 (3½-pound) beef tenderloin
¼ cup hot sauce
¼ cup teriyaki sauce
2 tablespoons Worcestershire sauce
1 tablespoon Creole seasoning

Vegetable cooking spray
Cocktail buns
Mustard-Horseradish Cream
Arugula (optional)

PLACE tenderloin in a large heavy-duty zip-top plastic bag. Combine hot sauce and next 3 ingredients. Pour over tenderloin. Seal bag; marinate in refrigerator 1½ hours, turning occasionally.

REMOVE tenderloin from marinade, discarding marinade.

PREPARE a hot fire by piling charcoal on 1 side of grill, leaving other side empty. Coat food rack with cooking spray; place rack on grill. Place tenderloin on rack over unlit side. Grill, covered with grill lid, 30 to 40 minutes or until meat thermometer inserted into thickest part of tenderloin registers 145° (medium-rare) or 160° (medium). Let stand at least 10 minutes before slicing. Serve on buns with Mustard-Horseradish Cream and, if desired, arugula. Yield: 24 appetizer servings.

Mustard-Horseradish Cream

¼ cup prepared horseradish
1 cup whipping cream

¼ cup Dijon mustard
1 tablespoon fresh lemon juice

PLACE horseradish in a fine wire-mesh strainer; press with back of a spoon against sides of strainer to squeeze out juice. Discard juice. Set horseradish aside.

BEAT whipping cream at high speed with an electric mixer until soft peaks form. Fold in horseradish, mustard, and lemon juice. Cover and chill thoroughly. Yield: 2½ cups.

The Artful Table
Dallas Museum of Art League
Dallas, Texas

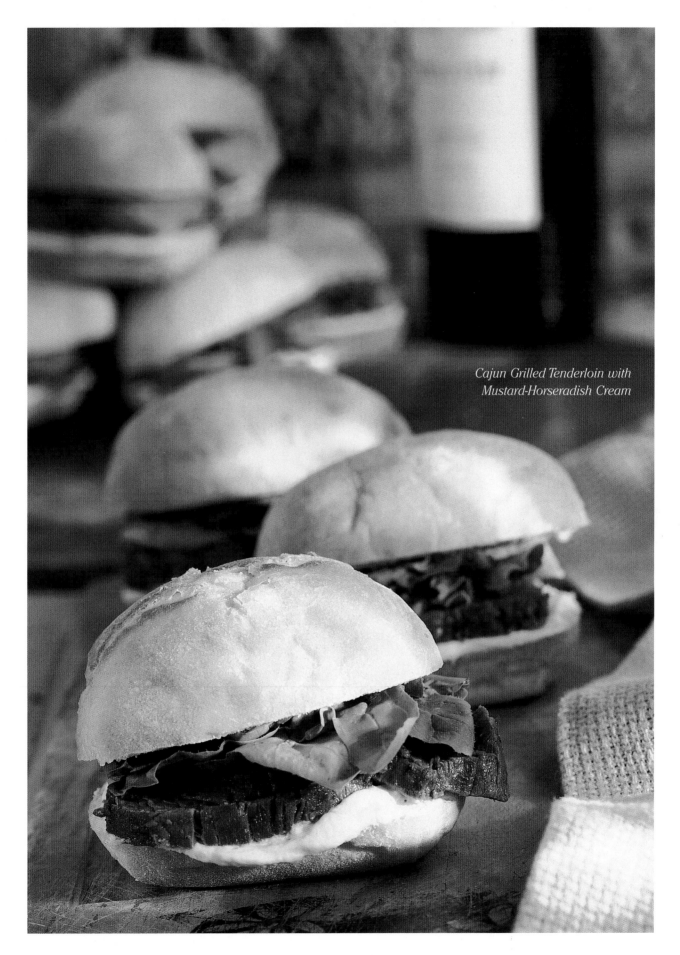

*Cajun Grilled Tenderloin with
Mustard-Horseradish Cream*

Lemon Honeyade

Lemon Honeyade QUICK & EASY

Lemon Ease
This recipe couldn't be easier. The hardest task is squeezing juice from a fresh lemon. You'll easily get 2 tablespoons juice from 1 lemon.

Here's a great recipe when you're craving fresh lemonade because you make it by the glass. Multiply the ingredients if you want to keep a stash in the fridge.

2 tablespoons fresh lemon juice
1 cup water

1 to 3 tablespoons honey

COMBINE lemon juice, water, and honey in a glass; serve over ice. Yield: 1¼ cups.

Will Smoot
Our Favorite Recipes from Coast to Coast
Hopeman Brothers/Lofton Corporation/AWH Associates
Waynesboro, Virginia

Watermelon Margaritas PARTY DRINK

There are some who wouldn't trade a slice of cold watermelon on a hot summer day for anything. But if they did, it'd be for a sip of this innovative melon margarita.

3 cups peeled, seeded, and cubed
    watermelon
Lime wedge
Salt
½ cup tequila

¼ cup orange liqueur
1 tablespoon sugar
2 tablespoons lime juice
2 cups ice cubes
Garnish: lime slices, orange slices

PLACE watermelon cubes in a heavy-duty zip-top plastic bag; seal bag, and freeze 2 hours.

RUB rims of cocktail glasses with wedge of lime. Place salt in a saucer; spin rim of each glass in salt. Set prepared glasses aside.

PROCESS frozen watermelon, tequila, and next 3 ingredients in a blender until smooth, stopping to scrape down sides. Add ice; blend well. Pour into prepared glasses. Garnish, if desired. Yield: 5 cups.

Sugar Baby
Sugar Baby is a popular watermelon variety in the South. It's a small round melon with a dark green rind. You'll know a Sugar Baby or any watermelon's ripe by thumping it; if it sounds hollow but feels heavy, buy it.

Chocolate Frostie

Cool off on a hot summer night with this frozen chocolate delight that resembles soft-serve ice cream. Serve it with either a spoon or a straw.

1 (14-ounce) can sweetened
    condensed milk
½ cup instant malted milk powder
1 cup chocolate syrup

6 cups chocolate milk
1 (16-ounce) container frozen
    whipped topping, thawed

COMBINE first 4 ingredients; fold in whipped topping. Pour mixture into freezer container of a 1-gallon hand-turned or electric freezer. Freeze according to manufacturer's instructions. Yield: about 4 quarts.

Sharon Craw
Culinary Tastes of Blue Mountain Cooks
Grand Terrace Branch Library: Friends
Grand Terrace, California

Plenty Sweet
Sweetened condensed milk and chocolate syrup provide the sweet flavor for this dessert drink. No sugar necessary.

Champagne Punch MAKE AHEAD PARTY DRINK

Affordable Bubbly

You don't need expensive champagne for this punch. Many other flavors blend with the bubbly anyway, so there's no need to break the budget.

Any occasion becomes more festive when you serve this sparkling drink. It's meant for wedding receptions or special celebrations.

2 cups sugar
2 cups water
2 cups apricot nectar
1 cup frozen lemon juice from concentrate, thawed
2 (64-ounce) bottles apple juice

1 (6-ounce) can frozen orange juice concentrate, thawed
2 (750-milliliter) bottles champagne, chilled
2 (12-ounce) cans ginger ale, chilled

COMBINE sugar and water in a Dutch oven; bring to a boil, stirring until sugar dissolves. Set aside, and let cool.

ADD apricot nectar and next 3 ingredients to sugar mixture; stir well. Pour mixture into 2 (12-cup) containers. Cover and freeze at least 8 hours.

REMOVE containers from freezer, and let stand at room temperature 30 minutes.

PLACE 1 block of frozen juice mixture in a punch bowl. Add 1 bottle champagne and 1 can ginger ale; stir gently. Add remaining frozen juice mixture, champagne, and ginger ale as needed. Yield: 32 cups.

Texas Tapestry
The Junior Woman's Club of Houston, Texas

Spiced Cider Punch QUICK & EASY

Simmering Cider

If your cooktop's crowded with other things, you can simmer this cider in a slow cooker. Just bring it to a simmer on HIGH; then turn cooker to LOW. Add more cider when punch begins to run low.

Looking for a simple party punch? This autumn sipper fits the bill. It takes only minutes to heat and fills your home with a spiced aroma.

4 cups water
¾ cup firmly packed light brown sugar
¾ cup sugar
4 (2-inch) cinnamon sticks

1½ cups fresh lemon juice
4 cups fresh orange juice
3 cups apple cider

COMBINE first 4 ingredients in a large saucepan. Bring to a boil; reduce heat, and simmer 5 minutes. Discard cinnamon sticks. Add lemon juice, orange juice, and cider. Cook until thoroughly heated (do not boil). Serve hot or cold. Yield: 14 cups.

Eloise Scott
Down Home Dining in Mississippi
Mississippi Homemaker Volunteers, Inc.
Water Valley, Mississippi

White Wine Sangría Cooler · PARTY DRINK

Slices of brightly colored oranges, lemons, and limes sparkle in this white wine version of the traditional Spanish drink.

2 oranges
2 lemons
2 limes
4 cups dry white wine
2 tablespoons brandy (optional)

2 tablespoons honey
1 (3-inch) stick cinnamon
1 cup seedless green grapes
1 quart ginger ale

CUT 1 orange, 1 lemon, and 1 lime in half, reserving one-half of each fruit. Slice remaining half of each fruit into thin slices for garnish; cover and chill fruit slices.

SQUEEZE juice from reserved fruit halves and remaining orange, lemon, and lime into pitcher. Add wine and next 4 ingredients. Cover and chill at least 1 hour. Just before serving, stir in ginger ale. Add reserved fruit slices; serve over ice. Yield: 10 cups.

Dorothy Wood
Appetizers from A to Z
Christ Child Society
Phoenix, Arizona

Sparkling Sangría

White wine Sangría is so pretty because the golden wine allows the multicolored fruit slices to stand out. For an extra chilly idea, freeze the grapes before adding them to the Sangría.

Spicy Bloody Marys · QUICK & EASY

Hot sauce, horseradish, and pepper give this wake-up drink its kick.

4½ cups tomato juice or spicy
   vegetable juice, chilled
¼ cup lemon juice, lime juice, or
   clam juice
3 tablespoons Worcestershire sauce
1 tablespoon prepared horseradish

1 teaspoon celery salt
½ teaspoon freshly ground pepper
¼ teaspoon hot sauce
1 cup vodka
Garnish: celery ribs

COMBINE first 7 ingredients; stir well, and chill thoroughly. Stir in vodka, and serve over ice. Garnish, if desired. Yield: 6 cups.

Alcohol-Free Option

Omit the vodka, and add 1 more cup tomato juice or spicy vegetable juice.

Hearty Mint Juleps MAKE AHEAD   PARTY DRINK

Pictured on page 79

Southerners love this potent drink that's made from a simple sugar syrup, a shot of bourbon, and lots of fresh mint.

2¼ cups sugar
1 cup water
½ cup packed fresh mint leaves

2 cups bourbon
Garnish: fresh mint sprigs

COMBINE sugar, water, and mint leaves in a medium saucepan. Bring to a boil; boil, stirring constantly, 5 minutes or until sugar dissolves. Remove from heat. Let stand 12 hours at room temperature, stirring occasionally.

POUR liquid through a wire-mesh strainer into a pitcher, discarding mint leaves. Stir in bourbon; chill. Serve over crushed ice. Garnish, if desired. Yield: 3½ cups.

Dining Al Fresco
Wolf Trap Associates
Vienna, Virginia

The Many Faces of Mint

Make this the year you grow mint in your garden. It's a prolific herb with dozens of varieties available. To extract the most mint flavor, bruise the leaves with the back of a spoon before adding leaves to saucepan.

Coffee Frappé PARTY DRINK   QUICK & EASY

This recipe serves a crowd, but easily halves, too. And if you want to spike it, just add a little coffee liqueur.

1 gallon vanilla ice cream, softened
1 quart double-strength coffee, chilled

1 pint whipping cream, whipped

COMBINE all ingredients in a large punch bowl; blend well. Serve immediately. Yield: 18 cups.

Allison Pelham
Designer's Recipes for Living
East Tennessee Interior Design Society
Knoxville, Tennessee

Frappé Finale

This 3-ingredient sweet ending definitely counts as dessert. Sweeten the pot by brewing flavored coffee and serving a simple shortbread or sugar cookie alongside.

Breads, Breakfasts & Brunches

*Salsa Eggs,
page 138*

Buttermilk Biscuits QUICK & EASY

Biscuits are a Southern staple as much as any food. Buttermilk makes these good. Biscuits are simple to make—all you need is a biscuit cutter and a baking sheet.

1 cup all-purpose flour
2 teaspoons baking powder
⅛ teaspoon baking soda

½ teaspoon salt
¼ cup shortening
½ cup buttermilk

COMBINE first 4 ingredients in a medium bowl; cut in shortening with a pastry blender until mixture is crumbly. Add buttermilk, stirring just until dry ingredients are moistened.

TURN dough out onto a lightly floured surface, and knead lightly 4 or 5 times. Roll dough to ½-inch thickness; cut with a 2½-inch biscuit cutter. Place on a lightly greased baking sheet. Bake at 425° for 13 to 14 minutes or until biscuits are lightly browned. Yield: ½ dozen.

Ann Nixon
Trinity Episcopal School, Classroom Classics
The Parents and Students of Trinity Episcopal School
Pine Bluff, Arkansas

Chill Out
When making biscuits, chill the shortening before cutting it into the dry ingredients. It's a step toward flaky biscuits. You can use whole or nonfat buttermilk in this recipe.

Sausage Gravy ONE PAN QUICK & EASY

This meaty gravy pours perfectly over your favorite fluffy biscuits. Try it on fried chicken, too.

¾ pound ground pork sausage
¼ cup all-purpose flour
2 cups half-and-half or milk

1 teaspoon salt
½ teaspoon freshly ground pepper

BROWN sausage in a large heavy skillet, stirring until it crumbles. Drain sausage on paper towels, reserving ½ cup drippings in skillet.

WHISK flour into sausage drippings until smooth. Cook over medium-high heat, whisking constantly, 3 minutes or until browned.

STIR in sausage. Gradually add half-and-half, and cook over medium heat, stirring constantly, until thickened and bubbly. Stir in salt and pepper. Serve gravy with biscuits. Yield: 3 cups.

Art Shealey
Grandad's Old Fashion Cookbook
St. Cloud, Florida

Essence of Sage
For an additional flavor boost, try sage-seasoned pork sausage in this cream gravy.

Hot Cheesy Biscuits QUICK & EASY

Drop Them Instead

This is the perfect recipe if you want to make biscuits and don't own biscuit cutters. You drop these lumpy favorites onto baking sheets just like cookie dough.

Sharp Cheddar cheese gives these free-form biscuits extra appeal.

2 cups all-purpose flour
2 teaspoons baking powder
½ teaspoon salt
½ teaspoon ground red pepper

1 cup (4 ounces) shredded sharp
   Cheddar cheese
¼ cup shortening
1 cup buttermilk

COMBINE first 4 ingredients in a bowl; cut in cheese and shortening with a pastry blender until mixture is crumbly. Add buttermilk, stirring just until dry ingredients are moistened.

DROP by heaping tablespoonfuls onto greased baking sheets. Bake at 450° for 9 minutes or until golden. Yield: 2 dozen.

Chad Bailey
Evening Shade, Volume II
Evening Shade School Foundation
Evening Shade, Arkansas

Pumpkin-Pecan Biscuits

Biscuit Cutters

Biscuit cutters are inexpensive and easy to find at kitchen shops. They typically come nestled in graduated sizes. You can use the cutters to cut out brownies, too.

Serve these tasty biscuits hot with butter and honey, or split, toast, and top them with ham—either way is bound to please.

2 cups all-purpose flour
¼ cup sugar
1 tablespoon plus 1 teaspoon baking
   powder
½ teaspoon salt
½ teaspoon ground cinnamon

½ teaspoon ground nutmeg
½ cup butter or margarine, cut into
   pieces
⅓ cup chopped pecans, toasted
⅔ cup canned pumpkin
⅓ cup half-and-half

COMBINE first 6 ingredients in a large bowl. Cut in butter with a pastry blender until mixture is crumbly; stir in pecans. Combine pumpkin and half-and-half; add to flour mixture, stirring just until dry ingredients are moistened.

TURN dough out onto a lightly floured surface; knead 4 or 5 times. (Add more flour if dough is sticky.) Roll dough to ½-inch thickness; cut with a 2-inch biscuit cutter. Place on a lightly greased baking sheet. Bake at 400° for 12 to 14 minutes or until lightly browned. Yield: 20 biscuits.

Gene Crystal
Recipes from the Flock
Mandarin Senior Citizens Center
Jacksonville, Florida

Beaten Biscuits via Food Processor

QUICK & EASY

Trade in your rolling pin for a food processor, and forget rolling for the perfect beaten biscuit. These compact biscuits with flaky layers split naturally to form perfect pockets for their traditional partner, country ham.

2 cups all-purpose flour
1 teaspoon salt

½ cup cold butter, cut into pieces
⅓ cup ice water

PROCESS flour and salt in a food processor 5 seconds; add butter, and process 10 seconds or until mixture is crumbly.

POUR water through food chute with processor running; process until mixture forms a ball. Turn dough out onto a lightly floured surface. Roll dough into a ⅛-inch-thick rectangle. Fold dough in half lengthwise; cut with a 1-inch biscuit cutter. Place on an ungreased baking sheet. Prick top of each biscuit with a fork 3 times. Bake at 400° for 20 minutes or until lightly browned. Yield: 28 biscuits.

Emory Seasons, Entertaining Atlanta Style
Emory University Woman's Club
Atlanta, Georgia

On Using Ice Water

Pastry recipes often call for ice water. This literally means floating ice cubes in a cupful of cool water and then measuring the amount of water you need. This extra chilly H_2O contributes to the flakiness of pastries (and these pastrylike biscuits).

Dried Cherry and Cream Scones

These pale scones are light in texture due to the abundance of whipping cream in the dough.

2 cups all-purpose flour
1 tablespoon baking powder
½ teaspoon salt
¼ cup sugar
¾ cup chopped dried cherries

1 tablespoon grated lemon rind
1¼ cups whipping cream
2 tablespoons unsalted butter, melted
2 tablespoons sugar
1 teaspoon grated lemon rind

COMBINE first 4 ingredients in a large bowl. Stir in cherries and 1 tablespoon lemon rind. Add whipping cream, stirring with a fork just until dry ingredients are moistened.

TURN dough out onto a lightly floured surface; knead lightly 4 or 5 times, just until dough holds together. Pat dough into an 8-inch circle on an ungreased baking sheet. Cut dough into 8 wedges; separate wedges slightly. Brush with melted butter. Combine 2 tablespoons sugar and 1 teaspoon lemon rind; sprinkle over dough.

BAKE at 400° for 23 minutes or until golden. Remove from pan. Serve warm, or cool on a wire rack. Yield: 8 scones.

A Capital Affair
The Junior League of Harrisburg, Pennsylvania

Chive-Parmesan Scones QUICK & EASY

Shapely Scones

This recipe gives directions for baking free-form scones. For rustic, round scones like the photograph shows, we patted the dough to ¾-inch thickness and cut them out with a 2½-inch biscuit cutter. Then we baked them 13 minutes.

Scones are close cousins of biscuits, though they're usually richer and sometimes contain cream and egg. They can be cut into wedges (triangles) or stamped out like biscuits.

1½ cups all-purpose flour
1 tablespoon baking powder
¼ teaspoon salt
¼ teaspoon black pepper
¼ cup butter, cut into pieces
1 cup fresh shredded Parmesan
    cheese
3 tablespoons chopped fresh chives

2 garlic cloves, pressed
½ cup whipping cream
1 large egg, lightly beaten
2 tablespoons honey
¼ cup fresh shredded Parmesan
    cheese
⅛ teaspoon ground red pepper
1 tablespoon whipping cream

COMBINE first 4 ingredients in a large bowl; stir well. Cut in butter with a pastry blender until mixture is crumbly. Stir in 1 cup cheese, chives, and garlic.

COMBINE whipping cream, egg, and honey; add to dry ingredients, stirring just until moistened. Combine ¼ cup cheese and red pepper.

DROP dough by 3 tablespoonfuls, 1 inch apart, onto a greased baking sheet. Brush 1 tablespoon cream over scones; sprinkle with cheese mixture. Bake at 400° for 12 minutes or until lightly browned. Serve warm. Yield: 10 scones.

Culinary Masterpieces
Birmingham Museum of Art
Birmingham, Alabama

Chive-Parmesan Scones

Fresh Lemon Muffins with Lemon Glaze

Moist Muffins

Poking holes in these slightly sweet muffins allows the glaze to drip down inside the muffins and keep them moist. For a change, serve the muffins for dessert with small scoops of vanilla ice cream.

An abundance of freshly squeezed lemon juice and grated lemon rind gives these muffins incredible zing. To make the lemons easier to juice, roll them on a flat surface, pressing firmly with the palm of your hand.

1¾ cups all-purpose flour
1½ teaspoons baking powder
½ teaspoon baking soda
¼ teaspoon salt
½ cup sugar
2 teaspoons grated lemon rind

2 large eggs, lightly beaten
⅔ cup fresh lemon juice
½ cup unsalted butter, melted
1 teaspoon lemon extract
¼ cup sugar
¼ cup fresh lemon juice

COMBINE first 6 ingredients in a large bowl; make a well in center of mixture.

COMBINE eggs and next 3 ingredients; add to flour mixture, stirring just until dry ingredients are moistened. Spoon batter into 8 paper-lined muffin pans. Bake at 400° for 20 to 25 minutes or until a wooden pick inserted in center comes out clean.

COMBINE ¼ cup sugar and ¼ cup lemon juice in a small saucepan; cook over medium heat, stirring constantly, until sugar dissolves.

REMOVE muffins from oven, and poke holes in tops of muffins with a wooden pick; drizzle with warm glaze. Cool muffins in pans 5 minutes; remove from pans, and cool completely on a wire rack. Yield: 8 muffins.

Sonya Loper
Recipes of Love
Alpha Delta Pi, Jackson Area Alumnae Association
Brandon, Mississippi

Orange Streusel Muffins

A cinnamon-sugar topping adds just the right amount of sweetness for these muffins to qualify as breakfast or dessert.

2 cups all-purpose flour
1 tablespoon baking powder
1 teaspoon salt
⅓ cup sugar
½ cup chopped pecans
1 large egg, lightly beaten
½ cup orange juice
¼ cup milk
¼ cup vegetable oil

1 tablespoon grated orange rind
½ cup orange marmalade
1 tablespoon all-purpose flour
¼ cup sugar
½ teaspoon ground cinnamon
¼ teaspoon ground nutmeg
1 tablespoon butter or margarine, softened

COMBINE first 5 ingredients in a large bowl; make a well in center of mixture. Set aside.

COMBINE egg and next 5 ingredients; add to dry ingredients, stirring just until moistened. Spoon batter into greased muffins pans, filling two-thirds full.

COMBINE 1 tablespoon flour and remaining 4 ingredients; sprinkle over batter. Bake at 375° for 15 minutes or until golden. Remove from pans immediately. Yield: 15 muffins.

Overhall Sam
Quilters Guild of Indianapolis Cookbook
Quilters Guild of Indianapolis, Indiana

Mix It Up with Marmalade

For variety, try another flavor of marmalade, such as pineapple, in these muffins. Or if you don't have marmalade on hand, use preserves.

Very Berry Muffins

Fresh blueberries and raspberries dot these fragrant muffins. A hint of orange and lemon complements the berry blend.

2 cups all-purpose flour
1 tablespoon baking powder
½ teaspoon salt
½ cup sugar
2 teaspoons grated lemon rind
2 teaspoons grated orange rind

1 large egg, beaten
½ cup butter or margarine, melted
½ cup fresh orange juice
¾ cup fresh blueberries
¾ cup fresh raspberries

COMBINE first 6 ingredients in a large bowl; make a well in center of mixture.

COMBINE egg, butter, and orange juice; add to dry ingredients, stirring just until moistened. (Batter will be very thick.) Gently fold berries into batter. Spoon batter into muffin pans coated with cooking spray or paper-lined muffin pans, filling three-fourths full.

BAKE at 400° for 18 to 20 minutes or until golden. Cool muffins in pan 1 minute; remove from pan, and cool completely on a wire rack. Yield: 1 dozen.

Dawn to Dusk, A Taste of Holland
The Junior Welfare League of Holland, Michigan

Cheddar and Bacon Muffins   WEEKNIGHT FAVORITE

For the perfect accompaniment with a bowl of hearty soup, you can't beat these savory muffins.

The Perfect Blend

Extra-sharp cheese mingles with Dijon mustard for great flavor in these muffins loaded with bacon. For a subtler flavor, try a milder Cheddar and less bacon.

1 pound bacon
1 cup finely chopped green onions
1 teaspoon salt
1 teaspoon freshly ground pepper
1½ teaspoons caraway seeds (optional)
3 cups all-purpose flour
2 teaspoons baking powder
1 teaspoon baking soda

2 tablespoons sugar
2 large eggs
1½ cups milk
3 tablespoons Dijon mustard
3 tablespoons shortening, melted and cooled
2 cups (8 ounces) shredded extra-sharp Cheddar cheese

COOK bacon until crisp. Drain bacon, reserving 2 tablespoons drippings. Crumble bacon, and set aside.

SAUTÉ green onions, salt, pepper, and, if desired, caraway seeds in reserved bacon drippings over medium heat until onion is tender; set aside.

COMBINE flour, baking powder, soda, and sugar; stir well.

COMBINE eggs, milk, mustard, shortening, and green onion mixture. Add to dry ingredients, stirring just until moistened. Stir in cheese and crumbled bacon.

SPOON batter into greased muffin pans. Bake at 375° for 20 minutes or until a wooden pick inserted in center comes out clean. Remove from pans immediately, and cool on wire racks. Yield: 1½ dozen.

Call to Post
Lexington Hearing and Speech Center
Lexington, Kentucky

Cheddar and Bacon Muffins

Oatmeal-Walnut Pancakes

Unbleached Explained

Unbleached flour is the freshest, highest quality flour you can buy, because the flavor hasn't been altered from bleaching. Many chefs claim it's the only way to go in baking. But if you have regular all-purpose flour in the pantry, it works fine in these pancakes as well.

Homemade pancakes are a great Saturday morning ritual. Try this healthy recipe loaded with oats and nuts, and laced with honey.

1 cup whole wheat flour	1 cup finely chopped walnuts
1 cup uncooked regular oats	2 large eggs, lightly beaten
½ cup plain cornmeal	2¼ cups milk
½ cup unbleached all-purpose flour	¼ cup honey
1 tablespoon baking powder	¼ cup vegetable oil
1 teaspoon salt	

COMBINE first 7 ingredients in a large bowl; make a well in center of mixture.

COMBINE eggs, milk, honey, and oil in a small bowl; add to dry ingredients, stirring mixture just until moistened. Let mixture stand 10 minutes.

POUR ¼ cup batter for each pancake onto a hot, lightly greased griddle or skillet. Cook until tops are covered with bubbles and edges look cooked; turn and cook other side. Yield: 20 (4-inch) pancakes.

Linda Cardone and Ed Metcalfe
Town Hill Playground Cookbook
Town Hill Playground Committee
Whitingham, Vermont

Out-of-This-World Pecan Waffles

Ground Pecans

Grind pecans easily in a food processor or mini chopper until they're very fine. Be careful not to process nuts too long or the oils will come out. Finely chopped pecans sub nicely for ground pecans.

Make breakfast a big party when you serve these nutty waffles. For extra flavor, toast the nuts before stirring them into the batter.

2½ cups all-purpose flour	2 large eggs, beaten
1½ tablespoons sugar	2¼ cups milk
1 tablespoon plus 1 teaspoon baking powder	¾ cup vegetable oil
¾ teaspoon salt	½ cup ground pecans

COMBINE first 4 ingredients in a large bowl. Combine eggs, milk, and oil; add to flour mixture, stirring just until moistened. Stir in pecans.

BAKE in a preheated, oiled waffle iron until golden. Yield: 22 (4-inch) waffles.

Cheryl and John Barron Harris
The Authorized Texas Ranger Cookbook
Texas Ranger Museum
Hamilton, Texas

Apple and Spice Baked French Toast

MAKE AHEAD

Tempt those late sleepers out of bed with the appetizing aroma of baked apples, cinnamon, and nutmeg coming from this mostly make-ahead French toast.

1 (1-pound) unsliced French or Italian
   bread
8 large eggs
1 cup sugar, divided
3½ cups milk
1 tablespoon vanilla extract

6 to 8 medium Granny Smith apples
1 tablespoon ground cinnamon
1 teaspoon ground nutmeg
2 tablespoons butter
Warm maple syrup
Whipped cream

SLICE bread into 1½-inch-thick slices. Arrange bread slices tightly together in a lightly greased 13- x 9-inch baking dish.

BEAT eggs, ½ cup sugar, milk, and vanilla with a wire whisk until blended. Pour half of egg mixture over bread.

PEEL, core, and slice enough apples to measure about 8½ cups. Place sliced apple over bread to cover. Pour remaining half of egg mixture over apple. Combine remaining ½ cup sugar, cinnamon, and nutmeg; sprinkle evenly over apple. Dot with butter. Cover and chill at least 8 hours.

BAKE, uncovered, at 350° for 1 hour. Remove from oven, and let stand 5 to 10 minutes before serving. Cut into squares, and serve with warm maple syrup; top with whipped cream. Yield: 8 servings.

Diane and Don Crosby
Flavors of Falmouth
Falmouth Historical Society
Falmouth, Massachusetts

Forgiving French Toast

You can use any kind of rustic European bakery bread to make French toast. And it won't even matter if it's a little stale.

Cream Cheese Coffee Cake

Cream Cheese Coffee Cake

Soft Cheese
To soften cream cheese for this recipe, unwrap it, and let it stand at room temperature about 20 to 30 minutes.

This old-fashioned coffee cake is easy to make. It looks rustic with a bumpy streusel top, which is what makes it so yummy.

½ cup butter, softened
1 (8-ounce) package cream cheese, softened
1½ cups sugar
2 large eggs
2 cups all-purpose flour

2 teaspoons baking powder
½ teaspoon baking soda
½ teaspoon salt
½ cup milk
1 teaspoon vanilla extract
Topping

BEAT butter and cream cheese at medium speed with an electric mixer until creamy; gradually add sugar, beating well. Add eggs, 1 at a time, beating after each addition.

COMBINE flour, baking powder, soda, and salt; add to butter mixture alternately with milk, beginning and ending with flour mixture. Mix at low speed just until blended after each addition. Stir in vanilla.

POUR batter into a greased 13- x 9-inch pan. Sprinkle with Topping. Bake at 350° for 40 minutes or until a wooden pick inserted in center comes out clean. Cool in pan on a wire rack. Yield: 12 servings.

Topping

½ cup all-purpose flour
½ cup firmly packed light brown sugar

½ cup chopped pecans
¼ cup butter, melted

COMBINE all ingredients. Yield: 1½ cups.

Michelle Jackson
Sharing Tasteful Memories
L.A.C.E. (Ladies Aspiring to Christian Excellence) of First Church of the Nazarene
Longview, Texas

Blueberry Coffee Cake

Fresh blueberries awaken the senses in this coffee cake. They're layered in the cake with a cinnamon streusel.

¼ cup firmly packed light brown sugar
1 tablespoon all-purpose flour
½ teaspoon ground cinnamon
¾ cup butter or margarine, softened
1½ cups sugar
4 large eggs
3 cups all-purpose flour

1½ teaspoons baking powder
¾ teaspoon baking soda
1 (8-ounce) container sour cream
1 teaspoon vanilla extract
1 pint fresh blueberries (2 cups)
1 cup sifted powdered sugar
2 tablespoons milk

COMBINE brown sugar, 1 tablespoon flour, and cinnamon; set aside.

BEAT butter at medium speed with an electric mixer until creamy; gradually add 1½ cups sugar, beating well. Add eggs, 1 at a time, beating after each addition.

COMBINE 3 cups flour, baking powder, and soda; add to butter mixture alternately with sour cream, beginning and ending with flour mixture. Mix at low speed after each addition until blended. Stir in vanilla. Pour one-third of batter into a greased and floured 10-inch tube pan. Sprinkle with half of blueberries and half of reserved brown sugar mixture. Repeat layers, ending with batter.

BAKE at 350° for 1 hour or until a wooden pick inserted in center comes out clean. Cool 20 minutes in pan on a wire rack. Remove cake from pan; cool completely on rack.

STIR together powdered sugar and milk; drizzle over cake. Yield: one 10-inch cake.

Mary MacDonald
Over the Bridge
Corpus Christie Women's Guild
East Sandwich, Massachusetts

Blueberry Boost
For a little extra assurance that blueberries won't sink to the bottom of the pan, toss them with 1 tablespoon flour before sprinkling them over the batter.

Apple-Cheddar Cornbread   WEEKNIGHT FAVORITE

Cornbread gets interesting in this recipe with the interplay of chopped apple and Cheddar cheese. If you're looking for a more traditional cornbread recipe, turn to page 13.

1 cup yellow cornmeal
1 cup all-purpose flour
1 tablespoon baking powder
½ cup sugar
1 large egg, beaten

1 cup milk
¼ cup butter or margarine, melted
2 small tart red apples, chopped
½ cup (2 ounces) shredded sharp
 Cheddar cheese

COMBINE first 4 ingredients; make a well in center of mixture. Combine egg, milk, and butter; add to dry ingredients, stirring just until moistened. Stir in apple and cheese.

PLACE a well-greased 9-inch cast-iron skillet or 9-inch square pan in a 425° oven for 5 minutes or until hot. Remove from oven; pour batter into hot skillet. Bake at 425° for 25 minutes or until golden. Yield: 9 servings.

Sarah Hardin
A Thyme to Remember
Dallas County Medical Society Alliance
Dallas, Texas

Caring for Cast Iron
Give cast iron a little attention and you're set for years of good cooking. Never place cast iron in a dishwasher. Instead, clean thoroughly with a nylon scouring pad after each use. If cast iron is badly caked, simply run it through a cycle in your self-cleaning oven.

*Beer and Tomato
Hush Puppies*

Beer and Tomato Hush Puppies

The name says it all. Beer and chopped tomato highlight these crispy, golden mouthfuls. They're great with fried fish.

1½ cups self-rising yellow cornmeal	1 tomato, finely chopped
¼ cup self-rising flour	1 large egg, lightly beaten
⅛ teaspoon salt	1½ teaspoons Worcestershire sauce
2 onions, finely chopped	⅛ teaspoon hot sauce
1 medium-size green bell pepper, finely chopped	½ cup beer
	Vegetable oil

COMBINE first 3 ingredients in a large bowl; stir well. Add onion, pepper, and tomato. Stir in egg, Worcestershire sauce, and hot sauce. Add beer, stirring well.

POUR oil to a depth of 2 inches into a Dutch oven; heat to 375°. Carefully drop batter by rounded tablespoonfuls into oil; fry hush puppies, a few at a time, 1 to 2 minutes or until golden, turning once. Drain well on paper towels. Yield: 3½ dozen.

By Special Request, Our Favorite Recipes
Piggly Wiggly Carolina Employees
Charleston, South Carolina

Freezer Facts
Hush puppies freeze well in zip-top plastic bags. Just thaw as many as you need in the microwave and reheat on a baking sheet at 350° until crisp.

Green Tomato Bread

Pluck your homegrown tomatoes before they ripen for a unique sweet bread that'll send you back to that vine again and again.

3 cups all-purpose flour	2 large eggs, lightly beaten
¼ teaspoon baking powder	1 cup vegetable oil
1 teaspoon baking soda	1 teaspoon vanilla extract
1 teaspoon salt	2 cups finely chopped green tomato (about 2 medium)
2 cups sugar	1½ cups chopped pecans
1 tablespoon ground cinnamon	

COMBINE first 6 ingredients in a large bowl; make a well in center of mixture. Combine eggs, oil, and vanilla; stir well. Add to dry ingredients, stirring just until moistened. Fold in tomato and pecans.

SPOON batter into 2 greased and floured 8½- x 4½-inch loafpans. Bake at 350° for 1 hour or until a wooden pick inserted in center comes out clean. Cool in pans on a wire rack 10 minutes. Remove from pans, and let cool completely on wire rack. Yield: 2 loaves.

Mary Solomon
Carolinas Heritage
47th National Square Dance Convention
Charlotte, North Carolina

Tomatoes in Bread?
Chopped tomato adds moisture to this quick bread in the way mashed banana does for banana-nut bread. Once you've baked the bread, you'd never guess tomato was in it.

Banana-Nut Bread

A.M. Option

For a breakfast treat, butter and toast a slice of nut bread, and spread a little cream cheese or apple butter on it, too.

Macadamia nuts add a tropical flair to this banana bread, but you can substitute an equal amount of any type of nut. Toast the nuts to flaunt their flavor.

2¼ cups all-purpose flour
1 tablespoon plus ½ teaspoon baking powder
½ teaspoon salt
¾ cup firmly packed light brown sugar
¼ cup sugar
1½ teaspoons ground cinnamon

1¼ cups mashed ripe banana
⅓ cup milk
3 tablespoons vegetable oil
1 large egg
1 teaspoon white vinegar
1 cup macadamia nuts, coarsely chopped

COMBINE first 6 ingredients in a large bowl; make a well in center of mixture. Combine banana, milk, oil, egg, and vinegar; beat with a wire whisk until blended. Add to dry ingredients, stirring just until moistened. Stir in macadamia nuts.

SPOON batter into a greased 9- x 5-inch loafpan. Bake at 350° for 1 hour or until a wooden pick inserted in center comes out clean. Cool in pan on a wire rack 10 minutes. Remove from pan, and cool completely on wire rack. Yield: 1 loaf.

Perfect Endings: The Art of Desserts
Friends of the Arts of the Tampa Museum of Art
Tampa, Florida

Spiced Applesauce Bread

Warm and toasty spices give this applesauce quick bread its sweet, homespun character. A generous amount of chopped pecans tucked inside and a crunchy pecan and brown sugar topping ensure nutty flavor in every bite.

1¼ cups applesauce
1 cup sugar
½ cup vegetable oil
2 large eggs, lightly beaten
3 tablespoons milk
2 cups all-purpose flour
½ teaspoon baking powder
1 teaspoon baking soda

¼ teaspoon salt
½ teaspoon ground cinnamon
¼ teaspoon ground nutmeg
¼ teaspoon ground allspice
1 cup chopped pecans, divided
¼ cup firmly packed light brown sugar
½ teaspoon ground cinnamon

COMBINE first 5 ingredients in a large bowl; stir well.

COMBINE flour and next 6 ingredients; add to applesauce mixture, stirring well. Fold in ½ cup pecans. Pour batter into a greased 9- x 5-inch loafpan. Combine remaining ½ cup pecans, brown sugar, and ½ teaspoon cinnamon; sprinkle over batter in pan.

BAKE at 350° for 1 hour or until a wooden pick inserted in center comes out clean. Cool in pan on a wire rack 10 minutes; remove from pan. Cool completely on wire rack. Yield: 1 loaf.

Nancy H. Hamill
Fishing for Compliments
Shedd Aquarium Society
Chicago, Illinois

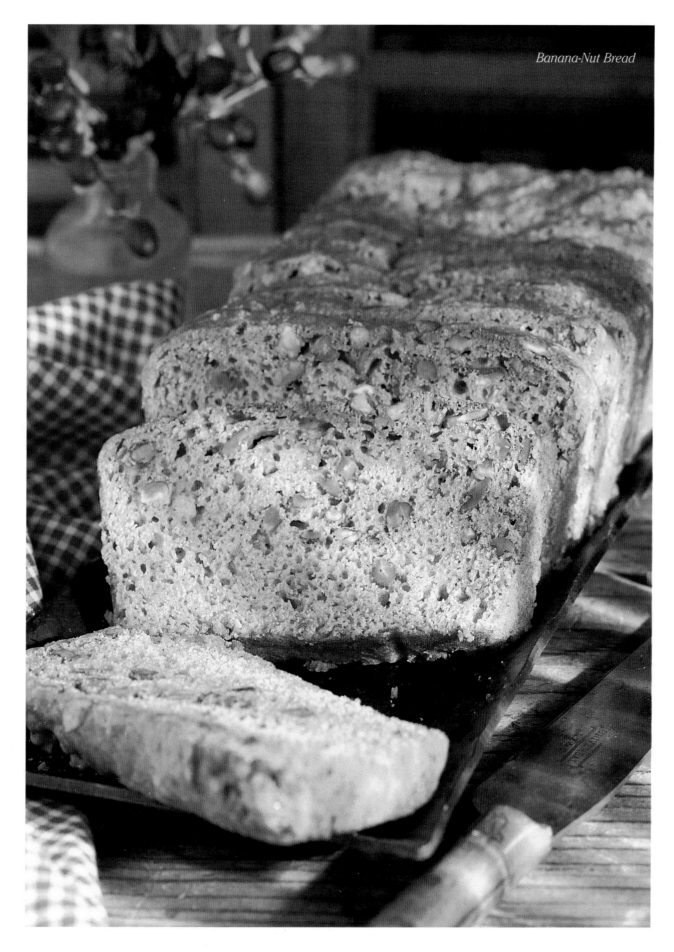

Sun-Dried Tomato and Provolone Bread

Tangy dried tomatoes, provolone cheese, pine nuts, and garlic mingle in this quick bread that tantalizes your taste buds with Mediterranean flair.

⅓ cup oil-packed dried tomatoes
2 garlic cloves
2½ cups all-purpose flour
2 teaspoons baking powder
½ teaspoon baking soda
1¼ teaspoons salt
1 cup (4 ounces) shredded provolone cheese
½ cup finely chopped green onions

2 teaspoons minced fresh parsley
1 teaspoon fresh or dried rosemary, crumbled
¾ teaspoon coarsely ground pepper
2 teaspoons shortening
2 teaspoons sugar
2 large eggs, lightly beaten
1¼ cups buttermilk
⅓ cup chopped pine nuts

DRAIN tomatoes, reserving 2 teaspoons oil; chop tomatoes, and set aside.

COOK garlic in small amount of boiling water 15 minutes; drain. Peel and mash garlic; set aside.

COMBINE flour, baking powder, soda, and salt; stir well. Add chopped tomatoes, cheese, and next 4 ingredients; stir well.

COMBINE reserved oil, shortening, and sugar; beat with a wire whisk until smooth. Add garlic, eggs, and buttermilk; stir well. Add chopped tomatoes, garlic mixture, and pine nuts to flour mixture, stirring just until blended.

SPREAD batter in a greased 8½- x 4½-inch loafpan; smooth top. Bake at 350° for 45 to 50 minutes or until golden. Cool in pan on a wire rack 5 minutes. Remove from pan; cool on wire rack. Yield: 1 loaf.

Special Selections of Ocala
Ocala Royal Dames for Cancer Research, Inc.
Ocala, Florida

Breakfast Roll

Starting the morning off with one of these bacon- and cheese-endowed rolls provides a luxurious breakfast-on-the-run.

1¾ cups biscuit mix
⅓ cup cold water
1 (3-ounce) package cream cheese,
    softened
¾ cup (3 ounces) shredded Cheddar
    cheese

½ pound bacon, cooked and
    crumbled (8 slices)
1 large egg, beaten
½ teaspoon poppy seeds

COMBINE biscuit mix and water in a medium bowl; stir until a soft dough forms. Turn dough out onto a lightly floured surface, and knead dough 10 times. Roll dough into a 12-inch square.

SPREAD cream cheese over dough, leaving a ¼-inch border. Sprinkle with cheese and bacon. Roll up dough, pressing firmly to eliminate air pockets; pinch seam to seal. Place dough, seam side down, on a lightly greased baking sheet. Brush dough with egg, and sprinkle with poppy seeds.

CUT slices at 1-inch intervals to, but not through, bottom of roll. Bake at 400° for 30 minutes or until rolls are golden. Serve warm. Yield: 4 servings.

Stephanie Winborn
The Art of Cooking
The Muscle Shoals District Service League
Sheffield, Alabama

Egg Wash
Brushing dough with a beaten egg before baking helps the dough brown nicely in the oven. The egg also helps toppings to adhere.

Rich Refrigerator Rolls

Shaping Rolls

The beauty of these rolls is that you choose the shape, depending on your needs. We like the cloverleaf shape (shown at right), because they're homey looking and will naturally tear apart into 3 bites.

Variety is a bonus with these great-tasting rolls. Choose your favorite shape—cloverleaf, miniature, Parker House, or crescent—or make a portion of each.

1 cup water
½ cup butter or margarine
4½ to 5 cups all-purpose flour
½ cup sugar

2 (¼-ounce) envelopes rapid-rise yeast
1 teaspoon salt
3 large eggs

COMBINE water and butter in a saucepan; heat until butter melts, stirring occasionally. Cool to 120° to 130°.

COMBINE 2 cups flour, sugar, yeast, and salt in a large mixing bowl. Gradually add liquid mixture to flour mixture, beating at low speed with an electric mixer. Add eggs, beating until moistened. Beat 3 more minutes at medium speed. Gradually stir in enough remaining flour to make a soft dough.

TURN dough out onto a lightly floured surface, and knead 3 or 4 times. Place in a large well-greased bowl, turning to grease top. Cover and chill at least 8 hours.

PUNCH dough down, and divide dough into fourths. Shape each portion into Cloverleaf, Miniature, Parker House, or Crescent rolls. Yield: dough for about 3 dozen rolls.

Cloverleaf Rolls

Using one-fourth of dough recipe, divide dough into 3 portions. Divide each portion into 6 pieces; shape each piece into a smooth ball. Place 3 balls in each greased muffin pan. Cover and let rise in a warm place (85°), free from drafts, 20 minutes or until doubled in bulk. Bake at 400° for 10 to 12 minutes or until golden. Yield: 6 rolls.

Miniature Rolls

Using one-fourth of dough recipe, divide dough into 3 portions. Divide each portion into 4 pieces; shape each piece into a smooth ball. Place 1 ball in each greased miniature (1¾-inch) muffin pan. Cover and let rise in a warm place (85°), free from drafts, 20 minutes or until doubled in bulk. Bake at 400° for 8 to 10 minutes or until golden. Yield: 1 dozen.

Parker House Rolls

Using one-fourth of dough recipe, roll dough to ¼-inch thickness on a lightly floured surface; cut with a 2-inch biscuit cutter. Brush tops lightly with melted butter. Make an off-center crease in each round, using the dull edge of a knife. Fold each round along crease, with larger half on top. Place folded rolls in rows 2 inches apart on lightly greased baking sheets. Cover and let rise in a warm place (85°), free from drafts, 20 minutes or until doubled in bulk. Bake at 400° for 8 to 10 minutes or until golden. Yield: 10 rolls.

Crescent Rolls

Using one-fourth of dough recipe, roll dough into a ½-inch circle on a lightly floured surface; brush with melted butter. Cut into 10 wedges. Starting with wide end of wedge, roll toward point. Place rolls 2 to 3 inches apart on greased baking sheets; curve to form a crescent shape. Cover and let rise in a warm place (85°), free from drafts, 20 minutes or until doubled in bulk. Bake at 400° for 8 to 10 minutes or until golden. Yield: 10 rolls.

Black Tie & Boots Optional
Colleyville Woman's Club
Colleyville, Texas

Rich Refrigerator Rolls

Grandmom Rice's Rolls

You'll wish Grandmom Rice was a relative of yours when you taste her tender potato rolls.

1 medium baking potato	1 cup milk (100° to 110°)
2 (¼-ounce) envelopes active dry yeast	3 tablespoons shortening
1 cup warm water (100° to 110°)	8 to 8¾ cups all-purpose flour, divided
4 large eggs	¾ cup plus 2 tablespoons sugar
	1½ teaspoons salt

COOK potato in boiling water to cover 30 minutes or until done. Peel and mash with a potato masher.

COMBINE yeast and warm water in a large mixing bowl; let stand 5 minutes. Add eggs, milk, shortening, sugar, salt, and mashed potato; beat at medium speed with a heavy-duty electric mixer until combined. Gradually add 8 cups flour, kneading with a dough hook until a soft dough forms, adding remaining ¾ cup flour as needed to make a soft dough.

COVER and let rise in a warm place (85°), free from drafts, 45 minutes or until doubled in bulk.

PUNCH dough down, and divide into thirds; shape each portion into 12 (2-inch) balls. Place 2 inches apart on greased baking sheets. Cover and let rise in a warm place, free from drafts, 20 to 30 minutes or until doubled in bulk.

BAKE at 375° for 14 minutes or until golden. Yield: 3 dozen.

A Century of Serving
The Junior Board of Christiana Care, Inc.
Wilmington, Delaware

Chocolate Cinnamon Rolls

For a chocolaty treat, you can't beat these yummy chocolate rolls filled with cinnamon sugar and pecans.

1 (¼-ounce) envelope active dry yeast	2½ cups all-purpose flour, divided
¾ cup warm water (100° to 110°)	1 tablespoon butter or margarine, softened
¼ cup butter or margarine, softened	1½ teaspoons ground cinnamon
1 teaspoon salt	3 tablespoons sugar
¼ cup sugar	½ cup chopped pecans
1 large egg	2 cups sifted powdered sugar
⅓ cup cocoa	2½ tablespoons milk

COMBINE yeast and warm water in a 2-cup liquid measuring cup; let stand 5 minutes.

COMBINE yeast mixture, ¼ cup softened butter, salt, ¼ cup sugar, egg, cocoa, and 1 cup flour in a large mixing bowl; beat at medium speed with an electric mixer until well blended. Gradually stir in enough remaining flour to make a soft dough. Place dough in a well-greased bowl, turning to grease top. Cover and let rise in a warm place (85°), free from drafts, 50 minutes or until doubled in bulk.

PUNCH dough down; turn out onto a lightly floured surface, and knead until smooth and elastic (about 2 minutes). Roll dough into a 12- x 9-inch rectangle, and spread 1 tablespoon softened butter over dough. Combine cinnamon and 3 tablespoons sugar; sprinkle over butter. Sprinkle pecans over cinnamon mixture. Roll up dough, starting at short side, pressing firmly to eliminate air pockets; pinch seams to seal. Slice dough into 9 rolls; place rolls on a greased baking sheet. Cover; let rise in a warm place, free from drafts, 15 minutes or until doubled in bulk. Bake at 425° for 8 minutes or until golden.

MEANWHILE, combine sifted powdered sugar and milk, stirring until blended. Drizzle powdered sugar glaze over hot rolls. Yield: 9 large rolls.

Dolores Wilson
Madalene Cooks—50 Years of Good Taste
Church of the Madalene
Tulsa, Oklahoma

Whole Wheat Spirals

This recipe spiraled its way through our Test Kitchens with our highest rating.

2 (¼-ounce) envelopes active dry yeast	½ cup butter or margarine, melted and divided
1¾ cups warm water (100° to 110°)	1 large egg, lightly beaten
½ cup sugar	2¼ cups whole wheat flour
2 teaspoons salt	2¼ to 2½ cups all-purpose flour

COMBINE yeast and warm water in a 2-cup liquid measuring cup; let stand 5 minutes.

COMBINE yeast mixture, sugar, salt, ¼ cup melted butter, egg, and whole wheat flour in a large mixing bowl; beat at medium speed with an electric mixer until well blended. Gradually stir in enough all-purpose flour to make a soft dough.

TURN dough out onto a well-floured surface, and knead until smooth and elastic (about 5 minutes). Place in a well-greased bowl, turning to grease top.

COVER and let rise in a warm place (85°), free from drafts, 30 minutes or until doubled in bulk.

PUNCH dough down, and divide in half; shape each portion into a 14- x 7-inch rectangle. Cut each rectangle into 12 (7- x 1-inch-wide) strips. Roll each strip into a spiral, and place in well-greased muffin pans.

COVER and let rise in a warm place, free from drafts, 20 minutes or until doubled in bulk.

BAKE at 400° for 8 to 10 minutes or until golden. Remove from pans, and cool on wire racks. Brush with remaining ¼ cup melted butter. Yield: 2 dozen.

Linda Brown
Blended Blessings
First Presbyterian Church
Salisbury, North Carolina

Two Flours

Yeast bread recipes are often made from a blend of whole wheat and all-purpose flours. The protein amounts differ for these flours, and when combined and blended with liquids, they form the ideal bread structure.

Easy Focaccia ONE PAN

Shortcut Focaccia

This shortcut version starts with frozen bread dough. All you do is thaw it, press it in the pan, and add toppings. Get creative and vary the toppings—try whole pitted olives, slivers of garlic and ham, and grape tomatoes.

Southern women have been turning out homemade bread for centuries. And so have Italians, evidenced by the popularity of focaccia, an Old World crusty flatbread laden with olive oil. A staple across Italy, focaccia has now made its way into the heart of the American South. It shows up in kitchens and on menus as an appetizer or a sandwich.

2 (1-pound) loaves frozen bread
  dough, thawed
¼ cup olive oil
1 small white or purple onion, thinly
  sliced and separated into rings
¼ cup freshly grated Parmesan
  cheese

2 tablespoons fresh or dried
  rosemary
½ teaspoon garlic powder
1 teaspoon coarse salt
½ teaspoon freshly ground pepper

PLACE each portion of dough on a lightly greased baking sheet; slightly flatten each dough into a 12- x 8- x ½-inch rectangle. Press your finger or knuckle into dough at 2-inch intervals to create "dimples." Brush with olive oil. Top with onion rings; sprinkle evenly with cheese, rosemary, garlic powder, salt, and pepper.

BAKE at 375° for 25 minutes or until lightly browned. Serve warm, or cool completely on wire racks. Yield: 2 loaves.

Valerie Viglione
Celebration: St. Andrew's School 30th Anniversary Book of Celebrated Recipes
St. Andrew's School Parents' Association
Boca Raton, Florida

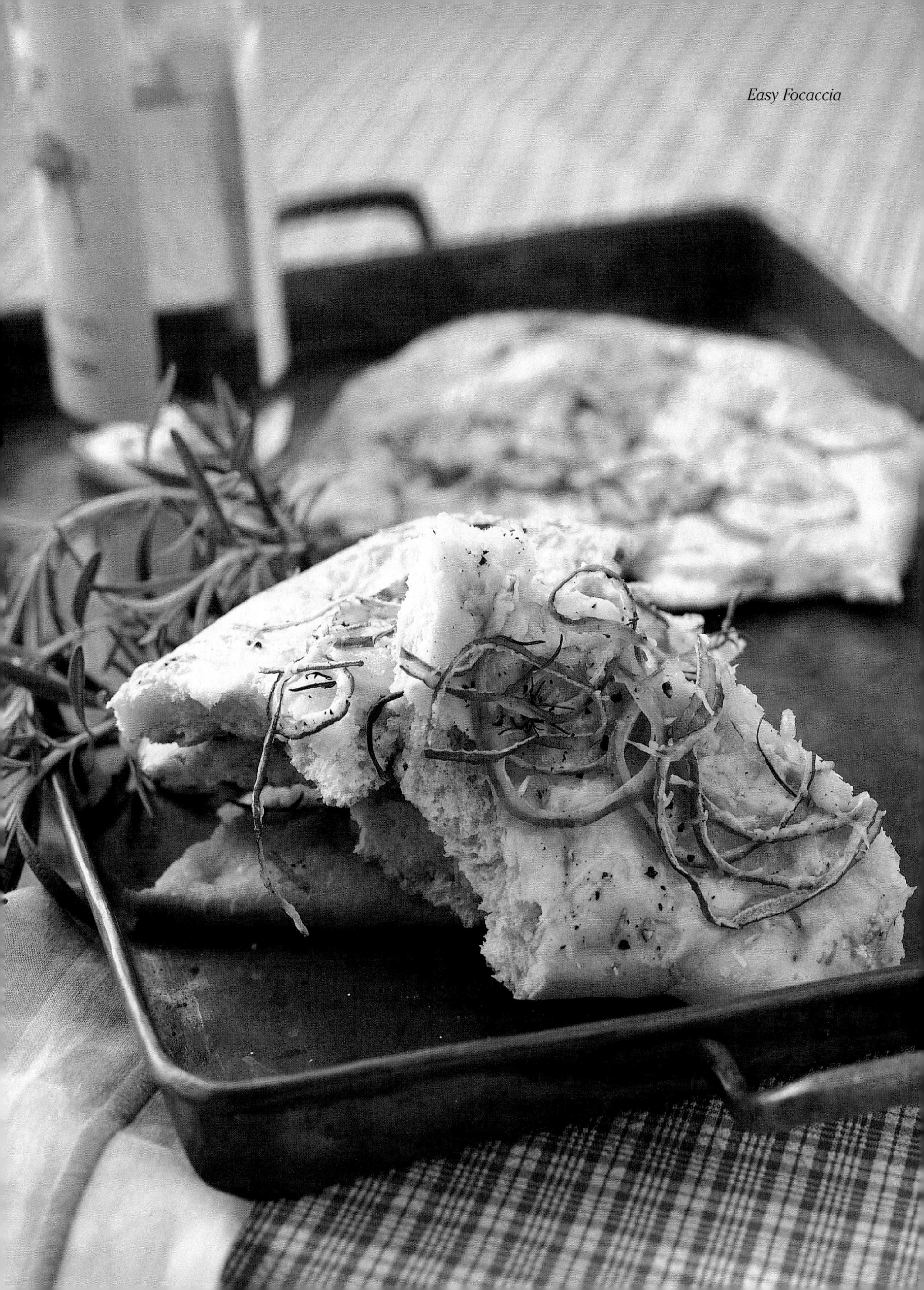
Easy Focaccia

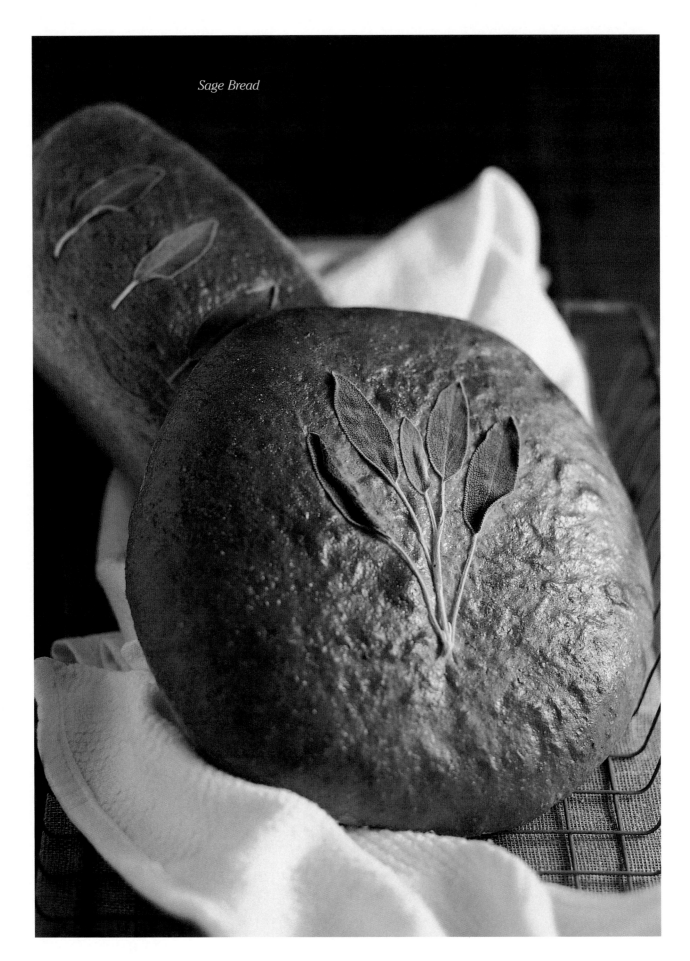

Sage Bread

Sage Bread

Fresh sage leaves top this savory bread, making an attractive presentation special enough for gift giving. We halved the recipe so it can be mixed with a regular mixer. If you have a heavy-duty mixer, you can double the recipe, if you'd like, and make three slightly larger loaves in 9- x 5-inch loafpans. They'll need a little more time to rise; bake the loaves at 375° for 30 minutes or until golden.

2¼ to 2½ cups all-purpose flour, divided
2 cups whole wheat flour
2 (¼-ounce) envelopes active dry yeast
1 tablespoon minced fresh sage
1¾ cups milk
¼ cup firmly packed light brown sugar

2½ tablespoons butter or margarine
1 teaspoon salt
¼ cup plus 2 tablespoons yellow cornmeal, divided
1 large egg, lightly beaten
1 tablespoon water
Fresh sage leaves

COMBINE 1 cup all-purpose flour, whole wheat flour, yeast, and minced sage in a large mixing bowl; stir well.

PLACE milk, brown sugar, butter, and salt in a saucepan; cook over low heat until butter melts, stirring often. Cool to 120° to 130°.

GRADUALLY add milk mixture to flour mixture, beating 30 seconds at low speed with an electric mixer. Beat 3 more minutes at medium-high speed. Gradually stir in ¼ cup cornmeal and remaining 1¼ to 1½ cups all-purpose flour to make a soft dough.

TURN dough out onto a floured surface, and knead until smooth and elastic (about 6 to 8 minutes). Shape into a ball. Place in a well-greased bowl, turning to grease top. Cover and let rise in a warm place (85°), free from drafts, 30 minutes or until doubled in bulk.

PUNCH dough down; turn out onto a lightly floured surface, and knead lightly 4 or 5 times. Divide dough in half. Cover and let rest 10 minutes.

LIGHTLY grease a baking sheet, and sprinkle with remaining 2 tablespoons cornmeal. Shape each half of dough into an 8½- x 4½-inch loaf. Place on prepared baking sheet.

COMBINE egg and water, stirring well. Brush loaves with egg mixture. Place sage leaves on top of loaves. Cover and let rise in a warm place, free from drafts, 20 minutes or until doubled in bulk. Brush again with egg mixture. (Do not brush sage leaves.)

BAKE at 375° for 25 to 35 minutes or until golden, covering with aluminum foil during last 15 minutes, if necessary, to prevent excessive browning. Remove loaves from baking sheet, and cool on a wire rack. Yield: 2 loaves.

Robin Westerick
Carnegie Hall Cookbook
Carnegie Hall, Inc.
Lewisburg, West Virginia

Fresh Sage

Fresh sage is a wonderful, earthy scented soft herb that grows strong in Southern gardens. In warmer climates, sage keeps growing right into the winter months.

Dill Pickle Rye Bread

The Shape of Things
Baking this bread in a loafpan gives it a nice, neat shape for sandwich slices.

Make your next ham sandwich memorable with this hearty rye bread. It's flavored with chopped dill pickles, dillseeds, and caraway seeds.

3 cups all-purpose flour
3 cups rye flour
2 (¼-ounce) envelopes active
    dry yeast
1 cup finely chopped dill pickles
1 cup water
½ cup liquid drained from dill pickles

½ cup buttermilk
¼ cup vegetable oil
2 tablespoons sugar
2 teaspoons dillseeds
2 teaspoons caraway seeds
1 teaspoon salt

COMBINE flours in a large bowl; stir well. Combine 2 cups flour mixture and yeast in a large mixing bowl; stir well.

COMBINE chopped dill pickle and remaining 8 ingredients in a medium saucepan. Heat until dill pickle mixture reaches 120° to 130°, stirring occasionally.

GRADUALLY add liquid mixture to yeast mixture, beating at low speed with an electric mixer until blended. Beat 2 more minutes at medium speed. Gradually stir in enough remaining flour mixture to make a soft dough.

TURN dough out onto a lightly floured surface, and knead until smooth and elastic (about 8 minutes). Place in a well-greased bowl, turning to grease top. Cover and let rise in a warm place (85°), free from drafts, 40 minutes or until doubled in bulk.

PUNCH dough down; turn out onto a lightly floured surface, and knead lightly 4 or 5 times. Divide dough in half. Roll 1 portion of dough into a 14- x 7-inch rectangle. Roll up dough, starting at short side, pressing firmly to eliminate air pockets; pinch ends to seal. Place dough, seam side down, in a well-greased 9- x 5-inch loafpan. Repeat procedure with remaining portion of dough.

COVER and let rise in a warm place, free from drafts, 40 minutes or until dough is doubled in bulk.

BAKE at 350° for 40 to 45 minutes or until loaves sound hollow when tapped. Remove bread from pans immediately; cool on wire racks. Yield: 2 loaves.

Ruth Fay Kilgore
The Nashville Cookbook
The Nashville Area Home Economics Association
Nashville, Tennessee

Cinnamon English Muffin Bread

Fresh Rise
Always check the date on a package of yeast to be sure it's fresh before adding it to a bread recipe.

These simple little cinnamon-raisin loaves boast the same texture and flavor as English muffins. They're thin, making them perfectly suited to popping in the toaster.

Cornmeal
½ cup water
2 cups milk
5 cups all-purpose flour, divided
2 (¼-ounce) envelopes active
    dry yeast

¼ teaspoon baking soda
2 teaspoons salt
1 tablespoon sugar
1½ teaspoons ground cinnamon
1 cup raisins

GREASE 2 (9- x 5-inch) loafpans, and coat with cornmeal. Set aside. Combine water and milk in a saucepan; heat over medium heat just until hot (120° to 130°).

COMBINE 3 cups flour, yeast, and next 4 ingredients in a large mixing bowl. Gradually add liquid mixture to flour mixture, beating at high speed with an electric mixer. Beat 2 more minutes at medium speed. Stir in raisins. Gradually stir in remaining 2 cups flour to make a soft dough.

SPOON dough into prepared loafpans. Sprinkle tops with cornmeal. Cover and let rise in a warm place (85°), free from drafts, 45 minutes or until doubled in bulk. Bake at 400° for 25 minutes. Remove bread from pans immediately; cool on wire racks. Yield: 2 loaves.

Pauline Moffatt
Party Pleasers
GFWC Philomathic Club
Duncan, Oklahoma

Raisin-Nut Cocoa Bread

If you're gonna make the effort for homemade bread, you might as well make 2 loaves. Keep one and give the other away, or freeze it for down the road.

2 cups water
1 cup uncooked regular oats
1 teaspoon salt, divided
6 cups all-purpose flour, divided
½ cup cocoa
2 (¼-ounce) envelopes active
    dry yeast

½ cup warm water (100° to 110°)
1 cup firmly packed light brown
    sugar
2 tablespoons butter, softened
1 cup chopped walnuts
1 cup raisins
Melted butter

Butter and Bread
Brushing melted butter on fresh baked bread gives it a pretty sheen and an extra nip of salty flavor.

COMBINE 2 cups water, oats, and ½ teaspoon salt in a medium saucepan. Bring to a boil; reduce heat, and simmer, uncovered, 5 minutes, stirring occasionally. Pour oat mixture into a large mixing bowl, and cool to lukewarm.

COMBINE 2 cups flour, cocoa, and remaining ½ teaspoon salt. Combine yeast and warm water in a 1-cup liquid measuring cup; let stand 5 minutes. Add flour mixture, yeast mixture, sugar, and softened butter to oat mixture. Beat at low speed with an electric mixer until moistened. Beat at medium speed 2 minutes. Stir in walnuts and raisins.

GRADUALLY stir in enough remaining flour to make a soft dough. Turn dough out onto a floured surface, and knead until smooth and elastic (6 to 8 minutes). Place dough in a well-greased bowl, turning to grease top. Cover and let rise in a warm place (85°), free from drafts, 45 minutes or until doubled in bulk. Punch dough down, and divide in half.

ROLL half of dough into a 15- x 7-inch rectangle on a lightly floured surface. Roll up dough, starting at short side, pressing firmly to eliminate air pockets; pinch seams and ends to seal. Place loaf, seam side down, in a greased 9- x 5-inch loafpan. Repeat procedure with remaining portion of dough. Cover and let rise in a warm place, free from drafts, 30 minutes or until doubled in bulk.

BAKE at 375° for 35 to 40 minutes or until loaves sound hollow when tapped. Remove bread from pans; immediately brush with melted butter. Cool completely on wire racks. Yield: 2 loaves.

Swap Around Recipes
Delmarva Square Dance Federation
Salisbury, Maryland

Salsa Eggs QUICK & EASY

Pictured on page 107

Speedy south-of-the-border scrambled eggs is what this recipe brings to the breakfast table.

6 large eggs, lightly beaten
1 (4.5-ounce) can chopped green
   chiles, drained
1 jalapeño pepper, seeded and minced
¼ teaspoon salt

Dash of ground red pepper
2 tablespoons butter
½ cup finely chopped red bell pepper
Salsa
Sour cream

STIR together first 5 ingredients in a bowl. Melt butter in a large skillet over medium-high heat, tilting pan to coat bottom. Add bell pepper; cook, stirring constantly, 3 minutes or until tender. Reduce heat to medium-low. Add egg mixture; cook, without stirring, until mixture begins to set on bottom. Draw a spatula across bottom of pan to form large curds. Continue cooking until eggs are thickened and firm, but still moist. Serve with salsa and sour cream. Yield: 3 servings.

Pick of the Crop, Two
North Sunflower PTA
Drew, Mississippi

Simple Scrambling

When cooking scrambled eggs in a skillet, you'll get the best results if you don't overstir them while they're cooking. Just use a wide spatula and gently stir a few times, allowing egg to form large curds.

Apple and Sausage Quiche

This cheese and sausage quiche is slightly sweet from the chopped apple. Prebaking the pastry, without the filling, ensures a crisp crust.

1 unbaked 9-inch pastry shell
1 cup peeled, chopped cooking apple
2 tablespoons sugar
1 tablespoon lemon juice
Dash of salt and pepper
¾ cup chopped onion
3 tablespoons butter, melted

½ pound ground pork sausage
4 large eggs, beaten
1 (8-ounce) container sour cream
⅛ teaspoon ground nutmeg
Dash of ground red pepper
½ cup (2 ounces) shredded Cheddar
   cheese

FIT pastry in a 9-inch quiche dish. Prick bottom and sides of pastry with a fork. Bake at 450° for 8 to 10 minutes; cool on a wire rack.

COMBINE apple and next 3 ingredients; toss well. Cook apple mixture and onion in butter in a large skillet over medium-high heat, stirring constantly, until onion is tender. Remove from heat, and cool 20 minutes.

BROWN sausage in a large skillet, stirring until it crumbles; drain well. Combine eggs and next 3 ingredients in a large bowl. Add apple mixture and sausage to egg mixture; stir well.

POUR mixture into prepared pastry shell. Gently stir in cheese. Bake, uncovered, at 350° for 35 minutes or until cheese melts and a knife inserted in center comes out clean. Let stand 10 minutes before serving. Yield: one 9-inch quiche.

Among the Lilies
Women in Missions, First Baptist Church of Atlanta, Georgia

Sausage Selections

Use mild pork sausage for a tamer-flavored quiche. Try hot pork sausage to pump up the flavor.

Apple and Sausage Quiche

Mexican Quiches

Long-Lasting Quiche

Bake, cool, and freeze these mini quiches up to a month. Thaw in refrigerator and reheat at 300° on a baking sheet.

These little mouthfuls make great brunch food or appetizers on a buffet. For spicier quiches, use Pepper Jack cheese.

½ cup butter or margarine, softened
1 (3-ounce) package cream cheese, softened
1 cup all-purpose flour
1 cup (4 ounces) shredded Monterey Jack cheese

1 (4.5-ounce) can chopped green chiles, undrained
2 large eggs
½ cup whipping cream
¼ teaspoon salt
⅛ teaspoon pepper

BEAT butter and cream cheese at medium speed with an electric mixer until smooth. Add flour, and beat well. Shape dough into a ball; cover and chill 20 minutes.

SHAPE dough into 36 (¾-inch) balls. Place in ungreased miniature (1¾-inch) muffin pans, and shape each ball into a shell. Divide shredded cheese and green chiles evenly among shells.

WHISK together eggs and remaining 3 ingredients. Spoon mixture evenly into shells. Bake at 350° for 35 minutes or until set. Serve warm. Yield: 3 dozen.

Toni Smith
Angels in the Kitchen
Grace Episcopal Church
Anderson, South Carolina

Country Breakfast Casserole

Make Ahead

Prepare this casserole up to the point of popping it into the oven to bake, then cover and refrigerate it overnight. This is a great make-ahead dish if you're hosting a brunch.

All your breakfast favorites—sausage, eggs, and grits—are cooked in one dish. Add hot biscuits and juice, and you'll be ready to tackle the day ahead.

1 pound ground mild pork sausage
3½ cups water
1 teaspoon salt
1 cup uncooked quick-cooking grits
1½ cups (6 ounces) shredded Cheddar cheese, divided

4 large eggs, lightly beaten
¾ cup milk
¼ cup butter or margarine, melted
¼ teaspoon pepper

BROWN sausage in a large skillet, stirring until it crumbles and is no longer pink; drain.

BRING water and salt to a boil in a medium saucepan; stir in grits. Return to a boil; cover, reduce heat, and simmer 5 minutes, stirring occasionally. Remove from heat; add 1 cup cheese, stirring until cheese melts. Stir in sausage, eggs, and remaining 3 ingredients.

POUR mixture into a greased 11- x 7-inch baking dish; sprinkle with remaining ½ cup cheese. Bake, uncovered, at 350° for 45 minutes or until set. Let stand 5 minutes before serving. Yield: 6 servings.

Secrets of Amelia
McArthur Family Branch YMCA
Fernandina Beach, Florida

Artichoke Brunch Casserole   PARTY FOOD

There's a lot to love in this savory breakfast casserole—fresh mushrooms, artichokes, and olives layered with plenty of melted Cheddar cheese.

1½ cups chopped onion
½ cup butter or margarine, melted
    and divided
12 large eggs, beaten
4 cups (16 ounces) shredded sharp
    Cheddar cheese
1 (8-ounce) package sliced fresh
    mushrooms
2 (14-ounce) cans artichoke hearts,
    drained and quartered

½ cup sliced ripe olives
3 tablespoons minced fresh parsley
2 garlic cloves, minced
¾ teaspoon dried oregano
½ teaspoon dried thyme
¼ teaspoon ground red pepper
¾ cup fine, dry breadcrumbs
    (store-bought)

COOK onion in ¼ cup plus 1 tablespoon butter in a large skillet over medium-high heat, stirring constantly, until tender.

COMBINE onion mixture, eggs, and next 9 ingredients in a large bowl; stir well. Pour into an ungreased 13- x 9-inch pan.

COMBINE remaining 3 tablespoons melted butter and breadcrumbs in a small bowl; stir well. Sprinkle over egg mixture. Bake at 350° for 40 to 45 minutes or until set and golden. Let stand 10 minutes before serving. Yield: 10 servings.

Food for the Journey
St. Francis Xavier College Church Choir
St. Louis, Missouri

Serving a Casserole

If you want to serve this casserole hot, set it into a woven or other type of casserole carrier. Carriers are attractive, allow you to serve the food while it's hot, and alert guests that the pan's hot.

Three-Pepper Frittata

A colorful trio of bell pepper strips peeks out from beneath a blanket of egg-soaked bread cubes, tender garden vegetables, and creamy cheeses.

Informal Frittata

Frittatas are more forgiving than omelets. You don't flip them in half and risk losing the filling. Typically, you send the skillet from cooktop to oven, but this recipe bakes in the oven exclusively in a springform pan. The pan gives the frittata nice edges for serving.

8 white bread slices, cubed and divided
1 large purple onion, thinly sliced (about 2¼ cups)
1 red bell pepper, cut into thin strips (about 1 cup)
1 yellow bell pepper, cut into thin strips (about 1 cup)
1 orange bell pepper, cut into thin strips (about 1 cup)
3 garlic cloves, minced
¼ cup olive oil, divided
2 yellow squash, thinly sliced (about 2⅓ cups)

2 zucchini, thinly sliced (about 3 cups)
1 (8-ounce) package fresh mushrooms, sliced
6 large eggs
¼ cup whipping cream
2½ teaspoons salt
2 teaspoons freshly ground pepper
2 cups (8 ounces) shredded Swiss cheese
1 (8-ounce) package cream cheese, cubed and softened

PRESS half of bread cubes into a lightly greased 10-inch springform pan. Wrap bottom and sides of pan with aluminum foil; set aside.

SAUTÉ onion and next 4 ingredients in 2 tablespoons oil in a large skillet over medium-high heat 5 minutes or until tender; drain and set aside.

SAUTÉ yellow squash and zucchini in 1 tablespoon oil in skillet over medium-high heat 7 minutes or until tender; drain and set aside.

SAUTÉ mushrooms in remaining 1 tablespoon oil in skillet over medium-high heat 4 minutes or until tender; drain and set aside.

WHISK together eggs and next 3 ingredients in a large bowl. Stir in sautéed vegetables. Stir in remaining half of bread cubes, Swiss cheese, and cream cheese. Spoon mixture into prepared pan; place pan on a baking sheet.

BAKE, uncovered, at 325° for 1 hour and 15 minutes or until set. Let stand 15 minutes. Carefully remove foil and sides of pan. Serve warm. Yield: 8 servings.

A Sunsational Encore
The Junior League of Greater Orlando, Florida

Breakfast Tortilla Torta

If you like to get an early start, prepare the potato and sausage mixtures for this egg and cheese dish the night before.

1 tablespoon olive oil
1 pound new potatoes, thinly sliced
1 cup sliced green onions, divided
    (about 8)
1 teaspoon chili powder
½ teaspoon salt, divided
6 large eggs
1 cup canned whole kernel corn,
    drained

½ teaspoon pepper
1 pound ground hot pork sausage
1 red bell pepper, finely chopped
1¼ cups salsa, divided
5 (10-inch) flour tortillas
½ cup (2 ounces) shredded Cheddar
    cheese
Salsa
Sour cream

HEAT oil in a large skillet over medium heat until hot; add potato, and cook 12 minutes or until tender, stirring occasionally. Add ⅓ cup green onions, chili powder, and ¼ teaspoon salt; cook 2 more minutes. Pour into a bowl; set aside.

WHISK together eggs, corn, remaining ¼ teaspoon salt, and pepper. Pour mixture into a lightly greased skillet, and cook over medium heat 2 to 3 minutes, stirring often (mixture will be slightly runny). Pour into a bowl; set aside.

BROWN sausage, red bell pepper, and remaining ⅔ cup green onions in skillet, stirring until sausage crumbles and is no longer pink. Drain and pat dry with paper towels. Wipe drippings from skillet with a paper towel. Stir in ¼ cup salsa.

LIGHTLY grease a 10-inch springform pan. Place a tortilla in pan. Spread potato mixture over tortilla. Top with a tortilla, pressing flat. Spread half of sausage mixture over tortilla. Top with another tortilla, egg mixture, tortilla, remaining half of sausage mixture, and remaining tortilla. Spread remaining 1 cup salsa over last tortilla. Sprinkle with cheese. Bake, uncovered, at 400° for 40 minutes or until set, shielding with aluminum foil after 20 minutes to prevent excessive browning. Let stand 10 minutes before serving. Serve with additional salsa and sour cream. Yield: 10 to 12 servings.

Eva Ann McLean
Southern Elegance: A Second Course
The Junior League of Gaston County
Gastonia, North Carolina

Torta Tactics
A torta can be a tart, pie, or cake. In this recipe it's a breakfast tart, stacked with layers of tortillas, potato, sausage, and peppers. This type of torta is easiest to serve if you let it stand a few minutes before slicing.

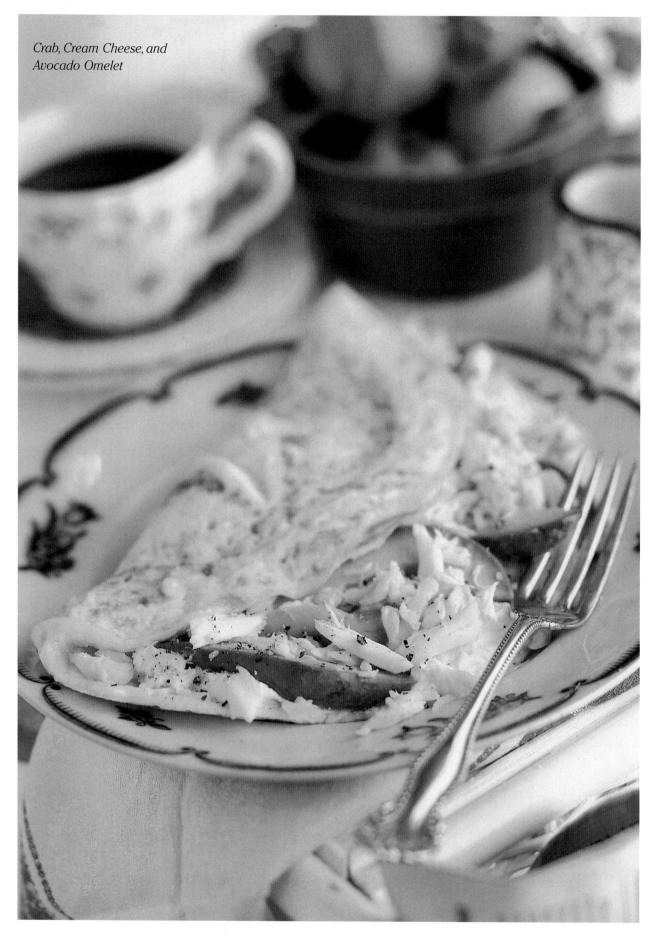

Crab, Cream Cheese, and Avocado Omelet

Crab, Cream Cheese, and Avocado Omelet

Nothing ordinary about this omelet. Flaky sweet crabmeat, cream cheese, and buttery avocado team up as the filling for this fancy brunch fare.

4 large eggs, lightly beaten
¼ cup milk
¼ teaspoon salt
⅛ teaspoon paprika
Dash of ground white pepper
1½ tablespoons butter

2 ounces cream cheese, cut into
    1-inch pieces and softened
½ ripe avocado, peeled and sliced
½ cup fresh lump crabmeat, drained
2 teaspoons lemon juice
Fresh chives

COMBINE first 5 ingredients; stir with a wire whisk until blended.

HEAT a 10-inch nonstick skillet over medium heat until hot enough to sizzle a drop of water. Add butter, and tilt pan to coat bottom evenly. Pour egg mixture into skillet. As mixture starts to cook, gently lift edges of omelet with a spatula, and tilt pan so uncooked portion flows underneath.

SPRINKLE cream cheese over half of omelet. Arrange avocado and crabmeat over cheese, and drizzle lemon juice over crabmeat. Fold omelet in half; cover and cook 2 to 3 minutes or until cheese melts. Top with chives. Serve immediately. Yield: 2 servings.

Virginia Fare
The Junior League of Richmond, Virginia

Omelet Encouragement
Once you've gathered your ingredients, making an omelet is a snap. Have a sturdy spatula handy to help you fold it.

Creole Deviled Eggs

Hot sauce and red pepper deliver a powerful punch to these stuffed eggs.

16 large hard-cooked eggs
½ cup mayonnaise
1 tablespoon lemon juice
5 drops of hot sauce
¼ teaspoon salt
½ teaspoon ground red pepper
2 tablespoons finely chopped fresh
    chives

2 tablespoons finely chopped fresh
    parsley
2 tablespoons finely chopped red
    bell pepper
Garnishes: red bell pepper strips,
    chopped chives, parsley sprigs
Ground red pepper

SLICE eggs in half lengthwise, and carefully remove yolks. Process yolks, mayonnaise, and next 4 ingredients in a food processor until smooth, stopping once to scrape down sides. Add chives, parsley, and chopped red bell pepper; pulse just until blended.

SPOON yolk mixture into egg whites. Garnish, if desired; sprinkle with additional ground red pepper. Chill thoroughly before serving. Yield: 16 servings.

Jan Lester
Somethin's Cookin' with Married Young Adults
Houston's First Baptist Church
Houston, Texas

Bigger is Better
Be sure to use large eggs when you make this recipe because you'll want the biggest bite possible of this Creole delicacy.

Smoked Salmon and Onion Cheesecake PARTY FOOD

Salmon Several Ways

If you prefer, serve this salmon cheesecake in small wedges as a plated appetizer.

A wedge of this rich salmon cheesecake and a fresh green salad make memorable luncheon fare.

¼ cup grated Parmesan cheese, divided
2 tablespoons fine, dry breadcrumbs (store-bought)
1 small Vidalia or other sweet onion, chopped
1 cup chopped green bell pepper
3 tablespoons butter or margarine, melted
3 (8-ounce) packages cream cheese, softened

⅓ cup evaporated milk
4 large eggs
¼ teaspoon salt
¼ teaspoon freshly ground black pepper
½ pound smoked salmon, finely chopped
½ cup (2 ounces) shredded Swiss cheese

COMBINE 2 tablespoons Parmesan cheese and breadcrumbs. Sprinkle crumb mixture evenly in bottom and up sides of a buttered 8-inch springform pan; set aside.

COOK onion and bell pepper in butter in a skillet over medium heat 3 minutes or just until tender, stirring occasionally; set aside.

COMBINE cream cheese, milk, and eggs in a large mixing bowl; beat at medium speed with an electric mixer until smooth. Stir in onion mixture, salt, and ground pepper; fold in salmon and Swiss cheese. Pour mixture into prepared pan.

BAKE, uncovered, at 300° for 1 hour and 40 minutes or until center is almost set. Turn oven off. Leave cheesecake in oven 1 hour. Remove from oven, and cool to room temperature on a wire rack; sprinkle top with remaining 2 tablespoons Parmesan cheese. Carefully remove sides of springform pan. Serve at room temperature, or cover and chill. Yield: 16 servings.

Carolina Sunshine, Then & Now
The Charity League of Charlotte, North Carolina

Make-Ahead Cheese Soufflé MAKE AHEAD

Good news! You can make this soufflé ahead. Just spoon the mixture into a soufflé dish; cover and chill it 8 hours. Place the soufflé in a cold oven. Turn oven to 350°, and bake 55 to 60 minutes or until it's puffed and set.

¼ cup plus 2 tablespoons butter or margarine
¼ cup plus 2 tablespoons all-purpose flour
1½ cups milk
1 teaspoon salt
½ teaspoon paprika

¼ teaspoon Worcestershire sauce
⅛ teaspoon onion salt
⅛ teaspoon dry mustard
⅛ teaspoon ground red pepper
3 cups (12 ounces) shredded sharp Cheddar cheese
6 large eggs, separated

MELT butter in a large heavy saucepan over low heat; add flour, stirring until smooth. Cook 1 minute, stirring constantly. Gradually add milk; cook over medium heat, stirring constantly, until mixture is thickened and bubbly. Remove from heat. Stir in salt, paprika, Worcestershire sauce, onion salt, mustard, and red pepper. Add cheese, stirring constantly until cheese melts.

BEAT egg yolks until thick and pale. Gradually stir about one-fourth of hot mixture into yolks; add to remaining hot mixture, stirring constantly. Beat egg whites in a large bowl at high speed with an electric mixer until stiff peaks form; gently fold beaten egg white, one-third at a time, into cheese mixture. Spoon into a buttered 2-quart soufflé dish. Bake at 350° for 55 to 60 minutes or until puffed and set. Serve immediately. Yield: 8 servings.

Mrs. Robert G. Allen
Party Potpourri
The Junior League of Memphis, Inc.
Memphis, Tennessee

Keep the Fluff

For this soufflé, be sure to follow the procedure of folding in beaten egg white one-third at a time. The reason for gradually folding in the fluff is so that it won't deflate. If you folded it in all at once too quickly, the soufflé wouldn't be quite so puffy.

Creamy Cheese Grits QUICK & EASY

This simple staple is daily comfort food on breakfast tables across the South. Folks outside the South may wonder the best way to eat grits. Try this cheesy version nestled near scrambled eggs or roast beef hash on your plate.

3 (10½-ounce) cans condensed
    chicken broth, undiluted
½ cup whipping cream

1 cup uncooked quick-cooking grits
2 cups (8 ounces) shredded sharp
    Cheddar cheese

COMBINE chicken broth and whipping cream in a large saucepan; bring to a boil. Stir in grits, and return to a boil. Cover, reduce heat, and simmer 5 to 7 minutes. Stir in cheese. Cool 10 minutes. Yield: 5¾ cups.

Terry L. Ward
Helena, Alabama

True Grit

If you can't locate quick grits in the marketplace, use 2⅓ cups instant grits and try a low-sodium chicken broth. Otherwise, you can use 1 cup regular grits and cover and cook 18 minutes or until grits are thickened.

Blue Cheese Grits

Grits get fancy with blue cheese, a break from the more traditional Cheddar take. These grits were a favorite in our Test Kitchens, even among those who don't consider themselves fond of blue cheese. We suggest serving these chunky grits at brunch or as a side dish with pork.

4 cups water
2 cups chicken broth
1 teaspoon salt
1 teaspoon pepper
2 cups uncooked regular grits

¼ cup butter
8 ounces firm blue cheese, crumbled
6 ounces creamy blue cheese
Garnish: chopped fresh chives

COMBINE first 4 ingredients in a saucepan; bring to a boil. Stir in grits and butter.
COOK grits according to package directions, stirring occasionally. Remove from heat; stir in cheeses. Garnish, if desired. Serve warm with sliced tomatoes, if desired. Yield: 8 servings.

Southern . . . On Occasion
The Junior League of Cobb-Marietta
Marietta, Georgia

Two Blues

There are many varieties of blue-veined cheese available on the market. For this recipe, pick a firm, crumbling cheese (such as Maytag) and a softer, creamy cheese (Baby Blue Saga), too. The combination of two types turns humble grits into an elegant dish.

Shrimp Gravy

Down in the Lowcountry of coastal South Carolina where shrimp boats run daily, shrimp gravy is a welcome dish on the dinner table. Spoon it over grits and add a little bacon.

It's the Shrimp that Counts

Use any type of grits for this dish—instant, quick, or regular. It's the sweet fresh shrimp that makes this gravy and the grits so good.

5 bacon slices
1 medium-size green bell pepper, chopped
2 tablespoons minced garlic
1 bunch green onions, sliced
4½ cups sliced fresh mushrooms (about 12 ounces)

1 tablespoon all-purpose flour
¾ cup chicken broth
1½ pounds unpeeled, medium-size fresh shrimp
1 teaspoon garlic salt
½ teaspoon pepper
3 cups hot cooked grits

COOK bacon in a large skillet until crisp; remove bacon. Drain skillet, reserving 2 tablespoons drippings. Crumble bacon, and set aside.

COOK green pepper, garlic, and green onions in bacon drippings over high heat, stirring constantly, until tender. Stir in mushrooms, and sauté 3 minutes. Add flour, stirring until smooth. Slowly add broth; bring to a boil. Add shrimp; cover and cook over medium heat 5 minutes or until shrimp turn pink, stirring often. Stir in garlic salt and pepper. Serve over grits, and sprinkle with crumbled bacon. Yield: 3 to 4 servings.

Tom Kapp
'Pon Top Edisto
Trinity Episcopal Church
Edisto Island, South Carolina

Desserts

Apple-Walnut Cake,
page 169

Colossal Chocolate Chip Cookies

Half is Fine, too

If you don't have a heavy-duty mixer to handle this large amount of stiff dough, cut the recipe in half.

Imagine jumbo chocolate chip cookies with extra chips, nuts, oats, and even chopped candy bars. This is the recipe.

2 cups butter or margarine, softened
2 cups sugar
2 cups firmly packed light brown sugar
4 large eggs
2 teaspoons vanilla extract
4 cups all-purpose flour
2 teaspoons baking powder
2 teaspoons baking soda

1 teaspoon salt
5 cups uncooked regular oats
2 cups (12 ounces) semisweet chocolate morsels
1 cup (6 ounces) semisweet chocolate morsels
1 (7-ounce) milk chocolate candy bar, coarsely chopped
2 cups chopped walnuts

BEAT butter at medium speed with a heavy-duty electric mixer until creamy; gradually add sugars, beating well. Add eggs and vanilla; beat well.

COMBINE flour and next 3 ingredients; gradually add to butter mixture, beating well.

PROCESS oats in a food processor until finely ground. Gradually add to butter mixture, beating well. Stir in chocolate morsels, chopped chocolate, and walnuts.

SHAPE cookie dough into 2-inch balls. Place 3 inches apart on ungreased baking sheets. Flatten each ball to a 2½-inch circle. Bake at 375° for 8 to 10 minutes or until lightly browned. Cool slightly on baking sheets; remove to wire racks to cool completely. Yield: 4 dozen.

Nikki Baron
Signature Cuisine
Miami Country Day School Parents' Association
Miami, Florida

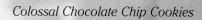
Colossal Chocolate Chip Cookies

Grand Slams

These mouthfuls get their crunch from a trio of pantry ingredients—cereal, coconut, and nuts.

Here's the Scoop

Use a cookie scoop or small ice cream scoop to portion out dough and to make uniform-size cookies.

1 cup shortening	1 teaspoon baking soda
1 cup sugar	½ teaspoon baking powder
1 cup firmly packed light brown sugar	1 teaspoon salt
2 large eggs	1 cup crispy rice cereal
2½ cups all-purpose flour	1 cup flaked coconut
	½ cup chopped pecans

BEAT shortening at medium speed with an electric mixer until fluffy. Gradually add sugars, beating mixture well. Add eggs, 1 at a time, beating well.

COMBINE flour and next 3 ingredients; gradually add to sugar mixture, beating until smooth. Stir in cereal, coconut, and pecans. Cover and chill 10 minutes.

DROP dough by rounded teaspoonfuls onto ungreased baking sheets. Bake at 325° for 10 minutes. Cool slightly on baking sheets; remove to wire racks to cool completely. Yield: 6 dozen.

Bully's Best Bites
The Junior Auxiliary of Starkville, Mississippi

The Very Best Oatmeal Cookies

Wholesome wheat flour, oats, and pecans give these cookies their hearty texture. The raisins are soaked in egg and vanilla to plump them up before adding them to the dough.

Keep the Canister

After you've made these comfort food cookies, save the (empty) oatmeal canister. It makes a great container for gift giving. Just wrap the canister in festive paper using a hot glue gun or white glue, and then fill with cookies.

4 egg whites, lightly beaten	1½ cups all-purpose flour
1 large egg, lightly beaten	1 cup whole wheat flour
1 teaspoon vanilla extract	2 teaspoons baking soda
1 cup raisins	1 teaspoon salt
1 cup butter or margarine, softened	1 teaspoon ground cinnamon
1 cup sugar	2 cups uncooked regular oats
1 cup firmly packed light brown sugar	¾ cup chopped pecans

COMBINE first 3 ingredients, stirring well. Add raisins; cover and chill 1 hour to rehydrate raisins.

BEAT butter at medium speed with an electric mixer until creamy; gradually add sugars, beating well.

COMBINE flours and next 3 ingredients; add to butter mixture, beating well. Add raisin mixture, beating well; stir in oats and pecans.

DROP dough by rounded teaspoonfuls onto greased baking sheets. Bake at 350° for 10 to 12 minutes or until lightly browned. Cool slightly on baking sheets; remove to wire racks to cool completely. Yield: 7 dozen.

Mary Lou Eitzman
Recipes from Our Home to Yours
Hospice of North Central Florida
Gainesville, Florida

Chocolate-Chocolate Chip Cookies

These double chocolate cookies will remind you of a gooey brownie. Two kinds of chocolate and toasted pecans make even the dough hard to resist.

½ cup butter
4 (1-ounce) squares unsweetened
 chocolate, chopped
3 cups (18 ounces) semisweet
 chocolate morsels, divided
1½ cups all-purpose flour

½ teaspoon baking powder
½ teaspoon salt
4 large eggs
1½ cups sugar
2 teaspoons vanilla extract
2 cups chopped pecans, toasted

COMBINE butter, chopped chocolate, and 1½ cups chocolate morsels in a large heavy saucepan. Cook over low heat, stirring constantly, until butter and chocolate melt; cool.

COMBINE flour, baking powder, and salt in a small bowl; set aside.

BEAT eggs, sugar, and vanilla in a medium mixing bowl at medium speed with an electric mixer. Gradually add flour mixture to egg mixture, beating well. Add chocolate mixture; beat well. Stir in remaining 1½ cups chocolate morsels and pecans.

DROP dough by 2 tablespoonfuls 1 inch apart onto parchment paper- or wax paper-lined baking sheets. Bake at 350° for 10 minutes. Cool slightly on baking sheets; remove to wire racks to cool completely. Yield: about 2½ dozen.

Janeyce Michel-Cupito
The Kansas City Barbeque Society Cookbook
Kansas City Barbeque Society
Kansas City, Missouri

Parchment Plan
Bake cookies on a parchment paper-lined pan and they'll brown evenly. And there'll be no dirty pan to scrub. Find parchment paper on the grocery baking aisle or near wax paper.

Honey-Roasted Peanut Crisps

These buttery cookies are chock-full of honey-roasted peanuts.

½ cup butter or margarine, softened
½ cup shortening
1 cup firmly packed light brown
 sugar
1 large egg
1 teaspoon vanilla extract

2 cups all-purpose flour
½ teaspoon baking powder
¼ teaspoon salt
2 cups honey-roasted peanuts
Sugar

BEAT butter and shortening at medium speed with an electric mixer until creamy; gradually add 1 cup brown sugar, beating well. Add egg and vanilla; beat well. Combine flour, baking powder, and salt; gradually add to butter mixture, beating well. Stir in peanuts.

SHAPE dough into 1¼-inch balls. Place 2 inches apart on ungreased baking sheets. Dip a flat-bottomed glass in sugar, and flatten each ball to ¼-inch thickness. Bake at 375° for 8 minutes or until edges are golden. Cool slightly on baking sheets; remove to wire racks to cool completely. Yield: 4 dozen.

Lazell Hudson
Cookin' with the Pride of Cove
Copperas Cove Band Boosters Club
Fort Hood, Texas

Soft Touch
For a softer cookie, drop this dough by rounded tablespoonfuls onto ungreased baking sheets, and bake at 375° for 7 to 8 minutes or until edges are golden.

Pecan Biscotti

Serrated Slicing
When slicing biscotti after the first baking, it's important to use the gentle sawing motion of a serrated knife. This helps the cookie keep its slender shape for dipping.

Biscotti is that long, slender, intensely crunchy Italian cookie, which can be softened by a dunk in your favorite beverage.

1¾ cups all-purpose flour
½ cup yellow cornmeal
1¼ teaspoons baking powder
¼ teaspoon salt
1 cup finely chopped pecans

¾ cup sugar
½ cup vegetable oil
⅛ teaspoon almond extract
2 large eggs

COMBINE first 5 ingredients in a large bowl. Combine sugar and remaining 3 ingredients; gradually add to flour mixture, stirring just until dry ingredients are moistened.

PLACE dough on a lightly floured surface; divide in half. With lightly floured hands, shape each portion of dough into a 12- x 1¼-inch log. Place logs 3 inches apart on a lightly greased baking sheet. Bake at 350° for 30 minutes. Cool 10 minutes.

CUT each log crosswise into ¾-inch slices, using a serrated knife. Place slices, cut sides down, on ungreased baking sheets. Bake at 350° for 15 minutes, turning cookies once. Cool slightly on baking sheets; remove cookies to wire racks to cool completely. Yield: 2½ dozen.

Nancy R. Kornegay
West Virginia DAR at Work for Our Schools
School Committee, West Virginia State Society
Daughters of the American Revolution
Peterstown, West Virginia

Teatime Gingersnaps

Sugared Sweets
Rolling cookie balls in sugar contributes to their crackly shape and crisp texture when baked.

Reminiscent of afternoon tea parties, these perfectly spiced, crisp delights are a cup of tea's gracious partner.

¾ cup shortening
1 cup sugar
1 large egg
¼ cup molasses
2 cups all-purpose flour
2 teaspoons baking soda

¼ teaspoon salt
1 teaspoon ground ginger
1 teaspoon ground cinnamon
1 teaspoon ground cloves
Sugar

BEAT shortening at medium speed with an electric mixer until fluffy. Gradually add 1 cup sugar, beating well. Add egg; beat well. Add molasses; beat until smooth.

COMBINE flour and next 5 ingredients; add to shortening mixture, beating well.

SHAPE dough into 1-inch balls; roll balls in sugar. Place 2 inches apart on lightly greased baking sheets. Bake at 375° for 10 minutes. Remove cookies to wire racks to cool completely. Yield: 4 dozen.

Cafe Oklahoma
The Junior Service League of Midwest City, Oklahoma

Butter Meltaways with Lemon Frosting

Recipe contributor Susie Walker recommends only butter for her recipe, and we agree. It makes these tea cookies wonderfully "short" (see right).

1 cup butter, softened
⅓ cup sifted powdered sugar
1¼ cups all-purpose flour

¾ cup cornstarch
Lemon Frosting

BEAT butter at medium speed with an electric mixer until creamy; gradually add powdered sugar, beating well.

COMBINE flour and cornstarch; gradually add to butter mixture, beating well. Shape dough into 2 (6-inch) logs, and wrap in wax paper dusted with powdered sugar. Chill at least 6 hours.

UNWRAP dough; cut each log into 18 slices, and place slices 2 inches apart on greased baking sheets. Bake at 350° for 12 minutes. Remove cookies to a wire rack to cool completely. Spread cookies with Lemon Frosting. Yield: 3 dozen.

Lemon Frosting

¼ cup butter, softened
1½ cups sifted powdered sugar

1 tablespoon grated lemon rind
1½ to 2 tablespoons fresh lemon juice

BEAT butter at medium speed with an electric mixer until creamy; gradually add sifted powdered sugar, beating until blended. Add lemon rind and lemon juice, beating until spreading consistency. Yield: ¾ cup.

Susie Walker
Simply Irresistible
The Junior Auxiliary of Conway, Arkansas

In Short

When a baked good is referred to as "short" in texture, you can bet it's a version of shortbread, as is the cookie on this page. Shortbread, the all-American butter cookie, is known for its fine crumb and melt-in-your-mouth appeal.

Pecan Shortbread Cookies

Chill Factor

Chilling cookie dough cutouts before baking helps them hold their shape in the oven.

Shortbread is simply good plain or enjoyed with a cup of hot tea. At its most basic description, it's a simple butter cookie made from four ingredients—butter, flour, sugar, and salt. This version adds a splash of flavorings and toasty nuts to sweeten the pot.

1 cup unsalted butter
½ cup sugar
½ teaspoon vanilla extract
⅛ teaspoon almond extract

1¾ cups all-purpose flour
¼ teaspoon salt
⅔ cup pecan pieces, toasted

BEAT butter at medium speed with an electric mixer until creamy; gradually add sugar, beating well. Stir in flavorings. Combine flour, salt, and pecans; add to butter mixture, beating well until pecans are broken up into small pieces. Cover and chill 1 hour.

ROLL dough to ¼-inch thickness on a lightly floured surface. Cut dough with a 2-inch round cookie cutter, and place 1 inch apart on ungreased baking sheets. Chill 10 minutes. Bake at 325° for 15 to 20 minutes or until edges are lightly browned. Cool 1 minute on baking sheets. Remove to wire racks to cool completely. Yield: 3 dozen.

Deborah Gragnani
Panthers' Pantry
Children's Educational Foundation
Madera, California

Lemon Bars Deluxe PARTY FOOD

Herbal Delight

Here's a tasty idea if you're in the mood for an herbal adventure. Stir 1 tablespoon chopped fresh rosemary into the dough before pressing it into the pan to bake. The flavor combination of lemon and rosemary is delicious.

These shortbread-based bars contain just the right amount of tangy lemon filling. Try cutting them with a heart-shaped cookie cutter instead of into bars for a loving touch.

2¼ cups all-purpose flour, divided
½ cup sifted powdered sugar
1 cup butter or margarine
½ teaspoon baking powder

4 large eggs, lightly beaten
2 cups sugar
⅓ cup lemon juice
Sifted powdered sugar

COMBINE 2 cups flour and ½ cup powdered sugar; cut in butter with a pastry blender until mixture is crumbly. Firmly press mixture into a greased 13- x 9-inch pan. Bake at 350° for 20 to 25 minutes or until lightly browned.

COMBINE remaining ¼ cup flour and baking powder in a small bowl; stir well. Combine eggs, 2 cups sugar, and lemon juice in a large bowl; stir in flour mixture. Pour over prepared crust. Bake at 350° for 25 minutes or until set and lightly browned. Cool completely in pan on a wire rack. Sprinkle with additional powdered sugar; cut into bars. Yield: 2½ dozen.

Julia Newhouse
Mountain Measures
The Junior League of Charleston, Inc.
Charleston, West Virginia

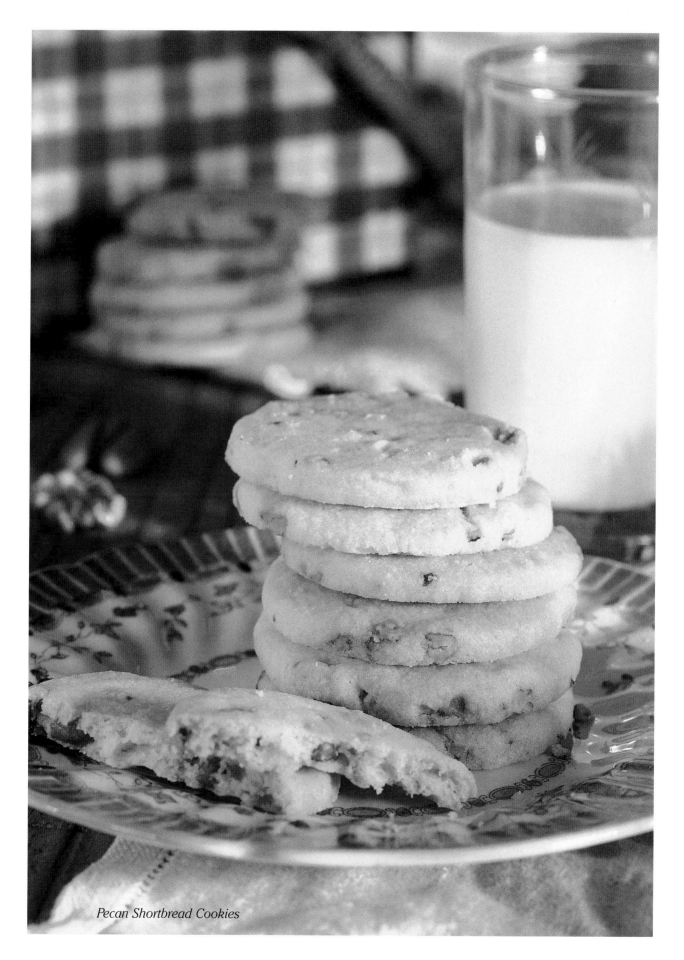

Pecan Shortbread Cookies

Double-Frosted Bourbon Brownies

Double-Frosted Bourbon Brownies

Bourbon and chocolate belong together. We think you'll agree once you taste these triple layered, satiny smooth, frosted favorites.

¾ cup all-purpose flour	1 teaspoon vanilla extract
¼ teaspoon baking soda	2 large eggs
¼ teaspoon salt	1½ cups chopped walnuts
½ cup sugar	¼ cup bourbon
⅓ cup shortening	White Frosting
2 tablespoons water	Chocolate Glaze
1 cup (6 ounces) semisweet	
chocolate morsels	

COMBINE first 3 ingredients in a medium bowl; stir well. Set flour mixture aside.

COMBINE sugar, shortening, and water in a medium saucepan. Bring to a boil over medium heat, stirring constantly; remove from heat. Add chocolate morsels and vanilla, stirring until smooth. Add eggs, one at a time, stirring after each addition. Add dry ingredients and walnuts; stir well. Spoon into a greased 9-inch square pan. Bake at 325° for 30 minutes or until a wooden pick inserted in center comes out clean.

SPRINKLE bourbon evenly over warm brownies. Cool completely in pan on a wire rack. Spread White Frosting on brownies. Pour warm Chocolate Glaze over frosting. Let stand until set. Cut into squares. Yield: 16 large brownies or 2½ dozen small brownies.

White Frosting

½ cup butter or margarine, softened	2 cups sifted powdered sugar
1 teaspoon vanilla extract	

COMBINE butter and vanilla in a large mixing bowl; beat at medium speed with an electric mixer until creamy. Gradually add powdered sugar, beating until smooth. Yield: 1¼ cups.

Chocolate Glaze

1 cup (6 ounces) semisweet	1 tablespoon shortening
chocolate morsels	

COMBINE chocolate morsels and shortening in top of a double boiler; bring water to a boil. Reduce heat to low; cook until chocolate morsels melt, stirring occasionally. Yield: ½ cup.

To Market, To Market
The Junior League of Owensboro, Inc.
Owensboro, Kentucky

Bourbon Boost
Bourbon is sprinkled over these warm brownies to keep them moist and to add an extra kick of Southern goodness.

Zucchini Brownies

Zucchini adds moistness and texture to these fudgy brownies. A generous spoonful of ground cinnamon adds a warm flavor note.

Vegetable brownies?
You bet. Grate zucchini on a box grater or in a food processor with a shredder disk and stir it into the chocolaty batter. After the brownies have baked, the zucchini almost disappears, yet it gives the brownies a moist texture.

3 cups all-purpose flour
¼ cup cocoa
1 teaspoon baking soda
½ teaspoon salt
2 teaspoons ground cinnamon
2 cups grated zucchini (about ¾ pound)
½ cup butter, melted

1¾ cups sugar
1 cup vegetable oil
2 large eggs, lightly beaten
1 teaspoon vanilla extract
2 cups (12 ounces) semisweet chocolate morsels
½ cup chopped walnuts

COMBINE first 5 ingredients in a bowl, stirring well. Combine zucchini and butter; add to flour mixture, stirring well. Combine sugar and next 3 ingredients; add to zucchini mixture, stirring 2 minutes.

POUR batter into a greased 15- x 10-inch jellyroll pan; top with chocolate morsels and walnuts. Bake at 350° for 30 minutes. Cut into bars. Yield: 32 brownies.

Florence Deeley
Howey Cook
Howey-in-the-Hills Garden and Civic Club
Howey-in-the-Hills, Florida

Chewy Oatmeal Spice Bars

Here's a soft oatmeal bar cookie that takes mere minutes to make—enjoy it with a tall glass of milk.

Silver Lining
Grease and line your pan with aluminum foil. Grease the foil and add the batter. Once baked, these uncut bars will be easy to lift right out of the pan using the foil as handles.

1 cup butter or margarine, softened
½ cup sugar
1½ cups firmly packed light brown sugar
2 large eggs
1 cup all-purpose flour
1 teaspoon baking soda
½ teaspoon salt

1 tablespoon ground cinnamon
1 teaspoon ground nutmeg
½ teaspoon ground ginger
2 teaspoons vanilla extract
2 cups uncooked quick-cooking oats
1 (3.5-ounce) can flaked coconut
1 cup raisins

BEAT butter at medium speed with an electric mixer until creamy; gradually add ½ cup sugar and 1½ cups brown sugar, beating well. Add eggs, one at a time, beating well after each addition.

COMBINE flour and next 5 ingredients; add to butter mixture, beating well. Stir in vanilla and remaining ingredients. Spoon batter into a greased 13- x 9-inch pan. Bake at 350° for 35 to 40 minutes or until a wooden pick inserted in center comes out clean. Cool slightly before cutting into bars. Yield: 2 dozen.

The Tailgate Cookbook
National Kidney Foundation of Kansas and Western Missouri
Westwood, Kansas

Chocolate-Raspberry Truffles PARTY FOOD

These double-chocolate delights have a hint of raspberry. They make a wonderful gift for any occasion.

1⅓ cups (8 ounces) semisweet
    chocolate morsels
2 tablespoons whipping cream
1 tablespoon butter
2 tablespoons seedless raspberry jam

6 ounces white chocolate or milk
    chocolate (we tested with
    Ghirardelli)
2 teaspoons shortening

COMBINE chocolate morsels, cream, and butter in a heavy saucepan. Cook over low heat, stirring constantly, until chocolate morsels melt; stir in jam. Remove from heat; cover and freeze mixture 30 minutes or until firm.

SHAPE mixture into ¾-inch balls. Place on wax paper-lined baking sheets; chill 5 minutes. If necessary, reroll to smooth balls. Freeze 8 hours.

PLACE white chocolate and shortening in top of a double boiler; bring water to a boil. Reduce heat to low; cook, stirring constantly, until chocolate and shortening melt.

PLACE each ball on a candy dipper or fork, and hold over double boiler. Quickly spoon melted chocolate mixture over each ball, allowing excess to drip back into double boiler. Return each ball to lined baking sheets; chill until firm. Store in an airtight container in refrigerator. Yield: 2½ dozen.

Secrets of Amelia
McArthur Family Branch YMCA
Fernandina Beach, Florida

A Fork That Fits
Find two-pronged plastic candy dipping forks in the cake-decorating section of your local crafts store.

Microwave Pralines

Praline Duty

Since praline candy is known for setting up quickly, two pairs of hands are beneficial for spooning pralines onto wax paper in a timely manner.

Pralines are easy to make using this microwave recipe. If your oven is 1,000 watts, use the lower time option.

2 cups sugar
2 cups pecans, chopped
1 (5-ounce) can evaporated milk

¼ cup butter or margarine
1 tablespoon vanilla extract

COMBINE all ingredients in a 2-quart microwave-safe liquid measuring cup. Microwave at HIGH 5 to 6 minutes, stirring well. Microwave 5 to 6 more minutes, stirring well. Working rapidly, drop by tablespoonfuls onto wax paper; let stand until firm. Yield: about 2½ dozen.

Jesse Messex
Somethin' to Smile About
St. Martin, Iberia, Lafayette Community Action Agency
Lafayette, Louisiana

Tiger Butter   PARTY FOOD

What's in a Name?

Tiger Butter candy resembles a tiger's skin once you swirl the 2 chocolates.

Try this easy-to-make nibble food with just three ingredients swirled together into a rich candy.

16 (1-ounce) white chocolate baking squares, finely chopped (we tested with Baker's)
¾ cup creamy peanut butter

2 cups (12 ounces) semisweet chocolate morsels

COMBINE white chocolate and peanut butter in a glass bowl. Microwave at HIGH 2 minutes or until melted, stirring twice. Pour into a wax paper-lined 15- x 10-inch jellyroll pan, spreading evenly.

MICROWAVE chocolate morsels in a glass bowl at HIGH 2 minutes or until melted, stirring twice. Pour over white chocolate mixture; swirl gently with a knife. Chill until firm. Break into pieces. Store in an airtight container in refrigerator. Yield: 2 pounds.

Marsha Schewe
Savory Secrets
Runnels School
Baton Rouge, Louisiana

Banana Pound Cake

Banana bread lovers will crave this dense, rich pound cake of the same persuasion.

1½ cups shortening
2 cups sugar
4 large eggs
2 cups mashed ripe banana
⅓ cup buttermilk

1 teaspoon vanilla extract
3 cups all-purpose flour
1¼ teaspoons baking soda
¼ teaspoon salt
½ cup chopped pecans

BEAT shortening at medium speed with an electric mixer 2 minutes or until creamy. Gradually add sugar, beating 5 to 7 minutes. Add eggs, 1 at a time, beating just until yellow disappears.

COMBINE banana, buttermilk, and vanilla. Combine flour, soda, and salt; add to shortening mixture alternately with banana mixture, beginning and ending with flour mixture. Mix at low speed after each addition just until blended. Stir in pecans. Spoon batter into a greased and floured 10-inch tube pan. Bake at 325° for 1½ hours or until a wooden pick inserted in center comes out clean. Cool in pan on a wire rack 15 minutes; remove cake from pan, and cool completely on wire rack. Yield: 1 (10-inch) cake.

Evelyn Criswell
Bread from the Brook
The Church at Brook Hills
Birmingham, Alabama

Black Russian Bundt Cake

This bodacious Bundt cake borrows vodka and coffee liqueur from the Black Russian cocktail.

1 (18.25-ounce) package yellow cake
    mix (we tested with Duncan Hines)
½ cup sugar
1 (3.9-ounce) package chocolate
    instant pudding mix
1 cup vegetable oil

4 large eggs
¼ cup vodka
½ cup coffee liqueur, divided
½ cup sifted powdered sugar
Sifted powdered sugar

COMBINE first 6 ingredients in a large mixing bowl; add ¼ cup liqueur. Beat at low speed with an electric mixer 1 minute; increase speed to medium, and beat 4 more minutes. Pour batter into a greased and floured 12-cup Bundt pan.

BAKE at 350° for 50 to 60 minutes or until a long wooden skewer inserted in center comes out clean. Cool in pan on a wire rack 15 minutes; invert onto a serving plate.

COMBINE remaining ¼ cup liqueur and ½ cup powdered sugar, stirring until smooth. Prick warm cake at 1-inch intervals with a long wooden skewer. Brush liqueur mixture over top and sides of cake; cool completely. Sprinkle additional powdered sugar over cake. Yield: 1 (10-inch) cake.

Myra McDonald
Recipes for Champions
Shebas of Khiva Temple Oriental Band
Amarillo, Texas

Lemon Buttermilk Cake
with Lemon Curd Sauce

Lemon Buttermilk Cake with Lemon Curd Sauce

Lemon lovers, this is your dream dessert—a tender, lemony pound cake soaked with a lemon syrup and topped with a thick, rich lemon curd.

1 cup butter, softened
2⅓ cups sugar, divided
3 large eggs
3 cups all-purpose flour
½ teaspoon baking soda
½ teaspoon salt
1 cup buttermilk

1½ tablespoons grated lemon rind
½ cup plus 3 tablespoons fresh
   lemon juice, divided
3 tablespoons fine, dry breadcrumbs
   (store-bought)
Powdered sugar (optional)
Lemon Curd Sauce

Lemon Aid
The easiest way to get maximum juice from a lemon is to roll it on the countertop briefly to release the juices, or heat the lemon in the microwave for about 10 seconds.

BEAT butter at medium speed with an electric mixer until creamy; gradually add 2 cups sugar, beating well. Add eggs, 1 at a time, beating after each addition.

COMBINE flour, baking soda, and salt; add to butter mixture alternately with buttermilk, beginning and ending with flour mixture. Mix at low speed after each addition until blended. Stir in rind and 3 tablespoons juice.

POUR into a buttered 12-cup Bundt pan coated with breadcrumbs. Bake at 350° for 55 minutes or until a wooden pick inserted in center comes out clean. Cool in pan on a wire rack 10 minutes; remove from pan, and place on wire rack.

COMBINE remaining ⅓ cup sugar and ½ cup lemon juice in a saucepan; cook over medium-low heat until sugar dissolves, stirring often. Prick cake at 1-inch intervals with a long wooden skewer or cake tester. Spoon juice mixture over top of warm cake; cool completely on wire rack. Dust with powdered sugar, if desired. Serve with Lemon Curd Sauce. Yield: 1 (10-inch) cake.

Lemon Curd Sauce

2 cups sugar
6 large eggs, lightly beaten
¼ cup grated lemon rind

¾ cup fresh lemon juice
¾ cup butter, softened

COMBINE first 4 ingredients in top of a double boiler; bring water to a boil. Reduce heat to medium; cook, stirring constantly, until mixture coats a spoon. Cool slightly. Add butter, 1 tablespoon at a time, whisking until blended. Serve immediately, or cover and chill until ready to serve. Yield: 4 cups.

Savour St. Louis
Barnes-Jewish Hospital Auxiliary Plaza Chapter
St. Louis, Missouri

Peanut Butter Pound Cake SUPPER CLUB

Think of plain pound cake as a blank canvas for additional flavor. Try this peanut butter take. It's luscious.

Pound Cake Popularity

Pound cake may have started out as an English creation, but it fast became a favorite in the American South. Pound cakes appear at church suppers, pot-luck parties, holiday buffets, family reunions, and a host of other occasions.

1 cup butter or margarine, softened
½ cup creamy peanut butter
2 cups sugar
1 cup firmly packed light brown sugar
5 large eggs
3 cups all-purpose flour
½ teaspoon baking powder
¼ teaspoon baking soda

½ teaspoon salt
1 cup milk
1 tablespoon vanilla extract
2 cups sifted powdered sugar
⅓ cup creamy peanut butter
¼ cup butter or margarine, melted
Dash of salt
¼ cup evaporated milk

BEAT 1 cup butter and ½ cup peanut butter at medium speed with an electric mixer 2 minutes or until soft and creamy. Gradually add 2 cups sugar and 1 cup brown sugar, beating at medium speed 5 to 7 minutes. Add eggs, 1 at a time, beating just until yellow disappears.

COMBINE flour, baking powder, soda, and ½ teaspoon salt; stir well. Add flour mixture to butter mixture alternately with 1 cup milk, beginning and ending with flour mixture. Mix at low speed just until blended after each addition. Stir in vanilla. Pour batter into a greased and floured 10-inch tube pan.

BAKE at 350° for 1 hour and 35 minutes or until a wooden pick inserted in center comes out clean. Cool in pan on a wire rack 10 to 15 minutes; remove from pan, and cool completely on a wire rack.

BEAT powdered sugar and next 3 ingredients at low speed until well blended. Add evaporated milk; beat at medium speed until smooth. Drizzle over cake. Yield: 1 (10-inch) cake.

Evelyn Barlowe
Preserving Our Heritage
Church of God Ladies Ministries
Charlotte, North Carolina

Apple-Walnut Cake

Pictured on page 151

A moist walnut-apple filling awaits in the center of this cream-cheese glazed Bundt cake.

1 cup finely chopped walnuts
1 cup peeled, finely chopped
   cooking apple
2 tablespoons brown sugar
½ teaspoon ground cinnamon
1 cup butter, softened
2 cups sugar

2 large eggs
1¾ cups all-purpose flour
1 teaspoon baking powder
¼ teaspoon salt
1 (8-ounce) container sour cream
1 tablespoon vanilla extract
Cream Cheese Glaze

COMBINE first 4 ingredients; set aside. Beat butter at medium speed with an electric mixer until creamy; gradually add 2 cups sugar, beating well. Add eggs, 1 at a time, beating after each addition.

COMBINE flour, baking powder, and salt; add to butter mixture alternately with sour cream, beginning and ending with flour mixture. Mix at low speed after each addition until blended. Stir in vanilla.

POUR half of batter into a well-greased and floured 12-cup Bundt pan. Spoon apple mixture over batter, leaving a ½-inch border around edges. Pour remaining batter over mixture. Bake at 350° for 50 to 55 minutes or until a wooden pick inserted in center comes out clean. Cool in pan on a wire rack 10 minutes. Remove from pan; cool on wire rack. Drizzle with glaze. Store in refrigerator. Yield: 1 (10-inch) cake.

Cream Cheese Glaze

1 (3-ounce) package cream cheese,
   softened
2 to 2½ teaspoons milk

1 teaspoon vanilla extract
Dash of salt
1½ cups sifted powdered sugar

COMBINE first 4 ingredients; beat at medium speed with an electric mixer until smooth. Gradually add sugar, beating at low speed until smooth. Yield: 1 cup.

With Love from the Shepherd's Center of North Little Rock
Shepherd's Center of North Little Rock, Arkansas

Toasty Goodness

For extra depth of flavor, toast and cool the walnuts before tossing them with the apple and spice into the batter.

Italian Cream Cheese Cake PARTY FOOD

For those who enjoy Italian Cream Cake, here's a version without rum. The lofty layer cake maintains its appeal to those who dream of coconut, cream cheese, and pecans.

Optimum Temp for Eggs

For general cake-baking guidelines, you'll achieve good results if eggs are at room temperature. An easy way to take the chill off is to slip eggs (in the shell) into a bowl of warm water for a few minutes before cracking.

1 cup butter or margarine, softened
2 cups sugar
5 large eggs, separated
2 cups all-purpose flour
1 teaspoon baking soda
¼ teaspoon salt
1 cup buttermilk
1 teaspoon vanilla extract
1 cup chopped pecans
1 cup flaked coconut
Italian Cream Cheese Cake Frosting

BEAT butter at medium speed with an electric mixer until creamy; gradually add sugar, beating well. Add egg yolks, 1 at a time, beating after each addition.

COMBINE flour, soda, and salt; add to butter mixture alternately with buttermilk, beginning and ending with flour mixture. Mix at low speed after each addition until blended. Stir in vanilla. Add pecans and coconut; stir well.

BEAT egg whites at high speed until stiff peaks form. Gently fold into batter. Spoon batter into 2 greased and floured 9-inch round cakepans. Bake at 350° for 30 to 35 minutes or until a wooden pick inserted in center comes out clean. Cool in pans on wire racks 10 minutes; remove from pans, and cool completely on wire racks.

SPREAD Italian Cream Cheese Cake Frosting between layers and on top and sides of cake. Cover and store in refrigerator. Yield: 1 (2-layer) cake.

Italian Cream Cheese Cake Frosting

1 (8-ounce) package cream cheese, softened
½ cup butter or margarine, softened
1 (16-ounce) package powdered sugar, sifted
1 cup chopped pecans, toasted
1 teaspoon vanilla extract

BEAT cream cheese and butter at medium speed until creamy; gradually add sugar, beating until smooth. Stir in pecans and vanilla. Yield: 3½ cups.

Earl R. Pearson and Gwenette Pearson
The Authorized Texas Ranger Cookbook
Texas Ranger Museum
Hamilton, Texas

Triple Chocolate Ecstasy

Three layers of rich chocolate cake, filling, and frosting stack up to be a chocoholic's dream dessert.

4 (1-ounce) squares semisweet
   chocolate
½ cup butter or margarine
1 cup finely chopped pecans
2 large eggs, lightly beaten
2 cups sugar
1½ cups all-purpose flour

1 teaspoon baking powder
½ teaspoon salt
1½ cups milk
1 teaspoon vanilla extract
Chocolate Filling
Chocolate Frosting

Lining the Pan
Lining cakepans with wax paper assures that the baked layers will come out of the pan intact. Be sure to peel off wax paper while cake layers are still warm.

GREASE 2 (9-inch) round cakepans; line with wax paper. Grease wax paper. Set aside.

COMBINE chocolate and butter in top of a double boiler; bring water to a boil. Reduce heat to low; cook until chocolate melts. Add pecans; stir well. Remove from heat.

COMBINE eggs and sugar in a mixing bowl. Beat at high speed with an electric mixer until thickened and pale. Stir in chocolate mixture. Combine flour, baking powder, and salt; add to chocolate mixture alternately with milk, beginning and ending with flour mixture. Stir in vanilla. Pour batter into prepared pans.

BAKE at 350° for 45 to 48 minutes or until a wooden pick inserted in center comes out clean. Cool in pans on wire racks 5 minutes; remove from pans, peel off wax paper and cool completely on wire racks.

SPREAD Chocolate Filling between layers of cake. Spread Chocolate Frosting on top and sides of cake. Yield: 1 (2-layer) cake.

Chocolate Filling

4 (1-ounce) squares semisweet
   chocolate
¼ cup butter or margarine

½ cup sifted powdered sugar
⅓ cup milk

COMBINE chocolate and butter in top of a double boiler; bring water to a boil. Reduce heat to low; cook until chocolate melts. Gradually add powdered sugar alternately with milk, beginning and ending with powdered sugar; stir until smooth. Cover and chill 30 minutes or until spreading consistency. Yield: 1 cup.

Chocolate Frosting

2 cups whipping cream
1 cup sifted powdered sugar

⅔ cup sifted cocoa
1 teaspoon vanilla extract

COMBINE all ingredients in a bowl; beat at high speed until stiff peaks form. Chill 30 minutes. Yield: 2½ cups.

True Grits: Tall Tales and Recipes from the New South
The Junior League of Atlanta, Georgia

Fudge Pecan Ripple Layer Cake

Pictured on cover and at right

Frost the Top Last

It's always a good practice to frost the top of a cake last. This way, the frosted cake has the best chance of standing upright.

A sweet cream cheese layer bakes atop these fudgy cake layers; then when you assemble, frost, and serve the cake, the cream cheese appears as swirly ripples in each slice.

½ cup shortening
1½ cups sugar
2 large eggs
1⅔ cups all-purpose flour
⅔ cup cocoa
1½ teaspoons baking soda
½ teaspoon salt
1½ cups buttermilk
1 tablespoon plus 1 teaspoon vanilla extract, divided
1 (8-ounce) package cream cheese, softened

2 tablespoons butter or margarine, softened
1 tablespoon cornstarch
1 (14-ounce) can sweetened condensed milk
1 large egg
⅔ cup butter, softened
5¾ cups sifted powdered sugar
1⅓ cups cocoa
1 cup plus 2 tablespoons milk
¾ cup chopped pecans or walnuts, toasted

GREASE 2 (9-inch) round cakepans; line with wax paper. Grease and flour wax paper. Set aside.

BEAT shortening at medium speed with an electric mixer until fluffy; gradually add 1½ cups sugar, beating well. Add 2 eggs, 1 at a time, beating until blended after each addition.

COMBINE flour and next 3 ingredients; add to shortening mixture alternately with buttermilk, beginning and ending with flour mixture. Mix at low speed after each addition until blended. Beat 3 more minutes at high speed, stopping once to scrape down sides. Stir in 2 teaspoons vanilla. Pour batter into prepared pans. Set aside.

BEAT cream cheese, 2 tablespoons butter, and cornstarch at medium speed until creamy; gradually add sweetened condensed milk, beating well. Add 1 egg; beat well. Stir in 1 teaspoon vanilla. Spoon cream cheese mixture evenly over batter.

BAKE at 350° for 40 minutes or until a wooden pick inserted in center comes out clean. Cool in pans on wire racks 10 minutes; remove from pans, and cool completely on wire racks.

BEAT ⅔ cup butter at medium speed until creamy. Combine powdered sugar and 1⅓ cups cocoa; add to butter alternately with 1 cup plus 2 tablespoons milk, beginning and ending with powdered sugar mixture. Beat until spreading consistency. Stir in remaining 1 teaspoon vanilla. Spread frosting between layers and on top and sides of cake. Sprinkle with toasted nuts. Yield: 1 (2-layer) cake.

Linda Thomas
Our Best Home Cooking
Citizens of Zion Missionary Baptist Church Women's Ministry
Compton, California

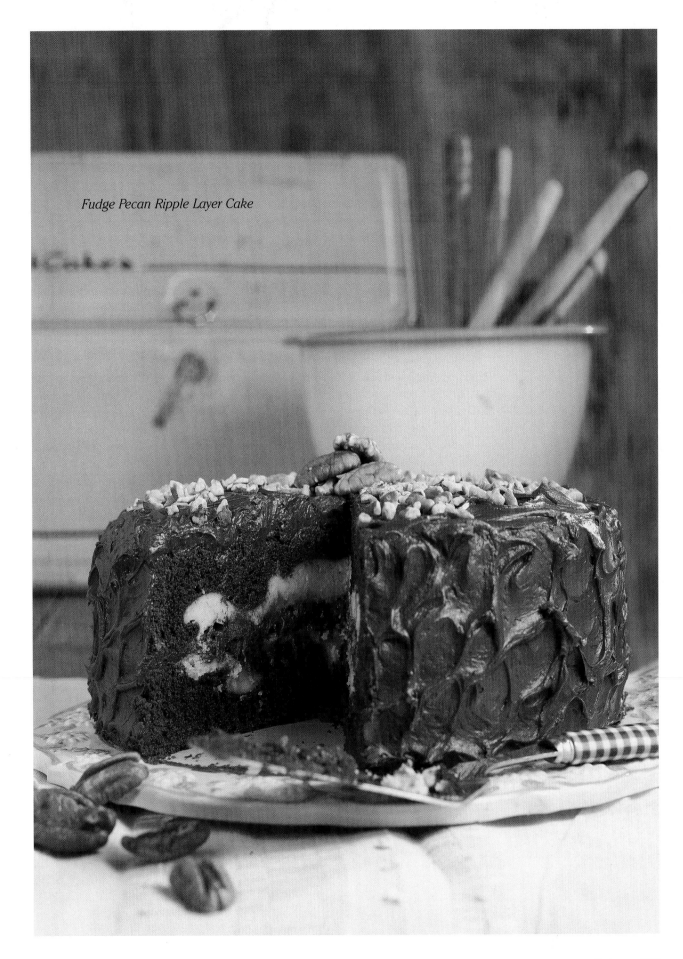

Fudge Pecan Ripple Layer Cake

Bananas Foster Cheesecake PARTY FOOD

Blending the Batter

One key to flawless cheesecakes is not overbeating the batter once eggs are added. Simply blend batter just until each egg is incorporated.

All the flavors of bananas Foster, the quintessential New Orleans dessert, are incorporated in this creamy delight.

¾ cup all-purpose flour
¾ cup finely chopped pecans
3 tablespoons brown sugar
2 tablespoons sugar
¼ cup unsalted butter, melted
1½ tablespoons vanilla extract, divided
2 (8-ounce) packages cream cheese, softened
1½ cups sugar, divided
2 tablespoons cornstarch
3 large eggs
2 cups mashed very ripe banana (about 4 large)

1 (16-ounce) container sour cream, divided
2 tablespoons fresh lemon juice
1½ teaspoons ground cinnamon, divided
⅛ teaspoon salt
½ teaspoon sugar
2 very ripe bananas
1 (12-ounce) jar caramel sauce (we tested with Smucker's)
¼ cup dark rum

COMBINE first 5 ingredients in a bowl; stir well. Stir in 2 teaspoons vanilla. Press in bottom of a 10-inch springform pan; set aside.

BEAT cream cheese at medium speed with an electric mixer until creamy. Gradually add 1¼ cups sugar and cornstarch, beating well. Add eggs, 1 at a time, beating after each addition. Stir in mashed banana, half the sour cream, lemon juice, 2 teaspoons vanilla, 1 teaspoon cinnamon, and salt. Pour batter into prepared pan.

BAKE at 350° for 1 hour or until center is set. Remove from oven, and set aside.

COMBINE remaining sour cream, ¼ cup sugar, and ½ teaspoon vanilla in a small bowl, stirring well. Spread over warm cheesecake; return to oven, and bake 10 more minutes. Turn oven off; let cheesecake cool in oven 2 hours or until room temperature. Cover and chill 8 hours.

CAREFULLY remove sides of springform pan. Combine ½ teaspoon sugar and remaining ½ teaspoon cinnamon in a small bowl; sprinkle over cheesecake. Peel and slice 2 bananas; arrange slices on top of cheesecake. Combine caramel sauce and rum in a small saucepan; cook over medium heat until warm. Drizzle some warm sauce over cheesecake, and serve with remaining sauce. Yield: 12 servings.

Capital Celebrations
The Junior League of Washington, DC

Chocolate-Coconut Cheesecake

MAKE AHEAD   PARTY FOOD

You know it's a great recipe when it's from a Southern Living® *Test Kitchen baker. Jan Moon is known for her glorious cakes, and this cheesecake is a scrumptious example. The flavors might remind you of a familiar candy bar.*

1½ cups chocolate wafer crumbs
    (about 30 wafers)
3 tablespoons sugar
¼ cup butter or margarine, melted
4 (8-ounce) packages cream cheese,
    softened
1 cup sugar
3 large eggs

1 (14-ounce) package flaked coconut
1 (11.5-ounce) package milk
    chocolate morsels
1 cup slivered natural almonds,
    toasted and divided
1 teaspoon vanilla extract
½ cup (3 ounces) semisweet
    chocolate morsels

STIR together first 3 ingredients; press mixture in bottom of a 10-inch springform pan. Bake at 350° for 8 minutes; cool.

BEAT cream cheese at high speed with an electric mixer until creamy; gradually add 1 cup sugar, beating well. Add eggs, 1 at a time, beating until blended after each addition. Stir in coconut, milk chocolate morsels, ½ cup almond slivers, and vanilla. Pour batter into prepared pan.

BAKE at 350° for 55 to 60 minutes or until cheesecake is almost set. Remove from oven; cool to room temperature in pan on a wire rack. Cover and chill at least 8 hours. Remove sides of pan.

PLACE semisweet chocolate morsels in a small heavy-duty zip-top plastic bag, and seal. Submerge bag in hot water until chocolate melts. Snip a tiny hole in 1 corner of bag, and drizzle melted chocolate over cheesecake. Sprinkle with remaining ½ cup almond slivers. Yield: 16 servings.

Jan Moon
Bread from the Brook
The Church at Brook Hills
Birmingham, Alabama

Leakproof Pan

Before baking a cheesecake, it's a good idea to wrap the outside of the springform pan with aluminum foil to prevent leaks during baking.

The Famous Stuart Hall Brown Sugar Pie ONE BOWL

Don't doubt the appeal of this pie just because it has a simple ingredient roster. It's sort of like a chess pie, except easier.

½ cup butter or margarine, melted
2 cups firmly packed light brown sugar

3 large eggs
1 teaspoon vanilla extract
1 unbaked 9-inch pastry shell

BEAT butter, sugar, eggs, and vanilla in a large mixing bowl at medium speed with an electric mixer until blended. Pour into pastry shell. Bake at 350° for 45 minutes. Cool completely on a wire rack. Yield: 1 (9-inch) pie.

Blakeslee Chase
Saints Alive!
Ladies' Guild of St. Barnabas Anglican Church
Atlanta, Georgia

Piecrust Options

When a recipe calls for an unbaked 9-inch pastry shell, you have a couple of options. One is to buy a refrigerated piecrust, unfold it, and press it into a glass pieplate. Another option is to buy a frozen deep-dish piecrust that comes in an aluminum pan.

Carrot Pie

Versatile carrots make the culinary leap from good-for-you vegetable to stellar dessert in this pumpkin-pielike recipe. Serve it at room temperature or chilled.

1 pound carrots, sliced
1½ cups water
1 teaspoon salt, divided
4 large eggs
1 (5-ounce) can evaporated milk
1 cup sugar
1 tablespoon all-purpose flour

1 teaspoon ground ginger
1 teaspoon ground cinnamon
½ teaspoon ground nutmeg
⅛ teaspoon ground cloves
1 unbaked 9-inch pastry shell
Whipped cream (optional)

COMBINE carrot, water, and ½ teaspoon salt in a medium saucepan, and bring to a boil. Cover, reduce heat, and simmer 20 minutes or until carrot is very tender. Drain well, and cool.

COMBINE cooked carrot, remaining ½ teaspoon salt, eggs, and next 7 ingredients in a blender; process until smooth, stopping to scrape down sides. Pour carrot mixture into pastry shell.

BAKE at 425° for 12 minutes; cover pie with aluminum foil to prevent excessive browning. Reduce oven temperature to 350°; bake 30 more minutes or until a knife inserted in center comes out clean. Cool completely on a wire rack. Serve with whipped cream, if desired. Yield: 1 (9-inch) pie.

The Best of Mayberry
The Foothills Lions Club of Mount Airy, North Carolina

Here's a clever takeoff on pumpkin pie using carrots. The easiest way to clean carrots is to use a vegetable peeler to shave off just the outermost layer.

Scraping Carrots

Butter Crunch Chocolate Pie

This pie's unique crust will tantalize your taste buds. What makes it so good is the taste of the brown sugar, butter, and nuts in the baked crust.

1 cup all-purpose flour
¼ cup firmly packed light brown
    sugar
½ cup butter or margarine
½ cup chopped walnuts
2 cups milk
1 cup sugar

⅓ cup all-purpose flour
1 tablespoon plus 1 teaspoon cocoa
¼ teaspoon salt
3 egg yolks, lightly beaten
¼ cup butter or margarine
1 teaspoon vanilla extract
1 cup whipping cream, whipped

COMBINE 1 cup flour and brown sugar in a medium bowl; cut in ½ cup butter with a pastry blender until mixture is crumbly. Stir in walnuts. Firmly press mixture in bottom and up sides of a 10-inch pieplate. Bake at 375° for 10 minutes or until golden. Cool completely on a wire rack.

COMBINE milk and next 4 ingredients in a heavy saucepan; stir well. Cook over low heat, stirring constantly, 25 minutes or until mixture is thickened and bubbly.

GRADUALLY add one-fourth of hot mixture to egg yolks. Add to remaining hot mixture, stirring constantly. Cook 5 minutes, stirring constantly. Remove from heat; add ¼ cup butter and vanilla, stirring until butter melts. Pour into prepared crust. Cool 30 minutes; cover and chill until firm. Serve with whipped cream. Yield: 1 (10-inch) pie.

A Slice of Paradise
The Hospital Service League of Naples Community Hospital
Naples, Florida

Butter Crunch
This pie is called "butter crunch" because of the combined flavor and texture from brown sugar, butter, and walnuts that bake into a sublime crust.

Ice Cream Pie MAKE AHEAD

Crackers vs. Cookies

You can use ¼ cup graham cracker crumbs instead of crushed vanilla wafers for this crust, if someone secretly finished off the vanilla wafers at your house.

In this easy ice cream dessert, vanilla ice cream gets dressed up with a coconutty cookie crust, streusel, and an easy brown sugar sauce.

1⅓ cups flaked coconut	½ cup chopped pecans or walnuts
¼ cup crushed vanilla wafers	1 teaspoon butter or margarine,
1 tablespoon sugar, divided	melted
2 teaspoons butter or margarine,	1 quart vanilla ice cream, softened
melted	Sauce
¾ cup flaked coconut	

COMBINE 1⅓ cups coconut, vanilla wafer crumbs, 2 teaspoons sugar, and 2 teaspoons butter; stir well. Firmly press crumb mixture in bottom and up sides of a 9-inch pieplate. Bake at 325° for 12 to 15 minutes or until lightly browned. Cool completely on a wire rack.

COMBINE ¾ cup coconut, chopped pecans, remaining 1 teaspoon sugar, and 1 teaspoon butter; stir well. Spread on an ungreased baking sheet. Bake at 325° for 5 to 7 minutes or until lightly browned, stirring often.

SPOON softened ice cream into cooled crust. Sprinkle coconut-pecan mixture over ice cream; lightly press into ice cream. Freeze at least 2 hours or until firm. Let stand at room temperature 5 minutes before serving. Serve with warm Sauce. Yield: 1 (9-inch) pie.

Sauce

½ cup butter or margarine	⅓ cup whipping cream
1 cup firmly packed light brown	2 teaspoons light corn syrup
sugar	

MELT butter in a small saucepan over low heat. Add brown sugar, whipping cream, and corn syrup, stirring well. Bring sauce mixture to a boil; reduce heat, and simmer 1 minute, stirring constantly. Yield: 1⅓ cups.

Kathy Burchfield
A Taste of History
University of North Alabama Women's Club
Florence, Alabama

Frozen Strawberry Margarita Pie

This frozen refresher stars all the makings of a cool strawberry margarita plus a salty pretzel crust. It's a slice of paradise.

1¼ cups finely crushed pretzels (we tested with 3½ cups whole Rold Gold Tiny Twists, crushed)
¼ cup sugar
½ cup plus 2 tablespoons butter or margarine, melted
1 (14-ounce) can sweetened condensed milk

1½ cups chopped fresh strawberries
⅓ cup lime juice
¼ cup tequila
2 tablespoons Triple Sec or other orange liqueur
3 drops red liquid food coloring (optional)
1½ cups whipping cream, whipped

COMBINE first 3 ingredients in a medium bowl; stir well. Press mixture firmly in bottom and up sides of a lightly buttered 10-inch pieplate.

COMBINE condensed milk and next 5 ingredients, stirring well. Fold in whipped cream; pour into prepared pieplate. Cover and freeze at least 4 hours or until firm. Let stand at room temperature 10 minutes before serving. Yield: 1 (10-inch) pie.

Sweet Home Alabama
The Junior League of Huntsville, Alabama

Pretzel Panache
You might not think that salty pretzels would be appealing in a piecrust. But once they're crushed, mixed with sugar and butter, and then topped with this berry concoction, you'll realize what a great sweet-salty match this dessert makes.

Mellow Mai Tai Pie

Fresh orange, lemon, and lime, along with coconut macaroons and pineapple, bring a taste of the tropics to this frozen pie.

2 cups macaroon cookie crumbs (about 18 cookies)
¼ cup butter, melted
1 pint pineapple sherbet, softened
1 pint vanilla ice cream, softened
1 tablespoon grated lime rind
1 teaspoon grated orange rind

1 teaspoon grated lemon rind
¼ cup fresh lime juice
2 tablespoons fresh orange juice
1 tablespoon fresh lemon juice
1 (20-ounce) can crushed pineapple, drained
Garnishes: pineapple slices, lime slices

COMBINE cookie crumbs and butter; press in bottom and up sides of a 10-inch pieplate. Chill.

COMBINE sherbet and ice cream; fold in lime rind and next 6 ingredients. Pour mixture into prepared crust. Cover and freeze 8 hours or until firm.

LET stand at room temperature 15 minutes before serving. Garnish, if desired. Yield: 1 (10-inch) pie.

Dee Dee Frazier
Camden's Back on Track
Missouri Pacific Depot Restoration
Camden, Arkansas

Macaroon Hunt
If you have a hard time locating macaroon cookies at your local supermarket, stop by a corner bakery and buy a dozen or so. You can use almond or coconut macaroons in this pie.

Chocolate-Macadamia Nut Pie MAKE AHEAD

Freeze Ahead

Make this showy pie several days ahead and store it tightly wrapped in the freezer.

This simple sweet looks smashing, in part because it's shaped in a springform pan. A chocolate-cream cheese mixture is softened with whipped cream before it's frozen. We liked it chilled, too.

1 cup (6 ounces) semisweet
    chocolate morsels
1⅔ cups crushed chocolate wafers
    (6 ounces)
¼ cup butter or margarine, melted
½ (8-ounce) package cream cheese,
    softened
¾ cup sugar

1½ teaspoons vanilla extract
1 (3½-ounce) jar macadamia nuts,
    coarsely chopped
2 cups whipping cream
Garnishes: unsweetened whipped
    cream, chocolate shavings, and
    toasted macadamia nuts

PLACE chocolate morsels in top of a double boiler; bring water to a boil. Reduce heat to low; cook until chocolate melts, stirring often. Remove from heat, and set aside.

COMBINE crushed wafers and butter. Firmly press mixture in bottom of a lightly buttered 9-inch springform pan.

COMBINE melted chocolate, cream cheese, sugar, and vanilla in a mixing bowl; beat at medium speed with an electric mixer until smooth. Fold in macadamia nuts.

BEAT 2 cups whipping cream at high speed until soft peaks form. Add about one-fourth of whipped cream to chocolate mixture, and beat until blended. Fold remaining whipped cream into chocolate mixture. Pour into crust.

COVER and freeze 4 hours or until firm.

TO SERVE, carefully remove sides of springform pan; let pie stand 10 minutes before serving. Garnish, if desired. Yield: 1 (9-inch) pie.

Azaleas to Zucchini
Smith County Medical Society Alliance
Tyler, Texas

Chocolate-Macadamia Nut Pie

Cranberry Tassies

Cranberry Tassies MAKE AHEAD

Serve these bite-size cranberry-nut gems when family and friends drop in during the holidays.

½ cup butter or margarine, softened
1 (3-ounce) package cream cheese, softened
1 cup all-purpose flour
1 large egg, beaten
¾ cup firmly packed light brown sugar

1 tablespoon butter or margarine, melted
1 teaspoon grated orange rind
½ cup chopped fresh cranberries
½ cup chopped pecans

BEAT ½ cup butter and cream cheese at medium speed with an electric mixer until creamy. Gradually add flour, beating well. Cover and chill 1 hour.

SHAPE dough into 24 (1-inch) balls; press balls into miniature (1¾-inch) muffin pans lightly coated with cooking spray. Set aside.

COMBINE egg and next 3 ingredients; stir in cranberries and pecans. Spoon 1 tablespoon mixture into each shell. Bake at 325° for 25 minutes or until filling is set. Remove from pans immediately, and cool completely on wire racks. Yield: 2 dozen.

Gracious Goodness Christmas in Charleston
Bishop England High School Endowment Fund
Charleston, South Carolina

Tassie Talk
Stack these little mouthfuls on a holiday tray and they'll be gone in minutes. They start with a 3-ingredient cream cheese pastry, which can be made ahead and chilled overnight.

Orange-Pecan Pie ONE BOWL

Any avid baker knows that good pecan pie recipes are a dime a dozen. But take a second look at this rendition. What makes it so memorable is the way orange enhances that familiar buttery nut filling.

3 large eggs, lightly beaten
¾ cup sugar
1 cup light corn syrup
2 tablespoons grated orange rind
¼ cup fresh orange juice

2 tablespoons butter or margarine, melted
1 cup coarsely chopped pecans
1 unbaked 9-inch pastry shell
Whipped cream

STIR together first 6 ingredients in a large bowl. Arrange pecans in pastry shell; pour filling over pecans. Bake at 325° for 50 minutes or until set. Cool on a wire rack. Serve with whipped cream. Yield: 1 (9-inch) pie.

Barbara Anderson
The Monarch's Feast
Mary Munford PTA
Richmond, Virginia

Fresh-Squeezed Flavor
Using freshly squeezed juice makes a flavor difference in this pie. Use your juicer machine or a citrus reamer. And depending on the size of the fruit, it may take only 1 orange to get the ¼ cup yield. Just remember to grate the rind before squeezing the juice.

Pear Pie

This fruit pie is exceptionally delicious with shredded sharp Cheddar cheese in the crust and a brown sugar streusel crumbled over fresh pears.

Pears and Cheese

What makes this pie so good? It's that winning combo of fruit and cheese together in an old-fashioned dessert. We liked Bartlett pears because they're large and have a musky, sweet flavor.

1 cup all-purpose flour
¼ teaspoon salt
⅓ cup shortening
½ cup (2 ounces) shredded sharp
    Cheddar cheese
3 to 4 tablespoons ice water
5½ cups peeled and sliced Bartlett
    pear (about 3 pounds)

2 teaspoons lemon juice
½ cup sugar
¼ cup all-purpose flour
¼ teaspoon ground cinnamon
¾ cup firmly packed light brown sugar
½ cup all-purpose flour
⅓ cup butter or margarine, cut into
    pieces

COMBINE 1 cup flour and salt; cut in shortening with a pastry blender until mixture is crumbly. Add cheese; sprinkle ice water, 1 tablespoon at a time, evenly over surface; stir with a fork until dry ingredients are moistened. Shape into a ball.

ROLL pastry to ⅛-inch thickness on a lightly floured surface. Place in a 10-inch glass pieplate; trim off excess pastry along edges. Fold edges under, and crimp. Set aside.

STIR together pear and next 4 ingredients in a large bowl. Spoon into pastry shell.

COMBINE brown sugar and ½ cup flour; cut in butter with pastry blender until mixture is crumbly. Sprinkle topping over pear filling.

BAKE at 375° for 1 hour or until golden. Cool completely on a wire rack. Yield: 1 (10-inch) pie.

Sounds Delicious: The Flavor of Atlanta in Food & Music
Atlanta Symphony Orchestra
Atlanta, Georgia

Pear Pie

Apple-Nut Pudding with Hot Rum Sauce PARTY FOOD

Pan or Dish?
In baking recipes, remember that "pan" refers to metal and "dish" refers to glass. Each makes a difference in how fast food browns and bakes in the oven.

This homey apple dessert is a cross between a cake and a pudding. Slice it into squares or scoop spoonfuls into dessert dishes before blanketing it with a generous amount of rum sauce.

½ cup butter, softened
2 cups sugar
2 large eggs
2 tablespoons water
2 teaspoons vanilla extract
½ teaspoon butter flavoring
2 cups all-purpose flour
2 teaspoons baking soda
½ teaspoon salt
2 teaspoons ground cinnamon
5 cooking apples, peeled and finely chopped (we tested with Granny Smith)
1 cup chopped pecans
Hot Rum Sauce

BEAT butter at medium speed with an electric mixer until creamy; gradually add sugar, beating well. Add eggs, 1 at a time, beating after each addition. Add water and flavorings, beating well.

COMBINE flour and next 3 ingredients; add to butter mixture, beating well. Stir in apple and pecans. Spoon mixture into a greased and floured 13- x 9-inch pan. Bake at 350° for 1 hour. Cut into squares or spoon into dessert dishes. Serve warm with warm sauce. Yield: 18 servings.

Hot Rum Sauce

1 cup sugar
1 cup water
½ cup butter
2 tablespoons all-purpose flour
⅛ teaspoon salt
2 teaspoons rum extract
1 teaspoon vanilla extract
¼ teaspoon butter flavoring

COMBINE first 5 ingredients in a medium saucepan; bring mixture to a boil over medium-high heat, stirring constantly. Stir in flavorings, and return to a boil, stirring constantly. Yield: 2⅓ cups.

Jennean McCutchen
Mounds of Cooking
Parkin Archeological Support Team
Parkin, Arkansas

Most Wonderful Winter Crisp

Cranberries, apples, and pecans—just thinking about these holiday ingredients can make you hungry for this simple fruit dessert.

3 Granny Smith apples, peeled and
    sliced
2 cups fresh cranberries
1 (8-ounce) can crushed pineapple in
    juice, undrained
½ cup sugar
1 cup firmly packed light brown
    sugar

¼ cup all-purpose flour
½ cup butter or margarine
1 cup uncooked regular oats
1 cup chopped pecans
   Sweetened whipped cream or vanilla
    ice cream

LAYER first 3 ingredients in a lightly greased 13- x 9-inch baking dish; sprinkle with ½ cup sugar.

COMBINE brown sugar and flour; cut in butter with a pastry blender until mixture is crumbly. Stir in oats and pecans. Sprinkle oat mixture evenly over fruit mixture. Bake, uncovered, at 375° for 30 minutes or until bubbly and thoroughly heated. Serve with whipped cream or ice cream. Yield: 8 servings.

Tested by Time
Porter Gaud Parents Guild
Charleston, South Carolina

Make-Ahead Option
To make this crisp ahead, cover and chill it overnight before baking. Let stand at room temperature 20 minutes before baking as directed.

Blackberry Grunt

"Old fashioned" best describes this berry dessert smothered in dumplings. It's a cousin to cobbler, but cooks on the stovetop instead of baking in the oven.

4 cups blackberries
¾ cup sugar
½ cup water
1 tablespoon butter
1 cup all-purpose flour
1½ teaspoons baking powder

¼ teaspoon salt
2 tablespoons sugar
½ cup milk
2 tablespoons butter, melted
   Sweetened whipped cream (optional)

COMBINE first 4 ingredients in a 3-quart saucepan. Bring to a boil over medium heat, stirring occasionally. Cover; reduce heat to low.

MEANWHILE, combine flour and next 3 ingredients in a bowl. Add milk and butter, stirring until smooth. Spoon dumpling mixture over berry mixture. Cover and simmer 15 minutes. (Do not remove cover.) Dumplings are done when a knife inserted in center comes out clean. Serve warm with sweetened whipped cream, if desired. Yield: 6 servings.

Laurie Trimm
The Cookbook Tour
Good Shepherd Lutheran Church
Plainview, Minnesota

Name Game
A "grunt" is a fruit dessert that's cooked on the stovetop. A thick biscuit dough is spooned on top of simmering fruit. The name probably came about because the fruit seems to "grunt" as it cooks. It's also known as a "slump."

Old-Fashioned Fried Pies

Tangy dried fruit encased in flaky pastry turnovers is the stuff of state fairs, but this recipe makes it easy enough to do in your own kitchen.

Oil for Frying

You'll want to use vegetable oil for frying these sweet pies. It has little to no flavor and is better suited for frying sweets than other oils. Remember to start heating the oil early on in recipe preparation, because it takes a little while for it to get good and hot.

2 cups dried peaches, apples, or apricots
½ cup sugar
2 tablespoons butter or margarine, melted
2 cups all-purpose flour
1 teaspoon salt
⅓ cup shortening
⅔ to 1 cup ice water
Vegetable oil
Sifted powdered sugar (optional)

PLACE fruit in a medium saucepan; cover with water. Bring to a boil; cook, uncovered, 30 minutes, adding water to cover, if necessary. Drain well. Finely chop fruit; place in a bowl. Stir in sugar and melted butter; set aside.

COMBINE flour and salt; cut in shortening with a pastry blender until mixture is crumbly. Sprinkle cold water, 1 tablespoon at a time, evenly over surface; stir with a fork until dry ingredients are moistened.

DIVIDE pastry into thirds; roll each portion to ⅛-inch thickness on a lightly floured surface, and cut with a 4½-inch round cutter.

PLACE 1 heaping tablespoon (about 1½ tablespoons) reserved fruit filling in center of each pastry circle. Moisten edges with water. Fold pastry over filling, pressing edges to seal. Crimp edges with a fork dipped in flour; pierce tops with fork.

POUR oil to a depth of 1 inch into a large heavy skillet; heat oil to 400°. Fry pies, 4 or 5 at a time, in hot oil 3 to 4 minutes or until golden, turning once. Drain on paper towels. Sprinkle with powdered sugar, if desired. Yield: 1½ dozen.

Montees Holloway
A Dab of This and a Dab of That
Bethlehem Baptist Church Senior Missionary
Ninety Six, South Carolina

Best-Ever Blueberry Cobbler

Fruit cobbler is the sum of all that's good about summer. Sweeten the pot by picking your own blueberries.

3 cups fresh blueberries
3 tablespoons sugar
⅓ cup orange juice
½ cup butter or margarine, softened
½ cup sugar

1 large egg
½ teaspoon vanilla extract
⅔ cup all-purpose flour
¼ teaspoon baking powder
Pinch of salt

TOSS together first 3 ingredients in an 8-inch square baking dish.

BEAT butter and ½ cup sugar at medium speed with an electric mixer until light and fluffy. Add egg and vanilla, beating until smooth. Gradually add flour, baking powder, and salt, beating at low speed. Drop batter in small clumps over berry mixture, covering as much surface as possible.

BAKE at 375° for 35 to 40 minutes or until crust is golden and filling is bubbly. Cool briefly on a wire rack.

SERVE warm with whipped cream or vanilla ice cream. Yield: 6 servings.

What Can I Bring?
Junior League of Northern Virginia, Inc.
McLean, Virginia

Fresh or Frozen

You can use frozen blueberries in this cobbler. Toss them with 1 tablespoon flour before adding to the recipe. This will help absorb extra moisture caused by the freezing process.

Skillet Apple Tart with Calvados Cream

Skillet Apple Tart with Calvados Cream

Also known as Tarte Tatin, this rustic, country dessert features apples snuggled in pastry. This dessert's drizzled with Calvados, a French apple brandy. If you don't taste enough brandy in the tart, it's also folded into the cream topping.

4 cups water
2¼ cups sugar, divided
1 tablespoon grated lemon rind
6 whole cloves
1 (3-inch) stick cinnamon
½ vanilla bean, split
4 Golden Delicious apples, peeled, cored, and halved crosswise

2 tablespoons unsalted butter
2 tablespoons Calvados or apple cider
1 tablespoon fresh lemon juice
1 teaspoon freshly grated nutmeg
½ (17¼-ounce) package frozen puff pastry, thawed
Calvados Cream

COMBINE water, 1½ cups sugar, lemon rind, and next 3 ingredients in a large saucepan; bring to a boil. Reduce heat, and simmer, uncovered, 10 minutes. Add apple halves, and simmer 7 more minutes. Remove apple halves from syrup, discarding syrup. Set apple halves aside.

SPRINKLE remaining ¾ cup sugar in a 10-inch cast-iron skillet; place over medium heat. Cook, stirring constantly, until sugar melts and turns light golden brown. Remove from heat. Arrange apple halves, cut side down, in skillet. Set aside.

COMBINE butter, Calvados, lemon juice, and nutmeg in a small saucepan; bring to a boil. Reduce heat, and simmer 5 minutes, stirring occasionally. Drizzle mixture over apple halves.

ROLL puff pastry into an 11-inch square. Cut pastry into an 11-inch circle. Place over apple halves, tucking edges of pastry into skillet. Bake at 425° for 28 to 30 minutes or until puffed and golden. Cool on a wire rack 10 to 15 minutes.

INVERT skillet onto a serving plate; scrape any remaining glaze from skillet onto tart. Cut into wedges; serve warm or at room temperature with Calvados Cream. Yield: 1 (10-inch) tart.

Calvados Cream

1 cup whipping cream
2 tablespoons Calvados or apple cider

1 tablespoon sugar

COMBINE all ingredients in a small mixing bowl; beat at high speed with an electric mixer until soft peaks form. Yield: 2 cups.

Sweet Home Alabama
The Junior League of Huntsville, Alabama

Skillet Dessert

Homestyle desserts often are made in cast-iron skillets; such is the case with this apple tart. Somewhat like pineapple upside down cake, you invert this apple delicacy onto a platter and spoon any gooey topping left in the skillet onto it before serving.

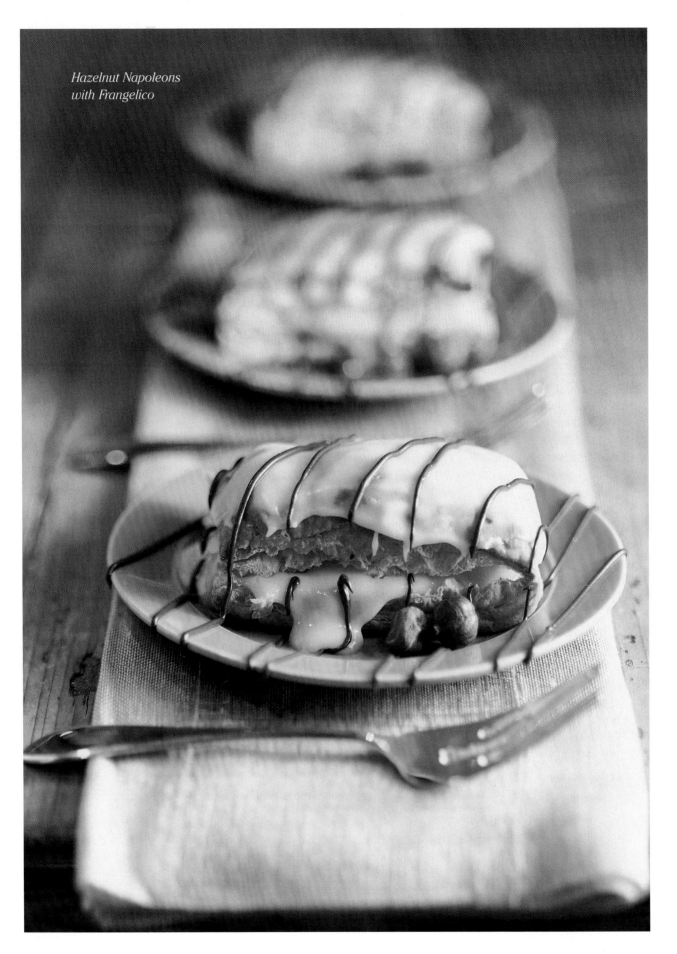

Hazelnut Napoleons with Frangelico

Hazelnut Napoleons with Frangelico

Puff pastry and a simple custard become a work of art in this recipe. Frangelico, a hazelnut liqueur, laces the custard, and a chocolate drizzle allows the cook to exhibit some artistic expression with garnish.

1 (17¼-ounce) package frozen puff pastry, thawed
2½ cups evaporated milk
1½ cups sugar
¼ cup plus 1 tablespoon all-purpose flour
4 egg yolks, lightly beaten
2 tablespoons butter

½ cup Frangelico or other hazelnut liqueur
1 teaspoon vanilla extract
2¼ cups sifted powdered sugar
3 tablespoons milk
¼ cup (1½ ounces) semisweet chocolate morsels
Garnish: whole hazelnuts

PLACE pastry on a lightly floured surface; cut into 3-x 4-inch rectangles. Transfer half of pastry to an ungreased baking sheet. Bake at 400° for 18 minutes or until pastry is puffed and golden. Gently remove pastry from baking sheet with a spatula, and cool on wire racks. Repeat procedure with remaining pastry.

COMBINE evaporated milk and next 4 ingredients in a heavy saucepan, stirring with a wire whisk until smooth. Cook over medium heat, stirring constantly, until mixture thickens and begins to bubble. Continue to cook 3 more minutes, stirring constantly. Remove from heat; stir in liqueur and vanilla. Cover and chill at least 2 hours.

CAREFULLY split each pastry in half horizontally, using a serrated knife. Spread each with about 1 tablespoon custard, and replace top of pastry.

COMBINE powdered sugar and milk, stirring until smooth; spoon glaze over tops of pastries, spreading evenly.

MELT chocolate in microwave oven according to package directions; cool slightly. Spoon chocolate into a pastry bag fitted with a small round tip. Or spoon chocolate into a zip-top plastic bag, seal bag, and snip a small hole in 1 corner. Pipe a decorative pattern across top of glaze. Let stand until set. Garnish, if desired. Yield: 3 dozen.

Southern . . . On Occasion
The Junior League of Cobb-Marietta
Marietta, Georgia

Lagniappe
There'll be a little of this custard left over. It's perfect for serving over pound cake, fresh berries, or all by itself. If you'd rather omit the liqueur in the custard, substitute ½ cup of any kind of milk.

Peach Ice Cream   MAKE AHEAD   SUPPER CLUB

Secret Ingredient

Marshmallows are novel in this home-made ice cream. Once melted, they add a unique creaminess to the churned results.

Melted marshmallows and succulent summer peaches sweeten this creamy classic.

1 cup half-and-half
1 cup milk
¼ cup plus 1 tablespoon sugar, divided
¼ teaspoon salt

1 (10-ounce) package large marshmallows
2 cups mashed ripe peaches (about 2½ pounds)
2 cups whipping cream, whipped

COMBINE half-and-half, milk, 3 tablespoons sugar, salt, and marshmallows in a large saucepan. Cook mixture over medium heat until marshmallows melt, stirring occasionally. Remove from heat, and cool completely.

COMBINE remaining 2 tablespoons sugar and peaches, stirring until sugar dissolves. Fold peach mixture into marshmallow mixture. Gently fold in whipped cream.

POUR mixture into freezer container of a 1-gallon hand-turned or electric freezer. Freeze according to manufacturer's instructions.

PACK freezer with additional ice and rock salt, and let stand 1 hour before serving. Yield: 2¼ quarts.

Eleanor Lowry
Blue Stocking Club Forget-Me-Not Recipes
Blue Stocking Club
Bristol, Tennessee

Butter Pecan Ice Cream   MAKE AHEAD

Double Boiler

It's important to use the gentle heat of a double boiler when cooking custard or your custard may curdle. Make your own double boiler by placing a large glass mixing bowl over a fairly large saucepan. Fill the saucepan with an inch or so of water before you begin. And be sure the glass bowl sits snugly over the pan. You don't want the bowl to touch the water; if it does, pour a little water out.

This ice cream is so good you may want to double or triple the recipe, and invite your friends over. If you do, make it in a gallon freezer.

¾ cup firmly packed light brown sugar
½ cup water
⅛ teaspoon salt
2 large eggs, lightly beaten

2 tablespoons butter
1 cup milk
1 teaspoon vanilla extract
1 cup whipping cream
½ cup finely chopped pecans, toasted

COMBINE first 3 ingredients in top of a double boiler; bring water in bottom of double boiler to a boil. Reduce heat to low; cook, stirring constantly, 3 to 4 minutes or until sugar dissolves. Gradually stir a small amount of hot mixture into eggs; add to remaining hot mixture, stirring constantly. Cook over medium heat, stirring constantly, until thermometer registers 160° and mixture thickens (about 4 to 5 minutes). Remove from heat; stir in butter, and cool. Stir in milk and remaining ingredients.

POUR mixture into freezer container of a 2-quart hand-turned or electric freezer. Freeze according to manufacturer's instructions.

PACK freezer with additional ice and rock salt, and let stand 1 hour before serving. Yield: 1 quart.

A Southern Collection, Then and Now
The Junior League of Columbus, Georgia

Butter Pecan Ice Cream

Peach Melba Ice Cream Cake MAKE AHEAD

Melba Sauce

The famed French chef Auguste Escoffier created this sauce for an Australian opera singer, Dame Nellie Melba. The sauce is made of pureed raspberries, sugar, and cornstarch, and is used to adorn any type of peach melba dessert.

If fresh peaches are not in season when you get a yen to make this fruity frozen cake, simply substitute thawed frozen peach slices.

1 cup melba toast crumbs
⅓ cup sugar
⅓ cup flaked coconut
¼ cup plus 2 tablespoons butter, melted
1 quart raspberry sherbet, softened
1 quart vanilla ice cream, softened

1 (10-ounce) package frozen raspberries, thawed
½ cup sugar
2 tablespoons cornstarch
1 tablespoon lemon juice
1 cup sliced fresh peaches, chilled

COMBINE first 4 ingredients, stirring well. Press mixture in bottom and up sides of a 9-inch springform pan. Bake at 350° for 10 minutes or until golden. Cool completely in pan on a wire rack. Cover and freeze at least 1 hour.

SPREAD raspberry sherbet in frozen crust. Freeze 30 minutes or until firm. Spread vanilla ice cream over sherbet. Cover and freeze 8 hours.

DRAIN raspberries, reserving liquid. Set raspberries aside. Combine ½ cup sugar and cornstarch in a saucepan. Add water to raspberry liquid to equal 1 cup. Stir liquid into sugar and cornstarch mixture. Cook over medium heat, stirring constantly, until mixture thickens and comes to a boil. Boil 1 minute, stirring constantly. Remove from heat; stir in raspberries and lemon juice. Cool; cover and chill.

TO SERVE, carefully remove sides of springform pan. Arrange peach slices on top of vanilla ice cream. Drizzle a small amount of raspberry sauce over peaches. Cut ice cream cake into wedges. Serve immediately with additional raspberry sauce spooned over each serving. Yield: 12 servings.

Here, There & Everywhere
Volunteers in Overseas Cooperative Assistance
Washington, DC

Ruby Grapefruit and Lemon Granita

A splash of red food coloring adds a flattering blush to this double citrus fruit delight.

2 cups sugar
4 cups water
2 tablespoons grated lemon rind
1 cup fresh lemon juice

1 tablespoon grated grapefruit rind
1 cup fresh ruby red grapefruit juice
1 drop red liquid food coloring

COMBINE sugar and water in a medium saucepan; bring to a boil, stirring until sugar dissolves. Boil 5 minutes. Remove from heat, and cool completely. Stir in lemon rind and remaining ingredients.

POUR mixture into a 13- x 9-inch pan; freeze until almost firm, stirring occasionally. Break frozen mixture into chunks. Process in a food processor until smooth. Return mixture to pan; cover and freeze until firm. Let stand at room temperature 20 minutes before serving. Scrape and shave granita with a fork until fluffy. Serve immediately. Yield: 6 cups.

Simple Pleasures: From Our Table to Yours
Arab Mothers' Club
Arab, Alabama

Italian Ice
Granita is an Italian icy dessert that's a frozen mixture of sugar, water, and either fruit juice, wine, or coffee. Stirring the slushy concoction as it freezes results in a desired granular texture.

Watermelon Granita   MAKE AHEAD

Call this drink a slush, and your kids will love it.

6 cups peeled, seeded, and cubed
   watermelon

¼ to ½ cup sugar
2½ tablespoons lemon juice

PROCESS watermelon in a blender or food processor until smooth (about 4 cups puree). Pour into a bowl; add sugar and lemon juice, stirring until sugar dissolves. Cover and chill.

POUR watermelon mixture into a 13- x 9-inch pan, and freeze, stirring occasionally, 3 hours or until firm.

SCOOP frozen mixture into balls using a large ice cream scoop, and serve in paper snow cone cups or dessert dishes. Yield: 4 cups.

How Sweet It Is
The sweetness of your melon will determine how much sugar you add to this recipe.

Sweet Cream

Sweet Cream MAKE AHEAD

A sublime blend of whipping cream and sour cream creates the perfect cushion for a sprinkling of fresh berries.

1 cup sugar	2 (8-ounce) containers sour cream
1 envelope unflavored gelatin	1 teaspoon vanilla extract
2 cups whipping cream	Fresh berries

COMBINE sugar and gelatin in a medium saucepan; stir in whipping cream, and let stand 1 minute. Cook over medium heat, stirring constantly with a wire whisk, 5 minutes or until gelatin dissolves. Remove from heat, and cool.

STIR sour cream and vanilla into gelatin mixture. Pour into a serving bowl; cover and chill 3 hours or until set. To serve, spoon mixture into dessert dishes, and top with berries. Yield: 4 servings.

Ruth Bliss
700 lbs. of Marmalade
The Woman's Club of Winter Park, Florida

Simple Cream

This simple dessert is actually named Swedish Cream. It's a rich custard, slightly tangy due to the sour cream and fairly firm due to the gelatin.

Old-Fashioned Banana Pudding

No homestyle cookbook would be complete without a classic banana pudding recipe.

¼ cup plus 2 tablespoons all-purpose flour	¼ cup butter
1 cup sugar	1 teaspoon vanilla extract
⅛ teaspoon salt	36 vanilla wafers
1 cup water	3 ripe bananas, sliced
1 cup evaporated milk	2 cups frozen whipped topping, thawed
2 large eggs, lightly beaten	

COMBINE first 3 ingredients in a medium saucepan; stir in water, milk, and eggs. Cook over medium heat, stirring constantly, until mixture thickens. Add butter and vanilla; cook, stirring constantly, until butter melts.

LAYER vanilla wafers and banana slices evenly in 6 individual dessert dishes; spoon pudding over banana slices. Top each serving with a dollop of whipped topping. Yield: 6 servings.

Thomas Huckabee
Mississippi Reflections: A Collection of Recipes Seasoned with Memories
Hospice of Central Mississippi
Brookhaven, Mississippi

Brickle and Banana

Try something new next time you whip up banana pudding. Sprinkle a layer of almond brickle chips over the pudding. The combination of brickle and bananas is scrumptious.

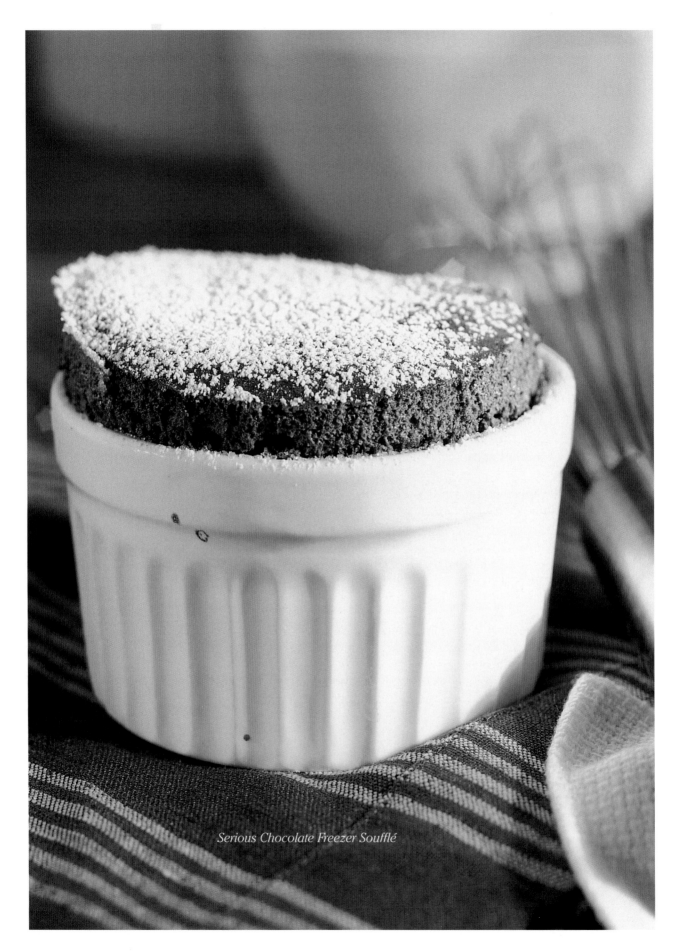

Serious Chocolate Freezer Soufflé

Serious Chocolate Freezer Soufflés

Those who are serious about their chocolate are sure to like these pretty chocolate puffs. Their make-ahead, freeze, and bake qualities add to their appeal.

½ cup all-purpose flour	2 tablespoons butter or margarine
¾ cup cocoa	1 teaspoon vanilla extract
1 cup sugar, divided	8 egg whites
¼ teaspoon salt	¼ teaspoon cream of tartar
2 cups milk	Hot fudge sauce or powdered sugar
6 egg yolks, lightly beaten	

BUTTER bottom and sides of 8 (6-ounce) custard cups, ramekins, or soufflé dishes, and sprinkle lightly with sugar. Set aside.

COMBINE flour, cocoa, ¾ cup sugar, and salt in a medium saucepan. Gradually whisk in milk. Cook mixture over medium heat, stirring constantly, until thick and bubbly. Remove from heat.

BEAT egg yolks until thick and pale. Gradually stir 2 tablespoons hot mixture into yolks; add to remaining hot mixture, stirring constantly. Stir in butter and vanilla. Cool.

BEAT egg whites and cream of tartar at high speed with an electric mixer until foamy. Add remaining ¼ cup sugar, 1 tablespoon at a time, beating until stiff peaks form and sugar dissolves (2 to 4 minutes). Fold into chocolate mixture. Spoon into prepared cups. Cover and freeze until firm.

WHEN ready to bake, uncover and place 1 inch apart on rack in cold oven. Set oven temperature to 350°. Bake 45 minutes or until tops are puffed. Cut a slit in top of each soufflé, and place 1 teaspoon fudge sauce into each slit. Serve immediately with additional fudge sauce or sprinkle with powdered sugar. Yield: 8 servings.

A Thyme to Remember
Dallas County Medical Society Alliance
Dallas, Texas

Egg Power

If you own a copper bowl, use it to beat egg whites for volume and stability. A clean glass bowl works fine as well.

Flan de Chocolate MAKE AHEAD

Caramel Cap

Flans have a layer of caramel in the bottom of the pan. After you add the custard, bake, chill, and invert the whole dessert, that caramel tops the flan as a thin delectable sauce.

Flan is a Spanish baked custard with a caramelized sugar cap. This flan takes on a new personality with the flavor of chocolate.

1 cup sugar
1¾ cups water, divided
2 tablespoons cocoa
1 tablespoon sugar

2 (14-ounce) cans sweetened
  condensed milk
4 large eggs
1 teaspoon vanilla extract

COMBINE 1 cup sugar and ¼ cup water in a heavy saucepan; cook over medium heat, stirring constantly with a wooden spoon, until sugar crystallizes into lumps (about 15 minutes). Continue to cook, stirring constantly, until sugar melts and turns golden brown (about 15 minutes). Quickly pour hot caramelized sugar into an ungreased 8-inch round cakepan, tilting to coat bottom evenly. Set aside (mixture will harden).

COMBINE remaining 1½ cups water, cocoa, and 1 tablespoon sugar in a small saucepan. Bring to a boil over medium heat, stirring often. Remove from heat, and let cool.

PROCESS milk, eggs, and vanilla in a blender just until blended. Add cocoa mixture; process until blended, stopping once to scrape down sides. Pour egg mixture over caramelized sugar in cakepan. Place cakepan in a large shallow baking dish. Add hot water to dish to depth of 1 inch.

COVER and bake at 350° for 1½ hours or until a knife inserted near center comes out clean. Remove pan from water, and let cool. Cover and chill 8 hours.

TO SERVE, loosen edge of flan with a spatula, and invert onto a serving plate. Yield: 6 servings.

Tropical Seasons, A Taste of Life in South Florida
Beaux Arts of the Lowe Art Museum of the University of Miami
Coral Gables, Florida

Meats, Poultry & Seafood

Country-Fried Steak with
Cream Gravy, page 210

Standing Rib Roast au Jus and Yorkshire Pudding PARTY FOOD

This grand holiday roast is well seasoned with garlic and slow roasted to perfect tenderness. Yorkshire Pudding and meat drippings called "jus" are traditional English accompaniments.

1 (8-pound) fully trimmed 3-rib roast
5 garlic cloves
½ teaspoon salt

½ teaspoon freshly ground pepper
Yorkshire Pudding
Jus

PLACE roast, rib side down, in a lightly greased shallow roasting pan. Cut small slits in meat, and insert whole garlic cloves. Rub salt and pepper into fat across top of roast. Tie roast with heavy string at 2-inch intervals. Insert a meat thermometer into roast, making sure it does not touch fat or bone.

BAKE, uncovered, at 325° for 3 hours or until thermometer registers 145° (medium-rare). Remove from oven; cover roast with aluminum foil, and let stand 20 minutes before slicing. (This allows juices to retreat back into the meat; the temperature of the roast will rise slightly.) Pour off pan drippings, reserving ½ cup drippings for Yorkshire Pudding. Leave browned bits in pan for Jus. Serve roast with Yorkshire Pudding and Jus. Yield: 12 servings.

Yorkshire Pudding

1½ cups all-purpose flour
¾ cup water
¾ cup milk

3 large eggs, beaten
¾ teaspoon salt
½ cup pan drippings from rib roast

PROCESS first 5 ingredients in a food processor 3 minutes or until smooth. Cover and chill 30 minutes. Add ½ cup pan drippings to a 13- x 9-inch pan. Heat pan in oven at 425° for 5 minutes. Quickly pour cold flour mixture into hot pan; do not stir. Bake at 425° for 18 minutes; reduce oven temperature to 350°, and bake 18 more minutes. Yield: 12 servings.

Jus

½ cup dry red wine
1½ cups water
4 teaspoons liquid beef concentrate
¼ teaspoon salt

¼ teaspoon pepper
2 teaspoons cornstarch
1 tablespoon water

ADD wine to roasting pan with browned bits; cook over high heat 2 minutes, stirring to loosen particles from bottom of pan. Add water and liquid beef concentrate; boil 3 minutes. Stir in salt and pepper. Combine cornstarch and water, stirring until smooth; stir into sauce. Cook, stirring constantly, until mixture is thickened and bubbly. Yield: 1½ cups.

Yuletide on Hilton Head: A Heritage of Island Flavors
United Way of Beaufort County
Hilton Head Island, South Carolina

Rosemary-Roasted Prime Rib

Fragrant rosemary leaves permeate this roast with their distinctive lemony-pine flavor magic.

1 (6-pound) boneless rib roast,
   trimmed
¼ cup olive oil
15 garlic cloves, chopped
   (about ½ cup)

½ cup fresh rosemary leaves
½ teaspoon salt
½ teaspoon pepper

RUB roast with 2 tablespoons olive oil. Combine garlic, rosemary, salt, and pepper; sprinkle mixture over roast, covering completely. Drizzle with remaining 2 tablespoons oil. Place roast on a lightly greased rack in a roasting pan. Insert a meat thermometer into thickest part of roast.

BAKE, uncovered, at 350° for 2 hours or until thermometer registers 145° (medium rare). Cover roast with aluminum foil to prevent excessive browning, if necessary. Let stand 15 minutes before slicing. Yield: 8 servings.

Sounds Delicious: The Flavor of Atlanta in Food & Music
Atlanta Symphony Orchestra
Atlanta, Georgia

Garlic Goodness

Don't panic about the abundance of garlic in this recipe. As garlic bakes, it mellows in flavor to a sweet, buttery finish.

Beef Tenderloin au Poivre

Peppercorns and mustard coat this entrée with savory goodness. Sometimes, a few simple ingredients can bake into incredible results.

1 (4-pound) beef tenderloin, trimmed
⅓ cup Dijon mustard
1½ tablespoons black peppercorns,
   crushed

1½ tablespoons white peppercorns,
   crushed

EVENLY shape tenderloin by tucking small end underneath; tie with string. Rub tenderloin with mustard.

COMBINE crushed peppercorns, and press evenly over surface of tenderloin. Place on a rack in a shallow roasting pan; bake, uncovered, at 425° for 45 minutes or until a meat thermometer inserted in thickest part of tenderloin registers 145° (medium rare) or 160° (medium). Let stand 10 minutes before slicing. Yield: 12 servings.

Women Who Can Dish It Out
The Junior League of Springfield, Missouri

Crushing Peppercorns

Crush peppercorns easily in a clean coffee grinder or by using a mortar and pestle.

Stuffed Tenderloin

Indirectly Done

This tenderloin gets grilled over indirect heat, which means the outside of the meat doesn't cook any faster than the inside since the meat doesn't sit directly over hot coals.

Snuggled between tender slices of beef tenderloin lie fresh mushrooms, green onions, garlic, and parsley. The stuffing mixture is melded with melted crumbles of blue cheese.

1 (3-pound) beef tenderloin
2 tablespoons butter or margarine
1 (8-ounce) package sliced fresh mushrooms
4 green onions, chopped

1 garlic clove, minced
2 tablespoons chopped fresh parsley
3 tablespoons crumbled blue cheese
1 tablespoon butter or margarine, melted

SLICE tenderloin lengthwise to, but not through, the center, leaving 1 long side connected; set aside.

MELT 2 tablespoons butter in a large skillet over medium-high heat. Add mushrooms and next 3 ingredients; cook 5 minutes or until tender, stirring often. Spoon mixture into opening of tenderloin, leaving a ½-inch border on all sides. Sprinkle cheese over mushroom mixture. Close tenderloin, and tie securely with heavy string at 2-inch intervals. Brush with melted butter.

PREPARE a hot fire by piling charcoal on 1 side of grill, leaving other side empty. (For gas grills, light only 1 side.) Coat food rack with cooking spray; place rack on grill. Arrange food on unlit side. Grill, covered with grill lid, 45 minutes or until meat thermometer inserted in thickest part of tenderloin registers 145° (medium rare) to 160° (medium). Let stand 10 minutes before slicing. Yield: 8 servings.

Montgomery Ranch
Taste of the Territory, The Flair and Flavor of Oklahoma
The Service League of Bartlesville, Oklahoma

Eye-of-Round with Horseradish Cream

Lean Roast Plus Red Wine

Red wine has chemical properties that tenderize meat as well as flavor it. You'll like the results of marinating this eye-of-round in red wine because it's a lean roast, which means it needs an acidic marinade such as wine to help make it tender.

Yes, the 20-minute cook time is correct for this recipe. By baking at the high temperature and keeping the oven door closed 2 hours, this roast cooks up extra tender and flavorful.

1 cup dry red wine
½ cup butter or margarine, melted
1 (4-pound) eye-of-round roast

1 tablespoon salt
1 teaspoon pepper
Horseradish Cream

COMBINE wine and butter in a large heavy-duty zip-top plastic bag; add roast. Seal and chill at least 8 hours or up to 24 hours, turning occasionally.

REMOVE roast from marinade, discarding marinade. Place roast in a 13- x 9-inch pan lined with heavy-duty aluminum foil. Combine salt and pepper, and rub over surface of roast.

BAKE, uncovered, at 500° for 20 to 30 minutes. Turn oven off. Do not open oven door for 2 hours. Meat thermometer should register 145° (medium rare) or 160° (medium). Thinly slice meat, reserving pan juices. Serve meat with pan juices and Horseradish Cream. Yield: 8 servings.

Horseradish Cream

1 (8-ounce) package cream cheese,
    softened
1½ tablespoons prepared
    horseradish

2 teaspoons Dijon mustard

COMBINE all ingredients, stirring until smooth. Cover and chill at least 2 hours. Yield: about 1 cup.

Linen Napkins to Paper Plates
The Junior Auxiliary of Clarksville, Tennessee

Melt-in-Your-Mouth Roast

This roast really lives up to its name. Its rich flavor is achieved by just a few simple ingredients. Be sure to cut the roast in half before placing it in the slow cooker—this ensures even cooking for large cuts of meat.

1 large onion, sliced
2 teaspoons salt
½ teaspoon pepper
1 (3- to 4-pound) rump roast, cut
    in half

1 tablespoon vegetable oil
2 tablespoons Worcestershire sauce
3 tablespoons all-purpose flour
¼ cup water

PLACE onion in a 4-quart electric slow cooker. Combine salt and pepper, and rub on all sides of roast. Cook roast in hot oil in a large skillet over medium-high heat until browned on all sides. Remove roast from skillet, and place on top of onion in slow cooker. Add Worcestershire sauce to skillet, deglazing skillet by scraping particles that cling to bottom. Pour Worcestershire sauce mixture over meat and onion.

COVER and cook on HIGH setting 1 hour. Reduce to LOW setting, and cook 7 hours or until meat is very tender. Remove meat and onion to a platter; cover and keep warm. Combine flour and water, stirring until smooth. Stir flour mixture into drippings in cooker. Cook, uncovered, on HIGH 10 minutes or until thickened and bubbly, stirring occasionally. Yield: 8 servings.

Stephanie Hightower Kraft
Savory Secrets
Runnels School
Baton Rouge, Louisiana

Start on High

Start cooking meat on HIGH in the slow cooker and then reduce heat to LOW. This ensures that the meat quickly gets to a safe simmering temperature.

Barbecue Beef Brisket GRILL LOVERS

The slow cooking of the meat made this barbecue melt in our mouths and get our best rating.

Against the Grain

When you cut meat against the grain, you're cutting through the meat fibers at an angle, actually breaking them. This slicing technique contributes to tender bites of brisket.

1 (5- to 6-pound) boneless beef brisket
2 teaspoons paprika
½ teaspoon pepper
1 (11- x 9-inch) disposable aluminum roasting pan
1 cup water
Hickory chunks
Sauce

SPRINKLE brisket with paprika and pepper; rub over surface of roast. Place roast in disposable pan; add 1 cup water, and cover with aluminum foil.

SOAK hickory chunks in water to cover 30 minutes; drain. Wrap chunks in heavy-duty foil, and make several holes in foil. Prepare a hot fire by piling charcoal on 1 side of grill, leaving other side empty. (For gas grills, light only 1 side.) Place foil-wrapped chunks directly on hot coals. Place food rack on grill. Arrange food over unlit side. Grill, covered with grill lid, 3½ to 4 hours or until tender. Turn brisket every hour, adding water as needed. Remove brisket from pan, reserving 1 cup pan drippings for sauce.

COAT grill rack with cooking spray; place rack over hot coals. Place brisket on rack; cover and grill 10 to 15 minutes on each side. Slice against grain into thin slices. Serve with Sauce. Yield: 12 servings.

Sauce

1 onion, finely chopped
1 tablespoon butter or margarine, melted
1 cup reserved pan drippings
½ teaspoon pepper
1½ cups ketchup
1 tablespoon lemon juice
1 tablespoon Worcestershire sauce
1 teaspoon hot sauce

SAUTÉ onion in butter in a large skillet over medium-high heat until tender. Stir in drippings and remaining ingredients. Bring to a boil; reduce heat, and simmer 15 minutes, stirring occasionally. Yield: 3 cups.

Ann Woolley
Discover Oklahoma Cookin'
Oklahoma 4-H Foundation
Stillwater, Oklahoma

Grilled Sirloin Steak with Stilton Sauce

GRILL LOVERS

Stilton cheese stars in this delectable sauce, which provides the perfect topping on grilled steak.

½ cup butter or margarine, melted
⅓ cup Worcestershire sauce
8 ounces Stilton cheese, crumbled
1 garlic clove, crushed

½ teaspoon salt
¼ teaspoon pepper
2 pounds lean boneless top sirloin
    steak (3 inches thick)

COMBINE first 4 ingredients in a medium saucepan. Cook over low heat until cheese melts, stirring constantly. Set aside ⅔ cup sauce; keep remaining sauce warm.

SPRINKLE salt and pepper over steak. Grill, covered with grill lid, over medium-high heat (350° to 400°) 18 minutes on each side or to desired degree of doneness, basting often with ⅔ cup sauce. To serve, cut steak diagonally across the grain. Serve with remaining sauce. Yield: 6 servings.

Savour St. Louis
Barnes-Jewish Hospital Auxiliary Plaza Chapter
St. Louis, Missouri

Creamy, Crumbly

Stilton cheese is a rich and creamy blue cheese with a slightly crumbly texture—perfect features for blending into a rich sauce for grilled steak.

Country-Fried Steak with Cream Gravy

WEEKNIGHT FAVORITE

Pictured on page 203

Chicken Fried or Country Fried

Some cookbooks differentiate between country-fried and chicken-fried steak. Country-fried steak has flour and seasonings pounded into the meat. It's then fried in an iron skillet and served with cream gravy made from goodness left in the pan. Chicken-fried steak was originally deep-fried and served *sans* gravy.

Crusty Country-Fried Steak is about as homestyle as supper can get, complete with the creamy peppered gravy, of course.

3 pounds boneless sirloin steak
   (½ inch thick)
1 tablespoon salt
1 tablespoon white vinegar
3 cups all-purpose flour
2 tablespoons freshly ground pepper

Vegetable oil
¼ cup all-purpose flour
2 cups milk
¼ teaspoon salt
½ teaspoon freshly ground pepper
Garnish: fresh parsley sprigs

TRIM excess fat from meat. Pound meat to ¼-inch thickness, using a meat mallet or rolling pin; cut into 10 to 12 serving-size pieces. Place in a large bowl; add water to cover. Stir in 1 tablespoon salt and vinegar. Cover and marinate in refrigerator 2 hours.

COMBINE 3 cups flour and 2 tablespoons pepper; stir well. Remove meat from marinade, discarding marinade. Dredge meat in flour mixture. Pour oil to depth of 2 inches into a large heavy skillet; heat to 375°. Fry meat, a few pieces at a time, in hot oil over medium heat 6 to 7 minutes on each side or until lightly browned. Remove from skillet, and drain well on paper towels. Transfer meat to a serving platter. Set aside, and keep warm.

DRAIN pan drippings, reserving 2 tablespoons drippings in skillet. Place skillet over low heat. Add ¼ cup flour, stirring until smooth. Cook 1 minute, stirring constantly. Gradually add milk; cook over medium heat, stirring constantly, until mixture is thickened and bubbly. Stir in ¼ teaspoon salt and ½ teaspoon pepper. Serve meat with gravy. Garnish, if desired. Yield: 10 to 12 servings.

Augusta Cooks for Company, Past and Present
The Augusta Council of the Georgia Association for Children and Adults
with Learning Disabilities
Augusta, Georgia

Slow-Cooked Pepper Steak

Round steak turns into fork-tender pepper steak when allowed to simmer long and slowly in the gentle heat of a slow cooker.

2   pounds top round steak (1 inch thick), trimmed
2   tablespoons vegetable oil
1   (14½-ounce) can peeled tomato wedges, undrained (we tested with Delmonte Fresh Cut Fancy Tomato Wedges)
2   large green bell peppers, cut into 1-inch-wide strips
1   cup chopped onion
¼   cup soy sauce
1   garlic clove, minced
1   teaspoon sugar
1   teaspoon salt
¼   teaspoon black pepper
¼   teaspoon ground ginger
1   tablespoon cornstarch
½   cup cold water
Hot cooked noodles or rice

CUT steak into 3-inch pieces; brown in hot oil in a large skillet over medium-high heat. Transfer steak to a 4-quart electric slow cooker. Add tomatoes and pepper strips.

COMBINE onion and next 6 ingredients; pour over mixture in slow cooker. Cover and cook on HIGH setting 7 hours.

COMBINE cornstarch and water, stirring until smooth. Stir into mixture in slow cooker; cook, uncovered, on HIGH 10 to 15 minutes or until mixture is thickened and bubbly. Serve over noodles or rice. Yield: 6 servings.

Pat Streeter
25 Years of Food, Fun & Friendship
Clifton Community Woman's Club
Clifton, Virginia

Natural Gravy

When you cook in a slow cooker, you don't lose much liquid. The lid keeps moisture intact, providing a juicy addition to the meat. This recipe adds a little cornstarch to thicken the juices, which creates a rich brown gravy to accompany the steak and pepper strips.

Beef Stroganoff   WEEKNIGHT FAVORITE

This rich, buttery stroganoff is a surefire family favorite.

2   pounds round steak
¼   cup all-purpose flour
⅓   cup butter or margarine
1½   teaspoons salt
⅛   teaspoon pepper
½   cup water
1   (10¾-ounce) can cream of mushroom soup
⅔   cup sour cream
⅓   cup milk
Hot cooked egg noodles
Garnish: chopped fresh parsley

CUT steak into 2- x ½-inch strips. Coat steak with flour; brown meat in batches in butter in a large skillet, stirring occasionally. Add salt, pepper, and water. Cover and simmer 45 minutes or until almost tender, stirring occasionally. Stir soup into skillet, and simmer, uncovered, 30 minutes or until meat is tender. Stir in sour cream and milk; cook until thoroughly heated. Serve over noodles. Garnish, if desired. Yield: 6 servings.

Betty Pawlowski
Our Saviors Lutheran Church 75th Anniversary Cookbook
Our Saviors Lutheran Church
Casper, Wyoming

Stroganoff Success

A good stroganoff can make a cook's reputation. What makes this recipe so luscious is the portion of butter that cooks with the meat.

*Grillades and Baked
Cheese Grits*

Grillades and Baked Cheese Grits

The traditional version of this Creole classic pairs the savory beef mixture with plain cooked grits. These cheesy grits ensure that this rendition becomes a classic in its own right.

4½ pounds round steak (½ inch thick)
2 teaspoons salt
2 teaspoons pepper
⅔ cup vegetable oil, divided
⅔ cup all-purpose flour
2 cups chopped onion
1½ cups chopped green bell pepper
½ cup chopped green onions
½ cup chopped celery

½ cup chopped fresh parsley
4 garlic cloves, minced
2 cups water
1 teaspoon dried thyme
2 (14.5-ounce) cans stewed tomatoes, undrained
3 bay leaves
Garnish: fresh parsley sprigs
Baked Cheese Grits

POUND steak to ¼-inch thickness, using a meat mallet or rolling pin. Cut steak into 12 serving-size pieces.

COMBINE salt and pepper; sprinkle evenly over both sides of beef. Cook beef, a few pieces at a time, in ⅓ cup hot oil in a large Dutch oven over medium-high heat until browned on both sides. Remove beef from Dutch oven, and set aside.

ADD remaining ⅓ cup oil to drippings in Dutch oven; gradually stir in flour. Cook over medium heat 5 minutes, stirring constantly. Stir in 2 cups onion and next 5 ingredients; cook over medium-high heat, stirring constantly, 7 minutes or until vegetables are tender.

STIR in water and next 3 ingredients. Add beef; bring to a boil. Cover, reduce heat, and simmer 1½ hours or until beef is tender, stirring and scraping bottom of Dutch oven often.

DISCARD bay leaves. Transfer beef mixture to a serving platter; garnish, if desired. Serve with Baked Cheese Grits. Yield: 12 servings.

Baked Cheese Grits

5 cups water
1 teaspoon salt
⅔ cup uncooked quick-cooking yellow grits
⅔ cup uncooked quick-cooking white grits

2 cups (8 ounces) shredded sharp Cheddar cheese
¼ cup butter or margarine
1 (15.5-ounce) can yellow hominy, drained (optional)
½ cup grated Parmesan cheese

BRING water and salt to a boil in a large saucepan; gradually stir in grits. Cover, reduce heat, and simmer 5 minutes, stirring occasionally. Add Cheddar cheese, butter, and, if desired, hominy, stirring until cheese and butter melt.

POUR mixture into a lightly greased 13- x 9-inch baking dish; sprinkle evenly with Parmesan cheese. Bake, uncovered, at 350° for 45 minutes or until set. Yield: 12 servings.

With Love from the Shepherd's Center of North Little Rock
Shepherd's Center of North Little Rock, Arkansas

Grillades Defined

Grillades and Grits is a New Orleans brunch dish. It's tender pieces of round steak swimming in a rich-brown tomato gravy. Creamy grits are typically puddled under this entrée to catch all the flavor. These baked grits are dolled up with an abundance of cheese, hominy, and 2 colors of grits. You can use all of 1 color of grits, and the recipe will turn out just fine.

Salisbury Steak ONE PAN   QUICK & EASY

Shortcut to Gravy

A can of mushroom soup provides a creamy substitution for the old-fashioned gravy that usually accompanies this chopped steak.

Serve these savory patties with plenty of mashed potatoes or hot cooked rice to soak up every bit of the mushroom gravy. These patties are comfort food at its best.

1 (10¾-ounce) can beefy mushroom soup, divided
1½ pounds ground chuck
1 large egg, beaten
½ cup fine, dry breadcrumbs (store-bought)

¼ cup finely chopped onion
⅛ teaspoon pepper
¼ cup water

COMBINE ¼ cup soup, ground chuck, and next 4 ingredients, mixing well. Divide meat mixture evenly into 6 portions. Shape each portion into a ½-inch-thick patty.

COOK patties in a large nonstick skillet over medium-high heat 3 to 4 minutes on each side or until browned.

COMBINE remaining soup and water, stirring well. Pour soup mixture over patties; cover, reduce heat, and simmer 20 minutes. Serve immediately. Yield: 6 servings.

Stepping Back to Old Butler
Butler Ruritan Club
Butler, Tennessee

Horseradish Meat Loaf WEEKNIGHT FAVORITE

Meat Loaf with Kick

You'll be amazed by how much pizzazz meat loaf gains with the addition of horse-radish. Try a leftover slice of this loaf on a sandwich.

Horseradish in the meat mixture and the saucy topping creates a pleasantly pungent flavor throughout this meat loaf.

2 pounds ground beef
¾ cup uncooked regular oats
1 large onion, chopped
½ cup ketchup
¼ cup milk
2 large eggs, lightly beaten
1 tablespoon prepared horseradish

1½ teaspoons salt
½ teaspoon pepper
½ cup ketchup
3 tablespoons brown sugar
1 tablespoon prepared horseradish
2 teaspoons spicy brown mustard

COMBINE first 9 ingredients in a large bowl; stir well. Form beef mixture into a loaf, and place in a 9- x 5-inch loafpan.

COMBINE ½ cup ketchup, brown sugar, 1 tablespoon horseradish, and mustard in a small bowl, stirring well. Spoon half of ketchup mixture over top of meat loaf. Bake, uncovered, at 375° for 1 hour and 15 minutes. Spoon remaining ketchup mixture over meat loaf, and bake 10 more minutes. Remove to a serving platter. Yield: 8 servings.

Maxine Johnston Scholtz
Pride of Gaithersburg
Gaithersburg Lioness Club
Gaithersburg, Maryland

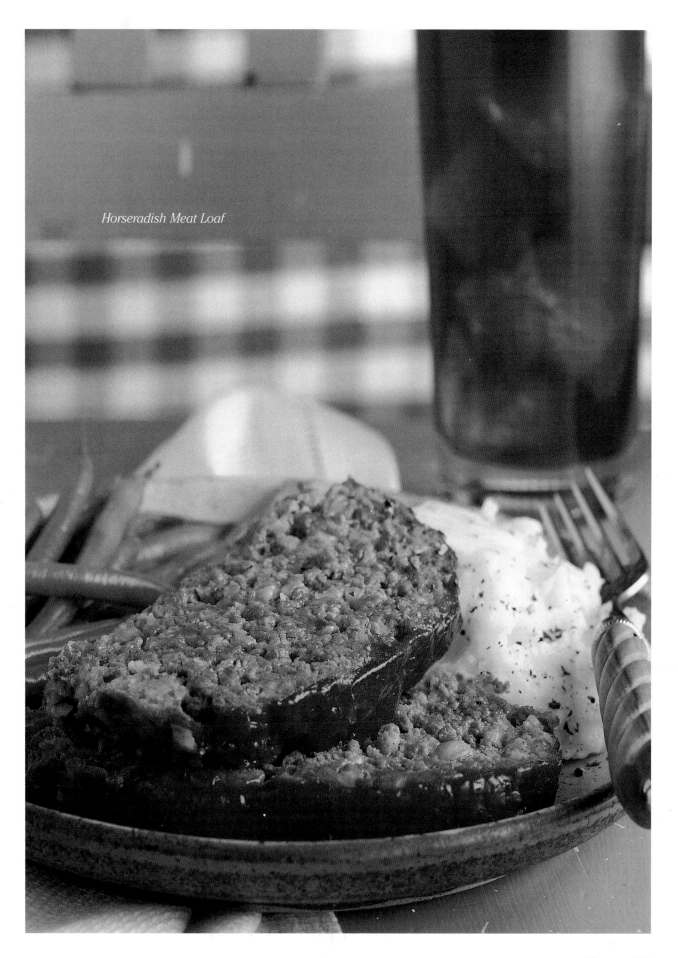

Horseradish Meat Loaf

Hot Tamales

Try Tamales

Savory tamales are quite popular in the United States. They're a Mexican dish of chopped meat or vegetable fillings covered in masa (cornmeal) dough and wrapped in dried corn husks to steam. When ready to eat, the husk is peeled away, not eaten.

Find dry corn husks in the produce section of most supermarkets.

½ (8-ounce) package corn husks or about 9 whole dried corn husks (we tested with Don Enrique)
¾ cup yellow cornmeal
½ cup plus 1 tablespoon chili powder
3 tablespoons onion powder
1 tablespoon plus 1 teaspoon salt
1 tablespoon garlic powder
2 tablespoons ground cumin
1 tablespoon ground red pepper
1 teaspoon black pepper
3 pounds ground beef
1 (8-ounce) can tomato sauce
¾ cup water
1 large egg
Tamale Sauce

PLACE whole corn husks in a large bowl (each husk should contain several layers); cover with hot water. Let stand 1 to 2 hours or until softened. Remove any silks; wash husks well. Drain well; pat dry.

COMBINE cornmeal and next 11 ingredients; stir well. Roll meat mixture into 24 (4-inch-long) logs. Separate layers of corn husks. Place 1 log in center of 1 layer of corn husk; wrap husk tightly around meat. Twist ends of husks; tie securely with narrow strips of softened corn husk or pieces of string. Cut off long ends of husks, if necessary. (You may not need all of the corn husk layers.)

LAYER tamales in a large Dutch oven. Pour Tamale Sauce over tamales; bring to a boil. Reduce heat; simmer, uncovered, 1½ hours, rearranging tamales every 30 minutes. Yield: 8 to 12 servings.

Tamale Sauce

1 (6-ounce) can tomato paste
¼ cup chili powder
2 tablespoons onion powder
1 tablespoon salt
1 tablespoon ground cumin
2 teaspoons garlic powder
9 cups water

COMBINE all ingredients in a large bowl, stirring until smooth. Yield: 9¼ cups.

Daniel Rigamer
Cooking from the Heart
Girl Scout Troop 669
Metairie, Louisiana

Philly Burgers GRILL LOVERS

Crispy French-fried onions cook inside these burgers and crown a cheese and mushroom mixture slathered on top after grilling. Sandwich the bounty in kaiser rolls for burgers your family won't soon forget.

1 pound ground chuck
2 tablespoons Worcestershire sauce, divided
4 teaspoons prepared mustard, divided
1 (2.8-ounce) can French fried onions, divided

1 (3-ounce) package cream cheese, softened
1 (2.5-ounce) jar sliced mushrooms, drained
1 teaspoon dried parsley flakes
4 kaiser rolls

COMBINE ground chuck, 1 tablespoon Worcestershire sauce, 3 teaspoons mustard, and half of onions. Shape mixture into 4 patties. Grill, without grill lid, over medium heat (300° to 350°) about 15 minutes or until a meat thermometer inserted into thickest part of 1 patty registers 160°, turning once.

MEANWHILE, combine cream cheese, remaining 1 tablespoon Worcestershire sauce, remaining 1 teaspoon mustard, mushrooms, and parsley. Spread mixture on cooked patties. Top with remaining half of onions. Broil 3 inches from heat 1 minute. Serve on rolls. Yield: 4 servings.

Karen Pett
Taste Buds—A Collection of Treasured Recipes
Alliance of the Illinois State Dental Society
Springfield, Illinois

Philly Food
This burger is smothered in the same good stuff as in Philly cheese steaks: melted cheese and mushrooms.

Grilled Lemon-Herb Veal Chops

GRILL LOVERS   QUICK & EASY

For a change in chops, marinate veal instead of pork in this herb-seasoned oil. Then quickly grill chops along with a few slices of tomato.

3 tablespoons fresh lemon juice
3 tablespoons olive oil
3 garlic cloves, quartered
2 teaspoons dried oregano

1 teaspoon freshly ground pepper
4 (1-inch-thick) veal loin chops
4 (¼-inch) slices firm ripe tomato

PROCESS first 5 ingredients in a food processor until well blended. Reserve 1 tablespoon marinade. Coat both sides of chops with marinade, and place in a shallow dish. Cover and marinate in refrigerator 2 hours.

SPREAD reserved marinade over 1 side of each tomato slice.

GRILL chops, uncovered, over medium-high heat (350° to 400°) 12 to 14 minutes, turning once. Cover and grill 10 to 12 minutes, turning once. Place tomato slices on grill during last 6 minutes of grilling time, turning once. Yield: 4 servings.

Beneath the Palms
The Brownsville Junior Service League
Brownsville, Texas

Virtuous Veal
When choosing veal, let the color of the meat be your guide. Look for meat that's creamy white. Veal that's pink turning to red means it's older than it should be. Veal's texture should be firm and smooth.

Veal Sentino

At first glance you'd think this was Veal Oscar with its slender veal cutlets and tender asparagus tucked under a blanket of Swiss cheese. But buttery mushrooms take the sensible place of pricey crabmeat for an entrée prepared to sensory satisfaction.

8 fresh asparagus spears
4 veal cutlets (about 12 ounces)
½ teaspoon salt
⅛ teaspoon pepper
¼ cup all-purpose flour
¼ cup plus 3 tablespoons butter or
    margarine, melted and divided

2 cups sliced fresh mushrooms
4 (1-ounce) slices Swiss cheese
2 tablespoons fresh lemon juice
Hot buttered noodles

SNAP off tough ends of asparagus. Cook asparagus in a small amount of boiling water 4 minutes or until crisp-tender. Drain and set aside.

PLACE veal between 2 sheets of heavy-duty plastic wrap, and flatten to ¼-inch thickness, using a meat mallet or rolling pin. Sprinkle cutlets with salt and pepper; dredge veal in flour. Cook veal in 2 tablespoons melted butter in a large skillet over medium-high heat until browned on both sides. Remove from skillet, and place in a 13- x 9-inch pan; set aside. Cook mushrooms in remaining ¼ cup plus 1 tablespoon butter in skillet, stirring constantly, until tender. Top veal with sautéed mushrooms, reserving pan drippings. Arrange asparagus spears over mushrooms, and top with Swiss cheese slices.

BROIL 5½ inches from heat 2 minutes or until Swiss cheese melts. Transfer to a serving platter. Mix lemon juice with reserved drippings in skillet; pour over veal. Serve with noodles. Yield: 4 servings.

Martha Durr Lemon
Homecoming: Special Foods, Special Memories
Baylor University Alumni Association
Waco, Texas

Grilled Lamb Chops   GRILL LOVERS   QUICK & EASY

Here's a simple supper for two. Since your grill will be hot, throw on some veggies to accompany the lamb.

¼ cup butter or margarine, softened
1½ tablespoons lemon juice
1 teaspoon paprika
1 teaspoon minced green onion
½ teaspoon minced garlic
¼ teaspoon salt
⅛ teaspoon pepper
4 (4-ounce) lamb chops

COMBINE first 7 ingredients in a small bowl; rub butter mixture on both sides of lamb chops. Grill, covered with grill lid, over medium heat (300° to 350°) 5 minutes on each side or to desired degree of doneness. Yield: 2 servings.

Stacey E. Pickering
Saints Alive!
The Ladies' Guild of St. Barnabas Anglican Church
Atlanta, Georgia

Lamb Lesson
Most cuts of lamb are tender enough to be cooked by dry heat methods, such as these chops that sizzle quickly on the grill.

Honey Mustard-Pecan Roasted Lamb

When company's coming, this rack of lamb is sure to impress. A pecan-breadcrumb mixture encrusts the elegant entrée, while Dijon mustard, molasses, garlic, and rosemary flatter the tender meat.

2 (1¼-pound) racks of lamb (8 chops each)
2 tablespoons olive oil
¼ cup Dijon mustard
1 tablespoon honey
1 tablespoon molasses
2 small garlic cloves, minced
½ cup pecan halves, toasted
3 tablespoons soft breadcrumbs (homemade)
1 teaspoon fresh rosemary

TRIM exterior fat on lamb racks to ¼ inch; brown lamb racks, 1 rack at a time, in olive oil in a large skillet over medium-high heat. Place lamb racks, fat side up, on a rack in a roasting pan.

COMBINE mustard and next 3 ingredients in a small bowl, stirring well. Brush mustard mixture over both sides of lamb racks.

PROCESS pecans, breadcrumbs, and rosemary in a food processor until pecans are finely chopped. Sprinkle lamb racks with pecan mixture.

INSERT a meat thermometer into thickest portion of 1 rack, making sure it does not touch fat or bone. Bake, uncovered, at 375° for 30 minutes or until thermometer registers 150° (medium rare) or 160° (medium). Let stand 10 minutes before slicing. Yield: 8 servings.

Sweet Home Alabama
The Junior League of Huntsville, Alabama

Plating the Food
Put on your chef's hat and get creative with presentation. Spoon your vegetable in the center of the plate, then lean 2 chops across each other over the veggies.

Charcoaled Bourbon-Marinated Lamb

Spreading out the Flavor

Cutting this leg of lamb into steaks gives you more meat and surface area to absorb the bourbon marinade flavor.

Guys will love grilling these large lamb steaks, pumped full of a robust marinade rich with bourbon and garlic flavor. Mashed potatoes make a winning side dish.

1 (8-pound) leg of lamb, cut into
  ½-inch-thick steaks
1½ cups bourbon
¾ cup olive oil
¾ cup soy sauce
3 large onions, thinly sliced
3 large garlic cloves, minced
Garnishes: chutney, Dijon mustard,
  sliced green onions

PLACE steaks in 2 large heavy-duty zip-top plastic bags. Combine bourbon and next 4 ingredients. Pour over steaks. Seal bags; marinate in refrigerator 8 to 24 hours, turning occasionally.

REMOVE steaks from marinade, discarding marinade. Grill steaks, in batches, covered with grill lid, over medium-high heat (350° to 400°) 7 minutes on each side or until steaks are done. Garnish, if desired. Yield: 16 servings.

Martha Kipcak
Flavors of Fredericksburg
St. Barnabas Episcopal Church
Fredericksburg, Texas

Grilled Butterflied Leg of Lamb with Mint Pesto   GRILL LOVERS

Vivid green pesto brightly contrasts with the subtle pink of the lamb in this company entrée. A surprise hint of mint in the pesto beautifully complements the richness of the meat.

1 (8-pound) leg of lamb, boned and
    butterflied
1 cup olive oil
¼ cup loosely packed fresh basil
    leaves
3 tablespoons chopped fresh mint
2 tablespoons chopped fresh
    rosemary

5 garlic cloves, chopped
1 (750-milliliter) bottle dry red wine
½ teaspoon salt
¼ teaspoon pepper
Mint Pesto

TRIM fat from lamb. Place lamb in a large heavy-duty zip-top plastic bag. Combine oil and next 5 ingredients in a blender; process until smooth, stopping to scrape down sides. Pour oil mixture over lamb; seal bag, and turn until lamb is well coated. Marinate in refrigerator 8 hours, turning bag occasionally.

REMOVE lamb from marinade, discarding marinade. Sprinkle lamb with salt and pepper. Grill lamb, without grill lid, over medium-high heat (350° to 400°) 50 minutes or until a meat thermometer inserted in thickest portion of lamb registers 150° (medium rare) or to desired degree of doneness, turning once. Let lamb stand 15 minutes. Slice diagonally across the grain into thin slices. Serve with Mint Pesto. Yield: 10 to 12 servings.

Mint Pesto

2½ cups loosely packed fresh mint
    leaves
1 cup loosely packed fresh basil
    leaves
1 cup chopped walnuts

½ cup loosely packed Italian parsley
8 garlic cloves, cut in half
1 cup olive oil
½ teaspoon salt
¼ teaspoon pepper

PROCESS first 5 ingredients in a food processor until finely chopped, stopping to scrape down sides.

WITH processor running, pour oil in a thin, steady stream through food chute, processing just until smooth. Stir in salt and pepper. Cover and chill. Yield: about 2 cups.

NOTE: You can store Mint Pesto in an airtight container in the refrigerator up to 2 days.

Loving Spoonfuls
Covenant House of Texas
Houston, Texas

Roasting Option
Grilled leg of lamb is awfully good, but if you'd rather bake it, here's how: Place lamb in a greased roasting pan and bake at 325° for 2½ hours or until a meat thermometer registers 160° (medium).

Rio Grande Pork Loin GRILL LOVERS

Flavor Boost
Add a little extra subtle flavor to this smoked entrée by substituting a flavorful liquid such as apple cider or beer instead of water to fill the water pan.

Hickory flavor permeates this pork loin which is slowly smoked and basted with a tangy sauce of chili powder and apple jelly.

Hickory or mesquite chunks
1 teaspoon chili powder, divided
½ cup apple jelly
½ cup ketchup
1 tablespoon white vinegar

½ teaspoon salt
½ teaspoon garlic salt
1 (4-pound) rolled boneless pork loin
    roast

SOAK hickory or mesquite chunks in water at least 1 hour. Prepare charcoal fire in smoker, and let burn 15 to 20 minutes. Drain chunks, and place on coals. Place water pan in smoker, and add water to depth of fill line.

COMBINE ½ teaspoon chili powder and next 3 ingredients in a small saucepan. Bring to a boil; reduce heat to medium, and cook, stirring constantly, 2 minutes. Reserve ¼ cup sauce for basting and ¾ cup sauce to serve with pork loin.

COMBINE remaining ½ teaspoon chili powder, salt, and garlic salt; mix well. Rub roast with seasoning mix; brush roast with reserved basting sauce.

COAT food rack with cooking spray, and place over coals. Place roast on rack; cover with smoker lid, and cook 5 hours or until a meat thermometer inserted in thickest part of roast registers 160° (medium), refilling water pan and adding charcoal as needed. Baste twice while cooking.

REMOVE roast from food rack. Let stand 10 minutes before slicing. Serve with reserved ¾ cup sauce. Yield: 10 to 12 servings.

Beneath the Palms
The Brownsville Junior Service League
Brownsville, Texas

Ric and Mickey's Jerk Pork GRILL LOVERS

A make-your-own seasoning mix turns pork tenderloin into a spice explosion. Simply double the seasoning mix to grill a package of 2 (1-pound) tenderloins. (They often come prepackaged.)

¼ cup lime juice
¼ cup soy sauce
1 teaspoon dried oregano

½ teaspoon dried thyme
1 (1-pound) pork tenderloin
Seasoning Mix

Spicy Seasoning

It's the special Jamaican Seasoning Mix that makes this grilled tenderloin so awesome. See page 67 for the whole story on jerk seasoning.

COMBINE first 4 ingredients in a large heavy-duty zip-top plastic bag; add pork. Seal bag securely, and turn to coat pork. Marinate in refrigerator at least 4 hours.

REMOVE pork from marinade, reserving marinade. Sprinkle pork with 2 tablespoons Seasoning Mix. Coat grill rack with cooking spray; place on grill over medium-high heat (350° to 400°). Place pork on rack; grill, covered with grill lid, 25 to 30 minutes or until a meat thermometer inserted in thickest portion of tenderloin registers 160°, turning once.

PLACE reserved marinade in a small saucepan; bring to a boil. Slice pork, and serve with marinade. Yield: 4 servings.

Seasoning Mix

1 tablespoon dried minced onion
1 tablespoon onion powder
2 teaspoons salt
2 teaspoons sugar
2 teaspoons dried chives
2 teaspoons ground thyme

1 teaspoon ground allspice
1 teaspoon coarsely ground black pepper
1 teaspoon ground red pepper
¼ teaspoon ground nutmeg
¼ teaspoon ground cinnamon

COMBINE all ingredients in a bowl; stir well. Yield: ⅓ cup.

Project Open Hand Cookbook
Project Open Hand Atlanta
Atlanta, Georgia

Pork Tenderloin with Maple Mustard Sauce

Serving Idea

Slice this tenderloin thinly and serve it with mayonnaise on cocktail buns for a tailgate party.

This pork tenderloin picks up lots of flavor from an array of spices and a maple-Dijon glaze.

⅓ cup maple syrup
2 tablespoons Dijon mustard
½ teaspoon nutmeg
½ teaspoon dried thyme, crushed
¼ teaspoon dried basil, crushed
¼ teaspoon ground red pepper
¼ teaspoon ground cloves
¼ teaspoon ground cinnamon
¼ teaspoon black pepper
⅛ teaspoon ground allspice
1 (12- to 16-ounce) pork tenderloin
3 bay leaves
Olive oil-flavored cooking spray

COMBINE maple syrup and mustard in a small bowl; stir with a wire whisk until blended. Set Maple Mustard Sauce aside.

COMBINE nutmeg and next 7 ingredients in a bowl; stir well. Rub mixture over tenderloin. Place tenderloin on a large sheet of heavy-duty plastic wrap. Place bay leaves along bottom of tenderloin. Wrap tenderloin in plastic wrap; marinate in refrigerator at least 2 hours.

REMOVE tenderloin from plastic wrap, and place tenderloin on a rack in a shallow roasting pan. Coat tenderloin with cooking spray. Bake at 425° for 25 to 35 minutes or until a meat thermometer inserted in thickest part of tenderloin registers 160°. Discard bay leaves. Place tenderloin on a serving platter; slice diagonally across the grain. Serve with reserved Maple Mustard Sauce. Yield: 3 to 4 servings.

A Taste of the Good Life from the Heart of Tennessee
Saint Thomas Heart Institute
Nashville, Tennessee

Bourbon-Basted Pork Chops   GRILL LOVERS

Quick Cookin' Pork

Keep in mind that today's lean pork cooks fairly quickly. And overcooking can rob meat of its juiciness and tenderness. Be sure to monitor the grill temperature closely and don't stray too far while the meat's cooking.

These thick chops take on a pronounced lemon tang from the simmered sauce that's brushed on them before grilling.

1 lemon
½ cup soy sauce
3 tablespoons butter or margarine
2 tablespoons bourbon
1 tablespoon minced onion
¼ teaspoon hot sauce
⅛ teaspoon salt
⅛ teaspoon pepper
4 (1-inch-thick) rib pork chops, trimmed

CUT lemon in half. Squeeze juice from both halves into a small saucepan; add lemon halves. Add soy sauce and next 6 ingredients, stirring to combine. Bring to a boil, reduce heat, and simmer 5 minutes. Reserve half of sauce.

BRUSH sauce evenly over both sides of pork chops. Grill, covered with grill lid, over medium-high heat (350° to 400°) 8 minutes on each side or until done, basting often with sauce. Serve chops with reserved sauce. Yield: 4 servings.

Virginia Fare
The Junior League of Richmond, Virginia

Grilled Sausages with Chunky Tomato Sauce GRILL LOVERS

Choose your favorite sausage for this sloppy grilled supper idea. Spoon the meat and tomato mixture onto buns, if you'd like.

1 large onion
3 large garlic cloves, chopped
3 tablespoons olive oil
1½ tablespoons fresh rosemary, chopped
¼ teaspoon dried crushed red pepper
2 (28-ounce) cans Italian-style tomatoes, drained and chopped
1 (8-ounce) package sliced fresh mushrooms
2 tablespoons tomato paste
¼ teaspoon salt
¼ teaspoon pepper
3 pounds assorted fresh sausages (Italian, Polish, or bratwurst)

COOK onion and garlic in hot oil in a large saucepan over medium-high heat, stirring constantly, 7 minutes or until tender. Add rosemary and red pepper; cook 1 minute, stirring constantly. Stir in tomatoes and next 4 ingredients; bring to a boil. Reduce heat, and simmer, uncovered, 20 minutes, stirring occasionally.

GRILL sausages, covered with grill lid, over medium-high heat (350° to 400°) 6 minutes on each side or until done. Serve with tomato mixture. Yield: 6 servings.

Jo Atwood
A Century of Cooking
Eden Chapel United Methodist Church
Perkins, Oklahoma

Sausage Selection

Just about any fat sausage links would be fine in this recipe. Some choices include sweet mild or hot Italian sausage, kielbasa, or bratwurst.

Adams' Ribs

Adams' Ribs GRILL LOVERS

These dark, succulent ribs have a spicy bite to them. The more basting sauce you use on the ribs during cooking, the more flavorful they'll be.

1 tablespoon garlic powder
1 tablespoon Creole seasoning
2 tablespoons pepper
1 tablespoon Worcestershire sauce

2 (3- to 4-pound) slabs pork spareribs
Basting Sauce
Serving Sauce

COMBINE first 4 ingredients; rub on all sides of ribs.

PREPARE a hot fire by piling charcoal on 1 side of grill, leaving other side empty. (For gas grills, light only 1 side.) Coat food rack with cooking spray, and place on grill. Arrange food over unlit side. Grill, covered with grill lid, over medium-low heat (275° to 325°) 2 to 3 hours, turning and basting with Basting Sauce every hour. The longer ribs cook, the more tender they will be.

GRILL, covered with grill lid, over medium-high heat (350° to 400°) 1 more hour, basting every 10 minutes. Serve with Serving Sauce. Yield: 8 to 10 servings.

Basting Sauce

3 cups red wine vinegar
1 cup dry white wine
1 cup water
¾ cup ketchup
¼ cup Worcestershire sauce
¼ cup firmly packed light brown sugar

¼ cup prepared mustard
2 tablespoons black pepper
1 to 2 tablespoons ground red pepper or dried crushed red pepper

COMBINE all ingredients in a saucepan; bring to a boil. Reduce heat to medium, and simmer, uncovered, 1 hour. Yield: about 4½ cups.

Serving Sauce

1 medium onion, finely chopped
1½ teaspoons minced garlic (about 4 cloves)
1 tablespoon butter or margarine, melted
1 cup ketchup
½ cup white vinegar

¼ cup lemon juice
¼ cup steak seasoning (we tested with Dale's)
2 tablespoons brown sugar
1 tablespoon Cajun seasoning
2 tablespoons liquid smoke

COOK onion and garlic in melted butter in a large skillet over medium heat, stirring constantly, 5 minutes or until tender. Add ketchup and remaining ingredients; bring to a boil. Reduce heat, and simmer, uncovered, 15 minutes. Yield: 2 cups.

Oscar W. Adams
Southern Settings
Decatur General Foundation, Inc.
Decatur, Alabama

Triple-Good Ribs

These ribs take some effort, but, boy, are they worth it! The secret to their flavor is the 2 sauces—a basting sauce for the grill and a serving sauce spiked with brown sugar and Cajun seasoning. It all comes together in a delicious finger-licking-good mess. Pass out bibs and towels for this one.

Chicken Pie WEEKNIGHT FAVORITE

Pastry Shortcut
This pot pie has a homemade flaky pastry crust that you can make ahead and keep wrapped in the refrigerator. Or use a refrigerated piecrust as a shortcut.

Here's comforting, old-fashioned flavor at its best. This thick, rich one-dish meal is loaded with tender chunks of chicken, potato, carrot, celery, and onion.

1 (2½- to 3-pound) broiler-fryer
1 medium onion, quartered
1 celery rib, cut into 1-inch pieces
1 bay leaf
1 teaspoon salt
1 teaspoon dried thyme
1 teaspoon dried rosemary
1 teaspoon dried basil
1 cup peeled, chopped potato
⅓ cup butter or margarine
1 cup chopped celery
1 cup chopped onion
1 cup chopped carrot

½ cup all-purpose flour
1½ cups half-and-half
¾ teaspoon salt
¼ teaspoon pepper
3 cups all-purpose flour
1 teaspoon salt
1 cup shortening, chilled
1 large egg, lightly beaten
1 tablespoon white vinegar
¼ cup plus 2 tablespoons water
1 large egg, lightly beaten
1 tablespoon milk

COMBINE first 8 ingredients in a large Dutch oven; add water to cover. Bring to a boil; cover, reduce heat, and simmer 1 hour. Remove chicken from broth, reserving broth; cool chicken. Bone chicken, and coarsely chop meat. Set aside. Strain broth, reserving 1½ cups.

COOK potato in butter in a large skillet over medium-high heat 5 minutes, stirring constantly. Add celery, onion, and carrot; cook 5 more minutes, stirring constantly. Add ½ cup flour, stirring well; cook 1 minute, stirring constantly. Gradually add reserved 1½ cups broth and half-and-half; cook over medium heat, stirring constantly, until mixture is thickened and bubbly. Stir in ¾ teaspoon salt, pepper, and reserved chicken. Set aside.

COMBINE 3 cups flour and 1 teaspoon salt; cut in shortening with a pastry blender until mixture is crumbly. Combine egg, vinegar, and water; sprinkle evenly over surface. Stir with a fork until dry ingredients are moistened. Shape into a ball.

ROLL two-thirds of pastry to ⅛-inch thickness on a floured surface. Fit pastry into a 2½-quart casserole. Spoon chicken mixture into prepared pastry. Roll remaining pastry to ⅛-inch thickness; cut into ¾-inch strips. Arrange strips in a lattice design over chicken mixture. Seal pastry edges. Combine remaining egg and milk; brush over pastry. Bake at 400° for 30 to 35 minutes or until golden and chicken mixture is hot and bubbly. Yield: 6 servings.

Catherine Hicks
The Heritage Cookbook
St. George's Episcopal Church
Fredericksburg, Virginia

Chicken Pie

Southwestern Roast Chicken

This chicken is seasoned with 3 ingredients often found in southwestern cooking—chili powder, jalapeño pepper, and sage.

½ cup peanut oil
3 tablespoons chili powder
½ teaspoon jalapeño pepper, chopped
2 garlic cloves
2 (3½-pound) whole chickens
½ cup dried sage, divided

2 garlic cloves, halved and divided
2 teaspoons red wine vinegar
1 teaspoon chopped purple onion
1 teaspoon prepared mustard
¼ teaspoon salt
¼ teaspoon pepper

PROCESS first 4 ingredients in a blender until smooth, stopping to scrape down sides.

REMOVE giblets, and rinse chickens with cold water; pat dry. Place ¼ cup sage and 1 halved garlic clove in cavity of each chicken. Tie ends of legs together with string. Lift wingtips up and over back, and tuck under bird. Place chickens on a lightly greased rack in a shallow roasting pan, breast side up. Insert meat thermometer into meaty portion of thigh of 1 chicken, making sure it does not touch bone.

BRUSH chickens with oil mixture. Bake, uncovered, at 500° for 10 minutes. Reduce oven temperature to 350°, and bake 55 more minutes or until meat thermometer registers 180°. Remove sage and garlic from chicken cavities; set sage mixture aside. Transfer chickens to a serving platter; set aside, and keep warm. Skim fat from pan drippings; reserve pan drippings.

PROCESS reserved sage, garlic, vinegar, and next 4 ingredients in blender until smooth, stopping to scrape down sides. Add reserved pan drippings; process until smooth, stopping to scrape down sides. Serve chicken with sauce. Yield: 8 servings.

Tastes and Traditions: The Sam Houston Heritage Cookbook
The Study Club of Huntsville, Texas

Crunchy Pecan Chicken WEEKNIGHT FAVORITE

Buttermilk biscuit mix, Creole seasoning, and finely chopped pecans join forces to make a crispy and flavorful coating for these chicken breast halves.

1 cup biscuit mix
½ cup finely chopped pecans
1 teaspoon paprika
½ teaspoon salt
½ teaspoon Creole seasoning

4 skinned and boned chicken breast halves
½ cup buttermilk
½ cup unsalted butter or margarine, melted

COMBINE first 5 ingredients in a medium bowl; stir well. Dip chicken in buttermilk; dredge in pecan mixture. Place chicken in an ungreased 13- x 9-inch pan. Drizzle butter over chicken. Bake, uncovered, at 350° for 50 minutes or until chicken is done. Yield: 4 servings.

Come On In!
The Junior League of Jackson, Mississippi

Simple Chicken
This nutty chicken is simple to put together and send into the oven. In the end, it will look like you went to a lot of trouble for the delicious results.

Mexican Chicken Kiev MAKE AHEAD

Monterey Jack cheese and green chiles mingle discreetly inside crispy coated chicken breasts. When cut, the buttery essence of the cheese and chiles oozes onto your dinner plate. You can make this dish ahead for company or treat your family to an ethnic delight.

8 large skinned and boned chicken breast halves
1 (4.5-ounce) can chopped green chiles, drained
4 ounces Monterey Jack cheese, cut into 8 strips
½ cup fine, dry breadcrumbs (store-bought)

½ cup grated Parmesan cheese
1 tablespoon chili powder
½ teaspoon ground cumin
½ teaspoon salt
⅛ teaspoon pepper
¼ cup plus 2 tablespoons butter or margarine, melted
Salsa

PLACE chicken between 2 sheets of heavy-duty plastic wrap, and flatten to ¼-inch thickness, using a meat mallet or rolling pin. Place chiles and cheese evenly on top of chicken breasts. Roll up chicken, starting with short end; secure with wooden picks.

COMBINE breadcrumbs and next 5 ingredients. Dip chicken rolls in melted butter; dredge in breadcrumb mixture. Place in a lightly greased 13- x 9-inch baking dish. Cover and chill 8 hours.

BAKE at 400° for 30 minutes or until chicken is done; discard wooden picks. Serve chicken with salsa. Yield: 8 servings.

Entertaining in Kingwood
Kingwood Women's Club
Kingwood, Texas

Kiev Pointers
The first few steps of this recipe are key to keeping the cheesy filling intact. Be sure to flatten the chicken thin enough so that it's easy to stuff and roll up; then poke the wooden picks into the rolls to keep the filling intact.

Chicken Basque ONE DISH

Chock-full of zucchini, roasted red peppers, Italian sausage, and chicken, this Mediterranean-inspired dish is easily served as a one-dish meal.

2 pounds zucchini, cut into ¾-inch-thick slices
2 tablespoons olive oil
1½ teaspoons salt
1 teaspoon pepper
¾ pound mild or hot Italian link sausage
1 tablespoon butter or margarine, melted
1 medium onion, chopped
8 ounces small fresh mushrooms
1 garlic clove, minced
¼ cup olive oil
1½ pounds skinned and boned chicken breast halves, left intact or cut into 1-inch pieces
1 cup all-purpose flour
1 cup dry vermouth
1 (15-ounce) jar roasted red peppers, coarsely chopped
1 tablespoon chopped fresh parsley
1 bay leaf
½ teaspoon dried basil
½ teaspoon dried thyme

SAUTÉ zucchini in 2 tablespoons hot olive oil in a large skillet over high heat 3 minutes or until browned. Sprinkle with salt and pepper; stir well. Remove from skillet with a slotted spoon; set aside.

REDUCE heat to medium-high. Add sausage to skillet; cook 8 minutes or until browned and no longer pink. Drain, reserving 1 tablespoon drippings in skillet. Cut sausage into ¾-inch-thick slices; set aside.

ADD butter and next 3 ingredients to skillet; cook, stirring often, until onion is tender and mushroom liquid evaporates. Remove vegetables from skillet, using a slotted spoon.

HEAT ¼ cup olive oil in same skillet over medium-high heat. Dredge chicken in flour; cook chicken in hot oil 8 minutes or until done, turning once. Stir in vermouth, roasted red pepper, reserved sliced sausage, reserved vegetables, parsley, bay leaf, basil, and thyme; bring to a boil. Reduce heat, and simmer, uncovered, 5 minutes; discard bay leaf. Yield: 10 cups.

Gracious Gator Cooks
The Junior League of Gainesville, Florida

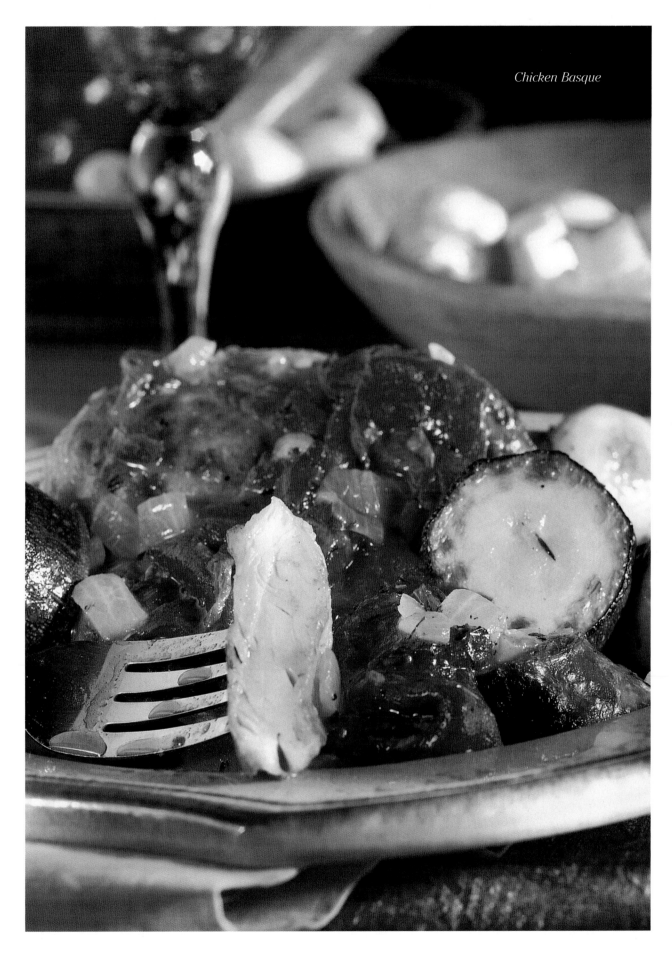

Chicken Basque

Grilled Chicken with Corn Salsa GRILL LOVERS

Make-Ahead Salsa

Make this colorful corn salsa up to a day ahead and store it in the refrigerator. If there's any salsa left, it's great for dipping chips.

Sprinkle these sizzling beer-lime-jalapeño-marinated chicken breasts with colorful corn salsa as they come off the grill.

4 skinned and boned chicken breast halves
½ cup light beer
1 tablespoon chopped fresh cilantro
1 tablespoon low-sodium soy sauce
2 teaspoons seeded, minced jalapeño pepper
2 teaspoons fresh lime juice
¼ teaspoon salt

¼ teaspoon pepper
1¼ cups frozen whole kernel corn, thawed
¼ cup chopped purple onion
¼ cup chopped sweet red pepper
¼ cup chopped fresh cilantro
1½ tablespoons fresh lime juice
2 teaspoons seeded, minced jalapeño pepper

PLACE chicken in a large heavy-duty zip-top plastic bag. Combine beer and next 6 ingredients; pour over chicken. Seal bag securely; turn to coat chicken. Marinate in refrigerator at least 1 hour, turning bag occasionally.

MEANWHILE, combine corn and remaining 5 ingredients; stir well. Cover and chill.

REMOVE chicken from marinade, discarding marinade. Grill chicken, covered with grill lid, over medium-high heat (350° to 400°) 5 minutes on each side or until done. Cut chicken diagonally into thin slices. Top evenly with corn salsa. Yield: 4 servings.

Women Who Can Dish It Out
The Junior League of Springfield, Missouri

Southwestern Grilled Chicken GRILL LOVERS

Spicy Cheese

If you want to turn up the heat in this dish, substitute Monterey Jack cheese with jalapeño peppers for the regular Monterey Jack cheese.

This chicken tastes subtly southwestern with its avocado, salsa, and lime garnish.

4 skinned and boned chicken breast halves
2 tablespoons cider vinegar
2 tablespoons olive oil
1 tablespoon Dijon mustard
¼ teaspoon onion salt
½ teaspoon coarsely ground pepper

½ teaspoon dried dillweed
½ teaspoon dried basil
1 ripe avocado, peeled and sliced
1 cup (4 ounces) shredded Monterey Jack cheese
Salsa
Lime slices (optional)

Place chicken in a large heavy-duty zip-top plastic bag; set aside. Combine vinegar and next 6 ingredients in a small bowl; stir well with a wire whisk. Pour marinade mixture over chicken. Seal bag securely, and marinate in refrigerator 30 minutes.

Remove chicken from marinade, discarding marinade. Grill, covered with grill lid, over medium-high heat (350° to 400°) 8 minutes on each side or until chicken is done. Place chicken on an ungreased baking sheet. Top chicken evenly with avocado slices and shredded cheese. Broil 5½ inches from heat 1 minute or until cheese melts. Serve chicken topped with salsa. Garnish with lime slices, if desired. Yield: 4 servings.

Food for Thought
The Junior League of Birmingham, Alabama

Deluxe Chicken Casserole

Deluxe Chicken Casserole

If this dish reminds you of similar casseroles you had growing up, then you'll enjoy it as much as we did. The chopped nuts are an added pleasure.

1½ cups diced cooked chicken
1½ cups cooked rice
1 cup chopped celery
½ cup chopped walnuts or pecans
1 (10¾-ounce) can cream of chicken
    soup, undiluted
2 teaspoons finely chopped onion
½ teaspoon salt

½ teaspoon black pepper
¼ teaspoon ground red pepper
1 tablespoon lemon juice
¾ cup mayonnaise
¼ cup water
3 hard-cooked eggs, sliced
2 cups coarsely crumbled potato
    chips

COMBINE first 10 ingredients in a large bowl. Combine mayonnaise and water; stir with a wire whisk until smooth. Add mayonnaise mixture to chicken mixture. Gently fold in egg slices.

SPOON mixture into a greased 11- x 7-inch baking dish; top with potato chips. Bake, uncovered, at 400° for 15 minutes or until bubbly. Yield: 6 servings.

Selina Lyman
'Pon Top Edisto
Trinity Episcopal Church
Edisto Island, South Carolina

Chip of Choice
We liked Ruffles potato chips on top of this casserole. The salty, crispy ridged chips add just the right finish to each bite, but other potato chips will work just as well.

Never-Fail Chicken and Dumplings

Dumpling Dos
The key to tender dumplings is to cook the dough strips in batches to be sure the water stays at a boil and cooks them evenly.

Nothing says comfort like a helping of homemade chicken and dumplings. Follow these directions for never-fail results every time.

1½ cups all-purpose flour
½ teaspoon salt
3 tablespoons shortening
1 large egg, lightly beaten
5 tablespoons cold water
3½ cups chicken broth or
    2 (14½-ounce) cans chicken broth

½ teaspoon freshly ground pepper
3 cups chopped cooked chicken or
    1 roasted chicken from the deli,
    meat pulled from the bone and
    shredded

COMBINE flour and salt; cut in shortening with a pastry blender until mixture is crumbly. Gently stir in egg and cold water; form dough into a ball, and knead 3 or 4 times.

COMBINE broth and pepper in a Dutch oven; bring to a boil over medium-high heat.

MEANWHILE, roll dough to ⅛-inch thickness on a lightly floured surface. Cut dough into 2- x ¾-inch strips; drop several dough strips at a time into boiling broth. Reduce heat to medium, and cook, uncovered, 7 minutes. Add chicken, and cook 4 to 6 minutes or until dumplings are tender and chicken is heated, stirring occasionally. Yield: 4 servings.

NOTE: To make your own broth, combine 3 bone-in chicken breast halves, 8 cups water, ¾ teaspoon salt, and ½ teaspoon freshly ground pepper in a Dutch oven. Bring to a boil; cover, reduce heat, and simmer 30 minutes or until chicken is tender. Remove chicken from broth, reserving broth in Dutch oven; cool chicken. Remove meat from bone, and shred. Prepare dumplings, and cook in homemade broth as directed above; do not add pepper from original recipe to homemade broth.

Sharon Hampton and Harold Mesimer
Blended Blessings
First Presbyterian Church
Salisbury, North Carolina

Crescent Chicken Squares

QUICK & EASY   WEEKNIGHT FAVORITE

Once you've made these chicken packets, you'll probably move them into your monthly weeknight repertoire. They're just that good.

1 (3-ounce) package cream cheese, softened
3 tablespoons butter or margarine, melted and divided
2 cups chopped cooked chicken
2 tablespoons milk

¼ teaspoon salt
⅛ teaspoon pepper
1 (8-ounce) can refrigerated crescent rolls
¾ cup seasoned croutons, crushed

COMBINE cream cheese and 2 tablespoons butter; stir in chicken and next 3 ingredients. Set aside.

UNROLL crescent dough, separating into 4 rectangles; press perforations to seal. Spoon one-fourth of chicken mixture into center of each rectangle; bring corners of each rectangle together over chicken mixture, and twist gently to seal.

BRUSH packets with remaining 1 tablespoon melted butter; dredge in crushed croutons, and place on an ungreased baking sheet. Bake, uncovered, at 350° for 20 to 25 minutes or until golden. Yield: 4 servings.

JoAnn Frazee
Premium Recipes That Really Rate
Insurance Women of Sussex County
Ocean View, Delaware

Go for the Gravy

Dress up these cheesy crescents with a drizzle of warm chicken gravy. It's easy when you use convenient canned heat-and-serve gravy.

Chicken Fajita Potatoes WEEKNIGHT FAVORITE

Quick Pick of the Chick

Pick up a deli roasted chicken on the way home, and shred the meat for this recipe. Taco seasoning makes the chicken taste spicy good on top of the potato.

This recipe turns a simple stuffed potato into a fantastic one-dish dinner. It's a mile-high meal once you pile on all the toppings—spicy chicken, cheese, olives, green chiles, sour cream, guacamole, and salsa.

4 large baking potatoes
1 medium-size red or green bell pepper, chopped
1 small onion, chopped
2 tablespoons butter or margarine, melted
1 tablespoon taco seasoning mix
1½ cups shredded cooked chicken breast (about 6 ounces)
½ cup (2 ounces) shredded Cheddar cheese

½ cup (2 ounces) shredded Monterey Jack cheese
1 (2¼-ounce) can sliced ripe olives, drained
2 tablespoons diced green chiles
1 cup salsa
Sour cream (optional)
Guacamole (optional)
Salsa (optional)

SCRUB potatoes; pat dry. Wrap in aluminum foil, and bake at 400° for 1 hour or until tender. Cook pepper and onion in butter in a medium saucepan until tender. Add taco seasoning mix. Cook 1 minute, stirring constantly; remove from heat. Stir in chicken, cheeses, olives, and chiles.

CUT a lengthwise slit in top of each potato. Press each potato open. Spoon chicken mixture into potatoes. Spoon ¼ cup salsa over each potato. If desired, serve with sour cream, guacamole, and additional salsa. Yield: 4 servings.

Debbie Yagoda
Doggone Good Cookin'
Support Dogs, Inc.
St. Louis, Missouri

238   Meats, Poultry & Seafood

Chicken Fajita Potatoes

Chicky Kowloon MAKE AHEAD

Put this Asian entrée on to simmer all day in the slow cooker, and when it comes time for supper, just cook some boil-in-bag rice to supplement.

3½ pounds chicken breast halves and thighs, skinned
½ teaspoon salt
¼ teaspoon pepper
1 cup chicken broth
1 garlic clove, minced
¼ teaspoon ground ginger
1 (8½-ounce) can sliced pineapple in heavy syrup, undrained
1 (4-ounce) can sliced water chestnuts, drained
4 green onions, diagonally sliced
¼ cup soy sauce
1 tablespoon white vinegar
¼ cup cornstarch
Chow mein noodles
Hot cooked rice

SPRINKLE chicken with salt and pepper; place in a 5-quart electric slow cooker.

COMBINE chicken broth, garlic, and ginger, stirring well. Drain pineapple, reserving syrup. Add syrup to broth mixture, stirring well; cut pineapple slices into fourths. Arrange pineapple and water chestnuts over chicken. Pour broth mixture over chicken. Cover and cook on HIGH setting 1 hour; reduce to LOW setting, and cook 6 to 7 hours.

ADD green onions to mixture in slow cooker. Combine soy sauce and vinegar; add cornstarch, stirring until smooth. Stir into broth mixture, gently moving chicken pieces. Cover and cook on HIGH setting 10 minutes or until slightly thickened. Serve with chow mein noodles over rice. Yield: 6 servings.

Pat Warner
Howey Cook
Howey-in-the-Hills Garden and Civic Club
Howey-in-the-Hills, Florida

Mexican Chicken with Orange, Cumin, and Olives

Soak up the extra sauce from this dish with a serving of hot cooked rice.

1 (14.5-ounce) can whole tomatoes, undrained
2 tablespoons cornstarch
2 tablespoons olive oil
12 skinned chicken thighs (about 4¾ pounds)
2 medium onions, halved lengthwise and thinly sliced
2 garlic cloves, minced
1 cup dry red wine
½ cup sliced ripe olives
¼ cup plus 2 tablespoons fresh orange juice
¼ cup golden raisins
2 bay leaves
1 tablespoon ground cumin
2 teaspoons grated orange rind
½ teaspoon salt
½ teaspoon ground cinnamon
¼ teaspoon ground red pepper
2 tablespoons chopped fresh parsley

CHOP and drain tomatoes, reserving tomato juice; set aside. Place ½ cup juice in a 1-cup liquid measure; add cornstarch, and stir until smooth. Set aside.

HEAT oil in a large skillet over medium-high heat; add chicken, in batches, and cook 6 minutes, turning once. Remove chicken, and set aside.

DRAIN skillet; reserving 2 tablespoons drippings in pan. Add onion and garlic to drippings; cook, stirring constantly, until onion is tender. Add wine; bring to a boil, scraping particles that cling to bottom. Add reserved tomato, remaining reserved tomato juice, olives, and next 8 ingredients; stir well. Return chicken to skillet; bring to a boil. Cover, reduce heat, and simmer 30 to 40 minutes or until chicken is done. Remove and discard bay leaves.

TRANSFER chicken to a large serving platter; set aside, and keep warm. Add reserved cornstarch mixture to mixture in skillet; cook over low heat, stirring constantly, until slightly thickened. Pour sauce over chicken. Sprinkle with parsley. Yield: 6 servings.

Praiseworthy
Foundation for Historic Christ Church
Irvington, Virginia

Try Thighs

Here's a great way to work chicken thighs into a menu. You can buy thighs already skinned. The dark meat has rich flavor and is nutrient dense.

Blackened Chicken Fettuccine

Blackened Chicken Fettuccine

Move over blackened redfish. The blackening technique has now been tried on all types of meat, and its effect on chicken is as good as it gets. Use a cast-iron skillet for best results.

1 tablespoon garlic powder
1 tablespoon onion powder
1 tablespoon dried thyme
1 tablespoon dried oregano
1 tablespoon paprika
1 tablespoon dried tarragon
1 tablespoon ground nutmeg
1 teaspoon salt
1 teaspoon ground red pepper
½ teaspoon black pepper
⅔ cup olive oil
½ cup Worcestershire sauce
5 skinned and boned chicken breast halves
¼ cup butter, melted
1 (12-ounce) package dried fettuccine

½ red bell pepper, cut into thin strips
½ yellow bell pepper, cut into thin strips
½ green bell pepper, cut into thin strips
2 celery ribs, sliced
1 medium onion, chopped
2 carrots, diagonally sliced
1 cup dry white wine
¾ cup whipping cream
3 medium tomatoes, chopped
2 tablespoons water
1 teaspoon cornstarch
Freshly shredded Parmesan cheese

COMBINE first 12 ingredients in a heavy-duty zip-top plastic bag; add chicken. Seal bag, and marinate in refrigerator 8 hours, turning bag occasionally.

REMOVE chicken from bag, discarding marinade. Cook chicken in melted butter in a large skillet over medium-high heat 5 minutes on each side or until well browned. Remove chicken from skillet, reserving drippings in skillet. Slice chicken diagonally, and set aside.

COOK pasta according to package directions; drain well. Set aside. Sauté peppers, celery, onion, and carrot in drippings in skillet 4 minutes or until vegetables are crisp-tender. Add wine, whipping cream, and tomato; simmer 5 minutes.

COMBINE water and cornstarch; stir well. Add to vegetable mixture in skillet. Bring to a boil; boil 1 minute or until thickened, stirring constantly. Remove from heat. Add chicken and pasta, tossing well; sprinkle with Parmesan cheese. Yield: 6 servings.

Linen Napkins to Paper Plates
The Junior Auxiliary of Clarksville, Tennessee

Tricolor Peppers

Red, yellow, and green bell peppers each bring a distinct flavor to this dish. Red and yellow peppers tend to be sweeter, while green peppers typically carry the best price. Peppers will stay fresh up to a week in the refrigerator.

Chicken Liver Sauté   QUICK & EASY

Liver Goodness
Chicken livers are an inexpensive source of protein, iron, and vitamin A.

Our Test Kitchens staff is hard to please when it comes to liver recipes, but this one was an easy sell. The livers are enhanced with mushrooms, garlic, white wine, and herbs for a fine finish over rice.

1 pound chicken livers
3 tablespoons butter, melted
1 (8-ounce) package sliced fresh mushrooms
1¼ cups chopped onion
1 garlic clove, minced
1 tablespoon all-purpose flour
½ cup dry white wine

1 (14½-ounce) can whole tomatoes, chopped and drained
¼ cup chopped fresh parsley
½ teaspoon dried thyme
¼ to ½ teaspoon fresh or dried rosemary
¼ teaspoon salt
Hot cooked rice

COOK livers in butter in a skillet over medium-high heat 7 to 9 minutes, stirring constantly. Remove livers, reserving drippings in skillet. Set livers aside; keep warm. Add mushrooms, onion, and garlic to drippings. Cook, stirring constantly, 5 minutes or until tender. Reduce heat to low. Stir in flour; cook 1 minute, stirring constantly. Stir in wine and next 5 ingredients. Bring to a boil; reduce heat, and simmer, uncovered, 5 minutes. Stir in livers; cook until heated, stirring occasionally. Serve over rice. Yield: 4 servings.

Lauralyn Pierce
Sweet Home Alabama Cooking
The 44th National Square Dancing Convention
Montgomery, Alabama

Chicken Liver Stroganoff   QUICK & EASY

Noodle News
You'll find egg noodles in various sizes. Wide or medium are best suited for this dish.

This chicken liver version of classic beef stroganoff, complete with the same smooth sour cream and egg noodle base, has what it takes to become a family favorite.

½ cup all-purpose flour
1 teaspoon salt
1 pound chicken livers
½ cup vegetable oil
2 medium onions, thinly sliced and separated into rings

½ cup water
1 teaspoon lemon-pepper seasoning
1 teaspoon dried parsley flakes
1 teaspoon pepper
1 (8-ounce) container sour cream
Toast points or hot cooked egg noodles

COMBINE flour and salt; dredge chicken livers in flour mixture. Fry livers in hot oil in a large skillet over medium-high heat until browned, turning occasionally. Remove livers from skillet; add onion, and cook, stirring constantly, until tender and browned. Remove onion, and carefully drain excess oil from skillet.
RETURN livers and onion to skillet. Add water and next 3 ingredients. Bring to a boil; reduce heat, and simmer, uncovered, 5 minutes. Stir in sour cream, and cook until thoroughly heated (do not boil). Serve over toast points or noodles. Yield: 4 servings.

Have You Heard . . . A Tasteful Medley of Memphis
Subsidium, Inc.
Memphis, Tennessee

Herbed Turkey   MAKE AHEAD

Several make-ahead steps lead to divine results—the turkey is slathered with a salty spice seasoning and left to marinate; then it gets rubbed with an herb butter and put over a hickory smoke fire.

1 (12-pound) turkey
2 tablespoons salt
1 tablespoon grated gingerroot
1 teaspoon cumin seeds
½ cup butter, melted
1 bay leaf
1½ teaspoons chopped fresh
    tarragon

1½ teaspoons chopped fresh
    rosemary
1½ teaspoons chopped fresh dill
½ cup dry sherry
1 tablespoon steak sauce
1 tablespoon honey

REMOVE giblets and neck, and reserve for another use. Rinse turkey with cold water; pat dry.

COMBINE salt, gingerroot, and cumin seeds; crush until pulverized, using a mortar and pestle. Rub cavity and skin of turkey with salt mixture. Wrap turkey with plastic wrap, and chill 8 hours.

COMBINE butter and next 4 ingredients; cover and chill 8 hours. Let butter mixture stand at room temperature until softened.

LOOSEN skin from turkey breast and thighs without totally detaching skin. Spread butter mixture under skin on breast and thighs.

COMBINE sherry, steak sauce, and honey; set aside.

SOAK hickory chunks in water at least 1 hour; drain. Wrap chips in heavy-duty aluminum foil, and make several holes in foil. Prepare a hot fire by piling charcoal on 1 side of grill, leaving other side empty. (For gas grills, light only 1 side.) Place foil-wrapped chips directly on hot coals. Coat grill rack on opposite side with cooking spray. Place food rack on grill. Arrange food over unlit side. Grill, covered with grill lid, basting occasionally with sherry mixture, 3 hours or until meat thermometer registers 180° when inserted into meaty portion of thigh, making sure it does not touch bone. Let stand 15 minutes before carving. Yield: 12 servings.

The Bess Collection
The Junior Service League of Independence, Missouri

Thawing the Bird

If you buy a frozen turkey, plan on 2 to 3 days for it to thaw in the refrigerator before cooking.

Peppered Turkey Breast

Turkey Breast

Bone-in turkey breast is a good choice if your family prefers white meat. You'll get more servings for your money.

Baking in an oven bag keeps this turkey breast moist.

1 (5½-pound) bone-in turkey breast	1 medium onion, chopped
½ cup pepper	3 tablespoons chopped fresh parsley
¼ cup salt	1 (10-ounce) bottle steak sauce
¾ cup cider vinegar	(we tested with A-1)
¼ cup vegetable oil	1 tablespoon all-purpose flour
3 garlic cloves, minced	1 large oven cooking bag

PLACE turkey breast in a large heavy-duty zip-top plastic bag or large shallow dish; set aside.

COMBINE pepper and next 7 ingredients, stirring well; pour over turkey breast, coating thoroughly. Seal or cover, and marinate in refrigerator 8 hours, turning occasionally.

REMOVE turkey breast from marinade, discarding marinade. Add flour to oven bag, shaking to coat; place in a 13- x 9–inch baking pan. Add turkey breast to oven bag. Close bag with nylon tie; cut 6 (½-inch) slits in top of bag. Bake at 325° for 1 hour and 35 minutes or until meat thermometer registers 170°. Let stand 15 minutes before carving.

CUT top of oven bag, and remove turkey breast to a serving platter, reserving drippings. Strain drippings, and serve with turkey. Yield: 10 servings.

Julie Jackson
Savory Secrets
Runnels School
Baton Rouge, Louisiana

Turkey Cutlets in Wine   QUICK & EASY

Thin Cutlets

Turkey cutlets are thin pieces that cook quickly and lend themselves to easy skillet suppers.

Cheese-coated panfried cutlets simmer quickly in a rich Marsala sauce and need only a salad and rice or mashed potatoes on the plate.

½ cup all-purpose flour	2 tablespoons olive oil
¼ cup grated Parmesan cheese	2 tablespoons butter or margarine,
½ teaspoon paprika	melted
¼ teaspoon salt	½ cup dry Marsala wine
¼ teaspoon pepper	2 tablespoons lemon juice
1 pound turkey breast cutlets	1 teaspoon garlic salt

COMBINE first 5 ingredients; dredge turkey in flour mixture. Cook turkey in oil and butter in a large skillet over medium-high heat 4 to 5 minutes on each side or until browned. Remove turkey to a serving platter, and keep warm.

ADD Marsala, lemon juice, and garlic salt to drippings in skillet. Cook over medium-high heat, stirring constantly, until bubbly. Reduce heat to medium; return turkey to skillet, and cook 2 minutes or until thoroughly heated. Yield: 4 servings.

Sandy Lockwood
Angel Food & Deviled Crab
Ann Street United Methodist Church
Beaufort, North Carolina

Cornish Hens with Apricot Sauce

A pair of these glazed hens will serve a dinner party of four.

4 (1- to 1½-pound) Cornish hens
1 cup apricot preserves, divided
¾ cup butter or margarine, divided
2 cups white bread cubes, toasted
½ cup sliced celery
¼ cup chopped green onions
¼ cup chopped fresh parsley

2 to 3 tablespoons dry white wine
¾ teaspoon dried marjoram or dried
    oregano, divided
½ teaspoon salt
¼ teaspoon pepper
¼ teaspoon dried basil

REMOVE giblets from hens; reserve for another use. Rinse hens thoroughly with cold water, and pat dry. Lift wingtips up and over back, and tuck under hens. Set hens aside.

COMBINE ½ cup preserves and ¼ cup butter in a small saucepan; cook over medium heat until melted, stirring often.

COMBINE preserves mixture, bread cubes, and next 4 ingredients in a large bowl. Add ¼ teaspoon marjoram, salt, pepper, and basil; stir mixture well.

SPOON bread cube mixture evenly into cavities of hens. Close cavities, and secure with wooden picks. Tie ends of legs together with string. Place hens, breast side up, on a lightly greased rack in a shallow roasting pan. Bake at 350° for 1 hour.

COMBINE remaining ½ cup preserves, ½ cup butter, and ½ teaspoon marjoram in a small saucepan. Cook over medium heat until butter is melted, stirring often. Remove hens from oven, and brush with ½ cup preserves mixture. Bake 30 more minutes or until done. Serve hens with remaining preserves mixture. Yield: 4 servings.

Texas Tapestry
The Junior Woman's Club of Houston, Texas

Smothered Quail

A savory gravy of sherry and chicken broth smothers these quail.

8 quail, dressed
½ cup butter or margarine
¼ cup all-purpose flour
2 cups chicken broth

½ cup dry sherry
1 teaspoon salt
¾ teaspoon pepper

BROWN quail, in batches, in butter in a large skillet over medium-high heat. Place quail, breast side up, in a lightly greased 9-inch square baking dish.

ADD flour to skillet, stirring until smooth. Cook 2 minutes, stirring constantly over medium heat. Gradually stir in broth and sherry; cook over medium heat, stirring constantly, until mixture is thickened and bubbly. Stir in salt and pepper. Pour sauce over quail. Bake, covered, at 350° for 1 hour. Yield: 4 servings.

V.V. Thompson
'Pon Top Edisto
Trinity Episcopal Church
Edisto Island, South Carolina

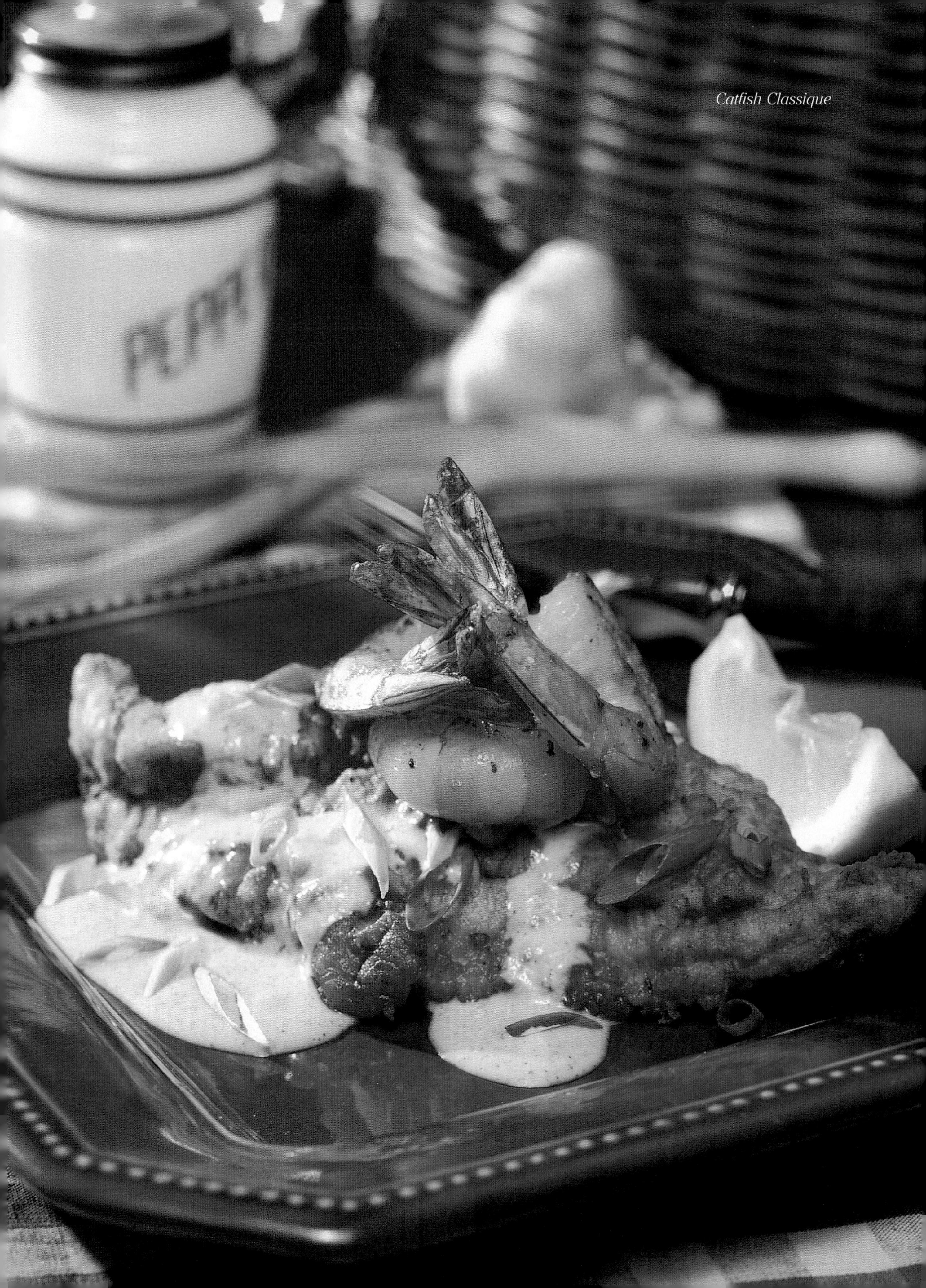

Catfish Classique

Catfish Classique

Fried catfish gets dressed up. Each crispy fillet is topped with a rich cream sauce and a few fresh shrimp. This is a great dish for company when you want to impress with 2 Southern favorites—shrimp and catfish.

1 large egg
½ cup milk
1½ cups all-purpose flour
1¼ teaspoons salt, divided
2½ teaspoons ground red pepper, divided
4 (6-ounce) catfish fillets (½ inch thick)
Vegetable oil

12 unpeeled, large fresh shrimp
1 tablespoon butter or margarine
2 teaspoons minced garlic (about 2 cloves)
¼ cup dry vermouth
2 cups whipping cream
¼ cup chopped green onions, divided
2 teaspoons fresh lemon juice
Garnish: lemon wedges

COMBINE egg and milk, stirring until blended. Combine flour, 1 teaspoon salt, and 1 teaspoon red pepper in a shallow dish. Dredge catfish fillets in flour mixture, dip in milk mixture, and dredge again in flour mixture.

POUR oil to a depth of 2 inches into a Dutch oven; heat to 375°. Fry fillets, 2 at a time, 6 minutes or until golden; drain on paper towels. Set aside, and keep warm.

PEEL and devein shrimp, if desired. Set aside. Melt butter in a large skillet over medium heat. Add shrimp and garlic; sauté 4 minutes or until shrimp turn pink. Remove shrimp from skillet, reserving drippings in pan. Set shrimp aside; keep warm.

ADD vermouth to skillet; bring to a boil, and cook 1 minute, stirring constantly. Add whipping cream, half of green onions, lemon juice, remaining ¼ teaspoon salt, and remaining 1½ teaspoons red pepper; cook sauce 15 minutes or until thickened, stirring often.

TO SERVE, place catfish on a serving platter, and drizzle with sauce. Top with shrimp, and sprinkle with remaining green onions. Garnish, if desired. Yield: 4 servings.

Linen Napkins to Paper Plates
The Junior Auxiliary of Clarksville, Tennessee

Fan the Tails
Leave the tails on the shrimp for a fancy presentation (see photograph). You can easily peel away the body shell and leave the tail shell intact during preparation.

Baked Fish with Lemon-Parsley Stuffing

Get Dressed

The term "pan-dressed" refers to small fish that have been eviscerated, scaled, and had head and fins removed.

Bass fishermen will enjoy this baked recipe with an herby, aromatic stuffing.

1 (1½-pound) pan-dressed bass
Lemon-Parsley Stuffing
1 tablespoon fresh lemon juice

Garnishes: fresh parsley sprigs, lemon
    wedges

RINSE fish, and pat dry. Fill cavity of fish with Lemon-Parsley Stuffing, and secure with skewers. Place fish in a greased 13- x 9-inch baking dish. Sprinkle with lemon juice.

BAKE, uncovered, at 350° for 40 minutes or until fish flakes easily with a fork. Garnish, if desired. Yield: 4 servings.

Lemon-Parsley Stuffing

¼ cup chopped onion
¼ cup chopped celery
1 garlic clove, minced
1 tablespoon butter or margarine,
    melted
2 tablespoons chopped fresh parsley
1 tablespoon fresh lemon juice

1 tablespoon dry white wine
½ teaspoon grated lemon rind
¼ teaspoon dried thyme, crushed
¼ teaspoon salt
⅛ teaspoon pepper
1½ cups soft whole wheat
    breadcrumbs (homemade)

COOK first 3 ingredients in butter in a medium skillet over medium-high heat, stirring constantly, 4 minutes or until vegetables are tender; remove from heat. Add parsley and next 6 ingredients, stirring well. Add breadcrumbs, and toss gently. Yield: 1½ cups.

Mississippi Reflections: A Collection of Recipes Seasoned with Memories
Hospice of Central Mississippi
Brookhaven, Mississippi

Rafe's Fried Grouper

Grouper Sandwich

Enjoy this crisp fish on a sandwich. Just use a large, hearty bun and add some lettuce, mayonnaise, and red onion slices.

A dusting of cornmeal is key to the crispy crust on these panfried grouper fillets. Serve them with a squirt of fresh lemon juice or a dollop of tangy tartar sauce to entice your taste buds.

1 cup milk
1 small onion, minced (about ¾ cup)
1 garlic clove, minced
1 pound grouper or other firm white
    fish fillets
⅔ cup all-purpose flour
⅓ cup white cornmeal

½ teaspoon dried basil
½ teaspoon dried oregano
¼ teaspoon salt
⅛ teaspoon black pepper
⅛ teaspoon ground red pepper
Vegetable oil
Lemon wedges

COMBINE first 3 ingredients in a large bowl; add fish fillets. Cover and marinate in refrigerator 30 minutes.

COMBINE flour and next 6 ingredients; stir well. Dredge fillets in flour mixture. Fry in ½ inch hot oil in a skillet over medium-high heat 5 to 6 minutes on each side or until golden. Drain on paper towels. Serve with lemon wedges. Yield: 4 servings.

Rafael Rosengarten
McClellanville Coast Seafood Cookbook
McClellanville Arts Council
McClellanville, South Carolina

Crab-Stuffed Flounder

These succulent flounder fillets sport a double dose of a fresh crabmeat and Parmesan mixture—they're stuffed as well as topped with the savory blend.

1 celery rib, chopped
3 green onions, chopped
2 garlic cloves, minced
¼ cup olive oil
½ pound fresh lump crabmeat,
      drained
1 cup soft breadcrumbs (homemade)
½ cup grated Parmesan cheese
1 plum tomato, chopped

1 large egg, lightly beaten
2 tablespoons fresh lemon juice
1 tablespoon chopped fresh parsley
¼ teaspoon salt
¼ teaspoon pepper
6 (4-ounce) flounder fillets
½ cup butter or margarine, melted
Garnish: lemon wedges

COOK celery, green onions, and garlic in hot oil in a large skillet over medium-high heat, stirring constantly, until tender. Remove from heat; add crabmeat and next 8 ingredients, stirring well.

BRUSH fillets with melted butter. Spoon 1 heaping tablespoon crabmeat mixture on top of each fillet. Roll up fillets, and secure each with a wooden pick. Place fillets in a lightly greased 13 - x 9-inch baking dish. Spoon remaining crabmeat mixture over each stuffed fillet, and drizzle with any remaining butter.

COVER and bake at 375° for 20 minutes. Uncover and bake 10 more minutes or until fish flakes with a fork. Garnish, if desired. Yield: 6 servings.

Texas Ties
The Junior League of North Harris County
Spring, Texas

Flounder Tips

For this recipe, look for long, thin flounder pieces. They'll be the easiest to stuff and roll up. And once you've rolled the fillets and secured them with picks, you can store them in the refrigerator for several hours before baking.

Orange Roughy with Strawberry-Star Fruit Salsa QUICK & EASY

Star Fruit

Star fruit, named for its striking shape, is at its showy best when purchased at its peak from summer's end to mid-winter.

Orange roughy is a tender, mild white fish that's easy to cook. Here, it's ready in just 5 minutes under the broiler. And you can make the citrusy salsa ahead; it gives a kiss of beautiful color to the white fish.

1 cup sliced fresh strawberries	1 tablespoon fresh lime juice
2 medium star fruit (carambola), thinly sliced	¼ teaspoon ground coriander
½ cup minced onion	⅛ teaspoon ground red pepper
1 tablespoon chopped jalapeño pepper	2 tablespoons fresh lime juice
1 tablespoon minced fresh cilantro	2 teaspoons butter or margarine, melted
1 teaspoon grated lime rind	6 orange roughy fillets
	Garnish: jalapeño peppers

COMBINE first 9 ingredients in a medium bowl to make salsa. Cover and chill 2 hours.

COMBINE 2 tablespoons lime juice and butter in a small bowl. Place orange roughy fillets on a lightly greased rack in a broiler pan. Brush with butter mixture. Broil 5½ inches from heat 5 minutes or until fish flakes with a fork. Serve with salsa. Garnish, if desired. Yield: 6 servings.

Simply Divine
Second-Ponce de Leon Baptist Church
Atlanta, Georgia

Herb-Crusted Salmon with Dill Sauce

A Happy Marriage

Salmon and fresh dill make a happy marriage of flavors. Dill is the predominant herb in this sauce, though there are other background herbs in the recipe, too.

Dinner for two can be ready in a jif if you're a salmon fan. A foursome of fresh herbs peppers the top of the salmon and sure smells good once it hits a hot skillet.

¼ cup chopped fresh parsley
2 tablespoons chopped fresh rosemary
2 tablespoons chopped fresh tarragon

2 tablespoons chopped fresh oregano
2 (6-ounce) salmon fillets
2 garlic cloves, minced
2 tablespoons olive oil
Dill Sauce

COMBINE first 4 ingredients in a shallow dish. Dredge fish in herb mixture (do not dredge skin side).

COOK garlic in hot oil in a medium ovenproof skillet over medium heat 30 seconds. Add fish, coated side down, and cook 5 minutes or until browned on coated side.

TURN salmon, skin side down, in skillet, and place, uncovered, in oven. Bake at 350° for 7 minutes or until fish flakes with a fork. Serve with Dill Sauce. Yield: 2 servings.

Dill Sauce

½ cup mayonnaise
½ cup sour cream
2 tablespoons finely chopped onion
2 tablespoons honey mustard
1 tablespoon chopped fresh dill
1½ teaspoons Worcestershire sauce

½ teaspoon chopped fresh tarragon
½ teaspoon chopped fresh basil
¼ teaspoon minced garlic
⅛ teaspoon salt
⅛ teaspoon pepper

COMBINE all ingredients in top of a double boiler; bring water to a boil. Reduce heat to low; cook 10 minutes or until onion is tender. Yield: 1 cup.

Taste of the Territory, The Flair and Flavor of Oklahoma
The Service League of Bartlesville, Oklahoma

*Herb-Crusted Salmon
with Dill Sauce*

Salmon with Basil, Tomato, and Capers QUICK & EASY

On Salmon

The white substance that sometimes appears on cooked salmon is coagulated protein. Simply wipe it off fish before serving for a better appearance.

Coat salmon fillets with a little olive oil, run them under the broiler, and top them with tangy tomatoes and capers for a fine Mediterranean supper.

1 pound plum tomatoes, seeded and chopped	1 tablespoon drained capers
¾ cup lightly packed fresh basil leaves, chopped	⅛ teaspoon salt
	⅛ teaspoon pepper
½ cup olive oil	4 (6-ounce) salmon fillets
1 shallot, chopped (2 tablespoons)	1 tablespoon olive oil
1½ tablespoons lemon juice	Garnish: lemon wedges (1 small lemon)

COMBINE first 8 ingredients in a small bowl, stirring well; set aside.

BRUSH both sides of salmon with 1 tablespoon olive oil. Place salmon on a rack of broiler pan coated with cooking spray. Broil 3 inches from heat 10 minutes or until fish flakes with a fork.

TO SERVE, transfer salmon to a serving plate; top with tomato mixture, and garnish, if desired. Yield: 4 servings.

Special Selections of Ocala
Ocala Royal Dames for Cancer Research, Inc.
Ocala, Florida

Grilled Fresh Tuna GRILL LOVERS

Perfect Pairings

Pair this grilled tuna with yellow rice, black beans, and a light white wine such as Sauvignon Blanc.

A sassy marinade of citrus juices and soy sauce flatters thick tuna steaks.

4 (4- to 5-ounce) yellowfin tuna steaks (¾ inch thick)	2 tablespoons chopped fresh parsley
¼ cup orange juice	1 tablespoon lemon juice
¼ cup soy sauce	1 garlic clove, minced
2 tablespoons ketchup	½ teaspoon dried oregano
	⅛ teaspoon ground white pepper

PLACE tuna in a large heavy-duty zip-top plastic bag. Combine orange juice and remaining 7 ingredients; pour over tuna. Seal bag; marinate in refrigerator 1 hour.

REMOVE tuna from marinade, reserving marinade. Pour marinade into a small saucepan; bring to a boil.

COAT food rack with cooking spray; place on grill over medium-high heat (350° to 400°). Place steaks on rack; grill, covered with grill lid, 3 to 4 minutes on each side or until fish flakes with a fork, turning and basting with reserved marinade. Yield: 4 servings.

Pat Chitty
Timeless Treasures
The Junior Service League of Valdosta, Georgia

Grace's Broiled Shrimp

Serve this informal fare over toasted French bread to soak up the rich garlic-lemon sauce.

2 pounds unpeeled, large fresh
    shrimp
½ cup vegetable oil
¼ cup soy sauce
3 tablespoons chopped fresh parsley

1 tablespoon lemon juice
2 garlic cloves, minced
8 (1-inch) slices French bread,
    toasted

PEEL shrimp, and devein, if desired, leaving tails intact. Place shrimp in a large shallow roasting pan or broiler pan.

COMBINE oil and next 4 ingredients; pour over shrimp. Cover and marinate in refrigerator 2 hours.

UNCOVER and broil 5½ inches from heat 7 to 8 minutes or until shrimp turn pink, stirring once. Serve immediately over French bread. Yield: 4 servings.

Sterling Service
The Dothan Service League
Dothan, Alabama

Shrimp Count
When you buy large shrimp, you should get approximately 26 to 29 shrimp per pound.

Cooper River Shrimp Creole

Golden raisins nicely sweeten this spicy Creole dish.

5 pounds unpeeled, medium-size
    fresh shrimp
2 large onions, chopped
2 medium-size green bell peppers,
    chopped
4 celery ribs, chopped
½ cup olive oil
1 cup golden raisins
1 cup chili sauce

1 cup dry white wine
2 teaspoons salt
1 teaspoon sugar
1 teaspoon curry powder
2 (14-ounce) cans crushed tomatoes,
    undrained
3 bay leaves
Hot cooked rice

PEEL shrimp, and devein, if desired; set aside.

SAUTÉ onion, green pepper, and celery in hot oil in a Dutch oven over medium-high heat until tender. Add raisins and next 7 ingredients. Bring to a boil; cover, reduce heat, and simmer 30 minutes, stirring occasionally. Add shrimp; cook 5 more minutes or until shrimp turn pink. Discard bay leaves. Serve over rice. Yield: 6 to 8 servings.

Tested by Time
Porter Gaud Parents Guild
Charleston, South Carolina

Creole Defined
"Creole" in this case refers to the tomato-based sauce that the shrimp are simmered in.

*Garlic-Skewered
Grilled Shrimp*

Garlic-Skewered Grilled Shrimp GRILL LOVERS

Whole cloves of garlic are the surprise ingredient on these shrimp skewers. Once they've been grilled, enjoy them with each bite of shrimp or rub them on crusty bread.

24 unpeeled jumbo fresh shrimp (2 pounds)	2 tablespoons chopped fresh basil
3 large garlic cloves, minced	2 tablespoons red wine vinegar
⅓ cup olive oil	½ teaspoon ground red pepper
¼ cup tomato sauce	18 large garlic cloves, peeled
	Garnish: fresh basil sprigs

PEEL shrimp, and devein, if desired. Combine minced garlic and next 5 ingredients in a medium bowl. Add shrimp; stirring well. Cover and marinate in refrigerator 30 minutes.

PLACE 18 garlic cloves in a small saucepan; add water to cover, and bring to a boil. Boil 3 to 5 minutes; drain well, and set aside.

REMOVE shrimp from marinade; reserving marinade. Bring marinade to a boil in a small saucepan; set aside.

THREAD shrimp and garlic cloves evenly onto 6 (10-inch) metal skewers. Grill, covered with grill lid, over medium-high heat (350° to 400°) 3 to 4 minutes on each side or until shrimp turn pink, basting with reserved marinade. Garnish, if desired. Yield: 6 servings.

The Wohlers Family
From Home Plate to Home Cooking
The Atlanta Braves
Atlanta, Georgia

Garlic in Sync
Boiling whole garlic cloves before grilling takes off the raw edge and ensures that shrimp and garlic will cook evenly.

Tequila-Lime Shrimp GRILL LOVERS

An easy trick to prevent shrimp from falling through the grill rack is to use 2 skewers and double thread each row of shrimp, or thread tail and neck of each shrimp onto skewers so shrimp will lie flat.

2½ pounds unpeeled, large fresh shrimp	2 shallots, chopped
½ cup olive oil	2 garlic cloves, minced
¼ cup fresh lime juice	1 teaspoon salt
¼ cup tequila	1 teaspoon ground cumin
	½ teaspoon pepper

PEEL shrimp, leaving tails intact; devein, if desired. Combine oil and remaining 7 ingredients in a bowl; stir in shrimp. Cover; chill 1 hour.

REMOVE shrimp from marinade, discarding marinade. Thread 9 shrimp on each of 6 (12-inch) metal skewers.

COAT food rack with cooking spray; place on grill over medium-high heat (350° to 400°). Place skewers on rack; grill, without grill lid, 3 to 4 minutes on each side or until shrimp turn pink. Yield: 6 servings.

A Sunsational Encore
The Junior League of Greater Orlando, Florida

Baking Option
You can bake these shrimp if you're not in the grilling mood. Remove shrimp from marinade, discarding marinade. Place shrimp in an ungreased 15- x 10-inch jellyroll pan. Bake, uncovered, at 400° for 10 to 12 minutes or until shrimp turn pink.

Étouffée PARTY FOOD   SUPPER CLUB

Crawfish Chat

Buy cooked, peeled crawfish tail meat and use boil-in-bag rice, and half the work's done for you. The whole thing freezes well, too, so you can stretch it to serve several meals.

Étouffée's a mainstay meal in Louisiana. This crawfish version serves a family or crowd of 10 friends.

1 cup butter, melted
½ cup plus 2 tablespoons all-purpose
    flour
1¼ cups finely chopped celery
    (about 3 ribs)
1 cup chopped green bell pepper
    (about 1 medium)
1 (14½-ounce) can chicken broth
2 cups water
¼ cup chopped fresh parsley
1 tablespoon tomato paste

1 bay leaf
¼ teaspoon salt
¼ teaspoon black pepper
⅛ teaspoon ground red pepper
2 (1-pound) packages cooked, peeled,
    and deveined crawfish tail meat,
    drained
½ cup chopped green onions (about
    1 bunch)
Hot cooked rice

COMBINE butter and flour in a large Dutch oven; cook over medium-high heat, stirring constantly, 8 to 10 minutes or until roux is caramel-colored. Add celery and green pepper; cook 4 minutes. Add chicken broth and next 7 ingredients; bring to a boil. Cover, reduce heat, and simmer 30 minutes, stirring occasionally.

ADD crawfish and green onions, and cook 5 minutes. Discard bay leaf. Serve Étouffée over rice. Yield: 10 servings.

Lynda Huggins
Food for Thought
Northeast Louisiana Chapter, Autism Society of America
Monroe, Louisiana

Étouffée

Stuffed Clams

Sizing Up Clams

Cherrystone clams are hard-shell, medium-size clams. The shell is typically 2½ inches in diameter, which makes it just the right size to stuff and bake for hors d'oeuvres or entrées.

To make the clams easier to shuck, bake them at 400° for 5 to 10 minutes or just until the clams begin to open.

9 pounds cherrystone clams, scrubbed
½ cup soft breadcrumbs (homemade)
¼ cup (1 ounce) shredded Swiss cheese
2 bacon slices, cooked and crumbled

2 tablespoons dry white wine
1 tablespoon minced fresh parsley
1 tablespoon butter or margarine, melted
1 teaspoon Worcestershire sauce
¼ teaspoon pepper

SHUCK clams; release meat from bottom shells, reserving 16 shells. Arrange shells on an ungreased baking sheet; set aside.

CHOP clam meat (about 1½ cups); drain. Combine clam meat, breadcrumbs, and remaining 7 ingredients in a bowl. Fill each clam shell with 1 heaping tablespoon clam mixture. Bake, uncovered, at 375° for 20 minutes. Serve immediately. Yield: 4 servings.

Pat Sowinski
A Perfect Measurement of Love
Little Flower Children's Services of New York
Wading River, New York

Carolina Crab Cakes with Basil Tartar Sauce

Perfect Crab Cakes

When combining ingredients for crab cakes, always add crabmeat last and gently toss it in with your hands. This preserves large lumps of crab in each cake.

These golden, crumb-coated cakes make an exceptional appetizer or light dinner. The basil tartar sauce has a fresh flavor and would be good atop other types of fish, too.

1 large egg, lightly beaten
1 egg yolk, lightly beaten
2 tablespoons chopped green onions
2 tablespoons chopped fresh parsley
1½ tablespoons half-and-half
1 teaspoon lemon juice
½ teaspoon ground red pepper
½ teaspoon dry mustard
¼ teaspoon ground black pepper

¼ teaspoon Worcestershire sauce
1 pound fresh lump crabmeat, drained
½ cup plus 2 tablespoons round buttery cracker crumbs, divided
2 tablespoons butter, melted
Basil Tartar Sauce

COMBINE first 10 ingredients; stir in crabmeat and 2 tablespoons cracker crumbs. Chill 30 minutes.

SHAPE crab mixture into 8 patties; dredge in remaining ½ cup cracker crumbs. Place patties on a baking sheet coated with cooking spray. Drizzle with melted butter.

BAKE at 475° for 10 minutes or until lightly browned. Serve with Basil Tartar Sauce. Yield: 4 servings.

Basil Tartar Sauce

½ cup firmly packed fresh basil
    leaves
½ cup mayonnaise
1 tablespoon sour cream
1 teaspoon lemon juice

½ teaspoon minced garlic
⅛ teaspoon salt
⅛ teaspoon ground red pepper
⅛ teaspoon hot sauce

PROCESS all ingredients in a food processor until smooth, stopping to scrape down sides; chill. Yield: ½ cup.

Back to the Table
Episcopal Church Women–Christ Church
Raleigh, North Carolina

Deviled Crab

This dressed-up crab is an elegant entrée the way it's presented in baking shells. See the option at right if you don't have the shells.

1 pound fresh lump crabmeat,
    drained
1½ teaspoons Worcestershire sauce
¾ teaspoon celery seeds
1 teaspoon dried parsley flakes
3 tablespoons minced green bell
    pepper
1 large egg, lightly beaten

2 tablespoons mayonnaise
3 tablespoons butter
3 tablespoons all-purpose flour
1 cup milk
2 tablespoons butter, melted
½ cup soft breadcrumbs
    (homemade)
Paprika

Crab Casserole
For a more casual approach to this recipe, omit the baking shells and bake the crab mixture in a casserole dish for the same amount of time.

REMOVE any bits of shell from crabmeat; set crabmeat aside.

COMBINE Worcestershire sauce and next 5 ingredients in a large bowl; gently add crabmeat; set aside.

MELT 3 tablespoons butter in a small saucepan over low heat; add flour, stirring until smooth. Cook 1 minute, stirring constantly. Gradually add milk; cook over medium heat, stirring constantly until thickened. Remove from heat; allow to cool 5 minutes.

GENTLY combine white sauce with crab mixture. Cover and chill 15 minutes. Combine 2 tablespoons melted butter with breadcrumbs; set aside.

DIVIDE crab mixture evenly between 6 lightly greased individual baking shells. Sprinkle with breadcrumbs and paprika. Bake at 350° for 30 to 32 minutes or until thoroughly heated and breadcrumbs are golden brown. Yield: 6 servings.

Mary Thayer
Dixon Fixins
Dixon Ambulatory Care Center
Westminster, Maryland

Mussels Steamed in White Wine

Flexing Mussels

Store fresh mussels in the coldest part of your refrigerator no more than 2 days. Shucked mussels should be plump, their liquid clear. The creamy tan meat is chewier than that of either oyster or clam, but some say the taste is sweeter.

You'll need about a half bottle of wine for this dish. Chill and serve remaining wine with the mussels and some crusty French bread.

2 pounds raw mussels in shell
2 garlic cloves, minced
1 large shallot, minced
6 fresh thyme sprigs
2 bay leaves
½ teaspoon freshly ground pepper

2 tablespoons olive oil
1½ cups dry white wine
1 tablespoon chopped fresh Italian parsley
½ teaspoon salt
2 tablespoons butter

SCRUB mussels with a brush; remove beards. Discard cracked or heavy mussels (they're filled with sand), or opened mussels that won't close when tapped.

SAUTÉ garlic and next 4 ingredients in hot oil in a Dutch oven over medium heat 2 minutes. Add mussels; increase heat to high. Cover and cook 1 minute, shaking Dutch oven several times. Add wine; cover and cook 1 to 2 minutes or until mussels open, shaking pan several times. Transfer mussels to a serving dish with a slotted spoon, discarding any unopened mussels. Cover and keep warm.

POUR remaining liquid in Dutch oven through a strainer into a skillet, discarding solids. Bring to a boil. Add parsley and salt; cook 2 minutes. Remove from heat; whisk in butter. Pour over mussels. Serve immediately. Yield: 2 to 3 servings.

Maureen O'Sullivan
Over the Bridge
Corpus Christie Women's Guild
East Sandwich, Massachusetts

Oyster Fritters

Select or Standard

Select oysters are the large size. Standard oysters are a bit smaller. Use large oysters when making fritters so you'll get a big, crunchy bite.

Complement these tasty fritters with a rémoulade or cocktail sauce.

1 cup all-purpose flour
1 teaspoon salt
⅛ teaspoon ground red pepper
⅔ cup water
2 tablespoons butter or margarine, melted

1 large egg, separated
Vegetable oil
3 (8-ounce) containers Select oysters, drained

COMBINE flour, salt, and pepper in a medium bowl. Combine water, butter, and egg yolk in a small bowl, beating well with a fork. Gradually add egg mixture to dry ingredients, stirring until blended. Beat egg white until soft peaks form; fold into batter.

POUR oil to a depth of 2 to 3 inches into a Dutch oven; heat to 375°. Dip oysters in batter; fry in batches in hot oil 2 to 3 minutes or until golden, turning once. Drain on paper towels. Serve immediately. Yield: 4 servings.

Melissa Sthrom
In the Breaking of Bread
Catholic Committee on Scouting and Camp Fire
Lake Charles, Louisiana

Salads

Chicken Salad, page 289

Field Greens, Crumbled Blue Cheese, and Spicy Pecans

Pecan Surplus

As a bonus, you'll have some of these spiced pecans left over to serve as an appetizer or a snack. When preparing the nuts, we suggest using a disposable aluminum baking sheet for easy cleanup.

This salad is crisp, tangy, and terrific with spicy-hot pecans, apple, and blue cheese.

⅔ cup sugar
⅔ cup white vinegar
3 tablespoons apple cider vinegar
2 tablespoons Worcestershire sauce
1½ tablespoons onion juice
1 teaspoon salt
1 teaspoon dry mustard
1 cup vegetable oil

4 cups loosely packed mixed greens
1 Granny Smith apple, unpeeled, cored, and chopped
4 ounces blue cheese, crumbled
¼ cup coarsely chopped Spicy Pecans
2 green onions, chopped

COMBINE first 7 ingredients, stirring until sugar dissolves. Slowly add oil, stirring constantly with a wire whisk until blended.

COMBINE greens and remaining 4 ingredients in a large bowl. Add desired amount of dressing, and toss gently. Serve immediately. Store any remaining dressing in refrigerator. Yield: 8 servings.

Spicy Pecans

2 egg whites
1½ teaspoons salt
¾ cup sugar
2 tablespoons Hungarian paprika
1½ teaspoons ground red pepper

2 teaspoons Worcestershire sauce
4½ cups pecan halves
¼ cup plus 2 tablespoons unsalted butter, melted

BEAT egg whites and salt with a wire whisk until foamy. Add sugar and next 3 ingredients, beating well. Stir in pecans and butter. Spread coated pecans on a heavily greased large baking sheet.

BAKE at 325° for 30 minutes or until pecans are crisp and browned, stirring every 10 minutes. Remove from pan; cool completely. Store pecans in an airtight container. Yield: 5½ cups.

Stop and Smell the Rosemary: Recipes and Traditions to Remember
The Junior League of Houston, Texas

NOTE: Some consider Hungarian paprika to be the superior variety of paprika. It's a little sweeter and hotter than other brands available in the supermarket.

*Spinach Salad
with Feta Cheese
and Basil Dressing*

Spinach Salad with Feta Cheese and Basil Dressing MAKE AHEAD SUPPER CLUB

A fresh spinach salad is a refreshing change from iceberg lettuce. This bowl of greens is bursting with an interesting mix of toppings, too. Avocado, feta cheese, pine nuts, and Greek olives make every bite one to savor.

½ cup olive oil
¼ cup red wine vinegar
2 teaspoons sugar
¼ teaspoon salt
¼ teaspoon pepper
5 fresh basil leaves, chopped
1 garlic clove, minced

1 pound fresh spinach
1 ripe avocado, peeled and sliced
1 cup crumbled feta cheese
½ cup pine nuts or chopped walnuts,
   toasted
Kalamata olives (optional)

Make-Ahead Options

Make this dressing ahead and prep the spinach by removing stems and rinsing leaves in a salad spinner. Then you can store the greens in the refrigerator until you're ready for supper.

COMBINE first 7 ingredients in a jar. Cover tightly, and shake vigorously. Chill 2 hours.

REMOVE stems from spinach; wash leaves thoroughly, and pat dry. Tear leaves into bite-size pieces, if desired.

COMBINE spinach, avocado, feta cheese, pine nuts, and olives, if desired, in a large bowl; toss gently. Pour dressing over salad, and toss gently. Serve immediately. Yield: 10 servings.

Saint Louis Days, Saint Louis Nights
The Junior League of St. Louis, Missouri

Raspberry Salad

Raspberry Salad QUICK & EASY

This is a salad for the summer months when plump pink raspberries are abundant at the produce stand.

½ cup olive oil
¼ cup raspberry vinegar
2 tablespoons honey
½ teaspoon pepper
¼ teaspoon salt

1 garlic clove, minced
1 (6½-ounce) package mixed baby
   salad greens
2 cups fresh raspberries

COMBINE first 6 ingredients in a jar. Cover tightly, and shake vigorously. Pour dressing over lettuce; toss gently to coat. Top with raspberries. Yield: 8 servings.

Joyce Sloop
Silver Selections
Catawba School Alumni
Rock Hill, South Carolina

Other Greens
If you don't want to buy a package of baby salad greens, use 8 cups of any mixture of torn lettuces.

Traditional Greek Salad

For variety, substitute wine vinegar for the lemon juice and mint for the oregano.

1 garlic clove, halved
6 cups tightly packed torn mixed
   salad greens
1 medium tomato, cut into wedges
1 medium-size green bell pepper,
   thinly sliced into rings
1 small cucumber, thinly sliced
4 radishes, thinly sliced
3 green onions, thinly sliced

½ cup crumbled feta cheese
¼ cup large pitted ripe olives
1 (2-ounce) can anchovy fillets,
   drained
½ cup olive oil
¼ cup lemon juice
½ teaspoon salt
¼ teaspoon dried oregano
¼ teaspoon freshly ground pepper

RUB the inside of a large wooden salad bowl with cut sides of garlic. Discard garlic.
ADD salad greens and next 8 ingredients to bowl; toss well. Combine olive oil and next 4 ingredients; stir well. Pour dressing over salad, and toss gently. Serve immediately. Yield: 6 servings.

Despina T. Saffo
A Greek Feast: A Book of Greek Recipes
The Daughters of Penelope
Wilmington, North Carolina

Flavorful Bowl
Rubbing the inside of a wooden salad bowl with garlic helps the salad greens and other ingredients take on some garlic flavor.

Southwestern Layered Salad with Cilantro-Jalapeño Dressing

Southwestern Layered Salad with Cilantro-Jalapeño Dressing SUPPER CLUB

Try this Western take on the classic seven-layer salad. It's a bowlful, brimming with color and crunch.

1 (15-ounce) can black beans, rinsed and drained
2 tablespoons vegetable oil
2 tablespoons white wine vinegar
½ teaspoon salt
½ cup chopped purple onion
2 cups loosely packed shredded iceberg or curly leaf lettuce
1½ cups peeled, seeded, and chopped tomato

1 (15-ounce) can white corn, drained
½ cup chopped green bell pepper
1 cup (4 ounces) shredded Monterey Jack cheese
1 ripe avocado, peeled and cut into 6 wedges or coarsely chopped
4 bacon slices, cooked and crumbled
Cilantro-Jalapeño Dressing

Dressing Dos
A zippy dressing ties all the flavors together in this lively salad. Drizzle some dressing on the salad when you've got about half of it layered in the bowl. This way, all the layers, not just the top, will absorb some dressing.

COMBINE first 4 ingredients in a bowl; cover and marinate in refrigerator 2 hours. Drain beans, discarding marinade. Reserve 2 tablespoons beans. Toss remaining beans with onion. Place lettuce in a bowl; spoon bean mixture over lettuce. Reserve 1 table-spoon tomato. Sprinkle remaining tomato over bean layer. Combine corn and green pepper; reserve 2 tablespoons corn mixture. Spoon remaining corn mixture over toma-to layer. Sprinkle with cheese; cover and chill.

TO serve, spoon avocado on top of salad. Spoon reserved beans, tomato, and corn mixture over avocado. Sprinkle with bacon. Drizzle lightly with Cilantro-Jalapeño Dressing and serve with remaining dressing. Yield: 6 servings.

Cilantro-Jalapeño Dressing

½ cup white wine vinegar
4 pickled jalapeño peppers, seeded
1 teaspoon salt

⅔ cup olive oil
½ cup packed fresh cilantro

PROCESS first 3 ingredients in a blender until smooth. With blender on high, gradu-ally add oil in a slow, steady stream. Process until thick and smooth, stopping to scrape down sides. Add cilantro, and blend until finely chopped. Cover and chill. Yield: 1¼ cups.

Sensational Seasons: A Taste & Tour of Arkansas
The Junior League of Fort Smith, Arkansas

Garden Bean and Potato Salad with Balsamic Vinaigrette WEEKNIGHT FAVORITE

Hot Potato Tip
Cut and toss the potatoes with this pungent vinaigrette while potatoes are still slightly warm. They'll absorb more flavor this way.

A balsamic vinaigrette featuring Dijon mustard and fresh lemon juice cloaks these garden vegetables with distinctive flavor.

1½ pounds small round red potatoes, peeled, if desired
¾ pound fresh green beans, trimmed

1 small purple onion, chopped
¼ cup chopped fresh basil
Balsamic Vinaigrette

ARRANGE potatoes in a steamer basket over boiling water; cover and steam 20 minutes or until tender. Place in a large serving bowl.

ARRANGE beans in steamer basket over boiling water; cover and steam 10 minutes or until crisp-tender.

HALVE potatoes; add beans, onion, and basil. Add Balsamic Vinaigrette to potato mixture, and toss gently. Serve immediately, or cover and chill. Yield: 6 servings.

Balsamic Vinaigrette

½ cup extra-virgin olive oil
¼ cup balsamic vinegar
2 tablespoons Dijon mustard
2 tablespoons fresh lemon juice

1 teaspoon salt
¼ teaspoon pepper
Dash of Worcestershire sauce
1 garlic clove, minced

COMBINE all ingredients in a jar; cover tightly, and shake vigorously. Yield: 1 cup.

Gourmet Our Way
Cascia Hall Preparatory School Parent Faculty Association
Tulsa, Oklahoma

Garden Bean and Potato Salad with Balsamic Vinaigrette

Broccoli and Orange Salad WEEKNIGHT FAVORITE

Bring on the Broccoli

This type of fresh broccoli salad is a popular choice for potluck suppers and family reunions. If you enjoy nibbling on raw broccoli buds, you'll like this salad.

This creamy broccoli salad isn't a new concept, but the little orange segments mixed with bacon and almonds update it.

¾ cup mayonnaise
¼ cup sugar
2 tablespoons white vinegar
1 large bunch broccoli, cut into florets, or 1 (16-ounce) package broccoli florets
½ cup golden raisins

½ small purple onion, thinly sliced and separated into rings
4 bacon slices, cooked and crumbled
1 (11-ounce) can mandarin oranges, drained
⅓ cup sliced almonds, toasted

STIR together mayonnaise, sugar, and vinegar in a large bowl. Add broccoli and raisins; toss well. Cover and chill thoroughly. Top with onion, crumbled bacon, mandarin oranges, and toasted almonds. Yield: 10 servings.

Peggy Boyd
The Monarch's Feast
Mary Munford PTA
Richmond, Virginia

Phyllis's Favorite Carrot Salad ONE BOWL

One Bag Will Do

A 1-pound bag of carrots should give you more than enough grated carrot for this picnic salad.

Celery and walnuts add crunch, while raisins and pineapple sweeten this vitamin-packed salad.

2 cups grated carrot (about 5 carrots)
1 (8-ounce) can pineapple tidbits in heavy syrup, undrained
½ cup raisins

½ cup sliced celery
½ cup chopped walnuts
¼ cup mayonnaise
1 tablespoon fresh lemon juice
¼ teaspoon salt

TOSS together all ingredients in a medium bowl. Cover and chill. Yield: 4 to 6 servings.

Phyllis Shelton
NPT's Community Cookbook
Neighborhood Pride Team
Portland, Oregon

Grilled Corn Salad GRILL LOVERS

Not much else says summer like a pile of golden ears of corn wrapped in their crisp, green husks. This grilled salad brings out the natural sweetness of fresh corn.

18 ears fresh corn in husks
1 large red bell pepper
5 green onions, chopped
½ cup plus 1 tablespoon cider
    vinegar

1½ tablespoons honey
¾ teaspoon ground cumin
½ teaspoon salt
¼ teaspoon pepper
⅓ cup vegetable oil

SOAK corn in husks in water 15 minutes.

CUT bell pepper in half lengthwise; remove and discard seeds and membrane, and flatten pepper with palm of hand. Set aside.

COAT food rack with cooking spray, and place on grill over medium-high heat (350° to 400°). Place bell pepper, skin side down, on rack; remove corn from water and add corn in husks to grill. Grill, covered with grill lid, 15 to 20 minutes or until corn is tender and slightly charred, turning occasionally, and pepper is charred. Cool corn. Place pepper in ice water until cool; peel and discard skin.

REMOVE husks, and cut kernels from cob; place kernels in a large bowl. Chop pepper; add pepper and green onions to corn.

COMBINE vinegar and next 4 ingredients. Gradually add oil, stirring constantly with a wire whisk. Pour dressing over corn salad; toss gently. Serve immediately, or chill thoroughly. Yield: 8 servings.

Very Virginia: Culinary Traditions with a Twist
The Junior League of Hampton Roads
Newport News, Virginia

Why Soak?
The reason for soaking corn husks in water before grilling is to prevent the husks from catching on fire while the corn grills.

Grilled Vegetable Salad with Goat Cheese Croutons GRILL LOVERS

Croutons topped with warm goat cheese and fresh thyme nestle in a medley of grilled vegetables and gourmet mixed baby salad greens.

All-in-One Salad

If you're one of those people who enjoys making a meal of salad, this recipe's for you. It's got salad greens, grilled vegetables, and gourmet cheese-topped croutons. It's a colorful meal in a bowl.

3 tablespoons balsamic vinegar
1 tablespoon minced purple onion
1 tablespoon honey
½ teaspoon salt
½ teaspoon freshly ground pepper
½ cup olive oil
4 new potatoes
2 cups fresh broccoli florets
1 red bell pepper, quartered
1 yellow bell pepper, quartered
1 zucchini, cut into ¼-inch-thick lengthwise slices

1 yellow squash, cut into ¼-inch-thick lengthwise slices
1 baby eggplant (about 8 ounces), cut lengthwise into ¼-inch-thick slices
¼ cup olive oil
4 cups loosely packed gourmet mixed baby salad greens
Goat Cheese Croutons

PROCESS first 5 ingredients in a blender 20 seconds, stopping to scrape down sides. Turn blender on high; gradually add ½ cup olive oil in a slow, steady stream. Cover dressing; chill at least 1 hour.

COOK potatoes in boiling salted water to cover 15 to 20 minutes or until tender. Drain; cool and cut into ¼-inch-thick slices.

COOK broccoli in boiling water to cover 3 minutes; drain. Plunge into ice water to stop the cooking process; drain.

BRUSH potato, broccoli, red pepper, and next 4 ingredients with ¼ cup olive oil. Grill vegetables, covered with grill lid, over medium-high heat (350° to 400°) 6 minutes; remove potato and broccoli. Grill remaining vegetables 4 to 6 more minutes or until tender, turning once. Peel skins from peppers, if desired. Toss vegetables with ¼ cup dressing.

TOSS salad greens with ¼ cup dressing; divide among individual salad plates. Top with grilled vegetables and Goat Cheese Croutons. Serve with remaining dressing. Yield: 4 servings.

Goat Cheese Croutons

8 (½-inch-thick) slices French baguette
2 tablespoons olive oil
¼ teaspoon salt
½ teaspoon freshly ground pepper, divided

8 (¼-inch-thick) slices goat cheese (about 4 ounces)
1 tablespoon chopped fresh thyme

PLACE baguette slices on a baking sheet, and brush with oil; sprinkle with salt and ¼ teaspoon pepper. Bake at 350° for 5 minutes or until toasted, turning once. Top with sliced goat cheese; sprinkle with remaining ¼ teaspoon pepper and thyme. Bake 3 to 4 more minutes or until goat cheese is warm. Yield: 8 croutons.

Always in Season
The Junior League of Salt Lake City, Utah

Grilled Vegetable Salad with
Goat Cheese Croutons

Greek Tomato Salad ONE BOWL MAKE AHEAD

Pitting Olives

Use a cherry pitter to remove pits from kalamata olives, or mash olives with the flat side of a chef's knife, and the pit should pop out. You also can buy whole pitted kalamatas in jars.

Mediterranean classics—olive oil, feta cheese, and kalamata olives—offer a taste of the region in this tomato salad.

6 medium tomatoes, cut into ½-inch cubes	⅛ teaspoon pepper
3 tablespoons olive oil	2 (4-ounce) packages crumbled feta cheese
1½ tablespoons lemon juice	½ cup kalamata olives, pitted
1 garlic clove, crushed	2 (5-ounce) packages mixed baby salad greens
1½ teaspoons dried oregano	
½ teaspoon salt	

COMBINE first 9 ingredients in a large bowl, and stir well. Cover and chill at least 3 hours. To serve, add greens, and toss gently. Yield: 8 servings.

Jeri Derscheid
A Cook's Tour of Gautier
Gautier Garden Club
Gautier, Mississippi

Four-Bean Marinated Salad MAKE AHEAD

Picnic Food

Take this salad on a picnic. It can sit out at room temperature for several hours, leaving room in the cooler for other food that needs to stay chilled.

This familiar bean salad shows up often at potluck suppers and family reunions. It's a faithful make-ahead salad that tastes better the second day.

1 (17-ounce) can lima beans, drained	1 small onion, chopped
1 (16-ounce) can cut green beans, drained	1 (2-ounce) jar diced pimiento, drained
1 (16-ounce) can cut wax beans, drained	¾ cup sugar
1 (16-ounce) can kidney beans, rinsed and drained	½ cup vegetable oil
1 small green bell pepper, chopped	½ cup white vinegar
	½ teaspoon salt
	½ teaspoon pepper

COMBINE first 7 ingredients in a large bowl; toss. Combine sugar and remaining 4 ingredients in a small saucepan; bring to a boil over low heat, stirring until sugar dissolves. Pour hot vinegar mixture over bean mixture; stir gently. Cover and chill at least 4 hours. Serve with a slotted spoon. Yield: 10 servings.

Basil-Fettuccine Salad

Wonderful peppery-scented basil abounds in this pasta salad and vinaigrette. This is a great recipe to try if you grow basil in your garden.

1 pound fresh green beans
1 (8-ounce) package fettuccine
Red Wine-Basil Vinaigrette
6 plum tomatoes
2 cups pitted ripe olives

1½ cups loosely packed, julienne-sliced fresh basil leaves
2 tablespoons chopped fresh parsley
4 ounces Parmesan cheese, shaved

Parmesan Shavings
You can easily shave a wedge of fresh Parmesan cheese with a vegetable peeler.

WASH beans and remove strings. Arrange beans in a steamer basket over boiling water. Cover and steam 4 minutes or until tender. Rinse beans with cold water; drain and set aside.

COOK pasta according to package directions. Drain and place in a large bowl. Toss with ½ cup Red Wine-Basil Vinaigrette; set aside.

CUT each tomato into 8 wedges. Add tomato, green beans, olives, basil, and parsley to pasta; toss gently. Pour remaining Red Wine-Basil Vinaigrette over pasta; toss gently. Sprinkle with cheese. Yield: 8 servings.

Red Wine-Basil Vinaigrette

½ cup red wine vinegar
2 garlic cloves, crushed
2 tablespoons Dijon mustard
1 teaspoon freshly ground pepper

1 cup light olive oil
½ cup loosely packed, julienne-sliced fresh basil leaves
½ cup chopped fresh parsley

COMBINE first 4 ingredients in a small bowl. Add oil in a slow, steady stream, whisking until blended. Stir in basil and parsley. Yield: 2 cups.

Lois Wroten Boatwright
Homecoming: Special Foods, Special Memories
Baylor University Alumni Association
Waco, Texas

Bev's Tortellini Salad MAKE AHEAD

Tortellini Talk

Tortellini is small pasta typically stuffed with meat, cheese, or herbs or any combination of these, folded over and shaped into a tight ring.

This easy pasta salad starts with packaged cheese tortellini that you cook and embellish with artichoke hearts, olives, and tomatoes.

¾ cup olive oil
¼ cup red wine vinegar
1 tablespoon dried basil
1 tablespoon Dijon mustard
¼ teaspoon salt
¼ teaspoon pepper
1 garlic clove
2 (9-ounce) packages refrigerated cheese tortellini
1 (6-ounce) jar marinated artichoke hearts, drained and chopped

1 (2¼-ounce) can sliced ripe olives, drained
½ cup dried tomato halves in oil, drained and cut into strips
¼ cup chopped fresh parsley
¼ cup freshly grated Parmesan cheese
1 green bell pepper, coarsely chopped

PROCESS first 7 ingredients in a blender until smooth, stopping to scrape down sides.

COOK tortellini according to package directions; rinse with cold water, and drain. Add artichoke hearts and remaining 5 ingredients; pour dressing over salad, and toss gently. Cover and chill at least 2 hours. Yield: 8 servings.

L. Kay Schultheis
Olivet Heritage Cookbook
Olivet Presbyterian Church
Charlottesville, Virginia

Tabbouleh Primavera

Tabbouleh Primavera MAKE AHEAD

Tamari imparts a mellow flavor, similar to soy sauce, to the vinaigrette that dresses this minted vegetable-bulghur side salad. Find tamari on the condiment aisle near the soy sauce.

1 cup bulghur wheat, uncooked
1 cup boiling water
1⅓ cups chopped tomato (about
    2 medium)
½ cup currants or raisins
½ cup salted dry-roasted sunflower
    kernels

⅓ cup shredded carrot
2 green onions, diagonally sliced
1 garlic clove, minced
2 tablespoons chopped fresh mint
1 tablespoon chopped fresh basil
Pinch of dried oregano
Vinaigrette

COMBINE bulghur and water in a large bowl; cover and let stand 20 minutes or until liquid is absorbed and bulghur is tender.

ADD tomato and next 8 ingredients to bulghur; toss well. Add Vinaigrette; toss. Cover and chill at least 2 hours. Yield: 5 servings.

Vinaigrette

¼ cup red wine vinegar
¼ cup tamari

¼ cup olive oil

COMBINE all ingredients in a small bowl, stirring well with a wire whisk. Yield: ¾ cup.

Miki Roth and Clara McNay
A Culinary Tour of Homes
Big Canoe Chapel Women's Guild
Big Canoe, Georgia

Tabbouleh

Tabbouleh is a Middle Eastern dish. It consists of bulghur wheat that you plump in boiling water and then add an assortment of flavorings, including garlic and mint. The salad is traditionally served cold along with lavosh, a crisp cracker bread.

Creamy Coleslaw

Shredded Shortcut

If you're in a hurry, you can buy already shredded cabbage and carrots to use in this slaw.

Use a food processor to quickly prepare the vegetables for this coleslaw; just be careful not to overprocess them.

1 small cabbage, finely shredded (about 1½ pounds)
1 small carrot, shredded
½ cup diced green bell pepper
½ cup diced celery
¼ cup diced onion
½ cup mayonnaise

½ cup sour cream
2 tablespoons sugar
2 tablespoons white vinegar
1 tablespoon prepared mustard
½ teaspoon salt
½ teaspoon paprika
¼ teaspoon pepper

COMBINE first 5 ingredients in a large bowl; toss well, and set aside. Combine mayonnaise and remaining 7 ingredients; stir well. Pour dressing over vegetables; toss gently. Yield: 8 servings.

Wilted Cabbage   MAKE AHEAD

What Wilts It?

A hot vinegar-and-oil dressing wilts the cabbage and melts the sugar, which helps make the slaw crispy.

This do-ahead slaw tastes great with barbecue sandwiches or sweet and tangy ribs.

1 small cabbage, finely shredded (about 6 cups)
1 large onion, finely chopped
1 medium-size green bell pepper, finely chopped
1 medium-size red bell pepper, finely chopped

¾ cup sugar
1 cup white vinegar
1 cup vegetable oil
1½ teaspoons salt
1 teaspoon sugar
1 teaspoon dry mustard
1 teaspoon celery seeds

COMBINE first 4 ingredients; add ¾ cup sugar, and toss well.
COMBINE vinegar and remaining 5 ingredients in a small saucepan; bring to a boil. Boil 1 minute. Pour hot dressing over cabbage mixture; toss well. Cover and chill at least 8 hours, tossing occasionally. Serve with a slotted spoon. Yield: 6 to 8 servings.

NOTE: Substitute 1 (10-ounce) package shredded angel hair cabbage, if desired.

Cajun Men Cook
The Beaver Club of Lafayette, Louisiana

Wilted Cabbage

Classic Potato Salad WEEKNIGHT FAVORITE

Yellow Potatoes

Yellow Finn potatoes have a buttery yellow flesh similar to Yukon gold potatoes, which would taste good in this recipe, too.

Potato salad is one of the most versatile side dishes around. It pairs perfectly with steak, burgers, kabobs, and chicken.

2½	pounds red potatoes or yellow Finn potatoes	2	green onions, chopped
1	celery rib, diced	1	cup mayonnaise
⅓	cup sweet pickle relish or ½ cup chopped sweet pickles	2	tablespoons lemon juice
2	large hard-cooked eggs, sliced	1	teaspoon salt
		¼	teaspoon pepper
		½	teaspoon dry mustard (optional)

COOK potatoes in boiling water to cover 25 minutes or just until potatoes are tender.
DRAIN well, and cool slightly. Peel and cube potatoes. Combine potato, celery, and next 3 ingredients in a large bowl; toss gently.
COMBINE mayonnaise, next 3 ingredients, and, if desired, dry mustard in a small bowl. Spoon mayonnaise mixture over potato mixture, tossing gently to combine. Serve warm or chilled. Yield: 7 servings.

Ambrosia MAKE AHEAD

Italian Fruits

This is the Italian rendition of ambrosia with native fruits such as cantaloupe, oranges, plums, and a rich balsamic vinegar drizzled into the dressing.

Five fresh fruits mingle in a sweet blend of peach nectar and honey balanced with pungent balsamic vinegar and lemon juice. This blissful salad is special enough to serve as a light dessert.

1	medium cantaloupe, peeled, seeded, and cut into chunks	¾	cup peach nectar
2	navel oranges, sectioned	¼	cup honey
2	cups fresh pineapple chunks	2	tablespoons balsamic vinegar
2	fresh plums, sliced	2	tablespoons lemon juice
1	cup seedless green or red grapes or ½ cup of each		

COMBINE first 5 ingredients in a large bowl. Combine peach nectar and remaining 3 ingredients, stirring with a wire whisk until blended. Pour dressing over fruit mixture, stirring gently to coat fruit. Cover and chill at least 1 hour, stirring occasionally. Yield: 8 servings.

Women Who Can Dish It Out
The Junior League of Springfield, Missouri

Ambrosia

Christmas Ambrosia   PARTY FOOD

Coconut Choices

Grate chunks of fresh coconut easily in a food processor, using a shredder disk. Or you can substitute 2 cups frozen grated fresh coconut, thawed.

Oranges, pineapple, and coconut—traditional ingredients for ambrosia—make a versatile fruit dish to serve as an accompaniment with meat or as a light dessert. Try adding some grapefruit or even chopped pecans or walnuts for a jazzy version you can call your own.

12 small oranges
1 (20-ounce) can crushed pineapple, undrained
2 cups grated fresh coconut

Whipped cream (optional)
Garnish: maraschino cherries with stems

PEEL and section oranges, catching juice in a large nonmetal bowl. Add orange sections, pineapple, and coconut to juice; toss gently. Cover and chill thoroughly.

TO serve, spoon fruit mixture into individual dishes; top each serving with a dollop of whipped cream, if desired. Garnish, if desired. Yield: 6 to 8 servings.

Village Fare
Stone Mountain Woman's Club
Stone Mountain, Georgia

Apple Salad   MAKE AHEAD

Shape It Yourself

If you have a small mold for salads, use it instead of the 9-inch square pan called for in this recipe.

Marshmallows dissolve and sweeten this congealed apple salad. Leave the peel on the apples for pretty color.

2 cups boiling water
1 (3-ounce) package lemon gelatin
20 large marshmallows
½ cup cold water

2 Red Delicious apples, diced
½ cup chopped pecans
Frozen whipped topping, thawed

STIR together first 3 ingredients until blended. Add ½ cup cold water, and chill 30 minutes or until consistency of unbeaten egg white.

STIR in apple and pecans. Pour mixture into a 9-inch square baking dish. Cover and chill 3 hours or until firm. Serve with whipped topping. Yield: 6 servings.

Bunnie George
Birmingham, Alabama

Frozen Orange-Pecan Salad MAKE AHEAD

Congealed salad may remind you of days gone by, but retro or not, this recipe will be well received at a ladies luncheon.

1 (8-ounce) package cream cheese,
    softened
¼ cup orange juice
½ cup chopped pecans, toasted
1 (8-ounce) can crushed pineapple in
    syrup, drained
½ cup chopped pitted dates

¼ cup chopped maraschino cherries
½ teaspoon grated orange rind
1 cup whipping cream
¼ cup sugar
Garnishes: leaf lettuce, orange slices,
    pecan halves

Garnish Counts
This salad will look impressive when you serve it with the recommended garnishes. Toast the pecans for a little extra flavor.

BEAT cream cheese and orange juice at medium speed with an electric mixer until fluffy. Stir in pecans and next 4 ingredients. Beat whipping cream and sugar at high speed until soft peaks form. Fold sweetened whipped cream into cream cheese mixture.

SPOON into a lightly greased 6-cup ring mold or a 9- x 5-inch loafpan. Cover and freeze 8 hours. Unmold ring or loaf pan onto a serving platter. Garnish, if desired. Yield: 10 to 12 servings.

It's About Time: Recipes, Reflections, Realities
National Association Teachers of Family and Consumer Sciences
Bowling Green, Kentucky

Shrimp and Tomato Aspic

Shrimp and Tomato Aspic   MAKE AHEAD

A tangy twosome of blue cheese and cream cheese crowns this savory congealed salad.

3 cups water
¾ pound unpeeled, medium-size
    fresh shrimp
1 (3-ounce) package lemon-flavored
    gelatin
1½ teaspoons unflavored gelatin
1¾ cups vegetable juice, divided
¾ cup minced green bell pepper

¾ cup finely chopped celery
¼ cup prepared horseradish
1 tablespoon Worcestershire sauce
1 (3-ounce) package cream cheese,
    softened
2 tablespoons crumbled blue cheese
2 to 3 tablespoons milk

BRING water to a boil; add shrimp, and cook 3 to 5 minutes or until shrimp turn pink. Drain well; rinse with cold water. Chill. Peel shrimp, and devein, if desired. Chop shrimp, and set aside.

COMBINE gelatins in a medium bowl. Bring 1 cup vegetable juice to a boil; add to gelatin mixture, and cook, stirring 2 minutes or until gelatins dissolve. Remove from heat. Stir in remaining ¾ cup vegetable juice. Chill until consistency of unbeaten egg white.

COMBINE chopped shrimp, green pepper, and next 3 ingredients; stir into gelatin mixture. Pour mixture into a lightly greased 6-cup ring mold; cover and chill until firm.

COMBINE cream cheese and blue cheese in a small mixing bowl; beat at medium speed with an electric mixer until blended. Gradually add enough milk to reach desired consistency, beating until blended. Serve aspic with cream cheese mixture. Yield: 6 servings.

O Taste & Sing
St. Stephen's Episcopal Church Choir
Richmond, Virginia

Save Some Shrimp

Set aside a few whole shrimp for garnish before chopping the cooked shrimp for the aspic.

Chicken Salad   WEEKNIGHT FAVORITE

Pictured on page 265

Chicken salad is comfort food anytime. This version is colored with red and green grapes for a sweet touch.

3 cups chopped cooked chicken
1 cup thinly sliced celery
2 tablespoons lemon juice
1 tablespoon minced onion
½ cup mayonnaise
½ teaspoon salt
½ teaspoon pepper

½ cup seedless green grapes,
    halved lengthwise
½ cup seedless red grapes,
    halved lengthwise
1 (2-ounce) package sliced almonds,
    toasted
Bibb lettuce

COMBINE first 4 ingredients; cover and chill at least 1 hour.

COMBINE mayonnaise, salt, and pepper. Add mayonnaise mixture, grapes, and almonds to chilled chicken mixture; toss gently. Serve chicken salad in lettuce cups. Yield: 6 servings.

Creative Containers

Here are several options for creative serving containers for chicken salad: a hollowed out tomato or orange; a lettuce leaf; or a bread bowl.

Greek-Style Tuna Salad MAKE AHEAD   QUICK & EASY

What's the Best Tuna?

This recipe puts canned tuna to good use, but if you want to take this salad over the top, use fresh tuna. Grill or broil a tuna steak, flake it, and add to the salad.

Tuna salad goes Greek with the addition of feta cheese, olives, and oregano.

1 cup orzo, uncooked
1 (6⅛-ounce) can solid white tuna, drained and flaked
2 cups chopped tomato
½ cup crumbled feta cheese
¼ cup chopped purple onion
3 tablespoons sliced ripe olives

½ cup red wine vinegar
2 tablespoons water
2 tablespoons olive oil
1 garlic clove, minced
½ teaspoon dried basil
½ teaspoon dried oregano
Green leaf lettuce (optional)

COOK orzo according to package directions; drain, rinse with cold water, and drain again. Combine orzo, tuna, and next 4 ingredients in a large bowl; toss gently.

PROCESS vinegar and next 5 ingredients in a blender until smooth, stopping to scrape down sides. Pour vinegar mixture over pasta mixture, and toss gently. Cover and chill thoroughly. Serve on lettuce leaves, if desired. Yield: 6 servings.

Beth Smith
Briarwood Recipes to Crown Your Table
Women's Ministries of Briarwood Presbyterian Church
Birmingham, Alabama

Party Taco Salad PARTY FOOD

Taco Salad Appeal

Kids of all ages will gobble up this taco salad in a bowl. Buy an extra bag of corn chips for dipping leftovers.

To serve this taco salad neatly and easily, just layer it in a big bowl and provide salad tongs. Serve it right away so the warm cheese sauce doesn't wilt the other ingredients.

1 pound lean ground beef
½ cup chopped green bell pepper
1 cup chopped onion
1 tablespoon chili powder
1½ pounds iceberg lettuce, shredded
2 large tomatoes, chopped

1 (10.5-ounce) package corn chips
1 (16-ounce) loaf process cheese spread, cut into pieces
1 (10-ounce) can diced tomatoes and green chiles

COOK first 4 ingredients in a large nonstick skillet over medium heat until beef is done, stirring to crumble beef; drain.

PLACE shredded lettuce in a large bowl; top with chopped tomato, corn chips, and beef mixture.

COMBINE cheese spread and diced tomatoes in a saucepan; cook over low heat, stirring often, until cheese melts. Pour cheese sauce over salad, and serve immediately. Yield: 6 to 8 servings.

Rene Ralph
Broken Arrow, Oklahoma

Sandwiches,
Soups &
Condiments

Brunswick Stew, page 311
Grilled Apple and Cheese
Sandwiches, page 292

Grilled Apple and Cheese Sandwiches

QUICK & EASY

Pictured on previous page

Tired of plain old grilled cheese sandwiches? Try this fabulous flavor teaser—a combination of shredded sharp Cheddar cheese, tart apple, and pimiento-stuffed olives.

1 cup (4 ounces) shredded sharp Cheddar cheese	¼ cup mayonnaise
1 cup finely chopped cooking apple	8 slices white or whole wheat bread
⅓ cup minced pimiento-stuffed olives	Melted butter or margarine

COMBINE cheese, apple, olives, and mayonnaise in a medium bowl, and stir well.

SPREAD cheese mixture evenly on 1 side of 4 slices of bread to within ¼ inch of edges. Top with remaining bread slices; brush top slices of bread with melted butter, and invert onto a hot griddle. Immediately brush other sides of sandwiches with melted butter; cook over medium heat until golden. Turn sandwiches, and brown other sides. Yield: 4 servings.

Joan K. Bartley
Culinary Classics, From Our Kitchens
Mountain State Apple Harvest Festival
Martinsburg, West Virginia

French Club Sandwiches

Tailgating takes a tasty turn when this winning cream cheese club sandwich is served.

2 (8-ounce) packages cream cheese, softened	2 tablespoons finely chopped onion
¼ cup mayonnaise	1 tablespoon lemon juice
¾ cup finely chopped celery	1 tablespoon Worcestershire sauce
½ cup (2 ounces) shredded Cheddar cheese	¼ teaspoon seasoned salt
⅓ cup chopped fresh parsley	2 (1-pound) French baguettes
	2 pounds thinly sliced cooked ham
	6 dill pickles, thinly sliced lengthwise

COMBINE cream cheese and mayonnaise; beat at medium speed with an electric mixer until mixture is creamy. Stir in celery and next 6 ingredients.

CUT baguettes horizontally in half lengthwise; spread cream cheese mixture over cut sides of bread. Place ham evenly on bottom halves of baguettes; top ham with pickles. Cover with tops of baguettes. Cut each baguette into 6 portions. Yield: 12 servings.

Down by the Water
The Junior League of Columbia, South Carolina

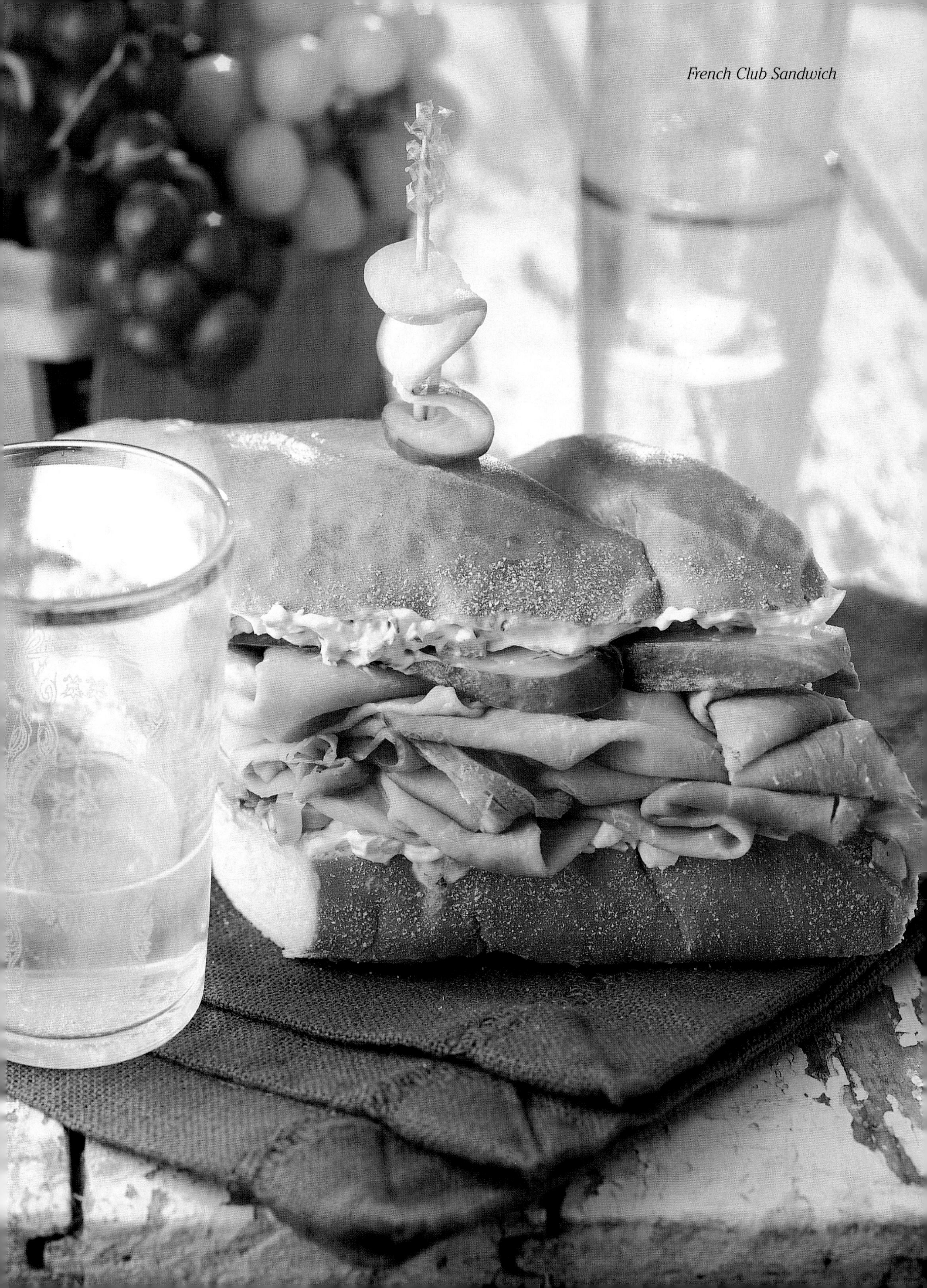

French Club Sandwich

Barbecue for Sandwiches

Barbecue for Sandwiches

Dump all the ingredients in the slow cooker and come back 7 hours later to this well-seasoned barbecue. Shred the meat easily at the end of cooking by mashing it against the side of the slow cooker with the back of a spoon.

1½ pounds beef stew meat	¼ cup white vinegar
1½ pounds lean cubed pork	1 tablespoon chili powder
1 green bell pepper, chopped	2 teaspoons salt
1 small onion, chopped (about 1 cup)	1 teaspoon dry mustard
1 (6-ounce) can tomato paste	2 teaspoons Worcestershire sauce
½ cup firmly packed light brown sugar	

COMBINE all ingredients in a 5-quart electric slow cooker. Cover and cook on HIGH setting 7 hours. Shred meat before serving. Yield: 6 servings.

Isabelle White
7 Alarm Cuisine
East Mountain Volunteer Fire Department
Gladewater, Texas

Stroganoff Steak Sandwiches

Tender slices of dark beer-marinated flank steak are nestled atop crusty portions of French bread, and then capped with sautéed onions and an ample dollop of sour cream.

2 pounds flank steak	4 medium onions, sliced
⅔ cup dark beer	½ teaspoon paprika
⅓ cup vegetable oil	2 tablespoons butter, melted
1 teaspoon garlic powder	12 (1-inch-thick) slices French bread
1 teaspoon salt	1 (8-ounce) container sour cream
¼ teaspoon pepper	

PLACE flank steak in a large heavy-duty zip-top plastic bag. Combine beer and next 4 ingredients; stir well. Pour marinade over steak. Seal bag securely; marinate in refrigerator 8 hours, turning occasionally.

REMOVE steak from marinade, discarding marinade. Place flank steak on a lightly greased rack of broiler pan; broil 3 inches from heat 10 minutes on each side or to desired degree of doneness. Cut steak diagonally across the grain into thin strips.

COOK onions and paprika in butter in a large skillet over medium-high heat, stirring constantly, until tender.

TO serve, place 2 slices French bread on serving plates; top with steak, onion, and sour cream. Yield: 6 servings.

Mary Shepley
Kimball Kub Grub
Kimball Elementary PTA
Kimball, Michigan

Cobb Sandwiches   GRILL LOVERS

Similar to the famous Cobb Salad, this sandwich boasts the same stack of great ingredients: chicken, bacon, tomato, avocado, and blue cheese.

4 skinned and boned chicken
    breast halves
½ teaspoon salt
½ teaspoon pepper
¼ cup olive oil
¼ cup balsamic vinegar
1 tablespoon Dijon mustard
Vegetable cooking spray
1 ripe avocado

1 teaspoon fresh lemon juice
⅓ cup mayonnaise
8 slices challah or other egg bread,
    toasted
4 Boston lettuce leaves
1 tomato, thinly sliced
8 ounces blue cheese, thinly sliced
8 bacon slices, cooked and crumbled

SPRINKLE chicken with salt and pepper; place in a shallow dish.

COMBINE oil, vinegar, and mustard; pour over chicken. Cover chicken, and marinate in refrigerator at least 30 minutes, turning occasionally. Drain, discarding marinade.

COAT grill rack with cooking spray; place on grill over medium-high heat (350° to 400°). Grill chicken, covered with grill lid, 5 minutes on each side or until done. Let chicken stand until cool to touch; cut chicken diagonally into thin slices.

SLICE avocado, and sprinkle with lemon juice. Spread mayonnaise evenly on 1 side of each bread slice. Layer 4 slices of bread with lettuce, tomato, avocado, cheese, bacon, and chicken; top with remaining bread slices. Yield: 4 servings.

Landmark Entertaining
The Junior League of Abilene, Texas

Rich Bread

Rather than sliced bread, this sandwich is made with braided challah, a traditional Jewish yeast bread rich with eggs. It has a light, airy texture and is great for sandwiches.

Shrimp Po' Boys

Serve this long crusty loaf with coleslaw and chips.

1 (1-pound) loaf unsliced French bread
¼ cup butter or margarine, melted
2 pounds unpeeled large fresh
   shrimp
1⅓ cups cornmeal mix
6 cups vegetable oil

⅓ cup mayonnaise
2½ tablespoons sweet pickle relish
1 tablespoon lemon juice
⅛ teaspoon hot sauce
1 cup shredded lettuce
1 large tomato, thinly sliced

SLICE off top third of loaf; hollow out bottom section, reserving crumbs for another use. Spread inside surfaces of bread with butter. Place bread on a baking sheet, and bake at 400° for 8 minutes. Set aside.

PEEL shrimp, and devein, if desired.

DREDGE shrimp in cornmeal mix. Fry shrimp, in batches, in deep hot oil (375°) 2 minutes or until shrimp float to the top and are golden. Drain shrimp well on paper towels; keep warm.

COMBINE mayonnaise and next 3 ingredients; stir well. Stir in lettuce. Spread lettuce mixture in hollowed bread. Top with tomato slices, shrimp, and top of loaf. Cut loaf into 4 portions. Yield: 4 servings.

Crumbs

Save the crumbs left over from hollowed out bread. Freeze crumbs in a zip-top plastic bag, and keep them until you need a breadcrumb topping for a casserole.

Oyster Loaf

Enjoy crusty fried oysters sandwiched into a French loaf with bacon, tomatoes, and a tangy horseradish mayonnaise.

1 cup mayonnaise
1 tablespoon plus 1 teaspoon
   prepared horseradish
6 to 8 bacon slices
3 (10-ounce) containers fresh Select
   oysters, drained
½ cup all-purpose flour

2 medium tomatoes, sliced
1 (16-ounce) loaf French bread
2 garlic cloves
3 tablespoons butter or margarine,
   melted
Garnish: lemon wedges

COMBINE mayonnaise and horseradish; stir well. Chill. Cook bacon in a large skillet until crisp; remove bacon, reserving drippings in skillet. Crumble bacon; set aside. Dredge oysters in flour. Fry oysters in drippings over medium heat 3 to 4 minutes or until golden, turning once. Remove oysters, reserving drippings in skillet. Drain oysters. Lightly sauté tomato in drippings; set aside.

CUT a thick slice from top of loaf. Using a gentle sawing motion, cut vertically to, but not through, bottom of loaf, ¼ inch from edge. Lift out center; reserve for another use. Cut garlic in half. Rub inside of loaf with cut sides of garlic; discard garlic. Drizzle butter inside of loaf. Place oysters in loaf; top with bacon and tomato slices. Cover with top of loaf. Wrap in aluminum foil. Bake at 350° for 10 minutes or until heated. Cut into slices; serve with mayonnaise mixture. Garnish, if desired. Yield: 8 servings.

Oyster Adage

Oysters are at their best during fall and winter (the months that end with "r"). Oysters spawn in the summer months and become soft and fatty.

A Feast for All Seasons
Mt. Lebanon Junior Women's Club
Pittsburgh, Pennsylvania

Oyster Loaf

Cream of Roasted Tomato Soup with Parsley Croutons

Roasting tomatoes brings out the sweet, intense flavor of the vine-ripened fruit. Thin, crispy croutons seasoned with garlic and topped with Muenster cheese grace each serving of this soup that's good year-round hot or cold.

With or Without Cream

We liked this soup every bit as much without the 1 cup of cream added near the end of cooking. We prepared it *sans* cream for the photograph at right, and the color's actually brighter.

3 pounds tomatoes, cut in half
    crosswise and seeded
3 tablespoons olive oil
1 small head fennel
3 tablespoons unsalted butter
3 small shallots, coarsely chopped
1 small carrot, coarsely chopped
3 cups chicken broth, divided

5 fresh tarragon sprigs
5 fresh parsley sprigs
1 cup whipping cream
¼ teaspoon salt
¼ teaspoon pepper
Parsley Croutons
Garnish: chopped tomato

BRUSH tomato halves with olive oil; place tomato halves, cut side down, in an aluminum foil-lined shallow baking dish. Bake, uncovered, at 400° for 45 minutes or until tomato is soft and skins are dark. Cool to touch; remove skins.

RINSE fennel thoroughly. Trim and discard bulb base. Trim stalks from bulb; discard stalks. Coarsely chop fennel bulb.

MELT butter in a large saucepan over medium heat; add fennel, shallot, and carrot, and cook 12 minutes or until vegetables are tender. Add 2 cups chicken broth, tarragon, and parsley. Reduce heat, and simmer, uncovered, 30 minutes. Remove from heat. Discard herb sprigs, and add tomato halves. Cool slightly.

POUR mixture into a blender; process until smooth, stopping to scrape down sides. Return puree to saucepan; stir in whipping cream. Bring just to a simmer; stir in remaining 1 cup chicken broth, salt, and pepper.

TO serve, ladle soup into individual bowls; top each serving with Parsley Croutons. Garnish, if desired. Yield: 7 cups.

Parsley Croutons

12 thin slices French baguette
3 tablespoons olive oil
2 garlic cloves, halved

½ cup (2 ounces) shredded
    Muenster cheese
¼ cup chopped fresh parsley

BRUSH both sides of baguette slices with olive oil; rub garlic halves over slices. Place slices on an ungreased baking sheet, and sprinkle evenly with cheese and parsley. Bake, uncovered, at 400° for 5 minutes or until golden. Yield: 1 dozen croutons.

Savour St. Louis
Barnes-Jewish Hospital Auxiliary Plaza Chapter
St. Louis, Missouri

Cream of Roasted Tomato Soup with Parsley Croutons

Red Bell Pepper Soup   MAKE AHEAD

Garnish Options
If you don't have green onions for garnishing this soup, use fresh herb sprigs or celery leaves.

Sweet red peppers are showcased in this chilled soup laced with sherry and heavy cream.

6 red bell peppers, chopped
1 large onion, chopped
2 celery ribs, chopped
4 cups chicken broth
1 (7-ounce) jar diced pimiento, drained
2 teaspoons fresh lemon juice

1 teaspoon salt
½ teaspoon curry powder
½ teaspoon pepper
1 cup whipping cream
2 tablespoons dry sherry
Garnish: chopped green onions

COMBINE first 4 ingredients in a Dutch oven; bring to a boil. Cover, reduce heat, and simmer 10 minutes or until vegetables are tender. Remove from heat; stir in pimiento.

LADLE half of vegetable mixture into a blender; process until smooth, stopping to scrape down sides. Repeat procedure with remaining half of vegetable mixture. Return mixture to pan; stir in lemon juice and next 3 ingredients. Bring to a boil; reduce heat, and simmer, uncovered, 10 minutes, stirring occasionally. Cover and chill at least 8 hours.

STIR whipping cream and sherry into chilled soup. Ladle soup into individual bowls; garnish, if desired. Yield: 8 cups.

Mary Peyton
Amazin' Grazin'
First United Methodist Church
Balmorhea, Texas

Vicki's Cheese Soup

Cheddar Choices
If you don't have mild Cheddar on hand, try medium, sharp, or even white Cheddar in this soup.

Chunky fresh vegetables highlight satiny-smooth cheese soup in this winter warmer.

1 medium onion, finely chopped
2 celery ribs, finely chopped
2 medium carrots, finely chopped
1 garlic clove, minced
½ cup butter or margarine, melted
1 cup chopped fresh broccoli
1 cup chopped fresh cauliflower
½ cup all-purpose flour

3 cups chicken broth
2½ cups milk
2 cups (8 ounces) shredded mild
      Cheddar cheese
1½ teaspoons Worcestershire sauce
½ teaspoon salt
Dash of pepper
½ cup sliced natural almonds, toasted

COOK first 4 ingredients in butter in a heavy 4-quart saucepan over medium-high heat 2 minutes, stirring constantly. Stir in broccoli and cauliflower; cook 3 minutes, stirring constantly.

STIR in flour; cook 1 minute, stirring constantly. Gradually add broth and milk; cook over medium heat, stirring constantly, until mixture is thickened and bubbly. Remove from heat; add cheese and next 3 ingredients, stirring until cheese melts.

LADLE soup into individual bowls; sprinkle evenly with almonds. Yield: 8 cups.

Emily Harper
Centennial Cookbook 1895-1995
First Associate Reformed Presbyterian Church
Rock Hill, South Carolina

Brie and Roasted Garlic Soup

Roasting the garlic makes it a sweet and mellow flavor base for this soup. Buttery Brie melts into the broth, making it rich, creamy, and in a class by itself. Grab a spoon and indulge.

2 large heads garlic
2 tablespoons olive oil
7 ounces Brie
2 celery ribs, finely chopped
1 medium onion, finely chopped
1 medium carrot, finely chopped
¼ cup olive oil

¼ cup all-purpose flour
6 cups chicken broth
1 teaspoon chopped fresh oregano
1 teaspoon chopped fresh parsley
½ teaspoon chopped fresh thyme
⅛ teaspoon ground white pepper

PEEL and discard outer skin from each garlic head. Cut off top one-third of each garlic head. Place garlic, cut side up, on an aluminum foil-lined baking sheet. Drizzle garlic with 2 tablespoons olive oil. Bake, uncovered, at 350° for 1 hour or until garlic is soft. Remove from oven; cool 10 minutes. Squeeze pulp from each clove; set pulp aside.

REMOVE and discard rind from cheese; coarsely chop cheese, and set aside.

COOK celery, onion, and carrot in ¼ cup olive oil in a large saucepan over medium-high heat, stirring constantly, 10 minutes or until tender. Add flour, stirring until smooth. Cook 1 minute, stirring constantly. Gradually add chicken broth; bring to a boil, stirring often. Reduce heat, and simmer, uncovered, 15 minutes or until vegetables are tender, stirring often.

PROCESS garlic pulp and 1 cup soup mixture in a food processor until smooth. Stir pureed mixture into remaining soup mixture; add oregano, parsley, and thyme. Bring to a simmer over medium-low heat. Add cheese, and cook, stirring constantly, until cheese melts. Stir in pepper. Yield: 6½ cups.

Apron Strings: Ties to the Southern Tradition of Cooking
The Junior League of Little Rock, Arkansas

The Goodness of Garlic

Roasted garlic is good with many foods such as roasted chicken or turkey, or mashed potatoes. Or you can simply spread it on grilled bread as an appetizer.

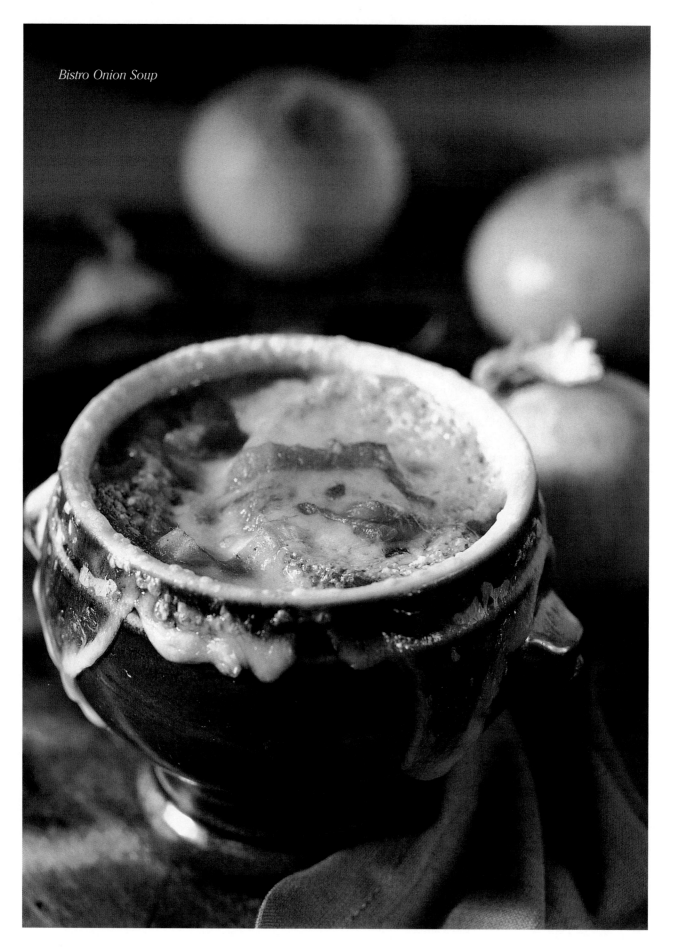

Bistro Onion Soup

Bistro Onion Soup

Creamy, oozing Gruyère cheese blankets a bowlful of caramelized onions and toasts swimming in a rich broth. This is casual comfort food at its best.

4 large onions (about 2 pounds),
    sliced and separated into rings
¼ cup butter or margarine, melted
2 tablespoons all-purpose flour
5¼ cups water
½ cup dry white wine
½ cup dry red wine
4 chicken bouillon cubes

4 beef bouillon cubes
2 bay leaves
½ teaspoon salt
½ teaspoon dried sage
¼ teaspoon pepper
8 (½-inch) diagonally sliced French
    bread slices, toasted
8 slices Gruyère cheese

SAUTÉ onion in butter in a Dutch oven over medium heat, stirring often, 15 to 20 minutes or until golden. Stir in flour; cook 1 minute. Add water and next 8 ingredients. Bring to a boil; reduce heat, and simmer, partially covered, 30 minutes. Discard bay leaves.

LADLE soup into 4 individual ovenproof soup bowls. Place on a baking sheet. Add 2 bread slices to each bowl, and cover each with 2 slices of cheese. Broil 5½ inches from heat 4 minutes or until cheese is bubbly. Serve immediately. Yield: 6 cups.

Gracious Gator Cooks
The Junior League of Gainesville, Florida

Caramelized Onions

The longer you sauté onion rings in butter, the deeper the color and caramelized flavor will be. You can even caramelize onions a day ahead, refrigerate them, and then reheat the next day and proceed with the recipe.

Baked Potato Soup   WEEKNIGHT FAVORITE

This family pleaser is the ever popular loaded and stuffed baked potato—soup style.

4 large baking potatoes
⅔ cup butter or margarine
⅔ cup all-purpose flour
7 cups milk
4 green onions, sliced
1 (12-ounce) package bacon, cooked
    and crumbled

1¼ cups (5 ounces) shredded
    Cheddar cheese
1 (8-ounce) container sour cream
¾ teaspoon salt
½ teaspoon pepper

BAKE potatoes at 400° for 1 hour or until done; cool. Cut potatoes in half lengthwise; scoop out pulp, mash to desired texture, and reserve. Discard shells.

MELT butter in a Dutch oven over low heat. Whisk in flour until smooth. Cook 1 minute, whisking constantly. Gradually whisk in milk; cook over medium heat, whisking constantly, until mixture is thickened and bubbly.

STIR in potato pulp and green onions; bring to a boil. Cover, reduce heat, and simmer 10 minutes. Add bacon and remaining ingredients; stir until cheese melts. Serve immediately. Yield: 14 cups.

Simple Pleasures: From Our Table to Yours
Arab Mothers' Club
Arab, Alabama

"Baked" Potato in a Bowl

This soup has all the yummy flavors and ingredients of a twice-baked potato in a bowl. It's perfect to take to a friend in need of a warm supper.

Curried Carrot Soup

Complexly flavored curry kisses this creamy carrot soup.

Curry's a Keeper

Curry and carrot make a delightful flavor pairing. Curry powder is a blend of many spices including cinnamon, cloves, fennel seed, nutmeg, pepper, cumin, and turmeric. Curry powder stays fresh up to 2 months.

1 medium onion, chopped
1 teaspoon dried thyme
1 bay leaf
2 tablespoons vegetable oil
4 medium carrots, cut into ½-inch pieces
3 (14½-ounce) cans chicken broth
1 (8-ounce) package cream cheese, softened
3 tablespoons chopped fresh parsley
1½ tablespoons curry powder
¼ teaspoon salt
Dash of ground red pepper

SAUTÉ first 3 ingredients in hot oil in a large saucepan over medium-high heat until onion is tender. Add carrot and chicken broth; bring to a boil. Reduce heat, and simmer, uncovered, 30 minutes or until carrot is tender. Discard bay leaf.

PROCESS half of carrot mixture and half of cream cheese in a blender until smooth. Repeat procedure with remaining half of carrot mixture and cream cheese. Stir in parsley, curry, salt, and red pepper. Return puree to saucepan, and cook until thoroughly heated. Yield: 6 cups.

Clinky Seabrook
Angels in the Kitchen
Grace Episcopal Church
Anderson, South Carolina

Hearty Lentil Soup   ONE POT

Smoked ham hocks permeate the broth, giving a richness to the legumes.

Little Lentils

Lentils are tiny legumes that are a staple throughout the Middle East and India. There are 3 varieties—red, yellow, and brown—the last of which is the most common lentil found in U.S. markets.

1 pound dried lentils
1½ pounds smoked ham hocks
4 cups beef broth
4 cups water
1 (28-ounce) can crushed tomatoes
1 (8-ounce) can tomato sauce
½ small cabbage, chopped
4 celery ribs, sliced
2 large onions, chopped
2 carrots, sliced
½ cup chopped fresh parsley
2 bay leaves
2 teaspoons salt
1 teaspoon dried basil
½ teaspoon pepper

COMBINE all ingredients in a Dutch oven; stir well. Bring to a boil; cover, reduce heat, and simmer 3 hours, stirring occasionally. Remove ham hocks; cool. Remove meat from bones; discard fat and bones. Cut meat into bite-size pieces; stir into soup. Cook over medium-high heat until heated. Discard bay leaves. Yield: 15 cups.

Cindy Blaser
Favorite Recipes
Tillamook County Dairy Women
Tillamook, Oregon

Fresh Vegetable Soup

Stir all your garden produce into this soul-satisfying soup. Then bake a skillet of cornbread for dunking.

1 (1-pound) meaty beef shank bone
2½ quarts water
1 (16-ounce) can stewed tomatoes,
    undrained and coarsely chopped
1½ cups fresh or frozen lima beans
1 cup cut corn
½ cup chopped onion
1 large potato, peeled and cubed
1 large carrot, sliced

1 tablespoon brown sugar (optional)
1 teaspoon salt
1 teaspoon dried Italian seasoning
½ teaspoon pepper
½ teaspoon hot sauce
1 bay leaf
1½ tablespoons all-purpose flour
1½ tablespoons water

BRING shank bone and 2½ quarts water to a boil in a large Dutch oven. Cover, reduce heat, and simmer 1 hour. Cover and chill 8 hours.

DISCARD solidified fat on top of broth. Strain broth; return to Dutch oven. Bring to a boil; add tomatoes and next 11 ingredients. Reduce heat, and simmer, uncovered, 1 hour.

COMBINE flour and water, stirring to make a paste; add to soup, stirring until blended. Cook, stirring constantly, until soup thickens. Discard bay leaf. Yield: 10 cups.

Slurry Defined

The flour and water paste that thickens this soup is called a "slurry." To make one, flour is blended with liquid until smooth. It's a safeguard against lumpy gravy or, in this case, soup.

Chicken Soup

Some say chicken soup has healing powers. This recipe won't disappoint. It's chock-full of familiar ingredients in each spoonful: chicken, rice, carrots, and celery.

1½ pounds chicken breast tenderloins
6 cups chicken broth
½ cup uncooked rice
3 medium carrots, thinly sliced
2 celery ribs, thinly sliced
½ cup thinly sliced green onions
2 small zucchini, diced

¼ cup chopped fresh parsley
6 tablespoons butter
6 tablespoons all-purpose flour
2 cups half-and-half
½ teaspoon salt
¼ teaspoon freshly ground pepper
½ cup chopped fresh mushrooms

ARRANGE chicken on a lightly greased 15- x 10-inch jellyroll pan in a single layer. Bake at 375° for 8 minutes; cool and coarsely chop. Set aside.

BRING chicken broth to a boil in a Dutch oven; add rice. Reduce heat; simmer, uncovered, 10 minutes. Add carrot, celery, and green onions; simmer 10 more minutes. Add zucchini and parsley; simmer 2 minutes. Remove from heat.

MELT butter in a medium saucepan over medium-high heat. Whisk in flour until smooth. Cook 1 minute, whisking constantly. Gradually add half-and-half and cook over medium heat 5 minutes, stirring constantly, until thickened and bubbly. Add 1 cup soup, salt, pepper and mushrooms; stir well.

ADD half-and-half mixture and reserved chopped chicken to soup; stir well. Bring to a boil; cook 2 minutes, stirring constantly. Serve immediately. Yield: 10½ cups.

Just Right

The consistency of this soup is perfect right off the stove. If it thickens as it cools, just add a little broth or half-and-half and reheat.

Mexican Lime Soup ONE POT

Tortilla Snack
Once you start nibbling on the crispy tortilla strips for this chicken soup, you won't be able to quit. Fry a few extras and enjoy them as an hors d'oeuvre.

This south-of-the-border chicken soup comes with an innovative and enticing garnish— crunchy strips of fried corn tortillas.

2 (14½-ounce) cans chicken broth
1 medium onion, thinly sliced and separated into rings
1 large green bell pepper, cut into very thin strips
1 large red bell pepper, cut into very thin strips
⅔ cup thinly sliced carrot
⅔ cup sliced celery
½ teaspoon salt
¼ teaspoon pepper
1 cup shredded cooked chicken breast
2 to 3 tablespoons chopped fresh cilantro
2 tablespoons fresh lime juice
Lime slices
Tortilla Strips

COMBINE first 8 ingredients in a large saucepan; bring to a boil. Cover, reduce heat, and simmer 10 minutes. Stir in chicken, cilantro, and lime juice; cook until thoroughly heated.

LADLE soup into individual bowls; top each serving with lime slices and Tortilla Strips. Yield: 7 cups.

Tortilla Strips

4 (6-inch) corn tortillas
2 tablespoons vegetable oil

CUT each tortilla into thin strips.

HEAT oil in a large skillet until hot. Add tortilla strips, and fry 3 to 4 minutes or until crisp. Drain tortilla strips on paper towels. Yield: 1½ cups.

Cherry Ring Peters
Chér . . . It's Good!
Louisiana Garden Club Federation
Lafayette, Louisiana

Mexican Lime Soup

Easy Corn and Crab Soup ONE POT

Fresh crab is enhanced with sweet corn in this soup, which is not quite as thick as chowder.

¼ cup butter
¼ cup all-purpose flour
2 cups chicken broth
2 cups half-and-half
1 pound fresh lump crabmeat, drained

1 (11-ounce) can whole kernel corn, drained
½ teaspoon salt
¼ teaspoon garlic powder
¼ teaspoon pepper

MELT butter in a heavy saucepan over low heat; add flour, stirring until smooth. Cook 1 minute, stirring constantly. Gradually add broth; cook over medium heat, stirring constantly, until thickened. Stir in half-and-half and remaining ingredients; cover, reduce heat, and simmer 20 minutes. Yield: 6 cups.

Pennyé L. Conner
Nun Better: Tastes and Tales from Around a Cajun Table
St. Cecilia School
Broussard, Louisiana

Fresh Corn Alternative

If you can and preserve corn in the summer months, this would be a great dish to use it. Just add about 1½ cups kernels in lieu of canned corn.

Seafood Gumbo

How Gumbo Got Its Name

Gumbo traces its roots to Africa where the word gumbo is derived from the African word for "okra." It's only fitting because this version is packed with 2 pounds of the little green pods. Once cooked, okra acts as a natural thickener for this stewlike meal.

2 pounds fresh okra
¼ cup vegetable oil
2 tablespoons vegetable oil
2 tablespoons all-purpose flour
2 small onions, finely chopped
2 celery ribs, chopped
1 green bell pepper, finely chopped
1 cup finely chopped green onions
2 garlic cloves, minced
1 (6-ounce) can tomato paste
3 large bay leaves
¼ teaspoon dried thyme
1 tablespoon salt

½ teaspoon hot sauce
¼ teaspoon ground red pepper
½ teaspoon freshly ground pepper
1 tablespoon Worcestershire sauce
1 (16-ounce) can whole tomatoes, undrained and chopped
7 cups water
1 pound fresh crabmeat
2½ pounds large fresh shrimp, peeled and deveined
2 tablespoons chopped fresh parsley
4 cups hot cooked rice

WASH okra; trim stem ends and cut into ½-inch slices. Sauté okra in ¼ cup hot oil in a large Dutch oven over high heat for 5 minutes. Reduce heat to medium-low, and cook 40 minutes, stirring often; set aside.

COMBINE 2 tablespoons oil and flour in a Dutch oven; cook over medium-high heat 5 minutes, stirring constantly. Add onion and celery; cook 5 minutes. Add bell pepper, green onions, and garlic; cook 3 minutes. Add tomato paste and next 7 ingredients; stir well. Gradually add tomatoes, water, and reserved okra; bring to a boil. Cover, reduce heat, and simmer 30 minutes. (Simmer gumbo uncovered for thicker results.)

MEANWHILE, drain and flake crabmeat, removing any bits of shell. Add crabmeat and shrimp; simmer 10 minutes. Stir in parsley. Discard bay leaves. Serve with rice. Yield: 15½ cups.

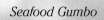
Seafood Gumbo

Oyster-Corn Chowder

On Oysters
Oysters need to cook only briefly, sometimes less than 5 minutes. As soon as their edges curl, they're ready for eating.

Oyster soups are popular during the holiday season. This recipe hails from South Carolina, where oyster harvesting comes easy during the fall and winter months.

1 large onion, chopped	1 (7-ounce) can cream-style corn
2 celery ribs, chopped	1 teaspoon salt
¼ cup butter	½ teaspoon sugar
2 new potatoes, cut into ¼-inch cubes	¼ teaspoon freshly ground pepper
2 medium carrots, cut into ¼-inch cubes	1 to 2 (12-ounce) containers fresh oysters, undrained
¼ cup chopped fresh Italian parsley	Garnish: chopped fresh Italian parsley
3 cups half-and-half, divided	

SAUTÉ onion and celery in butter in a Dutch oven over medium heat until tender. Add potato, carrot, and ¼ cup parsley; cook 1 minute. Add 2 cups half-and-half, and bring to a boil. Reduce heat, and simmer, uncovered, 15 minutes or until potato is tender. Stir in remaining 1 cup half-and-half, corn, and next 4 ingredients. Bring to a boil; reduce heat, and simmer, uncovered, 5 minutes or until edges of oysters curl. Serve immediately. Garnish, if desired. Yield: 8 cups.

Yuletide on Hilton Head: A Heritage of Island Flavors
United Way of Beaufort County
Hilton Head Island, South Carolina

Old-Fashioned Beef Stew

Onion Options
If you don't have boiling onions, just use a pound of the larger white or yellow onions, and cut them into small wedges.

Classic beef stew breathes new life into a soup supper. This stew's almost a one-dish meal. Just add some rolls and a salad.

4 pounds beef stew meat, cut into 1-inch pieces	1 teaspoon Worcestershire sauce
2 tablespoons vegetable oil	½ teaspoon paprika
2 cups water	½ teaspoon pepper
2 medium onions, sliced	6 carrots, quartered
1 garlic clove, minced	6 potatoes, peeled and quartered
2 bay leaves	1 pound boiling onions
1 tablespoon salt	¼ cup water
	2 tablespoons all-purpose flour

BROWN beef in batches in hot oil in a large Dutch oven. Add water and next 7 ingredients. Bring to a boil; cover, reduce heat, and simmer 1½ hours, stirring often.

ADD carrot, potato, and boiling onions; cover and cook 30 to 40 minutes or until meat and vegetables are tender. Discard bay leaves.

STIR together ¼ cup water and flour until smooth. Stir flour mixture into stew, and cook, stirring constantly, 3 minutes or until bubbly. Yield: 15 cups.

John T. Fagan
A Perfect Measurement of Love
Little Flower Children's Services of New York
Wading River, New York

Brunswick Stew

Pictured on page 291

The battle over authentic Brunswick stew is endless. Depending on which part of the country you're from, ingredients vary. But generally, the recipe includes chicken (and sometimes rabbit) and a host of vegetables cooked to a stewed consistency.

1 (3-pound) broiler-fryer
1½ teaspoons salt
1 cup peeled, chopped red potatoes
1 (15-ounce) can tomato sauce
1¾ cups frozen lima beans
⅔ cup chopped onion
1¾ cups frozen whole kernel corn

1 teaspoon sugar
¼ teaspoon salt
⅛ teaspoon pepper
⅛ teaspoon ground red pepper
⅛ teaspoon dried oregano
⅛ teaspoon poultry seasoning

PLACE chicken and 1½ teaspoons salt in a large Dutch oven; add water to cover. Bring to a boil; cover, reduce heat, and simmer 2 to 2½ hours or until done. Drain, reserving broth. Remove and discard skin from chicken. Bone chicken; shred meat. Set aside.

SKIM fat from reserved broth. Return broth to Dutch oven; bring to a boil. Reduce heat, and simmer, uncovered, until broth is reduced to 2 cups. Add potato, and simmer 10 minutes. Add tomato sauce, lima beans, and onion, and simmer 20 more minutes. Stir in reserved chicken, corn, and remaining ingredients, and simmer 10 more minutes or until vegetables are tender. Yield: 8½ cups.

Village Vittles
Grace Presbyterian Village Auxiliary
Dallas, Texas

How this Stew Got its Start
Brunswick Stew originated in Brunswick County, Virginia, in the early 1800s. Back then, squirrel was the meat of choice.

Frogmore Stew ONE POT

This seafood stew is a hallmark recipe of the Lowcountry. It's a mix of sausage, potatoes, corn, and shrimp seasoned with a bagged spice mix and boiled until everything's tender.

10 quarts water
1 (5-ounce) package crab boil
2 large onions, quartered
3 pounds smoked sausage, cut into
    1-inch pieces

3 pounds new potatoes
12 ears fresh corn, cut in half
3 pounds unpeeled, large fresh shrimp

BRING water to a boil in a large stockpot. Add crab boil, onion, sausage, and potatoes; return to a boil, and cook 35 minutes or until potatoes are tender. Remove onion, sausage, and potatoes with a slotted spoon to a large bowl or platter; keep warm.

ADD corn to stockpot; return to a boil, and cook 10 minutes. Add shrimp; cook 3 more minutes. Remove corn and shrimp with a slotted spoon to bowl with potato mixture. Serve immediately with cocktail sauce, if desired. Yield: 10 to 12 servings.

W. Frank Cason
A Dab of This and a Dab of That
Bethlehem Baptist Church Senior Missionary
Ninety Six, South Carolina

Frogmore History

The name "Frogmore" is the namesake of an old fishing community on St. Helena Island, S.C. According to legend, a fisherman developed the recipe when he couldn't find fish for stew. He scavenged for leftovers, added what shrimp and crab he did catch, and the rest is history.

Black Bean-Chicken Chili WEEKNIGHT FAVORITE

Ladle big bowlfuls of this thick, dark chili to warm up your family on a cold winter's night. Chicken is a nice surprise in it instead of beef.

2 skinned and boned chicken breast
    halves, cut into 1-inch pieces
1 medium onion, chopped
1 green bell pepper, chopped
2 garlic cloves, minced
2 tablespoons chicken broth
2 (28-ounce) cans stewed tomatoes,
    undrained

2 (15-ounce) cans black beans, rinsed
    and drained
2 cups medium salsa
2 tablespoons chili powder
1 teaspoon salt
1 teaspoon ground cumin
½ teaspoon hot sauce
Shredded Cheddar cheese (optional)

COOK first 4 ingredients in broth in a Dutch oven over medium-high heat 3 minutes or until onion is tender.

ADD tomatoes and next 6 ingredients; bring to a boil. Reduce heat, and simmer, uncovered, 30 to 35 minutes, stirring often.

TO serve, ladle chili into individual bowls. Top with shredded cheese, if desired. Yield: 13 cups.

Seaboard to Sideboard
The Junior League of Wilmington, North Carolina

Versatile Chili

Though Cheddar cheese is good on most all types of chili, a white cheese such as Monterey Jack also would be good in this black bean chili.

Turkey and Wild Rice Chili

Here's a white chili chock-full of white corn, white beans, and tender turkey. Green chiles, chili powder, and a shake of hot sauce put this chili in the spicy category.

1 tablespoon vegetable oil
1 medium onion, chopped
1 garlic clove, minced
1¼ pounds skinned and boned turkey breast, cut into ½-inch pieces
2 cups cooked wild rice
1 (15.8-ounce) can great Northern beans, drained
1 (11-ounce) can white whole kernel corn, drained
1 (10½-ounce) can reduced-sodium chicken broth

2 (4.5-ounce) cans diced green chiles, undrained
1 teaspoon salt
1 teaspoon ground cumin
2 teaspoons chili powder
⅛ teaspoon hot sauce
Shredded Monterey Jack cheese
Sour cream
Garnish: chopped fresh parsley or cilantro

HEAT oil in a Dutch oven over medium heat; add onion and garlic, and cook, stirring constantly, until vegetables are tender. Add turkey and next 8 ingredients. Bring to a boil; cover, reduce heat, and simmer 30 minutes or until turkey is done. Stir in hot sauce.

TO serve, ladle chili into individual bowls, and top with cheese and sour cream. Garnish, if desired. Yield: 8 cups.

Gracious Gator Cooks
The Junior League of Gainesville, Florida

Adding Herbs
Chopped fresh herbs add a finishing touch to soups. Always chop and add them just before serving for the best flavor.

Incredible Pimiento Cheese

Homemade pimiento cheese is treasured homestyle food. For many, this simple sandwich spread brings back childhood memories. This version gives you a big yield and is spiked with a little sugar.

1 (16-ounce) loaf process cheese spread, cubed
4 cups (16 ounces) shredded mild Cheddar cheese
4 cups (16 ounces) shredded sharp Cheddar cheese

2 cups mayonnaise
2 (4-ounce) jars diced pimiento, drained
3 tablespoons sugar
½ teaspoon salt
¼ teaspoon pepper

PROCESS half of all ingredients in a food processor until cheese mixture is blended. Remove processed cheese mixture to a large bowl. Repeat procedure with remaining half of all ingredients.

SERVE with assorted crackers, or use as a sandwich spread. Store in the refrigerator. Yield: 8 cups.

Karen Hansen Norman
Pass the Plate
Episcopal Church Women of Christ Episcopal Church
New Bern, North Carolina

Freezer Tip
Pop some of this three-cheese spread into the freezer up to a month, and you'll still have plenty left over to store in the refrigerator for tasty cheese sandwiches throughout the week.

Chili Dog Sauce

Dressed-Up Dogs

For big smiles, top chili dogs with some creamy coleslaw or Cheddar cheese sauce.

Simmer this easy chili for just 30 minutes; then grill some dogs or burgers and serve them to your kids for lunch or supper.

2 pounds ground beef	1 teaspoon ground ginger
1 medium onion, minced	1 teaspoon salt
4 garlic cloves, minced	1 tablespoon pepper
3 tablespoons chili powder	2 cups tomato juice
1 tablespoon ground cumin	

COOK ground beef and onion in a Dutch oven over medium-high heat until beef is browned, stirring until it crumbles; drain well.

ADD garlic, chili powder, and ground cumin; cook 3 minutes, stirring constantly. Add ground ginger and remaining ingredients; bring to a boil. Reduce heat; simmer, uncovered, 30 minutes or until thickened. Serve hot over frankfurters in buns. Yield: 5 cups.

Barbecue Sauce ONE PAN

Store this Sauce

This recipe makes quite a bit of Barbecue Sauce. Set some aside before basting to serve with ribs, chicken or whatever you choose to grill; then store any leftover sauce in an airtight container in the refrigerator up to a month.

You know this barbecue sauce has got to be good because it comes from Memphis, home of the annual Memphis in May BBQ cook-off.

2 cups water	3 tablespoons salt
2 cups white vinegar	3 tablespoons sugar
2 cups ketchup	3 tablespoons chili powder
½ cup chopped onion	3 tablespoons pepper

COMBINE all ingredients in a large saucepan. Bring to a boil; reduce heat, and simmer, uncovered, 1½ hours, stirring often. Yield: 3 cups.

Heart & Soul
The Junior League of Memphis, Tennessee

Grilled Tomato Sauce GRILL LOVERS

Smoky Summer Sauce

Try this fresh tomato sauce in the summer months when multi-colored tomatoes are in their prime. The sauce is great on pasta or as a burger topping.

Grill thick slices of yellow and plum tomatoes to create the smoky foundation of this distinctive sauce. Dried crushed red pepper sparks a bit of heat, while marjoram, basil, and thyme lend their herbed freshness.

8 large yellow tomatoes, cut into ½-inch slices	2½ tablespoons chopped fresh marjoram
8 large plum tomatoes, cut into ½-inch slices	2 tablespoons chopped fresh basil
¼ cup olive oil, divided	1 tablespoon chopped fresh thyme
1 onion, chopped	1 tablespoon dried crushed red pepper
3 garlic cloves, minced	2 tablespoons balsamic vinegar
2 cups dry red wine	1 teaspoon salt

BRUSH tomato slices evenly with 2 tablespoons olive oil. Coat grill rack with cooking spray; place tomato slices on grill rack. Grill, covered with grill lid, over medium-high heat (350° to 400°) 10 minutes, turning once. Coarsely chop tomato; set aside.

COOK onion in remaining 2 tablespoons oil in a large Dutch oven over medium-high heat, stirring constantly, 5 minutes or until tender. Add tomato, garlic, and remaining ingredients; simmer, uncovered, 20 minutes or to desired consistency. Serve warm over pasta. Yield: 8 cups.

Under the Canopy
GFWC Tallahassee Junior Woman's Club
Tallahassee, Florida

Puttanesca Sauce for Garlic Lovers

ONE PAN

Spoon this easy, aromatic tomato sauce over mounds of your favorite hot cooked pasta.

1 cup pitted, halved ripe olives
½ cup dried tomatoes, cut into
  thin strips
¼ cup olive oil
1 (3½-ounce) jar capers, drained

8 large garlic cloves, chopped
6 anchovy fillets, mashed
3 cups quartered plum tomatoes
¼ cup pesto
1 teaspoon dried crushed red pepper

COMBINE first 6 ingredients in a large saucepan; bring to a boil. Add tomato, pesto, and red pepper; bring to a boil. Reduce heat, and simmer, uncovered, 10 minutes, stirring occasionally. Serve over pasta. Yield: 4 cups.

Carolyn Hughes
Collard Greens, Watermelons, and "Miss" Charlotte's Pie
Swansboro United Methodist Women
Swansboro, North Carolina

Another Great Italian Sauce
"Puttanesca" is an Italian sauce rich with capers, anchovies, and olives.

Pecan Tartar Sauce   MAKE AHEAD   QUICK & EASY

Toasted pecans make this fish and seafood flatterer thick and chunky.

½ cup chopped pecans, toasted
½ cup mayonnaise
1 tablespoon minced fresh parsley
1 tablespoon minced gherkin pickle

1 tablespoon apple cider vinegar
1 teaspoon grated lemon rind
½ teaspoon dry mustard
¼ teaspoon salt

COMBINE all ingredients in a small bowl, stirring well; cover and chill thoroughly. Serve with fish, crab cakes, or shrimp. Yield: about 1 cup.

The Cook's Canvas
St. John's Museum of Art
Wilmington, North Carolina

Try this Tartar
Sure, you can buy tartar sauce at the grocery store, but this homemade sauce is a cut above the rest, and is good on just about any seafood.

Cocktail Sauce ONE BOWL   QUICK & EASY

Ketchup or Chili?

If you don't have ketchup on hand, use chili sauce instead. It's common in Cocktail Sauce recipes.

What would shrimp be without its best partner, tangy Cocktail Sauce?

1½ cups ketchup
2 tablespoons prepared horseradish
1 tablespoon Worcestershire sauce
1 tablespoon lemon juice

1½ teaspoons sugar
¼ teaspoon hot sauce
Salt and pepper to taste

COMBINE all ingredients in a small bowl; cover and chill. Yield: 1⅔ cups.

Danny Pietrocollo
Healthy Cooking for Kids—and You!
Children's Wish Foundation
West Melbourne, Florida

Pesto

Pesto Pleasure

Pesto is a versatile sauce based on a leafy green ingredient such as basil, parsley, or mint leaves, along with olive oil, Parmesan, and nuts such as pine nuts or walnuts. Pesto's delicious tossed with pasta, spooned on baked potatoes or burgers, or served as an appetizer spread with bread.

Pine nuts are found in the pine cones of several varieties of pine trees. Because pine nuts have a high fat content, store them in an airtight container in the refrigerator or freeze them up to 9 months.

½ cup pine nuts
1½ cups freshly grated Parmesan
  cheese
4 garlic cloves

⅛ teaspoon salt
¾ cup olive oil
2 cups loosely packed fresh basil
  leaves

BAKE pine nuts in a shallow pan at 350°, stirring twice, 5 minutes or until toasted.
PULSE pine nuts, Parmesan cheese, garlic, and salt in a food processor 10 to 15 times or until a paste forms. With processor running, gradually pour olive oil through food chute. Add basil, and process until blended. Store in an airtight container in refrigerator. Serve pesto over hot cooked pasta, stir into soups, or use as a sauce for pizza. Yield: 1½ cups.

Paseur Family
Cookin' with Friends
National Presbyterian School Class of 2000
Washington, D.C.

Pesto

"Lightning" Black Bean Salsa MAKE AHEAD

Whip up this 5-ingredient salsa in lightning speed using the food processor.

1 (15-ounce) can black beans,
    drained
1 (12-ounce) jar mild salsa

¼ cup chopped fresh cilantro
¼ teaspoon ground cumin
2 tablespoons fresh lime juice

PULSE beans 1 or 2 times in a food processor or until beans are chopped. Stir in salsa and remaining ingredients. Cover and chill at least 8 hours, or serve immediately. Serve with tortilla chips or fresh vegetables. Yield: 2¼ cups.

Brenda Brandon
Texas Sampler
The Junior League of Richardson, Texas

Mashed Beans

Mash beans slightly with a fork rather than process, if desired. Mashing the beans gives salsa the consistency of bean dip.

Roasted Red Peppers MAKE AHEAD PARTY FOOD

Roasted Red Peppers add a splash of color to salads and sandwiches.

8 medium-size red bell peppers
½ cup olive oil
2 tablespoons balsamic vinegar
1 tablespoon fresh lemon juice

1 garlic clove, minced
1 teaspoon pickling salt
¼ teaspoon pepper

WASH and dry peppers; place on an aluminum foil-lined baking sheet. Broil 5½ inches from heat 5 minutes or until peppers look blistered. Place peppers in a heavy-duty zip-top plastic bag; close bag, and let stand 10 minutes. Peel peppers; remove core and seeds. Cut peppers into ½-inch strips.

COMBINE peppers, oil, and remaining ingredients in a large bowl. Cover and let stand 30 minutes. Store in refrigerator up to a week. Yield: 2½ cups.

Sensational Seasons: A Taste & Tour of Arkansas
The Junior League of Fort Smith, Arkansas

Roasted Pepper Popularity

Roasted peppers in oil are all over grocery store shelves due to their popularity in recent years. This recipe shows you how easy it is to roast and store your own fresh peppers.

Vidalia Onion Jelly

Serve this sweet onion jelly on biscuits with slivers of roast beef or ham.

2 pounds Vidalia onions or other
    sweet onions, thinly sliced
    (about 9 cups)
2 cups water

1 (1¾-ounce) package powdered
    fruit pectin
¾ cup white vinegar (5% acidity)
5½ cups sugar

COMBINE onion and water in a large Dutch oven. Bring to a boil. Remove from heat, and cool. Press onion through a jelly bag or cheesecloth to extract juice. If necessary, add water to juice to measure 3 cups. Discard onion pulp.

COMBINE onion liquid, pectin, and vinegar in a large saucepan; stir well. Bring to a boil, stirring constantly. Stir in sugar; return to a boil. Boil 1 minute, stirring constantly. Remove from heat; skim off foam.

POUR onion jelly quickly into hot, sterilized jars, filling to ¼ inch from top. Remove air bubbles; wipe jar rims. Cover at once with metal lids, and screw on bands. Process in boiling-water bath 5 minutes. Yield: 6 half pints.

Lillian Huber
Ribbon Winning Recipes
South Carolina State Fair
Columbia, South Carolina

Onions All Year Long
Onion jelly provides a great way of preserving sweet Vidalia onions, so you can enjoy them year-round.

Blueberry Jam

Discover the thrill of picking fresh blueberries. You can eat them by the handful for instant gratification, but we recommend "putting them up" with this simple recipe so you can enjoy the plump gems all year long.

6 cups stemmed blueberries, crushed
1 teaspoon grated lemon rind
2 tablespoons fresh lemon juice

7 cups sugar
2 (3-ounce) packages liquid pectin

COMBINE first 4 ingredients in a Dutch oven. Bring to a boil; cook until sugar dissolves, stirring occasionally. Boil 2 minutes, stirring often; remove from heat. Add pectin to mixture, and stir 5 minutes. Skim off foam with a metal spoon.

QUICKLY pour hot mixture into hot, sterilized jars, leaving ¼-inch headspace; wipe jar rims. Cover at once with metal lids, and screw on bands. Process in boiling-water bath 5 minutes. Yield: 8 half pints.

Seasoned with Love
Mahoning County Foster Parent Association
Youngstown, Ohio

Freezing Berries
Store fresh blueberries by freezing them, uncovered, in a single layer on a jellyroll pan. Once frozen, transfer berries to a large zip-top bag, and seal up to 1 year.

Mission Inn's Peach and Ginger Relish

Peachy Keen

Enjoy this peach relish over pork tenderloin, ham, or chicken.

Curry and ginger season sweet slices of peaches, onion, and sweet red pepper. Apple cider vinegar and lemon juice provide tangy balance to this uncommon relish.

2 medium-size red bell peppers, chopped
1 small onion, chopped
12 medium-size fresh peaches, peeled and sliced
½ cup coarsely chopped fresh cilantro

½ cup firmly packed light brown sugar
½ cup apple cider vinegar
2 tablespoons curry powder
1½ ounces grated fresh ginger or 1½ teaspoons ground ginger
2 tablespoons lemon juice
½ teaspoon ground red pepper

COOK sweet red pepper and onion in a large nonstick skillet over medium-high heat, stirring constantly, until vegetables are tender. Add peaches and remaining ingredients, stirring well; cook until mixture is thoroughly heated. Serve relish warm as a topping for grilled chicken. Yield: 10 cups.

Howey Cook
Howey-in-the-Hills Garden and Civic Club
Howey-in-the-Hills, Florida

Dixie Relish

Bowled Over

A big glass bowl or pottery bowl is a good choice to use for soaking these chopped vegetables. These types of bowls won't react with the food.

We're not just whistling "Dixie" when we tell you this tangy relish received a high rating from our Test Kitchens staff. Try it on your next hot dog.

4 cups chopped cabbage
2 cups chopped onion
2 cups chopped green bell pepper
2 cups chopped red bell pepper
½ cup salt
2 quarts water

1 quart cider vinegar (5% acidity)
1 cup water
2 tablespoons mustard seeds
2 tablespoons celery seeds
½ teaspoon dried crushed red pepper

COMBINE first 4 ingredients in a large nonmetal container; toss well. Sprinkle with salt. Add 2 quarts water; cover and let stand 1 hour. Drain well. Rinse with cold water, and drain again.

PLACE vegetables in a large Dutch oven; add vinegar and remaining ingredients. Bring to a boil; reduce heat, and simmer, uncovered, 20 minutes, stirring occasionally.

SPOON relish quickly into hot jars, filling to ½ inch from top. Remove air bubbles; wipe jar rims. Cover at once with metal lids, and screw on bands. Process in boiling-water bath 15 minutes. Store in refrigerator after opening. Yield: 9 half pints.

Hoyt Lewis
Georgia Hospitality
Georgia Elks Aidmore Auxiliary
Conyers, Georgia

Green Tomato Relish

Green tomatoes are a Southern favorite. This relish highlights them in their best form.

4 cups finely chopped onion
4 cups finely chopped cabbage
4 cups finely chopped green
   tomatoes
2 cups finely chopped green
   bell pepper
2 cups finely chopped red bell
   pepper

½ cup salt
6 cups sugar
1 tablespoon celery seeds
2 tablespoons mustard seeds
1½ teaspoons ground turmeric
4 cups apple cider vinegar (5% acidity)
2 cups water

COMBINE first 5 ingredients in a large nonaluminum pan or bowl. Add salt; stir well. Cover and marinate in refrigerator at least 8 hours.

DRAIN vegetables in a large colander; rinse well, and let drain 15 minutes. Transfer vegetables to a large Dutch oven.

COMBINE sugar and remaining 5 ingredients; pour over vegetables. Bring mixture to a boil; reduce heat, and simmer, uncovered, 3 minutes.

DIVIDE vegetable mixture evenly among 7 hot jars; fill each jar with liquid to ½ inch from top. Discard remaining liquid. Remove air bubbles; wipe jar rims.

COVER at once with metal lids, and screw on bands. Process in boiling-water bath 10 minutes. Yield: 7 pints.

Apple Butter ONE PAN

Apple Butter is an old-fashioned favorite and an ideal use for the abundance of fruit on your apple trees.

6 pounds cooking apples, peeled,
   cored, and coarsely chopped
1 cup water
4 cups sugar

½ cup white vinegar
2 teaspoons ground cinnamon
½ teaspoon ground allspice
½ teaspoon ground cloves

COMBINE apple and water in a large Dutch oven; bring to a boil. Cover, reduce heat, and simmer 20 to 25 minutes or until apple is tender. Mash apple. Stir in sugar and vinegar; bring to a boil. Reduce heat, and simmer, uncovered, 2½ hours or until mixture is very thick. Stir in cinnamon, allspice, and cloves. Store in refrigerator up to 1 month. Yield: 8 cups.

Shirley Lowe
Treasured Gems
Hiddenite Center Family
Hiddenite, North Carolina

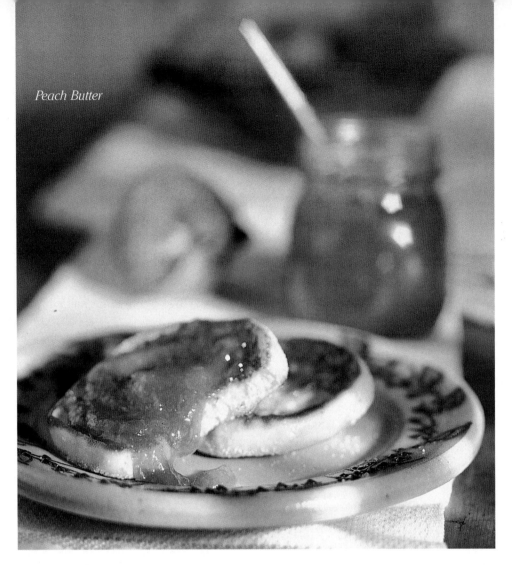

Peach Butter

Peach Butter

Peaches 101

How do you know if a peach is really ripe for a recipe like this? A fragrant aroma is your best clue, and if the peach yields to pressure when touched, that's another hint. Store peaches in a bowl at room temperature, check them daily, and eat the softest fruit first.

There's no butter in this recipe, just fragrant summer ripe peaches cooked down to a smooth puree laced with honey and spices. It's great on biscuits, English muffins, pancakes, or spooned over ice cream.

3 cups sliced fresh peaches (about 4 large)
¼ cup orange juice
¾ cup sugar

2 tablespoons honey
½ teaspoon grated orange rind
⅛ teaspoon ground allspice

COMBINE peaches and orange juice in a saucepan; bring to a boil. Cover, reduce heat, and simmer 8 minutes or until tender, stirring occasionally. Process mixture in a blender or food processor until smooth, stopping to scrape down sides.

RETURN peach mixture to saucepan; add sugar and remaining ingredients. Bring to a boil; reduce heat, and simmer, uncovered, 25 minutes or until thickened, stirring occasionally. Spoon into jars; cover and store in refrigerator. Yield: 1½ cups.

Sande Knapp
Flavors of Fredericksburg
St. Barnabas Episcopal Church
Fredericksburg, Texas

Side Dishes

Mashed Potatoes with Shallots, Goat Cheese, and Herbs, page 342

Pasta with Asparagus, Prosciutto, and Wild Mushrooms

Brie adds its buttery goodness to a medley of fresh asparagus, salty prosciutto, and meaty shiitake mushrooms.

1 (16-ounce) package spaghetti
1 teaspoon olive oil
1 pound fresh asparagus spears
¼ cup diced shallot
2 tablespoons minced garlic
¼ cup olive oil
3 ounces prosciutto, cut into
    thin strips
1 (3½-ounce) package shiitake
    mushrooms, sliced

1 cup chicken broth
¼ cup plus 2 tablespoons dry
    white wine
½ teaspoon salt
¼ teaspoon pepper
4 ounces Brie cheese, cut into
    thin slices

COOK spaghetti according to package directions; drain. Add 1 teaspoon olive oil; toss. Set spaghetti aside, and keep warm.

SNAP off tough ends of asparagus. Cut asparagus into 2-inch pieces. Set aside.

SAUTÉ shallot and minced garlic in ¼ cup olive oil in a large skillet over medium-high heat until golden.

ADD asparagus and prosciutto. Cook 2 minutes, stirring constantly. Add mushrooms; cook 5 minutes, stirring constantly. Add broth, wine, salt, and pepper; cook 2 minutes, stirring constantly.

COMBINE prosciutto mixture and reserved spaghetti in a large bowl, and toss gently. Add cheese slices, and toss gently. Serve immediately. Yield: 6 servings.

Patricia Hitner
Irish Children's Summer Program 10th Anniversary Cookbook
Irish Children's Summer Program
Greenville, South Carolina

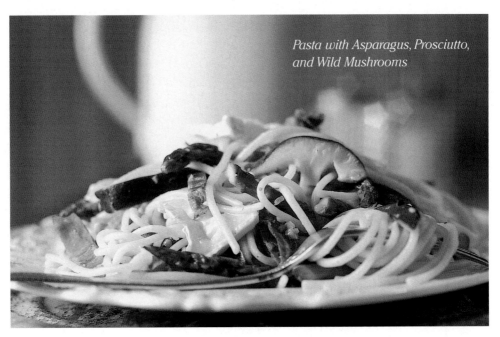

Pasta with Asparagus, Prosciutto, and Wild Mushrooms

Barley with Smoked Ham and Peas

Barley with Smoked Ham and Peas

With ham, onion, and peas sautéed in bacon drippings, this recipe must have been created by Southern hands.

3 cups water
1 cup uncooked pearl barley (we
    tested with medium)
½ teaspoon salt
2 bacon slices
3 ounces smoked ham, cut into
    thin strips
1 medium onion, finely chopped

1 (10-ounce) package frozen
    English peas
2 tablespoons chicken broth
4 fresh sage leaves, minced, or
    ¼ teaspoon dried sage
½ teaspoon fresh marjoram, minced,
    or ⅛ teaspoon dried marjoram

Pearl Barley
Pearl barley is a tiny grain that has been steamed and polished. Look for it in 3 sizes: coarse, medium, and fine. Besides being tasty in side dishes like this one, pearl barley makes a nice addition to soups.

BRING water to a boil in a medium saucepan; add barley and salt. Reduce heat, and simmer, uncovered, 40 minutes or until liquid is absorbed. Set aside.

COOK bacon in a large skillet until crisp; remove bacon, reserving drippings in skillet. Crumble bacon, and set aside.

COOK ham in drippings in skillet over medium heat until edges of ham are lightly browned, stirring often. Remove ham from skillet, reserving drippings in skillet.

COOK onion in drippings in skillet 2 minutes, stirring often. Add peas; cook, stirring constantly, 2 to 3 minutes or until peas are thoroughly heated. Add reserved barley, ham, and chicken broth; cook over medium-low heat until thoroughly heated, stirring occasionally. Stir in sage and marjoram. Sprinkle with crumbled bacon. Yield: 6 servings.

Special Selections of Ocala
Ocala Royal Dames for Cancer Research, Inc.
Ocala, Florida

John's Famous Beans ONE POT

What makes these beans famous is perhaps the memorable blend of garlic, cilantro, cumin, and chili powder that simmers long and slow with the beans.

Natural Thickener
Simmering beans and soups uncovered helps to thicken them as the liquid evaporates.

1 pound dried pinto beans
10 cups water
2 teaspoons vegetable oil
1 medium onion, diced
4 garlic cloves, crushed
1 (16-ounce) can stewed tomatoes, undrained and chopped
¼ cup Worcestershire sauce

2 tablespoons mild picante sauce
1 teaspoon chopped fresh cilantro
1 teaspoon salt
1 teaspoon ground cumin
¼ teaspoon chili powder
1 cup (4 ounces) shredded sharp Cheddar cheese

SORT and wash beans; place in a large Dutch oven. Cover with water 2 inches above beans; let soak at least 8 hours. Drain. Add 10 cups water and vegetable oil to beans; bring to a boil. Reduce heat, and simmer, uncovered, 1½ hours.

ADD onion and next 8 ingredients; bring to a boil. Reduce heat, and simmer, uncovered, 1½ hours.

TO serve, ladle beans into individual serving bowls. Top evenly with cheese. Yield: 7 servings.

Cynthia Lancaster
Coastal Cuisine, Texas Style
The Junior Service League of Brazosport
Lake Jackson, Texas

Baked Beans WEEKNIGHT FAVORITE

Here's a slow cooker bean recipe that frees up your oven for other casseroles.

Beef 'n' Beans
These baked beans go main dish with a hefty portion of ground beef in the pot. The one thing slow cookers can't do is brown meat. That's why you'll need a skillet, too.

2 pounds ground chuck
1 large onion, chopped
3 (16-ounce) cans pork and beans
1 (12-ounce) jar chili sauce
1 (8-ounce) can crushed pineapple, drained

1 cup firmly packed light brown sugar
1 tablespoon dry mustard
1 tablespoon Worcestershire sauce
6 bacon slices, cooked and crumbled

BROWN meat and onion in a large skillet, stirring until meat crumbles and onion is tender; drain. Combine meat mixture, pork and beans, and remaining ingredients in a 4-quart electric slow cooker, stirring well. Cover and cook on HIGH setting 3½ hours. Yield: 10 servings.

Hope Weatherly
Carolina Cuisine: Nothin' Could Be Finer
The Junior Charity League of Marlboro County
Bennettsville, South Carolina

Lima Beans

Crisp bits of bacon and melted Monterey Jack liven up these limas.

1½ cups water
½ teaspoon salt
2 (10-ounce) packages frozen
    lima beans
8 bacon slices, diced
1 cup chopped onion

½ cup chopped celery
1½ cups (6 ounces) shredded
    Monterey Jack cheese
¼ teaspoon pepper
Dash of Worcestershire sauce

COMBINE water and salt in a large saucepan; bring to a boil. Add lima beans; cover, reduce heat, and simmer 8 to 10 minutes or until tender. Drain beans, reserving ½ cup liquid; set aside.

COOK bacon in a large skillet until crisp; remove bacon, reserving 3 tablespoons drippings in skillet. Set bacon aside.

SAUTÉ onion and celery in drippings in skillet until tender.

COMBINE reserved lima beans, reserved liquid, onion mixture, cheese, pepper, and Worcestershire sauce. Spoon into a lightly greased 2-quart baking dish. Sprinkle with bacon. Bake, uncovered, at 350° for 25 minutes or until heated. Yield: 6 servings.

Gayle Hara
Sharing Tasteful Memories
L.A.C.E. (Ladies Aspiring to Christian Excellence) of First Church of the Nazarene
Longview, Texas

Lima Lesson
There are 2 types of lima beans—Fordhook and baby limas. Both are pale green, plump, and have a slight curve to their shape. Fordhook limas are larger and have a fuller flavor than baby limas. In the South, we call dried limas butter beans.

Lima Beans

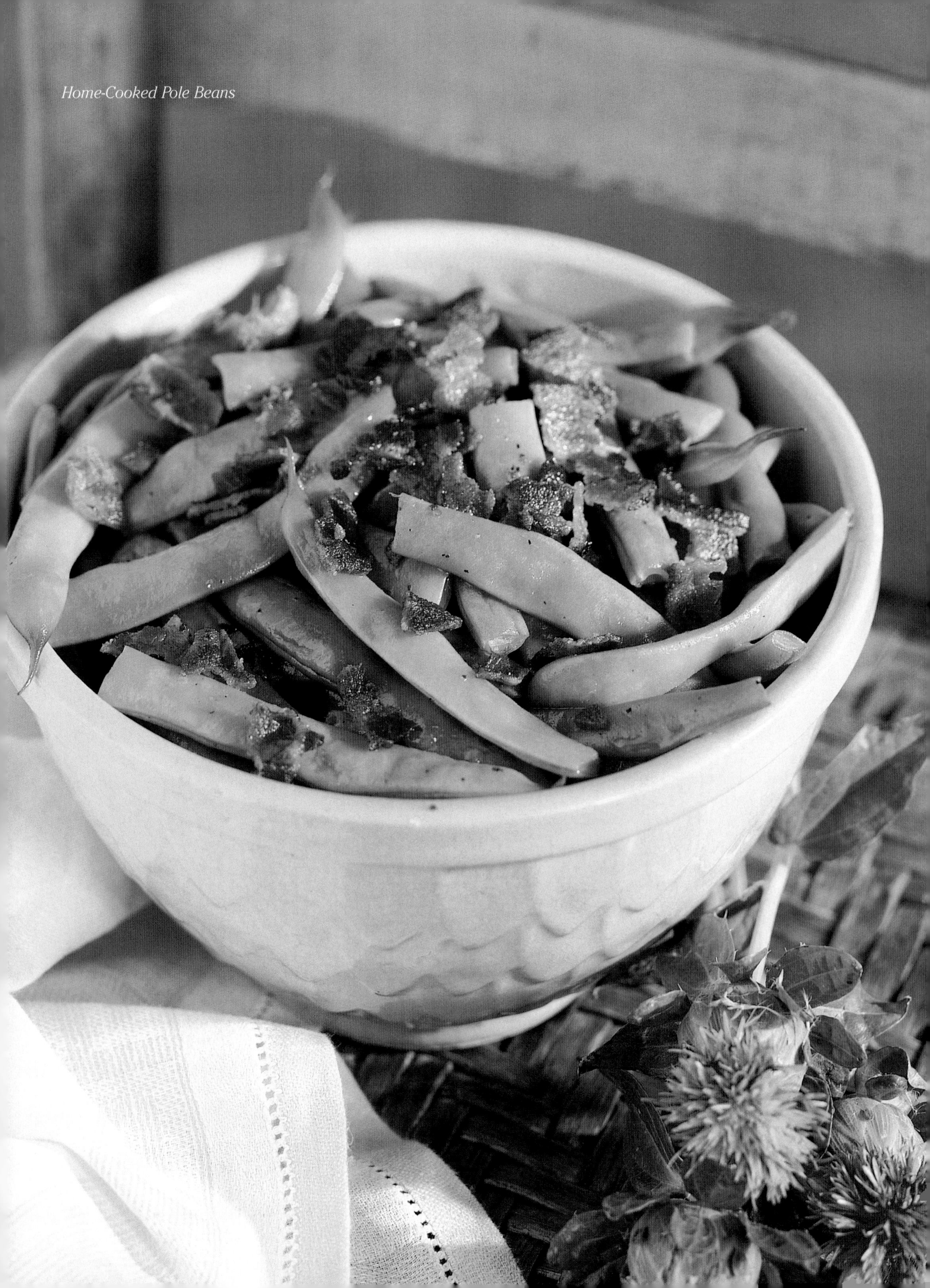

Home-Cooked Pole Beans

Home-Cooked Pole Beans   QUICK & EASY

Here's a classic, easy bean recipe flavored with bacon drippings and enhanced with a little sugar.

2 pounds fresh pole beans	1 teaspoon salt
3 bacon slices	¼ teaspoon sugar
1 cup water	¼ teaspoon pepper

WASH beans; trim stem ends. Snap beans in half, and set aside.

COOK bacon in a large saucepan until crisp; remove bacon, reserving drippings in pan. Crumble bacon, and set aside.

ADD water and remaining 3 ingredients to saucepan; bring to a boil over high heat. Add beans; cover, reduce heat to medium, and cook 15 minutes or to desired doneness. Sprinkle with crumbled bacon. Serve with a slotted spoon. Yield: 6 to 8 servings.

Louise Crawford
Coldwater, Mississippi

Don't Forget the Strings
Be sure to remove strings from beans before snapping them. A vegetable peeler makes an easy task of it.

Savory Green Beans and Mushrooms

QUICK & EASY

Sliced mushrooms and a warm herb vinaigrette make these green beans extraordinary.

1½ pounds fresh green beans, trimmed	1 tablespoon fresh lemon juice
½ pound sliced fresh mushrooms	1 tablespoon chopped fresh parsley
1 tablespoon thinly sliced green onions	2 tablespoons chopped fresh savory or 1 teaspoon dried savory
3 tablespoons butter or margarine, melted	1 teaspoon sugar
⅓ cup vegetable oil	1 teaspoon salt
1 tablespoon white wine vinegar	⅛ teaspoon pepper
	4 bacon slices, cooked and crumbled

COOK green beans in boiling water to cover 10 minutes or until crisp-tender; drain.

COOK mushrooms and green onions in butter in a large skillet over medium heat, stirring constantly, 5 minutes or until vegetables are tender. Toss with beans.

COMBINE oil and next 7 ingredients in a small saucepan; bring to a boil. Pour over bean mixture. Stir to coat evenly; sprinkle with bacon, and serve immediately. Yield: 6 servings.

Gourmet Our Way
Cascia Hall Preparatory School Parent Faculty Association
Tulsa, Oklahoma

Savory
Savory is one of the herbs used to flavor the oil and vinegar dressing for these beans. It's a strong flavored herb that tastes like a cross between mint and thyme.

Broccoli with Garlic Butter and Cashews   QUICK & EASY

A slightly sweet garlic butter sauce and roasted cashews top these green spears, which pair well with most any meat.

1½ pounds fresh broccoli
⅓ cup butter or margarine
1 tablespoon brown sugar
3 tablespoons soy sauce

2 teaspoons white vinegar
¼ teaspoon pepper
¼ teaspoon minced garlic
⅓ cup salted roasted cashews

REMOVE and discard broccoli leaves and tough ends of stalks; cut into spears. Cook broccoli in a small amount of boiling water 8 minutes or until crisp-tender. Drain well. Arrange broccoli on a serving platter. Set aside, and keep warm.

MELT butter in a small skillet over medium heat; add brown sugar and next 4 ingredients. Bring to a boil; remove from heat. Stir in cashews. Pour sauce over broccoli, and serve immediately. Yield: 4 servings.

Jean Harbison
Saxony Sampler
GFWC Saxonburg District Woman's Club
Saxonburg, Pennsylvania

Broccoli Bits
Did you know "broccoli" comes from the Italian word for cabbage sprout? It's a relative of cabbage, brussels sprouts, and cauliflower. Refrigerate broccoli, unwashed, in an airtight bag up to 4 days.

Broccoli Dressing   MAKE AHEAD

Swiss cheese and broccoli add a new twist to homemade pan dressing as they mingle deliciously with standbys onion, celery, and soft breadcrumbs.

½ cup chopped onion
1½ cups chopped celery
½ cup butter or margarine, melted
1 large egg, lightly beaten
1 teaspoon salt
½ teaspoon poultry seasoning
⅛ teaspoon pepper

4 cups soft bread cubes, lightly toasted
1 (8-ounce) package Swiss cheese, cubed
1 (10-ounce) package frozen chopped broccoli, thawed

SAUTÉ onion and celery in butter in a large skillet over medium-high heat until crisp-tender.

COMBINE egg and next 3 ingredients in a large bowl; gently stir in bread cubes, cheese, and broccoli. Spoon mixture into a greased 11- x 7-inch baking dish. Bake, uncovered, at 325° for 35 minutes or until golden. Yield: 8 servings.

Brenda Kirchmann
Recipes and Remembrances
Kirchmann-Witte Families
North Bend, Nebraska

Make-Ahead Dressing
It's handy to make a pan of dressing ahead and have it ready to pop in the oven later on. You can assemble this dressing in the baking dish and refrigerate, covered, up to a day ahead. Then, all you have to do is bake it the next day.

Cabbage with Apples and Walnuts

ONE POT

Braised cabbage is at its best in this colorful, sweet-and-sour side dish.

6 bacon slices
½ cup firmly packed light brown
    sugar
½ cup water
⅓ cup cider vinegar
½ medium cabbage, shredded

½ medium-size red cabbage,
    shredded
2 medium cooking apples, thinly
    sliced
⅓ cup chopped walnuts, toasted

COOK bacon in a large Dutch oven over medium heat until crisp; remove bacon, reserving 3 tablespoons drippings in pan. Crumble bacon, and set aside.

ADD sugar, water, and vinegar to drippings; cook over medium-high heat 3 to 4 minutes or until liquid is reduced to ¾ cup. Add cabbage; cook, stirring constantly, 4 minutes or until cabbage wilts. Add apple; toss gently. Remove from heat. Sprinkle with bacon and walnuts. Serve immediately. Yield: 6 servings.

The Bountiful Arbor
The Junior League of Ann Arbor, Michigan

Apple Tip
Leave the peel on your apples for this sauté. It makes the dish attractive and helps the apple hold its shape.

Golden Grated Carrots   QUICK & EASY

What makes these zippy microwave carrots "golden" is the sauce, which is made with curry powder and golden raisins. Try them with pork, chicken, or ham.

1 pound carrots, shredded
2 tablespoons dry white wine
1 tablespoon butter or margarine
1 tablespoon honey

2 teaspoons lemon juice
⅓ cup golden raisins
1½ teaspoons brown sugar
1 teaspoon curry powder

PLACE carrot in a lightly greased 1½-quart baking dish. Add wine and next 3 ingredients, stirring well. Cover tightly with heavy-duty plastic wrap; fold back a small corner of wrap to allow steam to escape. Microwave at HIGH 5 to 6 minutes or until carrot is crisp-tender. Uncover and stir in raisins, brown sugar, and curry powder. Cover and microwave at HIGH 1 to 2 minutes or until thoroughly heated. Let stand, covered, 2 minutes. Uncover and stir; serve immediately. Yield: 5 servings.

O Taste & Sing
St. Stephen's Episcopal Church Choir
Richmond, Virginia

Shredding Carrots
Shred carrots easily using the largest holes of a box grater or the shredder disk of a food processor.

Cauliflower Suisse

Two things make this cauliflower casserole great: a double cheesy sauce and a buttery breadcrumb and bacon topping.

Cauliflower Class

Cauliflower is a versatile vegetable that can be enjoyed raw or cooked. Look for firm cauliflower with compact florets. The size of the head doesn't affect the quality. Wrap and refrigerate raw cauliflower up to 5 days.

1 medium cauliflower (about 2 pounds), cut into florets
½ cup sour cream
½ cup (2 ounces) shredded Swiss cheese
½ cup (2 ounces) shredded Monterey Jack cheese

¼ cup mayonnaise
½ cup soft breadcrumbs (homemade)
2 tablespoons butter or margarine, melted
4 bacon slices, cooked and crumbled

COOK cauliflower in boiling water to cover 8 minutes; drain. Place cauliflower in an ungreased 11- x 7-inch baking dish; set aside.

COMBINE sour cream and next 3 ingredients in a small heavy saucepan; cook over low heat, stirring constantly, 16 minutes or until cheese sauce is smooth. Spoon cheese sauce over cauliflower.

COMBINE breadcrumbs and melted butter; sprinkle breadcrumbs over cheese sauce. Sprinkle crumbled bacon over breadcrumbs. Bake, uncovered, at 350° for 30 minutes or until casserole is lightly browned. Yield: 4 servings.

Fern Warnecke
Recipes for Champions
Shebas of Khiva Temple Oriental Band
Amarillo, Texas

Fresh Corncakes

Fresh, sweet corn, just cut from the cob, is so good in this Southern side dish, a cross between a pancake and a fritter. Serve these cakes as part of a veggie dinner.

Scraping the Cob

Once you've sliced the tips of corn from the cob, scrape the cob with a vegetable peeler to remove milk and pulp. Some may find it more comfortable than using a knife.

6 ears fresh corn
2 large eggs
3 tablespoons all-purpose flour
2 tablespoons sugar

1 teaspoon baking powder
½ teaspoon salt
Melted butter or margarine

SLICE tips of corn from cobs; scrape cobs with a vegetable peeler or knife to remove milk and pulp. Measure 2 cups corn mixture, reserving remaining for another use.

BEAT eggs at high speed with an electric mixer until thick and pale; add flour and next 3 ingredients, beating until blended. Stir in 2 cups corn mixture.

DROP batter by heaping tablespoonfuls onto a hot, buttered griddle. Cook over medium heat 2 minutes or until golden. Turn and cook other side. Yield: 2 dozen.

Blanche Lemee
A Shining Feast
First Baptist Church of Shreveport, Louisiana

Fresh Corncakes

Herbed Corn

GRILL LOVERS

Freshness Factor

Once you've picked or bought fresh corn, plan to use it within a day for the most delicious results.

Fresh corn flavor is really enhanced on the grill. Each ear is wrapped in foil, so the flavor is sealed in and cleanup is minimal.

8 ears fresh corn
½ cup butter, softened
2 tablespoons minced fresh parsley
2 tablespoons chopped fresh chives

1 tablespoon chopped fresh thyme
½ teaspoon salt
¼ teaspoon ground red pepper

REMOVE husks and silks from corn. Combine butter and remaining 5 ingredients in a small bowl. Spread 1 tablespoon mixture over each ear of corn. Wrap each ear in heavy-duty aluminum foil. Grill, covered with grill lid, over medium heat (300° to 350°) 10 minutes, turning once, until corn is done. Yield: 8 servings.

Sharing Our Best
Hackensack American Legion Auxiliary Unit 202
Hackensack, Minnesota

Corn, Okra, and Tomatoes

ONE PAN

Garden Smorgasbord

Here's a different take on okra and tomatoes. Corn and bell pepper speckle it with sweetness and extra color. To get 2½ cups of corn, count on 4 medium ears or 8 small ears.

Raid your garden for this savory summer side dish that received raves in our Test Kitchens.

1 large onion, chopped (1½ cups)
1 large green bell pepper, chopped (1 cup)
2 garlic cloves, minced
¼ cup plus 2 tablespoons butter or margarine

2 cups chopped plum tomatoes
2½ cups fresh corn, cut from the cob (about 4 ears)
1 cup sliced fresh okra
1 teaspoon salt
½ teaspoon freshly ground pepper

COOK first 3 ingredients in butter in a skillet over medium-high heat, stirring constantly, until tender. Add tomato; bring to a boil. Reduce heat, and simmer, uncovered, 15 minutes. Add corn and remaining ingredients; bring to a boil. Reduce heat, and simmer 9 minutes or until corn is tender. Yield: 6 servings.

Peg Grames
Exclusively Corn Cookbook
Coventry Historical Society
Coventry, Connecticut

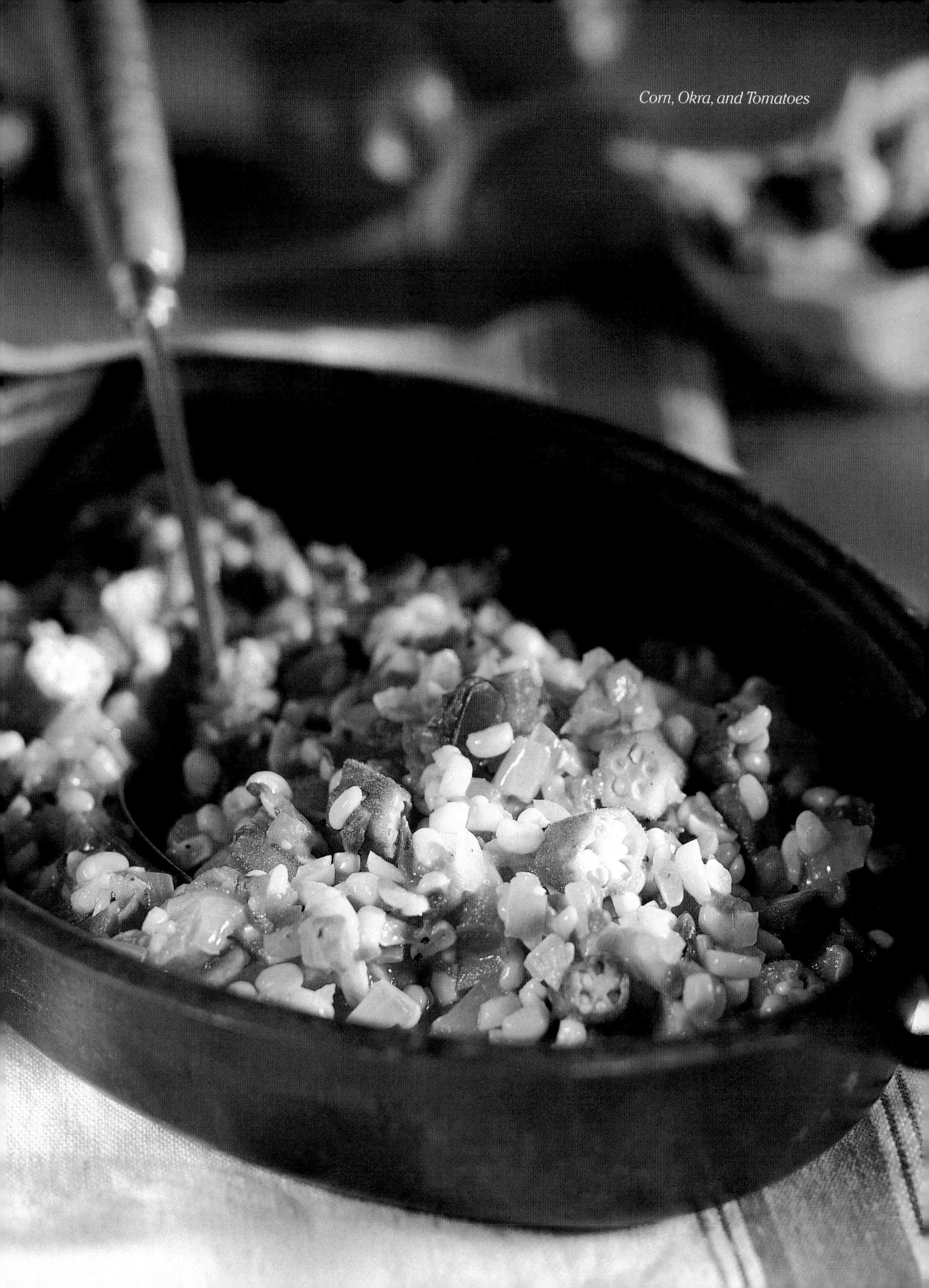

Corn, Okra, and Tomatoes

Grilled Portobello Steaks

Big Brown Mushrooms

A portobello is actually just a mature brown mushroom. Under its cap are exposed gills and a woody stem, which is often discarded before cooking.

Eating a grilled portobello cap is akin to biting into a big, juicy burger. That's why this recipe is called "steaks." Portobellos have a real meaty quality.

4 large portobello mushrooms (about 3 to 4 ounces each)
½ cup olive oil
2 garlic cloves, minced
1 teaspoon salt

2 teaspoons Worcestershire sauce or balsamic vinegar
½ teaspoon freshly ground pepper
Garnish: fresh rosemary

CUT stems off mushrooms near the cap. Reserve stems for other uses. Place mushroom caps, gill side up, on a plate. Combine olive oil and next 4 ingredients. Spoon oil mixture evenly into gills of each mushroom. Cover and chill until ready to grill. Place mushrooms, gill side up, on grill rack. Grill, covered with grill lid, over medium heat (300° to 350°) 4 minutes. Turn mushrooms; grill, covered, 4 minutes or just until tender. Garnish, if desired. Yield: 4 servings.

Jory Family
Cookin' with Friends
National Presbyterian School Class of 2000
Washington, D.C.

Grilled Portobello Steaks

Creamy Artichoke and Mushroom Penne

Creamy Artichoke and Mushroom Penne

Tender artichoke hearts, plump slices of fresh mushrooms, and a luscious cream sauce make this pasta the perfect choice for a romantic dinner. If you prefer, serve it as a side dish with your favorite steak.

12 ounces penne pasta, uncooked
½ small onion, minced (about ¼ cup)
1 garlic clove, crushed
3 tablespoons butter, melted
1 (8-ounce) package sliced fresh
    mushrooms
1 (15-ounce) can artichoke hearts,
    drained and chopped or cut
    lengthwise

1 cup whipping cream
2 tablespoons capers, drained
¼ teaspoon salt
¼ teaspoon freshly ground pepper
½ cup freshly grated Parmesan
    cheese
2 tablespoons chopped fresh parsley

COOK pasta according to package directions; drain well.

WHILE pasta is cooking, cook onion and garlic in butter in a medium skillet over medium-high heat, stirring constantly, until tender. Add mushrooms, and cook 5 minutes. Add artichokes, and cook 2 minutes or until thoroughly heated. Remove vegetables from skillet; set aside, and keep warm.

ADD whipping cream to skillet; bring to a boil, and cook, stirring constantly, until whipping cream is reduced by half. Add artichoke mixture, capers, salt, and pepper, stirring well. Toss artichoke mixture with pasta. Sprinkle with cheese and parsley. Serve immediately. Yield: 6 servings.

Stop and Smell the Rosemary: Recipes and Traditions to Remember
The Junior League of Houston, Texas

Pasta Water

Save a few tablespoons of pasta water to splash with the hot cooked pasta and other ingredients. It stretches the sauce and ensures a creamy mouthful.

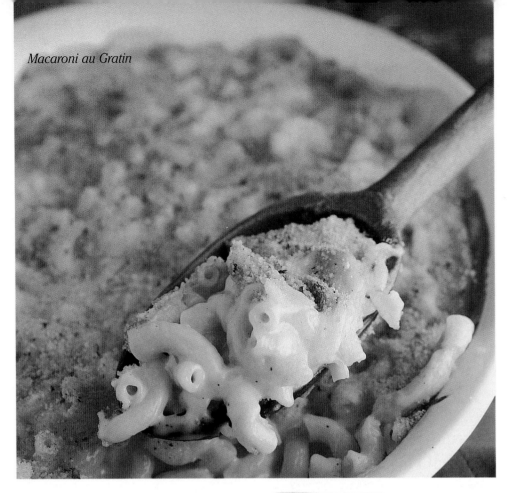

Macaroni au Gratin

Macaroni au Gratin   WEEKNIGHT FAVORITE

Shapely Side Dish

Tired of the expected elbow macaroni in this dish? Spiff it up by trying a new shaped pasta such as penne or bow ties.

This homey dish never goes out of style. This version is spiked with a little Worcestershire sauce and dry mustard, and dusted with breadcrumbs to keep it moist.

1 (8-ounce) package elbow macaroni (about 2 cups)
¼ cup butter or margarine
¼ cup all-purpose flour
2 cups milk
8 ounces process American cheese, cubed
1 tablespoon minced onion

½ teaspoon salt
½ teaspoon Worcestershire sauce
¼ teaspoon pepper
¼ teaspoon dry mustard
2 tablespoons Italian-seasoned breadcrumbs
Butter or margarine

COOK macaroni according to package directions; drain. Place in a greased 2-quart baking dish; set aside.

MELT ¼ cup butter in a large heavy saucepan over low heat; whisk in flour until smooth. Cook 1 minute, whisking constantly. Gradually whisk in milk. Cook over medium heat, whisking constantly, until mixture is thickened and bubbly. Reduce heat, and add cheese, onion, salt, Worcestershire sauce, pepper, and mustard; stir until cheese melts. Pour cheese mixture over macaroni, and mix well. Sprinkle with breadcrumbs, and dot lightly with additional butter. Bake, uncovered, at 375° for 30 minutes. Yield: 4 to 6 servings.

Favorite Recipes Taste of Tradition
B.A. Ritter Senior Citizen Center
Nederland, Texas

Spanish Okra ONE PAN QUICK & EASY

This is meaty okra and tomatoes. Ground chuck bestows hearty main-dish status to these few simple ingredients.

1 pound ground chuck
1 cup chopped onion
2 cups sliced okra
1 cup chopped tomato

1 cup tomato juice
2 teaspoons Worcestershire sauce
½ teaspoon salt
Hot cooked rice

BROWN ground chuck and onion in a large skillet, stirring until meat crumbles and is no longer pink; drain. Add okra; cook 5 minutes, stirring often.

ADD tomato and next 3 ingredients; bring to a boil. Cover, reduce heat, and simmer 15 minutes or until okra is tender. Serve over rice. Yield: 4 servings.

NOTE: For added heat, substitute 1 (14.5-ounce) can diced tomatoes and green chiles for the chopped tomato, if desired.

Jennifer Kinnaird
To Serve with Love
Christian Women's Fellowship of the First Christian Church
Duncan, Oklahoma

One-Dish Dinner
Serve this beefy recipe over rice for a family-pleasing, one-dish dinner.

Spanish Okra

Okra Fritters QUICK & EASY

These aren't your standard fritters—they're flavored with curry and studded with bits of okra, onion, and tomato.

1 cup thinly sliced fresh okra
½ cup chopped onion
½ cup chopped tomato
1 large egg, beaten
¼ cup all-purpose flour
¼ cup cornmeal
½ teaspoon salt
½ teaspoon curry powder
¼ teaspoon pepper
Peanut oil

COMBINE first 9 ingredients in a medium bowl, stirring well.

POUR oil to a depth of 2 inches into a Dutch oven; heat to 360°. Using a tablespoon dipped in hot water, drop cornmeal mixture into hot oil. Fry 1 minute on each side or until golden. Drain on paper towels. Serve immediately. Yield: 16 fritters.

Millie Cathey
Sharing Recipes
Hook & Ladder Association of Holly Lake Volunteer Fire Department
Big Sandy, Texas

Caramelized Onion Pudding

Be patient when preparing this pudding. The key to creating sweetly caramelized onions is cooking them slowly and stirring them often.

½ cup butter or margarine
6 cups sliced onions (about 3 large onions)
6 large eggs
2 cups heavy whipping cream
¼ cup sugar
3 tablespoons all-purpose flour
2 teaspoons baking powder
2 teaspoons salt

MELT butter in a Dutch oven over medium heat. Add onion; sauté 45 minutes or until onion is browned. Remove from heat; set aside.

STIR together eggs and remaining 5 ingredients; add to onion. Pour mixture into a greased 13- x 9-inch baking dish.

BAKE, uncovered, at 350° for 45 minutes or until golden. Let stand 5 minutes before serving. Yield: 10 servings.

Kathy Cary
Look Who's Cooking in Louisville
Pitt Academy
Louisville, Kentucky

Lovin' Onions

Cheddar and Monterey Jack cheeses, plus a little jalapeño pepper, spice up this dish a bit. So what's not to love about these onions?

1 tablespoon butter or margarine
7 medium onions, coarsely chopped
    (about 2¾ pounds)
½ cup self-rising flour
½ teaspoon salt
¼ teaspoon pepper

1¼ cups (5 ounces) shredded
    Cheddar cheese
1¼ cups (5 ounces) shredded
    Monterey Jack cheese
1 tablespoon chopped canned
    jalapeño pepper

MELT butter in a large skillet over medium heat; add onion, and sauté 10 minutes or until tender.

COMBINE flour, salt, and pepper. Combine cheeses. Add 1 cup cheese to flour mixture; stir well. Add onion and jalapeño pepper to flour mixture; stir well. Pour into a greased 3-quart baking dish. Top with remaining cheese mixture. Bake, uncovered, at 350° for 30 minutes or until cheese melts and mixture is bubbly. Yield: 6 servings.

Dolly Sloan
We're Cooking Up Something New: 50 Years of Music, History, and Food
Wichita Falls Symphony League
Wichita Falls, Texas

No More Tears
Onions are best known for their ability to make a cook cry. A few preventive tips: Freeze onions 20 minutes before slicing; run water over onion after peeling it; or wear glasses or goggles while chopping.

Green Peas with Pine Nuts and Rosemary QUICK & EASY

These just might be the finest peas you'll ever taste, thanks to the addition of fresh rosemary and buttery pine nuts.

½ cup chicken broth
2 (10-ounce) packages frozen
    English peas
3 green onions, cut into ½-inch pieces
½ teaspoon sugar

¾ cup pine nuts
3 tablespoons butter or margarine,
    melted
1 tablespoon chopped fresh rosemary
Salt and pepper to taste

BRING chicken broth to a boil in a medium saucepan over medium-high heat. Add peas, green onions, and sugar; cover, reduce heat, and simmer 5 minutes or until peas are tender. Drain well, and set aside.

COOK pine nuts in butter in a saucepan over medium heat, stirring constantly, 2 to 3 minutes or until golden. Add pea mixture, rosemary, and salt and pepper to taste; cook, uncovered, 2 minutes or until thoroughly heated. Yield: 8 servings.

Eat Your Dessert or You Won't Get Any Broccoli
The Sea Pines Montessori School
Hilton Head Island, South Carolina

Quick Peas
No need to thaw green peas for this recipe. Just open the 2 packages and add them to the boiling broth.

Mashed Potatoes with Shallots, Goat Cheese, and Herbs

Pictured on page 323

Pictured on page 323

Spud Know-How

Some say the best way to achieve fluffy mashed potatoes is to drain the cooked potatoes really well, return them to the warm pan, and heat over low heat to further dry the potatoes. Then use a potato masher, not a mixer of any type, to blend in other ingredients.

Mashed potatoes are more popular than ever. Shallots, goat cheese, and fresh herbs transform an old standby into gourmet fare.

¾ cup chopped shallot (about 4 large)
2 teaspoons olive oil
2½ pounds Yukon gold or round red potatoes
1 cup milk
10 ounces soft goat cheese

1 tablespoon chopped fresh thyme
1 tablespoon chopped fresh parsley
1 tablespoon chopped fresh chives
¾ teaspoon salt
¼ teaspoon freshly ground pepper
Garnishes: fresh thyme sprigs, fresh parsley sprigs

COOK shallot in oil in a large skillet over medium heat 4 to 5 minutes or until tender and golden. Set aside.

COOK potatoes in boiling water to cover 30 to 35 minutes or until tender. Drain well. Cool 5 minutes. Peel and mash potatoes with a potato masher. (Do not use a food processor.) Return potatoes to warm pan.

HEAT milk in a small saucepan until warm; add milk to potato. Stir in shallot, goat cheese, and next 5 ingredients. Mash gently. Spoon into a serving dish. Garnish, if desired. Yield: 10 servings.

Marge Eastman
A Culinary Tour of Homes
Big Canoe Chapel Women's Guild
Big Canoe, Georgia

Roasted Garlic Mashed Potatoes

Garlic lovers, wait'll you try these spuds mashed with roasted garlic puree. They're great with steak, chicken, or pork.

Best Mashers

Starchy russet potatoes are the best choice for mashing and blending because they absorb milk or cream easily.

2 pounds baking potatoes, peeled and cut into 3-inch pieces
½ teaspoon salt
Roasted Garlic Puree
2 tablespoons unsalted butter

2 tablespoons olive oil
⅛ teaspoon ground white pepper
⅔ cup half-and-half
2 tablespoons chopped fresh parsley

COOK potato in boiling salted water to cover 15 minutes or until tender; drain. Mash potatoes in a large bowl; stir in Roasted Garlic Puree and next 3 ingredients.

HEAT half-and-half in a small saucepan just until warm (do not boil). Gradually stir warm half-and-half into potato mixture to desired consistency. Remove potato mixture to a serving bowl, and sprinkle with parsley. Yield: 3 servings.

Roasted Garlic Puree

2 large heads garlic

PEEL outer skins from garlic. Cut off top one-fourth of each garlic head. Place garlic, cut side up, in center of a piece of heavy-duty aluminum foil; fold foil over garlic, sealing tightly. Bake at 350° for 1 hour or until soft. Remove from oven; cool. Remove and discard skins from garlic. Scoop out pulp; mash and stir until smooth. Yield: 2 tablespoons.

Palette Pleasers
St. Luke Simpson United Methodist Women
Lake Charles, Louisiana

Tennessee Sippin' Yams

Tennessee cooks know a thing about cooking with whiskey. The Jack Daniels distillery's right there. This casserole with a pecan streusel and whiskey sauce is over the top.

4 pounds sweet potatoes, peeled, cooked, and mashed	¼ cup whiskey
½ cup butter, melted	¾ teaspoon salt
⅓ cup packed light brown sugar	½ teaspoon ground allspice
⅓ cup orange juice	Pecan Crumble
	Whiskey Sauce

COMBINE first 7 ingredients; stir well. Spoon into a greased 2½-quart casserole. Sprinkle with Pecan Crumble. Bake at 350° for 45 minutes or until lightly browned and bubbly around the edges. Serve with warm Whiskey Sauce. Yield: 13 servings.

Pecan Crumble

1 cup firmly packed light brown sugar	½ cup all-purpose flour
1 cup chopped pecans	1 cup grated coconut (optional)
	⅓ cup cold butter

COMBINE first 3 ingredients; add coconut, if desired. Cut in butter with a pastry blender until crumbly. Yield: 4 cups.

Whiskey Sauce

⅔ cup packed light brown sugar	¼ cup butter
⅓ cup light corn syrup	⅛ teaspoon ground mace
¼ cup water	½ cup whiskey

COMBINE first 5 ingredients in top of a double boiler; bring water to a boil. Reduce heat to medium; cook until thickened, stirring often. Remove from heat; stir in whiskey. Yield: 1½ cups.

Sadie LeSueur
Linen Napkins to Paper Plates
The Junior Auxiliary of Clarksville, Tennessee

Is It Yams Yet?

Yams and sweet potatoes often are confused with one another. In the South the terms are used interchangeably. They're both root vegetables, but that's where the similarities end. Yams are sweeter and moister than sweet potatoes. Unlike sweet potatoes, though, yams aren't widely available in the United States.

Summer Risotto

Summer Risotto

Serve this incredibly light dish with grilled chicken, a crusty loaf of bread, and a freshly tossed green salad. The blue cheese adds a distinctive, but subtle, note to the risotto-vegetable blend.

4½ cups reduced-sodium chicken
    broth
2 tablespoons butter, divided
2 garlic cloves, minced
2 shallots, minced
1¼ cups Arborio rice, uncooked
¼ teaspoon salt
¼ teaspoon pepper
¼ cup thinly sliced purple onion
¼ cup julienne-sliced or shredded
    carrot

¼ cup thinly sliced zucchini
¼ cup thinly sliced yellow squash
¼ cup arugula
3 tablespoons chopped fresh basil
2 tablespoons chopped fresh oregano
⅓ cup crumbled blue cheese
3 tablespoons chopped walnuts,
    toasted
Garnish: fresh oregano sprigs

Creamy Italian
Arborio rice, a high-starch Italian grain, soaks up the broth as it simmers and leads to risotto's characteristic creamy finish.

BRING chicken broth to a simmer in a saucepan, and keep warm over low heat.

MELT 1 tablespoon butter in a 3-quart saucepan over medium-high heat. Add garlic and shallot; cook 2 minutes, stirring constantly. Reduce heat to medium; add rice, and continue to cook 5 more minutes or until rice is translucent, stirring constantly.

ADD warm chicken broth to rice mixture, ½ cup at a time, stirring constantly. Allow liquid to be absorbed after each addition before adding more chicken broth. Stir in salt and pepper; set aside.

MELT remaining 1 tablespoon butter in a large skillet over medium-high heat. Add onion and carrot; cook 2 minutes, stirring constantly. Reduce heat to medium; add zucchini and squash, and cook 2 minutes or until vegetables are tender, stirring often. Add vegetable mixture to rice mixture; stir gently. Stir in arugula, basil, and oregano; sprinkle with blue cheese and walnuts. Garnish, if desired. Serve immediately. Yield: 8 servings.

Call to Post
Lexington Hearing and Speech Center
Lexington, Kentucky

Texas Rice

Onion Bunch

One big bunch of green onions will produce the 1 cup chopped onion needed for this recipe.

This dressed-up rice dish has appeal for all ages. It's flecked with ham, cheese, and green chiles. It's the kind of casserole that'll get gobbled up quickly at a potluck supper.

1 cup chopped cooked ham
1 cup chopped green onions
¼ cup butter or margarine, melted
3 cups cooked rice
1 (8-ounce) container sour cream
1 cup (4 ounces) shredded sharp
    Cheddar cheese
½ cup small-curd cottage cheese

1 (4.5-ounce) can chopped green
    chiles, undrained
½ teaspoon salt
⅛ teaspoon ground white pepper
⅛ teaspoon ground bay leaves
Garnishes: paprika, fresh parsley
    sprigs

COOK chopped ham and green onions in butter in a large skillet over medium-high heat, stirring constantly, until green onions are tender. Remove from heat. Stir in rice and next 7 ingredients. Spoon into a lightly greased 11- x 7-inch baking dish. Bake, uncovered, at 375° for 20 minutes or until thoroughly heated. Garnish, if desired. Yield: 6 servings.

Tastes and Traditions: The Sam Houston Heritage Cookbook
The Study Club of Huntsville, Texas

Wild Rice with Grapes

Wild about Rice

Also called "Indian rice," wild rice is known for its nutty flavor and chewy texture. It also can take up to an hour to cook.

This healthy rice side dish sports beautiful colors with the addition of red and green grapes. Stir in some chopped cooked chicken and serve it as an entrée.

2 tablespoons butter or margarine,
    divided
2 tablespoons sliced almonds
¼ cup chopped green onions
1 (14½-ounce) can chicken broth
3 tablespoons water

½ teaspoon salt
¼ teaspoon pepper
⅔ cup uncooked wild rice
½ cup seedless green grapes, halved
½ cup seedless red grapes, halved

MELT 1 tablespoon butter in a large saucepan over medium heat; add almonds, and cook 2 minutes, stirring constantly, until golden. Remove almonds from pan; set almonds aside.

MELT remaining 1 tablespoon butter in pan. Add green onions; cook, stirring constantly, until tender. Add broth and next 3 ingredients; bring to a boil. Stir in rice; return to a boil. Cover, reduce heat, and simmer 1 hour or until rice is tender. Drain any liquid. Stir in grapes. Sprinkle with almonds. Yield: 4 servings.

Linda Norton
With Love from the Shepherd's Center of North Little Rock
The Shepherd's Center of North Little Rock, Arkansas

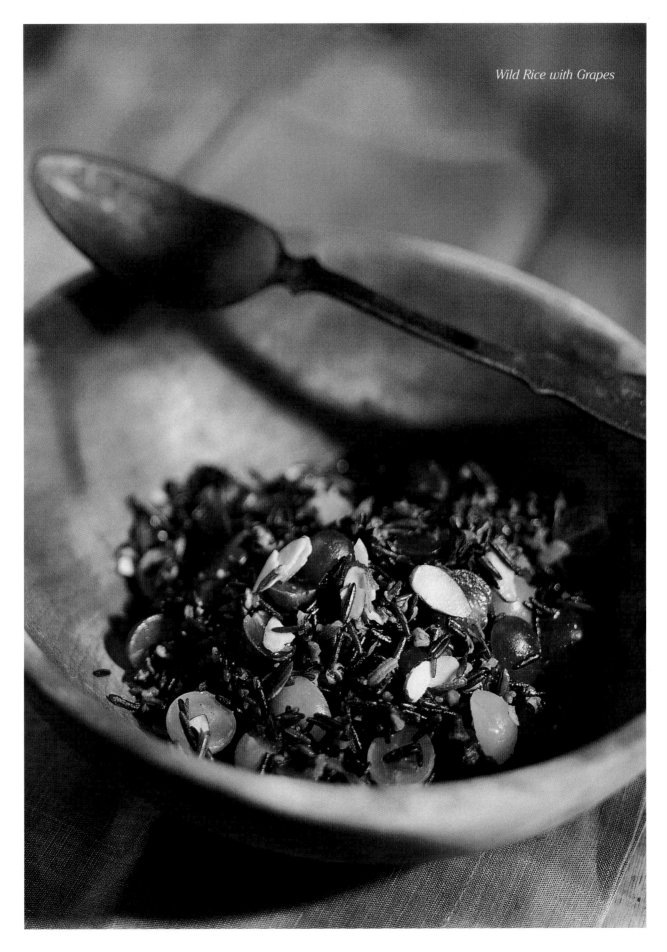

Wild Rice with Grapes

German-Style Spinach QUICK & EASY

Popeye's Pick

Spinach is an excellent source of folic acid, iron, and vitamins A and C.

A sprinkling of nutmeg and some bacon put German flair into these greens.

2 (10-ounce) packages frozen chopped spinach	2 garlic cloves, minced
6 bacon slices	1 large onion, chopped
2 tablespoons butter or margarine, melted	½ teaspoon salt
	½ teaspoon ground nutmeg
	⅛ teaspoon pepper

COOK spinach according to package directions. Drain well, and set aside.

COOK bacon in a large skillet until crisp; remove bacon, reserving 2 teaspoons drippings in skillet. Crumble bacon, and set aside.

ADD butter to drippings in skillet. Sauté garlic and onion in butter and drippings over medium-high heat until tender. Stir in salt, nutmeg, and pepper. Stir in cooked spinach and bacon; cook over medium heat until thoroughly heated. Serve immediately. Yield: 6 servings.

Wilda Ward
A Taste of Leavenworth
Washington State Autumn Leaf Festival Association
Leavenworth, Washington

Samford University Squash Croquettes

Croquettes Defined

The term "croquette" simply refers to a tasty mixture that's formed into rounds or ovals, dipped in egg, rolled in breadcrumbs, and deep-fried to golden status. It looks a lot like a hush puppy.

Yellow squash give these crisp, golden croquettes moisture and sweetness. Use your favorite cornbread recipe for the crumbs or purchase a ready-made loaf at the local deli or bakery to save time.

2 pounds yellow squash, sliced	1 teaspoon salt
1 to 2 cups cornbread crumbs	1 teaspoon pepper
2 large eggs, beaten	1 cup fine, dry breadcrumbs
½ cup finely chopped onion	(store-bought)
¼ cup butter or margarine, melted	Vegetable oil
1 tablespoon sugar	

PLACE squash in a medium saucepan; add water to cover. Bring to a boil; reduce heat, and simmer, uncovered, 20 minutes or until tender. Drain well.

COMBINE squash, cornbread crumbs, and next 6 ingredients; stir well. Shape mixture by ⅓ cupfuls into balls. Carefully dredge each ball in breadcrumbs.

POUR oil to a depth of 3 inches into a Dutch oven; heat to 375°. Fry in batches in hot oil 1 to 2 minutes or until golden. Drain and serve immediately. Yield: 8 servings.

Anna Schepker
Cougar Bites
Crestline Elementary School
Birmingham, Alabama

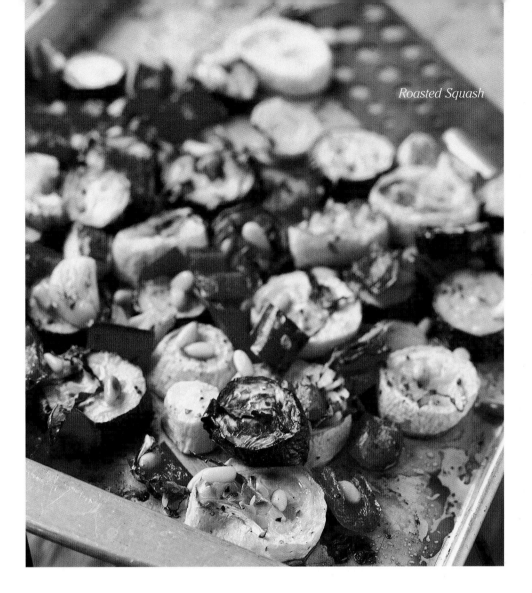

Roasted Squash

Roasted Squash   QUICK & EASY

High-temperature roasting has drawn universal attention in the kitchen. It's fast, flavorful, and healthy.

2 medium zucchini, sliced
2 medium-size yellow squash, sliced
1 red bell pepper, cubed
5 garlic cloves, crushed
2 tablespoons olive oil
1 teaspoon salt

½ teaspoon freshly ground pepper
1 tablespoon balsamic vinegar
2 tablespoons pine nuts, toasted
8 fresh basil leaves, cut into very
　　thin strips

COMBINE first 4 ingredients in a large bowl; drizzle with oil, and sprinkle with salt and pepper. Toss well. Place vegetable mixture in an ungreased 15- x 10-inch jellyroll pan. Bake, uncovered, at 500° for 10 to 20 minutes. Remove vegetables from oven, and toss with vinegar, pine nuts, and basil. Serve immediately. Yield: 4 servings.

Betty Ray
Immacolata Cookbook
Immacolata Church Ladies Society
St. Louis, Missouri

Roasting the Right Way

When roasting vegetables, cut pieces all the same size so they'll cook evenly. And be sure vegetables aren't crowded in the pan or they'll steam instead of roast.

Oven-Roasted Ratatouille

Salting Vegetables

Sprinkling zucchini and eggplant with salt draws out excess moisture, making vegetables better suited for roasting.

Ratatouille is a Provençal vegetable dish of stewed eggplant, squash, peppers, and tomatoes. Serve it hot or at room temperature.

2 medium zucchini, coarsely chopped (about 2 cups)
1 small eggplant, coarsely chopped (about 3 cups)
2 teaspoons salt
1 pound cherry tomatoes
1 red bell pepper, cut into 1-inch pieces
1 yellow bell pepper, cut into 1-inch pieces

1 medium onion, cut into 1-inch pieces
1 cup lightly packed torn fresh basil leaves (about 1 bunch)
2 large garlic cloves, minced
½ teaspoon pepper
3 tablespoons olive oil

PLACE zucchini and eggplant in a colander; sprinkle with salt. Cover with a small plate, and let stand at room temperature 1 hour. Pat dry with paper towels.

ARRANGE zucchini, eggplant, tomatoes, and next 3 ingredients in a single layer on an ungreased 15- x 10-inch jellyroll pan. Sprinkle with basil, garlic, and pepper. Drizzle with oil. Bake, uncovered, at 400° for 40 minutes. Yield: 6 to 8 servings.

Have You Heard . . . A Tasteful Medley of Memphis
Subsidium, Inc.
Memphis, Tennessee

Squash and Apple Casserole

Squash Talk

Generally, squash are divided into 2 categories—summer squash and winter squash. Winter squash, such as butternut and spaghetti squash, have hard, thick skins and seeds. The flesh is firmer than summer squash, and as a result requires longer cooking.

A brown sugar and spice topping sprinkled over butternut squash and apples creates a sweet side dish that pairs deliciously with pork.

1¼ pounds butternut squash, peeled and cut into 1-inch pieces
4 to 5 medium Granny Smith apples, peeled and cut into 8 wedges each
½ cup firmly packed light brown sugar

1 tablespoon all-purpose flour
1 teaspoon salt
¼ teaspoon ground cinnamon
¼ teaspoon ground nutmeg
¼ cup butter or margarine

COMBINE squash and apple in an ungreased 13- x 9-inch baking dish. Stir together brown sugar and next 4 ingredients in a small bowl. Cut in butter with a pastry blender until mixture is crumbly.

SPRINKLE sugar mixture over squash and apples. Bake, uncovered, at 350° for 50 to 60 minutes or until squash and apple are tender. Yield: 8 servings.

Out of the Ordinary
The Hingham Historical Society
Hingham, Massachusetts

Spaghetti Squash

The beauty of spaghetti squash is that it makes its own serving shell once you've baked it and scooped out the insides.

1 (3-pound) spaghetti squash
1 medium onion, chopped
1 garlic clove, minced
2 tablespoons vegetable oil
1 cup chopped fresh Swiss chard
3 large eggs, lightly beaten
1 cup plus 2 tablespoons fine, dry
    breadcrumbs, divided
    (store-bought)

½ cup freshly grated Parmesan
    cheese
1½ teaspoons salt
1 teaspoon dried parsley flakes
1 teaspoon dried Italian
    seasoning
¼ teaspoon pepper

CUT squash in half lengthwise; discard seeds.

PLACE squash, cut side up, in a Dutch oven; cover with water. Bring to a boil; cover, reduce heat, and simmer 20 minutes or until tender. Using a fork, remove spaghetti-like strands, leaving 2 (¼-inch-thick) shells; set shells aside. Place strands in a large bowl; set aside.

COOK onion and garlic in hot oil in a large skillet over medium-high heat, stirring constantly, 3 minutes or until onion is tender.

COMBINE squash and Swiss chard. Add to onion mixture; cook, uncovered, 3 to 5 minutes or until Swiss chard is wilted and tender. Add eggs, 1 cup breadcumbs, and next 5 ingredients.

PLACE reserved squash shells into an ungreased 13- x 9-inch baking dish. Spoon squash mixture evenly into shells. Sprinkle with remaining 2 tablespoons breadcrumbs. Coat breadcrumbs with cooking spray. Bake, uncovered, at 350° for 45 minutes. Yield: 4 to 6 servings.

Mary J. Dussault
Green Thumbs in the Kitchen
Green Thumb, Inc.
Arlington, Virginia

Cutting Squash

Sometimes cutting raw winter squash can be a tough task. To make it easier, prick squash and microwave at HIGH for 1 minute; then cut squash.

Fall Family Dinner, page 365

Homestyle Weeknight Meals

*W*ho says weeknight dinners have to be harried? In this chapter, we offer a variety of menu ideas, complete with grocery lists and game plans.

Vegetable Plate Supper

Serves 6

- Vegetable Slaw* *page 72*

- Ranch-Style Beans* *page 73*

- Tomato-Stuffed Yellow Squash*
  page 73

- Corn Sticks* *page 56*

- Mint Tea* *page 54*

*A*ny true Southerner loves an old-fashioned veggie dinner. We've put 4 healthy recipes on the plate to make this comforting meal. And, of course, we had to include iced tea.

Prep Plan

1. Prepare Mint Tea up to a day ahead. Cover and chill.
2. Soak pinto beans 1 hour.
3. While beans soak, chop and measure ingredients for beans. Prepare Vegetable Slaw; chill up to 2 hours.
4. Prepare Ranch-Style Beans, and simmer 2 hours.
5. Prepare and stuff yellow squash for baking. Set aside.
6. Prepare batter, and bake Corn Sticks.
7. Reduce oven temperature, and bake squash.

Denotes a light recipe.

Market Order

Staples on Hand

- salt
- pepper
- ground red pepper
- chili powder
- dry mustard
- baking powder
- all-purpose flour
- yellow cornmeal
- sugar
- fine, dry bread-crumbs
- garlic (4 cloves)
- white vinegar
- Worcestershire sauce
- vegetable oil
- olive oil
- vegetable cooking spray
- 8 regular-size tea bags

Grocery List

- 1 small cabbage (3 cups shredded)
- broccoli florets (1 cup)
- cauliflower florets (1 cup)
- 10 plum tomatoes
- 3 medium-size yellow squash
- 1 large white onion
- 1 purple onion
- 1 red bell pepper
- 1 small green bell pepper
- fresh oregano
- fresh mint
- 10-ounce can diced tomatoes and green chiles
- 11-ounce can sweet whole kernel corn
- 1 pound dried pinto beans
- shredded Parmesan cheese
- ¾ cup 1% low-fat milk
- ½ cup egg substitute
- 2 eggs (whites)
- light mayonnaise
- light sour cream
- 46-ounce can pineapple juice
- 6-ounce can frozen lemonade concentrate

Sloppy Joe Supper

Serves 5

- Sloppy Joes *page 41*
- Wilted Cabbage *page 282*
- Baked onion rings
- Fresh fruit and frozen yogurt

A simple sloppy joe supper is a great solution for busy weeknights. This menu weaves in a make-ahead slaw and frozen onion rings for ease.

Prep Plan

1. Prepare cabbage up to a day ahead; chill at least 8 hours.
2. Bake onion rings according to package directions.
3. Prepare Sloppy Joes. Toast buns.
4. Wash fruit, and scoop yogurt for dessert.

Market Order

Staples on Hand

- ☐ salt
- ☐ pepper
- ☐ sugar
- ☐ dry mustard
- ☐ celery seeds
- ☐ light brown sugar
- ☐ ketchup
- ☐ sweet pickle relish
- ☐ prepared mustard
- ☐ white vinegar
- ☐ vegetable oil

Grocery List

- ☐ 1 pound ground chuck
- ☐ 1 large onion
- ☐ 1 medium onion
- ☐ 1 medium-size green bell pepper
- ☐ 1 medium-size red bell pepper
- ☐ 1 small cabbage or 1 (10-ounce) package shredded angel hair cabbage
- ☐ (20-ounce) package frozen onion rings
- ☐ frozen yogurt
- ☐ fresh strawberries, blueberries, or other fruit
- ☐ hamburger buns

Keeping your Kitchen Tools Handy

Low on kitchen storage space? Store your kitchen tools in an antique tin, and display them on the kitchen counter. Then they'll be within easy reach when you need them.

Beef Stroganoff Splurge

Serves 6

- Green salad

- Beef Stroganoff *page 211*

- Peas and carrots

- Quick Chocolate Mousse *page 37*

C omfort your family with tender beef stroganoff smothered in a creamy, sour cream sauce. Then serve this 2-ingredient dessert—they'll think you've been cooking all day long.

Prep Plan

1. Melt and then cool mousse ingredients; cover and chill at least 8 hours.
2. Prepare Beef Stroganoff, and simmer.
3. Meanwhile, bring water to a boil for noodles.
4. Cook egg noodles.
5. Cook peas and carrots according to package directions.
6. Prepare salad.
7. Beat mousse until thickened, and spoon into dessert dishes.

Market Order

Staples on Hand

- salt
- pepper
- all-purpose flour
- butter or margarine
- salad dressing

Grocery List

- 2 pounds round steak
- head lettuce or bag of salad greens
- tomatoes and fresh mushrooms for salad
- fresh parsley
- egg noodles (12 to 16 ounces dried)
- 10¾-ounce can cream of mushroom soup
- 8-ounce container sour cream
- 1¼ cups whipping cream
- ⅓ cup milk
- 5 ounces dark chocolate
- 16-ounce package frozen peas and carrots

Quick Chocolate Mousse

Easy Italian Night

Serves 4

- 20-Minute Chicken Parmesan
  page 43

- Green salad

- Garlic bread

- Pecan Biscotti *page 156*

- Coffee

Market Order

Staples on Hand

- ☐ salt
- ☐ baking powder
- ☐ all-purpose flour
- ☐ yellow cornmeal
- ☐ ½ cup Italian-seasoned breadcrumbs
- ☐ sugar
- ☐ vegetable oil
- ☐ almond extract
- ☐ butter or margarine
- ☐ salad dressing

Grocery List

- ☐ 4 skinned and boned chicken breast halves
- ☐ bag of salad greens
- ☐ ¼ cup chopped fresh parsley
- ☐ 3 large eggs
- ☐ 2 ounces mozzarella cheese
- ☐ 1 tablespoon grated Parmesan cheese
- ☐ jar spaghetti sauce (1¾ cups)
- ☐ ½ (16-ounce) package spaghetti
- ☐ garlic bread
- ☐ 1 cup finely chopped pecans
- ☐ coffee

*S*tir up this fast Italian feast in mere minutes. Chicken Parmesan comes together quickly in a hot skillet. And in the time it takes to toss a salad, the garlic bread will be ready to pull out of the oven.

Prep Plan

1. Prepare biscotti dough, and bake up to a day ahead. Store in an airtight container.
2. Preheat oven for garlic bread.
3. Prepare Chicken Parmesan.
4. Bake garlic bread according to package directions.
5. Toss salad.
6. Brew coffee to accompany dessert.

Beauty of Old Wooden Bowls

Fill a wooden bowl with nature's produce, and display it on your coffee table, kitchen island, or breakfast table as a simple centerpiece. Use an antique oblong dough bowl for the same idea. In the fall and winter, fill the bowl with kindling or pine cones, and display it on your fireplace hearth.

Slow Cooker Dinner

Serves 8

- Melt-in-Your-Mouth Roast
  page 207

- Smoky Mashed Potato Bake*
  page 75

- Green beans

- Easy Cheddar Biscuits *page 34*

- Angel Toast *page 38*

Market Order

Staples on Hand	Grocery List
❏ salt	❏ 1 (3- to-4-pound) rump roast
❏ pepper	❏ 3½ pounds new potatoes
❏ garlic (3 cloves)	❏ 2 pounds green beans
❏ baking powder	❏ 1 large onion
❏ all-purpose flour	❏ 2 or 3 canned chipotle peppers in adobo sauce
❏ Worcestershire sauce	❏ 4 ounces sharp Cheddar cheese
❏ vegetable oil	❏ 3 ounces smoked Gouda cheese
❏ olive oil	❏ 4 ounces fat-free cream cheese
❏ shortening	❏ ½ cup light margarine
❏ vegetable cooking spray	❏ 1 cup fat-free half-and-half
❏ butter	❏ ½ cup milk
❏ sugar	❏ angel food cake from bakery
❏ light brown sugar	❏ ½ gallon coffee ice cream

*P*repare this roast in a slow cooker to free your oven for the side dishes and biscuits. This menu combines traditional full-fat recipes with a light recipe to make a filling meal.

Prep Plan

1. Cook roast in slow cooker for 8 hours.

2. Put water on to boil for potatoes and green beans. Trim green beans.

3. Prepare and bake Smoky Mashed Potato Bake, and keep warm.

4. Meanwhile, cook green beans in a small amount of boiling water for 15 minutes or until desired doneness. Drain and season beans; keep warm.

5. Just before the meal, thicken gravy for roast in slow cooker.

6. Increase oven temperature. Bake biscuits.

7. After dinner, prepare Angel Toast for dessert.

*Denotes a light recipe.

Fall Family Dinner

Serves 4

- Spiced Cider Punch *page 104*

- Bourbon-Basted Pork Chops *page 224*

- Broccoli Dressing *page 330*

- Cabbage with Apples and Walnuts
  page 331

- Apple-Nut Pudding with Hot Rum Sauce
  page 186

Consider this pork chop dinner in the fall of the year when apples and nuts and hot cider punch appeal to the palate. Serve the cider punch before the meal or with dessert.

Prep Plan

1. Prepare cider punch and hot rum dessert sauce up to a day ahead. Cover and chill.

2. Two to three hours before dinner, prepare and bake Apple-Nut Pudding.

3. Meanwhile, prepare Broccoli Dressing. When pudding is baked, reduce oven temperature, and bake dressing.

4. Shred cabbage, and slice apples.

5. Prepare basting sauce for pork chops. Grill pork chops.

6. Cook cabbage with apples in Dutch oven.

7. Reheat punch and rum dessert sauce before serving, if desired.

Market Order

Staples on Hand

- salt
- pepper
- hot sauce
- poultry seasoning
- ground cinnamon
- 4 cinnamon sticks
- all-purpose flour
- baking soda
- sugar
- light brown sugar
- butter or margarine
- 3 large eggs
- cider vinegar
- soy sauce
- vanilla extract
- butter flavoring
- rum extract
- enough bread to get 4 cups cubes

Grocery List

- 4 (1-inch-thick) rib pork chops
- 6 bacon slices
- 1 medium-size green cabbage
- 1 medium-size red cabbage
- 7 medium cooking apples
- 1 small onion
- 1 lemon
- 1½ cups chopped celery
- 10-ounce package frozen chopped broccoli
- 4 cups fresh orange juice (about 12 oranges)
- 1½ cups fresh lemon juice (6 to 8 lemons)
- 3 cups apple cider
- 8 ounces Swiss cheese
- ⅓ cup walnuts
- 1 cup chopped pecans
- bourbon

Streusel Shortcake, page 386

Casual Entertaining

*S*how off Southern hospitality with these easy-paced menus. Grab a deviled egg off our picnic plate, or sip some Homemade Lemonade while the kids enjoy July Fourth fireworks. Our casual menus make visiting the main focus.

July Fourth Fun

Menu

Serves 8

- Hamburgers and hot dogs

- Grilled Marinated Vegetable Salad

- Chips and pickles

- Granny Smith Apple Pie *page 369*

- Chocolate-Glazed Brownies
  page 370

- Homemade Lemonade *page 370*

*L*ight your grill and add to the celebration and fireworks with some good ol' burgers and hot dogs. Toast the buns on the grill, too, for a little added texture. Bring an assortment of chips for the kids and a bag of ice for the lemonade. The vegetable salad is portable and tastes great served chilled or at room temperature. The salad, brownies, and lemonade can be made a day ahead.

Grilled Marinated Vegetable Salad

4 tablespoons olive oil, divided
3 tablespoons honey
2 tablespoons balsamic vinegar
1 teaspoon salt
½ teaspoon pepper
3 large yellow squash
3 large zucchini
2 medium-size green bell peppers
2 medium-size red bell peppers
2 medium-size orange bell peppers
2 medium-size yellow bell peppers
1 pound fresh green beans

STIR together 1 tablespoon oil, honey, and next 3 ingredients until blended. Set aside.

SLICE squash and zucchini; cut bell peppers into 1-inch pieces, and trim green beans. Toss squash, zucchini, and bell pepper with 2 tablespoons oil. Toss green beans with remaining 1 tablespoon oil.

GRILL squash, zucchini, and bell pepper in a grill wok, covered with grill lid, over medium-high heat (350° to 400°), stirring occasionally, 5 to 7 minutes or until vegetables are tender. Remove from wok.

GRILL green beans in grill wok, covered with grill lid, over medium-high heat, stirring occasionally, 5 to 7 minutes or until tender.

TOSS vegetables with honey mixture; cover and chill 8 hours. Yield: 8 to 10 servings.

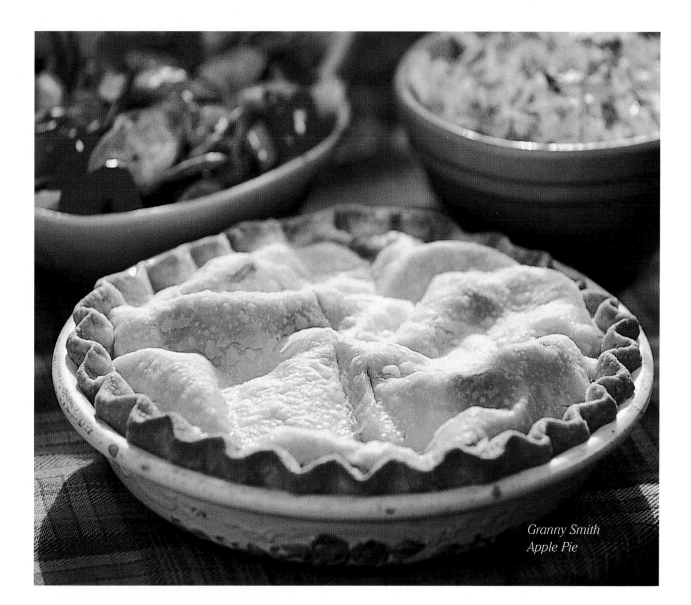

Granny Smith Apple Pie

Granny Smith Apple Pie

1½ (15-ounce) packages refrigerated
    piecrusts, divided
6 medium Granny Smith apples,
    peeled and sliced
1½ tablespoons lemon juice
¾ cup firmly packed light brown sugar
½ cup sugar
⅓ cup all-purpose flour
1 teaspoon ground cinnamon
½ teaspoon ground nutmeg

STACK 2 piecrusts; gently roll or press together. Fit pastry into a 9-inch deep-dish pieplate.

TOSS together apple and lemon juice in a large bowl. Combine brown sugar and remaining 4 ingredients; sprinkle over apple mixture, and toss to coat. Spoon into prepared piecrust.

ROLL remaining piecrust to press out fold lines; place over filling. Fold edges under, and crimp; cut slits in top for steam to escape.

BAKE at 450° for 15 minutes. Reduce oven temperature to 350°, and bake 35 more minutes. Yield: 1 (9-inch) pie.

Chocolate-Glazed Brownies

1 cup sugar
⅔ cup butter or margarine
¼ cup water
4 cups semisweet chocolate morsels, divided
1 teaspoon vanilla extract
1½ cups all-purpose flour
½ teaspoon baking soda
½ teaspoon salt
4 large eggs
1 cup chopped pecans, toasted

COOK first 3 ingredients in a large saucepan over high heat, stirring constantly, until sugar melts. Add 2 cups chocolate morsels and vanilla extract, stirring until mixture is smooth. Cool 15 minutes.

ADD flour, baking soda, and salt to cooled chocolate mixture, stirring until blended; stir in eggs and chopped pecans until blended. Spread brownie batter into a greased and floured 13- x 9-inch pan.

BAKE at 325° for 30 minutes. Sprinkle remaining 2 cups chocolate morsels evenly over warm brownies, and let stand 5 minutes to soften. Spread over top. Cool on a wire rack. Yield: 18 brownies.

Homemade Lemonade

1½ cups sugar
½ cup boiling water
2 teaspoons grated lemon rind
1½ cups fresh lemon juice
5 cups cold water
Garnish: lemon slices

STIR together sugar and ½ cup boiling water until sugar dissolves.

STIR in lemon rind, lemon juice, and 5 cups cold water. Chill 8 hours. Garnish, if desired. Yield: 8 cups.

LIMEADE: Substitute 2 teaspoons grated lime rind for lemon rind and 1½ cups fresh lime juice for lemon juice.

Picnic Basket
Pack a small utensil caddy basket with tall glasses stuffed with sunflowers or other wildflowers. Add rolled up napkins, flatware, and a corkscrew, and you'll have the makings for a simple picnic.

Barbecue Fest

Menu

Serves 6

• Smoked Pork Shoulder

• Peppery Vinegar Sauce or
Cider Vinegar Barbecue Sauce
page 372

• Creamy Coleslaw *page 282*

• Baked beans

• Squash Puppies *page 372*

• Key Lime Pie *page 373*

*S*tart cooking this pork early in the day so it
will be good and tender and ready for suppertime.
Two tangy sauces give you a sampling of Carolina
'cue at its best. Enjoy slaw, beans, and crisp
squash puppies with the pork. And be sure to save
some room for refreshing Key Lime Pie.

Smoked Pork Shoulder

Hickory wood chunks
1 (5- to 6-pound) pork shoulder or Boston butt
      pork roast
2 teaspoons salt
10 pounds hardwood charcoal, divided

SOAK wood chunks in water at least 1 hour.

SPRINKLE pork with salt; cover and chill 30 minutes.

PREPARE charcoal fire with half of charcoal in grill;
let burn 15 to 20 minutes or until covered with gray ash.

PUSH coals evenly into piles on both sides of grill.
Carefully place 2 hickory chunks on top of each pile,
and place food rack on grill.

PLACE pork, meaty side down, on rack directly in
center of grill. Cover with lid, leaving ventilation holes
completely open.

PREPARE an additional charcoal fire with 12 bri-
quets in an auxiliary grill or fire bucket; let burn 30 minutes or until covered with gray ash. Carefully add 6 bri-
quets to each pile in smoker; place 2 more hickory
chunks on each pile. Repeat procedure every 30
minutes.

COOK, covered with grill lid, 5½ hours or until meat
thermometer inserted into thickest portion registers
at least 165°, turning once the last 2 hours. (Cooking the
pork to 165° makes the meat easier to remove from
the bone.)

REMOVE pork; cool slightly. Chop and serve with
Cider Vinegar Barbecue Sauce (recipe on following
page) or Peppery Vinegar Sauce. Yield: 6 servings.

Peppery Vinegar Sauce

1 quart cider vinegar
1 tablespoon dried crushed red pepper
1 tablespoon salt
1½ teaspoons pepper

STIR together all ingredients; blend well. Yield:
4 cups.

Cider Vinegar Barbecue Sauce

This sauce is often referred to as Lexington-Style Dip, but there are many variations. Most folks can't resist adding their own touch.

1½ cups cider vinegar
⅓ cup firmly packed light brown sugar
¼ cup ketchup
1 tablespoon hot sauce
1 teaspoon browning and seasoning sauce
½ teaspoon salt
½ teaspoon onion powder
½ teaspoon pepper
½ teaspoon Worcestershire sauce

STIR together all ingredients in a medium saucepan; cook over medium heat, stirring constantly, 7 minutes or until sugar dissolves. Cover and chill sauce until ready to serve. Serve with Smoked Pork Shoulder. Yield: 2 cups.

NOTE: For testing purposes only, we used Texas Pete Hot Sauce and Kitchen Bouquet Browning & Seasoning Sauce.

Squash Puppies

These crisp hush puppies showcase the delicate fresh flavor of yellow squash.

¾ cup self-rising cornmeal
¼ cup all-purpose flour
½ teaspoon salt
¼ teaspoon black pepper
⅛ teaspoon ground red pepper
6 medium-size yellow squash, cooked and mashed
½ cup buttermilk
1 small onion, minced
1 large egg
Vegetable oil
½ teaspoon salt

COMBINE first 5 ingredients in a large bowl.
STIR together squash and next 3 ingredients; add to cornmeal mixture, stirring until blended.

Squash Puppies

POUR oil to a depth of ½ inch into a deep cast-iron skillet; heat to 350°. Drop batter by tablespoonfuls, in batches, into oil; fry 3 minutes on each side or until golden brown. Drain on paper towels; sprinkle evenly with ½ teaspoon salt. Yield: 20 squash puppies.

Virginia Harvey
Bella Vista, Arkansas

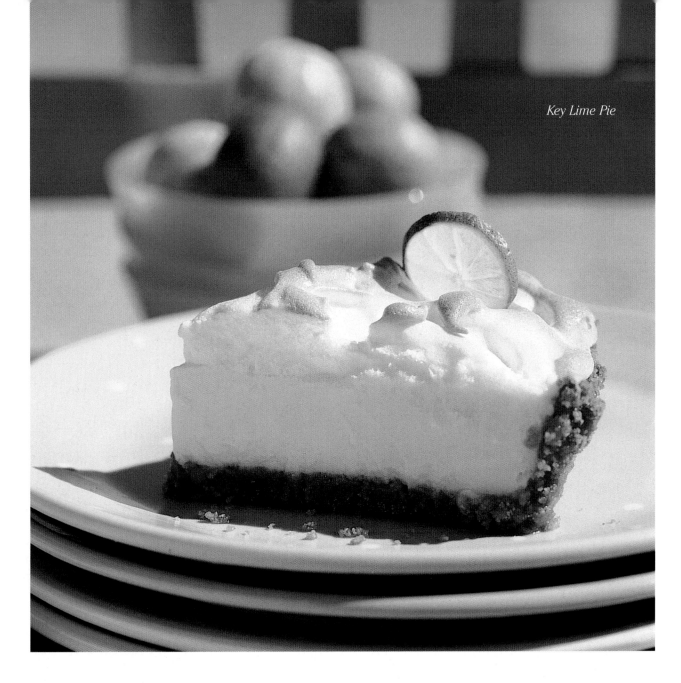

Key Lime Pie

Key Lime Pie

1¼ cups graham cracker crumbs
¼ cup firmly packed light brown
  sugar
⅓ cup butter or margarine, melted
2 (14-ounce) cans sweetened
  condensed milk
1 cup fresh Key lime juice
2 egg whites
¼ teaspoon cream of tartar
2 tablespoons sugar
Garnish: lime slices

COMBINE first 3 ingredients. Press crumb mixture into a 9-inch pieplate.

BAKE at 350° for 10 minutes; cool.

STIR together condensed milk and lime juice until blended. Pour into crust.

BEAT egg whites and cream of tartar at high speed with an electric mixer just until foamy. Add sugar, 1 tablespoon at a time, beating until soft peaks form and sugar dissolves (2 to 4 minutes).

SPREAD meringue over filling.

BAKE at 325° for 25 to 28 minutes. Chill 8 hours. Garnish, if desired. Yield: 1 (9-inch) pie.

Mike Smith
Kissimmee, Florida

Family Reunion

Menu

Serves 12

- Coyote Caviar

- Southern Spareribs *page 375*

- New-Fashioned Corn Relish
page 375

- Phyllis's Favorite Carrot Salad
page 274

- Classic Potato Salad *page 284*

- Toffee Cookie Bars *page 375*

- Peach and Blueberry
Pound Cake *page 376*

- Watermelon

Gather your clan and celebrate under a cool shade tree. Let the men do the grilling and slicing of the icy cold watermelon. The smoky spareribs serve 6, so double the recipe for a crowd. The appetizers and side dishes all have make-ahead potential. See our cool tips at right for ways to pack and serve the corn relish and carrot salad. Plan games for the kids to play while the spareribs are cooking.

Coyote Caviar

1 (15-ounce) can black beans, rinsed and drained
1 (4¼-ounce) can chopped ripe olives
1 (4.5-ounce) can chopped green chiles
1 small onion, finely chopped
1 garlic clove, minced
¼ cup chopped fresh cilantro
2 tablespoons vegetable oil
2 tablespoons lime juice
2 teaspoons chili powder
1 teaspoon black pepper
¼ teaspoon salt
¼ teaspoon dried crushed red pepper
¼ teaspoon ground cumin
1 (8-ounce) package cream cheese, softened
2 hard-cooked eggs, peeled and chopped
2 tablespoons chopped green onions
Tortilla chips

STIR together first 13 ingredients in a bowl. Cover and chill at least 2 hours.

TO serve, spread softened cream cheese on a round serving platter. Spoon bean mixture over cream cheese. Sprinkle egg around edge of bean mixture. Sprinkle green onions over bean mixture. Serve with tortilla chips. Yield: 12 appetizer servings.

Patti Hunter
Southern Elegance: A Second Course
The Junior League of Gaston County
Gastonia, North Carolina

Jarring Ideas

Here's a great time to use those wonderful old glass jars that were passed down to you. Wash the jars; then spoon the corn relish into a large jar or two. Spoon the carrot salad into another. Add lids, and nestle the jars in a cooler along with the watermelon. Serve straight from the jars when the picnic begins.

Southern Spareribs

Dark beer delivers the best flavor to these smoked ribs. And if you want to spice up things a bit, add a sprinkling of ground red pepper or hot sauce to the marinade.

4 pounds spareribs
1 (12-ounce) can beer
¼ cup soy sauce
2 tablespoons brown sugar
2 tablespoons chili sauce
2 tablespoons ketchup
2 tablespoons lemon juice
1 teaspoon onion powder
½ teaspoon salt
¼ teaspoon pepper
Hickory chunks

PLACE ribs in a shallow dish. Combine beer and next 8 ingredients; pour beer mixture over ribs, turning to coat well. Cover and marinate in refrigerator 8 hours.

SOAK hickory chunks in water at least 1 hour. Prepare charcoal fire in smoker, and let burn 15 to 20 minutes. Drain chunks, and place on hot coals. Place water pan in smoker, and add water to depth of fill line.

COAT food rack with cooking spray, and place over coals. Place ribs on rack; cover with smoker lid, and smoke 5 hours or until ribs are tender, refilling water pan and adding charcoal as needed. Yield: 6 servings.

Matt McCarter
Diamond Delights
Diamond Hill Elementary School
Abbeville, South Carolina

New-Fashioned Corn Relish

1 small onion, chopped (about 1 cup)
½ cup sugar
½ cup cider vinegar
2 teaspoons celery seeds
½ teaspoon mustard seeds
1 (15.25-ounce) can whole kernel corn, drained
½ cup chopped celery
¼ cup sweet pickle relish
1 (2-ounce) jar diced pimiento, drained

STIR together first 5 ingredients in a 3-quart saucepan; bring to a boil. Reduce heat, and simmer, uncovered, 10 minutes.

STIR together corn and remaining 3 ingredients in a large bowl; pour hot vinegar mixture over corn mixture, and stir gently. Cool completely (about 2 hours). Store relish in an airtight container in refrigerator. Yield: 2½ cups.

Jeanne Hancock
Recipes for Champions
Shebas of Khiva Temple Oriental Band
Amarillo, Texas

Toffee Cookie Bars

Look for almond toffee bits and English toffee bits on the baking aisle of your grocery store.

½ cup butter or margarine
1½ cups graham cracker crumbs (about 12 rectangle crackers)
1 (14-ounce) can sweetened condensed milk
1¼ cups almond toffee bits
1¼ cups English toffee bits or crushed English toffee candy bars
1 cup (6 ounces) semisweet chocolate morsels
1 cup chopped pecans
½ cup sliced natural almonds

PLACE butter in a 13- x 9-inch baking dish; bake at 325° for 4 minutes or until butter melts.

LAYER graham cracker crumbs and remaining 6 ingredients in baking dish with melted butter. Firmly press mixture in dish.

BAKE at 325° for 25 minutes or until edges are lightly browned. Cool completely in dish on a wire rack. Cut into bars. Yield: 2 dozen.

Picnics, Potlucks & Prizewinners
Indiana 4-H Foundation, Inc.
Indianapolis, Indiana

Peach and Blueberry Pound Cake

Here's a summertime stunner. Juicy ripe peaches and succulent fresh blueberries abound in this cream cheese pound cake. It takes on even more flavor from the fruits if allowed to set overnight before slicing.

½ cup unsalted butter, softened
½ (8-ounce) package cream cheese, softened
2 cups sugar
5 large eggs
¼ cup peach brandy, peach schnapps, or
      peach nectar
2 cups all-purpose flour
1 teaspoon baking powder
¼ teaspoon salt
1¼ cups diced fresh ripe peaches
1 cup fresh blueberries

GENEROUSLY grease and sugar a 10-inch tube pan; set aside.

BEAT butter and cream cheese at medium speed with an electric mixer about 2 minutes or until creamy. Gradually add sugar, beating 5 to 7 minutes. Add eggs, 1 at a time, beating just until yellow disappears. Stir in brandy.

COMBINE flour, baking powder, and salt; add to butter mixture, beating at low speed just until blended. Fold in peaches and blueberries. Pour batter into prepared pan.

BAKE at 325° for 1 hour and 25 minutes or until a long wooden skewer inserted in center of cake comes out clean. Cool in pan on a wire rack 15 minutes; remove from pan, and cool on wire rack. Yield: 1 (10-inch) cake.

Lois Tyler
Sharing Our Best
The Arrangement Hair Salon
Columbus, Ohio

Peach and Blueberry Pound Cake

Southern Picnic

*R*oll up your favorite quilt, pack for an old-fashioned picnic, and head for the great outdoors. Get things started with stuffed eggs and jars of watermelon rind pickles for snacking. Fry up a double batch of chicken to bring along. And be sure to take advantage of the fact that you can make the salads and desserts up to a day ahead.

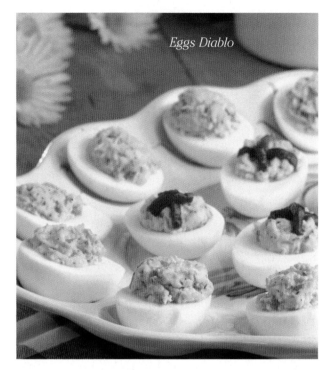
Eggs Diablo

Eggs Diablo

A spoonful of green chiles and picante sauce adds magic to these stuffed eggs.

6 hard-cooked eggs, peeled
2 tablespoons finely shredded Monterey
    Jack cheese
2 tablespoons finely chopped green onions
2 tablespoons canned chopped green chiles,
    undrained
2 tablespoons mayonnaise
2 tablespoons picante sauce
¼ teaspoon salt
¼ teaspoon pepper
Garnish: roasted sweet red pepper strips

CUT eggs in half lengthwise, and carefully remove yolks. Mash yolks; stir in cheese and next 6 ingredients. Spoon mixture into egg whites. Garnish, if desired. Yield: 12 servings.

Savoring the Southwest Again
Roswell Symphony Guild
Roswell, New Mexico

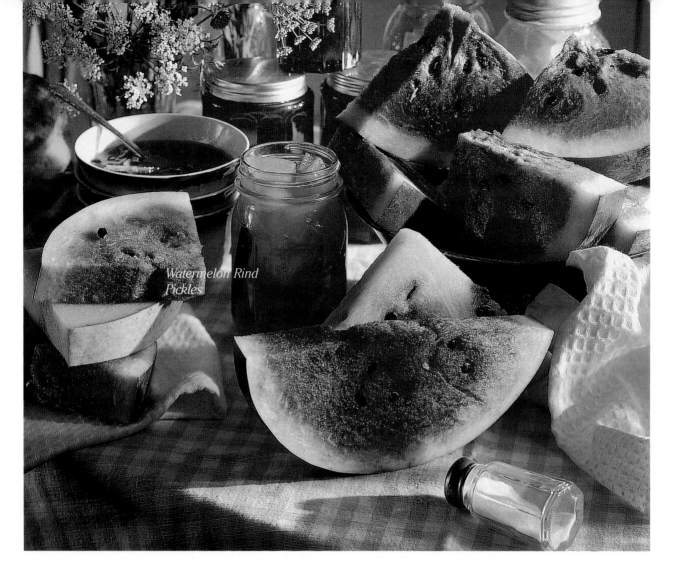

Watermelon Rind Pickles

Watermelon Rind Pickles

1 large watermelon, quartered
¾ cup salt
3 quarts water
2 quarts ice cubes
1 tablespoon whole cloves
1 tablespoon whole allspice
9 cups sugar
3 cups white vinegar
3 cups water
1 lemon, thinly sliced
5 (3-inch) cinnamon sticks

PEEL watermelon; remove pulp, and reserve for another use. Cut rind into 1-inch cubes; reserve 12 cups rind cubes in a large container.

STIR together salt and 3 quarts water; pour over rind. Add ice; cover and let stand 8 hours. Rinse well, and drain.

COOK rind and water to cover in a Dutch oven over high heat 10 minutes or until tender. Drain.

PLACE cloves and allspice on a 3-inch square of cheesecloth; tie with a string.

STIR together sugar, vinegar, and 3 cups water; add spice bag, and bring to a boil. Boil 5 minutes, and pour over rind. Stir in lemon slices. Cover and let stand 8 hours.

BRING rind and syrup mixture to a boil; reduce heat, and simmer, stirring occasionally, 1 hour. Remove and discard spice bag.

PACK rind mixture into hot jars, filling ½ inch from top. Add 1 cinnamon stick to each jar. Remove air bubbles; wipe jar rims. Cover at once with metal lids, and screw on bands.

PROCESS in a boiling-water bath 10 minutes. Yield: 5 (12-ounce) jars.

Lee Wells
Knoxville, Tennessee

Pound Cake Cookies

These cookies garnered a blue ribbon at a state fair competition. Once you taste these buttery gems, you'll agree that they're a hands-down winner for any occasion.

1 cup butter, softened
1 cup sugar
1 egg yolk
1 teaspoon rum or ½ teaspoon imitation rum flavoring
½ teaspoon vanilla extract
2¼ cups sifted cake flour
½ teaspoon salt
About 42 pecan halves

BEAT butter at medium speed with an electric mixer until creamy; gradually add sugar, beating well. Add egg yolk, rum, and vanilla; beat well.

COMBINE flour and salt in a bowl; gradually add to butter mixture, beating well. Cover and chill at least 2 hours or until firm.

SHAPE dough into 1-inch balls; place 2 inches apart on ungreased baking sheets. Press 1 pecan half into each cookie.

BAKE at 350° for 12 to 14 minutes or until edges are lightly browned. Cool 2 minutes on baking sheets; remove to wire racks to cool completely. Yield: about 3½ dozen.

Down by the Water
The Junior League of Columbia, South Carolina

Turtle Cake

Caramel, chocolate, and pecans—what's not to love? This decadent, rich cake is worth every calorie.

1 (18.25-ounce) package German chocolate cake mix with pudding (we tested with Betty Crocker)
3 cups chopped pecans, divided
¾ cup butter, melted
⅓ cup evaporated milk
1 (14-ounce) package caramels (about 50 caramels)
½ cup evaporated milk
2 cups (12 ounces) semisweet chocolate morsels

COMBINE cake mix, 2 cups pecans, butter, and ⅓ cup evaporated milk in a large bowl; stir well. Reserve half of cake mix mixture for topping. Press remaining half of mixture into a greased and floured 13- x 9-inch pan.

BAKE at 350° for 8 minutes. Remove pan from oven, and set aside.

MEANWHILE, combine caramels and ½ cup evaporated milk in a small heavy saucepan. Cook over low heat until caramels melt, stirring often.

SPRINKLE remaining 1 cup pecans and chocolate morsels evenly over cake. Drizzle caramel mixture over pecans and chocolate morsels. Crumble reserved cake mix mixture evenly over caramel mixture.

BAKE at 350° for 20 more minutes. Cool in pan on a wire rack. Yield: 12 servings.

Cyndi Bradt
Moments, Memories & Manna
Restoration Village
Rogers, Arkansas

Ladies Lunch

Menu

Serves 6

- Hazel's Curry Sauce for Melon or Fresh Fruit

- Cucumber Sandwiches *page 381*

- Chicken Salad *page 289*

- Shrimp and Tomato Aspic *page 289*

- Linda Bath's Cocktail Cheese Muffins *page 381*

- Lemon Buttermilk Cake with Lemon Curd Sauce *page 167*

- Peachy Tea *page 381*

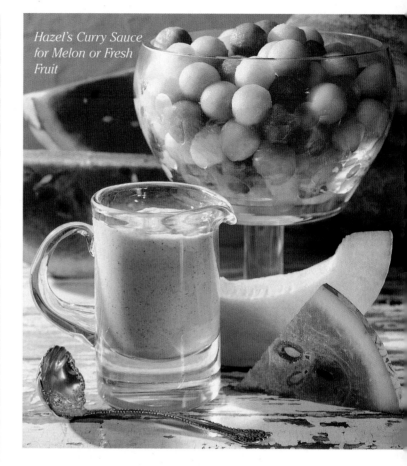

Hazel's Curry Sauce for Melon or Fresh Fruit

Invite your book club over for this light lunch spread. Start things off by offering your guests petit Cucumber Sandwiches and curry sauce with fresh fruit. Serve the two salads together on lunch plates along with muffins and tall glasses of tea that you can make a day ahead. Then finish the meal with buttermilk cake and lemon curd as you discuss the latest literary wonders.

Hazel's Curry Sauce for Melon or Fresh Fruit

1 cup mayonnaise
½ cup sour cream
½ cup spicy brown mustard
4 teaspoons curry powder
2 tablespoons sugar
½ teaspoon salt
¼ teaspoon pepper

COMBINE all ingredients in a small bowl; cover and chill. Serve with melons, apples, or grapes. Yield: 2 cups.

Hazel Carr Nicholson
Cooking in Harmony: Opus II
Brevard Music Center
Brevard, North Carolina

Cucumber Sandwiches

These teatime canapés are superquick.

3 tablespoons mayonnaise
⅛ teaspoon hot sauce
1 (8-ounce) package cream cheese, softened
1 (0.7-ounce) envelope Italian dressing mix
1 (12-ounce) loaf cocktail rye bread
1 large cucumber, thinly sliced into 36 slices
Garnish: fresh dill sprigs

COMBINE first 4 ingredients in a medium mixing bowl; beat at medium speed with an electric mixer until smooth.

SPREAD cream cheese mixture over bread slices. Top each with a cucumber slice. Garnish, if desired. Yield: 3 dozen.

Nathan Loes
Angel Food
St. Vincent de Paul School
Salt Lake City, Utah

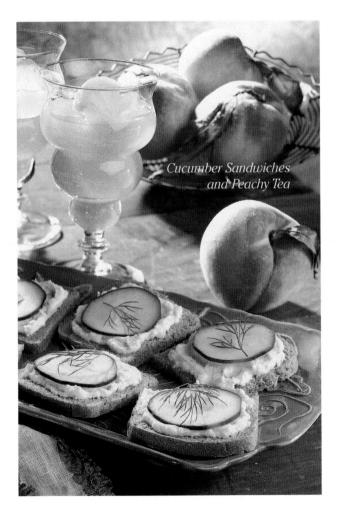

Cucumber Sandwiches and Peachy Tea

Linda Bath's Cocktail Cheese Muffins

¾ cup butter or margarine
2 cups (8 ounces) shredded sharp Cheddar
    cheese
2 cups self-rising flour
1 (8-ounce) container sour cream
2 tablespoons frozen chopped chives

MELT butter in a medium saucepan over medium heat. Add Cheddar cheese, and cook 2 minutes, stirring constantly. Stir in flour, sour cream, and chives.

SPOON batter into ungreased miniature (1¾-inch) muffin pans, filling two-thirds full. Bake at 375° for 20 to 22 minutes. Remove muffins from pans immediately. Yield: 4 dozen.

Mary Ann Marks
Georgia Land
Medical Association of Georgia Alliance
Atlanta, Georgia

Peachy Tea

Spiced tea bags infuse sweet peach nectar with honey and cinnamon flavors, while fizzy club soda lends pizzazz to this refresher.

2½ cups peach nectar
2 honey- and cinnamon-flavored tea bags
1 (10-ounce) bottle club soda, chilled
Garnish: lemon wedges

COMBINE peach nectar and tea bags in a glass jar; cover tightly, and shake vigorously. Chill at least 8 hours.

REMOVE and discard tea bags. Add club soda to peach nectar mixture just before serving; stir gently. Serve over ice. Garnish, if desired. Yield: 4 cups.

NOTE: We tested this recipe using Lipton Soothing Moments honey- and cinnamon-flavored tea bags.

Mary Muresan
The Lincoln Park Historical Society Cooks!
Lincoln Park Historical Society
Lincoln Park, Michigan

Lowcountry Dining

Frogmore Stew, page 312

Menu

Serves 10 to 12

- Frogmore Stew *page 312*
- French bread
- Beer
- Benne Seed Wafers *page 383*
- Easy Homemade Vanilla Ice Cream *page 383*

𝓘n the Carolina Lowcountry, Frogmore Stew is a meal in itself with seafood, sausage, and assorted vegetables. Just add some crusty bread and a homemade dessert. Pack your drinks on ice in a galvanized tub for dining outdoors. If you're picnicking, the best way to enjoy the meal is to spread newspaper on the table; then friends and family can be as messy as they'd like, and cleanup's still a breeze. As for dessert, make the wafer cookies a day in advance, but churn the ice cream on the scene.

Benne Seed Wafers

Benne seed (sesame seed) wafers are traditional in Charleston, South Carolina.

½ cup sesame (benne) seeds
½ cup butter or margarine, softened
1 cup sugar
1 large egg
½ teaspoon vanilla extract
1¾ cups all-purpose flour
2 teaspoons baking powder
½ teaspoon baking soda
½ teaspoon salt

COOK sesame seeds in a heavy skillet over medium heat 5 minutes or until toasted, stirring often.

BEAT butter at medium speed with an electric mixer until creamy; gradually add sugar, beating well. Stir in sesame seeds, egg, and vanilla.

COMBINE flour and remaining 3 ingredients; stir into butter mixture. Cover dough, and chill at least 1 hour.

SHAPE dough into ½-inch balls; place on lightly greased baking sheets. Flatten to ¹⁄₁₆-inch thickness with floured fingers or a flat-bottomed glass.

BAKE at 325° for 10 minutes or until lightly browned. Transfer to wire racks to cool. Store in airtight containers. Yield: 10 dozen.

Clementa Florio
Wadmalaw Island, South Carolina

NOTE: Natural food stores sell benne (sesame) seeds in bulk.

Easy Homemade Vanilla Ice Cream

No ice cream is easier—no cooking or chilling in advance is required.

1 (14-ounce) can sweetened condensed milk
1 quart half-and-half
1 tablespoon vanilla extract

POUR all ingredients into freezer container of a 4-quart hand-turned or electric freezer. Freeze according to manufacturer's instructions.

PACK freezer with additional ice and rock salt, and let stand 1 hour before serving. Yield: 6 cups.

FRESH FRUIT ICE CREAM: Decrease half-and-half to 3 cups. Add 1 to 1½ cups fresh fruit puree, using fruits such as peaches, strawberries, bananas, or raspberries. Yield: 7 cups.

MINT CHOCOLATE CHIP ICE CREAM: Decrease half-and-half to 2 cups, and omit vanilla. Add 2 teaspoons peppermint extract, 2 cups whipping cream, and ¾ cup miniature semisweet chocolate morsels. Add a few drops of green food coloring, if desired. Yield: 7 cups.

Picnics, Potlucks & Prizewinners
Indiana 4-H Foundation
Indianapolis, Indiana

Caddy Creativity
Use a handsome wooden caddy to store mix-and-match flatware and napkins. Kitchenware such as these family heirlooms should be out on display—ready at a moment's notice and for everyone's enjoyment.

*Peach-Glazed
Virginia Ham*

Sunday Company

Menu

Serves 8

• Peach-Glazed Virginia Ham

• Baked Beans Quintet *page 386*

• Macaroni au Gratin
page 338

• Wilted Cabbage *page 282*

• Streusel Shortcake *page 386*

*I*n the South, the Sunday afternoon meal is often the biggest event of the week. Entrées and vegetables are served family style on the table, so everyone is sure to get his fill. This glazed ham feeds a crowd, and the side dishes complement it well. Be sure your guests save room for the ever-popular strawberry shortcake.

Peach-Glazed Virginia Ham

1 (8-pound) Virginia smoked fully cooked ham half (shank end)
½ cup peach preserves
1 tablespoon stone-ground mustard
¾ teaspoon hot sauce
⅛ teaspoon ground cloves
Peach-Corn Piccalilli
2 large ripe peaches, pitted and halved

SCORE fat on ham in a diamond design. Place ham, fat side up, on a rack in a roasting pan. Insert a meat thermometer, making sure it does not touch fat or bone. Bake, uncovered, at 325° for 1 hour and 45 minutes or until meat thermometer registers 135°.

COMBINE peach preserves and next 3 ingredients. Remove ham from oven, and brush with glaze. Bake 20 more minutes or until thermometer registers 140°.

PLACE ham on a platter. Spoon piccalilli into peach halves. Arrange peach halves on platter. Yield: 16 servings.

Peach-Corn Piccalilli

1 tablespoon vegetable oil
1 red bell pepper, chopped
2 green onions, sliced
1 (15¼-ounce) can whole kernel corn, drained
2 tablespoons brown sugar
2 tablespoons cider vinegar
1 teaspoon hot sauce
¼ teaspoon salt
1 large ripe peach, peeled and chopped

HEAT oil in a saucepan over medium heat until hot. Add pepper and onions; sauté 3 minutes. Add corn and next 4 ingredients; bring to a boil. Stir in peach. Cover, reduce heat, and simmer 5 minutes. Yield: 2¾ cups.

Shirley Downing
Our Favorite Recipes
Claremont Society for the Prevention of Cruelty to
Animals Serving Sullivan County
Claremont, New Hampshire

Baked Beans Quintet

Five types of beans make this just about the best-looking and best-tasting bean dish around.

6 bacon slices
1 cup chopped onion
1 garlic clove, minced
1 (16-ounce) can butter beans, drained
1 (15¼-ounce) can lima beans, drained
1 (15-ounce) can pork and beans
1 (15¼-ounce) can red kidney beans, drained
1 (19-ounce) can garbanzo beans, drained
¾ cup ketchup
½ cup molasses
⅓ cup firmly packed light brown sugar
1½ tablespoons Worcestershire sauce
1 tablespoon prepared mustard
½ teaspoon pepper

COOK bacon in a large skillet until crisp; remove bacon, reserving drippings in skillet. Crumble bacon, and set aside.

COOK onion and garlic in bacon drippings, stirring constantly, until tender; drain.

COMBINE bacon, onion mixture, butter beans, and remaining ingredients in a large bowl.

SPOON mixture into a lightly greased 2½-quart bean pot or baking dish. Cover and bake at 375° for 1 hour or until beans are tender. Yield: 8 servings.

Carolyne M. Carnevale
Ormond Beach, Florida

Streusel Shortcake

3 cups biscuit mix
⅔ cup milk
¼ cup butter or margarine, melted
½ cup firmly packed light brown sugar
½ cup chopped walnuts
¼ cup butter or margarine
1 (8-ounce) container frozen whipped topping, thawed
2 pints fresh strawberries, sliced

COMBINE first 3 ingredients in a large bowl; stir until a soft dough forms. Spread dough evenly in 2 greased 8-inch square pans.

COMBINE sugar and walnuts; cut in ¼ cup butter with a pastry blender until mixture is crumbly. Sprinkle nut mixture over dough.

BAKE, uncovered, at 400° for 18 minutes or until a wooden pick inserted in center comes out clean. Cool in pans on wire racks 10 minutes; remove from pans, and cool completely on wire racks.

PLACE 1 cake layer on a serving plate. Spread half of whipped topping over layer, and arrange half of sliced strawberries on top. Repeat procedure with remaining layer, whipped topping, and strawberries. Chill until ready to serve. Yield: 1 (8-inch) cake.

Pat Trzaskos
Just Desserts
Amsterdam Free Library
Amsterdam, New York

Streusel Shortcake

Mexican Fiesta

*K**ick off your next party with pitchers of slushy margaritas and colorful Fiesta Cheesecake. Serve the entrée enchiladas, loaded with chicken and spinach, alongside the chopped salad for a filling meal. But save a little room for a sweet chocolate finale—decadent Fudge Pie.*

Blue Margaritas

For leftover margarita mix, recap the can of mix, and store it in the freezer. Or go ahead and make a second batch of margaritas, and freeze it in a plastic pitcher. The alcohol keeps the drink from freezing solid; all it needs is a quick stir and it's ready to serve.

½ (10-ounce) can frozen margarita mix
¾ cup tequila
¼ cup blue curaçao
2 tablespoons lime juice

COMBINE all ingredients in a blender. Add ice to 5-cup level; process until smooth. Serve in glasses with salt-crusted rims, if desired. Yield: about 5 cups.

Apron Strings: Ties to the Southern Tradition of Cooking
The Junior League of Little Rock, Arkansas

Sin-Free Sangría

1 (12-ounce) can frozen white grape juice
  concentrate
1 (12-ounce) can frozen apple juice concentrate
1 (12-ounce) can frozen cranberry juice
  concentrate
1 (12-ounce) can frozen limeade concentrate
2 (2-liter) bottles lemon-lime carbonated beverage
Garnish: lemon or lime slices

COMBINE first 4 ingredients in a 6-quart punch bowl; beat with a wire whisk until smooth. Add lemon-lime beverage, stirring well. Garnish, if desired. Yield: 23 cups.

Stephanie Guidry
In the Breaking of Bread
Catholic Committee on Scouting and Camp Fire
Lake Charles, Louisiana

Fiesta Cheesecake

This Mexican cheesecake appetizer is destined to become your party favorite. It boasts an impressive wagon-wheel arrangement of toppings.

1½ cups finely crushed tortilla chips
¼ cup butter, melted
2¾ cups (11 ounces) shredded Monterey Jack cheese, divided
2 (8-ounce) packages cream cheese, softened
2 large eggs
1 (4.5-ounce) can chopped green chiles, drained
¼ teaspoon ground red pepper
1 (8-ounce) container sour cream
½ cup chopped green bell pepper
½ cup chopped yellow bell pepper
½ cup chopped red bell pepper
½ cup sliced green onions
½ cup seeded, chopped tomato
⅓ cup chopped ripe olives
Tortilla chips

COMBINE tortilla chips, butter, and ¼ cup Monterey Jack cheese; firmly press mixture in bottom of a lightly greased 9-inch springform pan. Bake at 325° for 15 minutes. Set aside.

BEAT cream cheese at medium speed with an electric mixer until creamy; add eggs, 1 at a time, beating after each addition. Stir in remaining 2½ cups Monterey Jack cheese, green chiles, and ground red pepper. Pour mixture into prepared pan.

BAKE, uncovered, at 325° for 30 minutes. Cool in pan on a wire rack 10 minutes. Carefully remove sides of springform pan; cool completely on wire rack. Spread sour cream on top of cheesecake. Cover and chill thoroughly.

ARRANGE green pepper and remaining ingredients over sour cream, spoke fashion, creating a wheel design. Serve with tortilla chips. Yield: 1 (9-inch) cheesecake (16 appetizer servings).

Sterling Service
The Dothan Service League
Dothan, Alabama

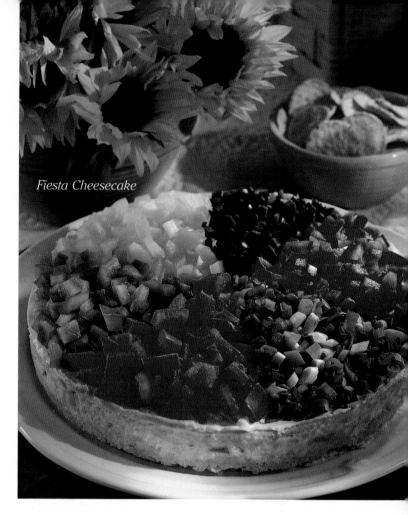

Fiesta Cheesecake

Green Enchiladas

Stuffed with chicken, spinach, chiles, and sour cream, these savory enchiladas received our highest rating. For extra zip, use Monterey Jack cheese with peppers. If you'd like to get a jump start on this recipe using leftover chicken, you'll need 6 cups shredded.

4 cups water
2 pounds skinned and boned chicken breast halves
1 medium onion, finely chopped
¼ cup butter or margarine
1 (10-ounce) package frozen chopped spinach, thawed and drained
1 (16-ounce) container sour cream
1 (8-ounce) container sour cream
1 (4.5-ounce) can chopped green chiles, drained
¾ cup milk
1 teaspoon ground cumin
¼ teaspoon salt
¼ teaspoon pepper
12 (6-inch) flour tortillas
1 (16-ounce) package Monterey Jack cheese, shredded

BRING water to a boil in a large nonstick skillet over medium heat. Add chicken; cover, reduce heat, and simmer 15 minutes or until tender. Remove chicken, and shred; set aside.

SAUTÉ onion in butter in a large skillet over medium-high heat until tender. Remove from heat; add spinach and next 7 ingredients, stirring well.

COMBINE half of spinach mixture with chicken; stir well. Spoon one-third cup chicken mixture evenly down center of each tortilla; roll up tortillas, jellyroll fashion. Place tortillas, seam side down, in 2 lightly greased 11- x 7-inch baking dishes. Sprinkle one-fourth of cheese evenly over each casserole. Spoon remaining spinach mixture over cheese; sprinkle with remaining cheese. Bake, uncovered, at 350° for 30 minutes. Yield: 6 servings.

Pamela Hamza
Somethin's Cookin' with Married Young Adults
Houston's First Baptist Church
Houston, Texas

Chopped Cilantro Salad

6 fresh tomatillos, husked
⅔ cup loosely packed fresh cilantro
6 tablespoons fresh lime juice (about 3 limes)
2 garlic cloves, halved
2 teaspoons chopped jalapeño pepper (about 1 small)
¾ cup vegetable oil
1 cup finely chopped green onions
1 teaspoon salt
½ teaspoon pepper
5 cups loosely packed, coarsely chopped Romaine lettuce
4 cups loosely packed, coarsely chopped cabbage
2 medium tomatoes, seeded and chopped (about 1½ cups)
1½ cups chopped, peeled jícama
1½ cups fresh corn kernels (about 3 ears)
½ cup crumbled feta cheese
2 ripe avocados, chopped
Tortilla chips (optional)

CUT tomatillos into quarters. Process tomatillos, cilantro, and next 3 ingredients in a blender 20 seconds or until pureed; pour into a medium bowl. Whisk together cilantro puree and oil; add green onions, salt, and pepper, stirring well.

STIR together Romaine lettuce and next 5 ingredients in a large bowl. Gently toss avocado and lettuce mixture with cilantro mixture. Serve with tortilla chips, if desired. Yield: 8 servings.

Sounds Delicious: The Flavor of Atlanta in Food & Music
Atlanta Symphony Orchestra
Atlanta, Georgia

Fudge Pie

Strong brewed coffee brings out the rich, fudgy flavor of this easy chocolate pie—it's a "must try." If you usually use instant coffee granules, use 2 teaspoons of the granules per 1 cup of water to make the strong coffee.

2 cups (12 ounces) semisweet chocolate morsels
¼ cup butter or margarine, softened
¾ cup firmly packed light brown sugar
3 large eggs
2 teaspoons strong brewed coffee
1 teaspoon vanilla extract
1½ cups chopped pecans, divided
¼ cup all-purpose flour
1 unbaked 9-inch pastry shell
1 cup whipping cream, whipped

PLACE chocolate morsels in top of a double boiler; bring water to a boil. Reduce heat to low; cook until chocolate melts, stirring occasionally. Set aside, and cool slightly.

BEAT butter at medium speed with an electric mixer until creamy; gradually add sugar, beating well. Add eggs, 1 at a time, beating after each addition. Stir in melted chocolate, coffee, and vanilla. Gradually add 1 cup pecans and flour, stirring well. Spoon chocolate mixture into pastry shell; sprinkle with remaining ½ cup pecans.

BAKE at 375° for 30 minutes or until a knife inserted in center of pie comes out almost clean. Cool completely on a wire rack. Serve pie with whipped cream. Yield: 1 (9-inch) pie.

Almost Chefs, A Cookbook for Kids
Palm Beach Guild for the Children's Home Society
West Palm Beach, Florida

Index

398   Index

Credits

Oxmoor House wishes to thank the following Birmingham, AL, merchants:

Attic Antiques

Hanna Antiques, Inc.

Henhouse Antiques

Tricia's Treasures

With special thanks to Cynthia Ann Briscoe, Cybil A. Brown, Donna Florio, Andria Scott Hurst, and Scott Jones for their well-coined words about some of our favorite Southern foods in "Taste of the South."

Metric Equivalents

The recipes that appear in this cookbook use the standard United States method for measuring liquid and dry or solid ingredients (teaspoons, tablespoons, and cups). The information on this chart is provided to help cooks outside the U.S. successfully use these recipes. All equivalents are approximate.

METRIC EQUIVALENTS FOR DIFFERENT TYPES OF INGREDIENTS

A standard cup measure of a dry or solid ingredient will vary in weight depending on the type of ingredient. A standard cup of liquid is the same volume for any type of liquid. Use the following chart when converting standard cup measures to grams (weight) or milliliters (volume).

Standard Cup	Fine Powder (ex. flour)	Grain (ex. rice)	Granular (ex. sugar)	Liquid Solids (ex. butter)	Liquid (ex. milk)
1	140 g	150 g	190 g	200 g	240 ml
¾	105 g	113 g	143 g	150 g	180 ml
⅔	93 g	100 g	125 g	133 g	160 ml
½	70 g	75 g	95 g	100 g	120 ml
⅓	47 g	50 g	63 g	67 g	80 ml
¼	35 g	38 g	48 g	50 g	60 ml
⅛	18 g	19 g	24 g	25 g	30 ml

USEFUL EQUIVALENTS FOR LIQUID INGREDIENTS BY VOLUME

¼ tsp					=	1 ml		
½ tsp					=	2 ml		
1 tsp					=	5 ml		
3 tsp	=	1 tbls		=	½ fl oz	=	15 ml	
		2 tbls	=	⅛ cup	=	1 fl oz	=	30 ml
		4 tbls	=	¼ cup	=	2 fl oz	=	60 ml
		5⅓ tbls	=	⅓ cup	=	3 fl oz	=	80 ml
		8 tbls	=	½ cup	=	4 fl oz	=	120 ml
		10⅔ tbls	=	⅔ cup	=	5 fl oz	=	160 ml
		12 tbls	=	¾ cup	=	6 fl oz	=	180 ml
		16 tbls	=	1 cup	=	8 fl oz	=	240 ml
		1 pt	=	2 cups	=	16 fl oz	=	480 ml
		1 qt	=	4 cups	=	32 fl oz	=	960 ml
						33 fl oz	=	1000 ml = 1 l

USEFUL EQUIVALENTS FOR DRY INGREDIENTS BY WEIGHT

(To convert ounces to grams, multiply the number of ounces by 30.)

1 oz	=	¹⁄₁₆ lb	=	30 g
4 oz	=	¼ lb	=	120 g
8 oz	=	½ lb	=	240 g
12 oz	=	¾ lb	=	360 g
16 oz	=	1 lb	=	480 g

USEFUL EQUIVALENTS FOR LENGTH

(To convert inches to centimeters, multiply the number of inches by 2.5.)

1 in					=	2.5 cm	
6 in	=	½ ft			=	15 cm	
12 in	=	1 ft			=	30 cm	
36 in	=	3 ft	=	1 yd	=	90 cm	
40 in					=	100 cm	= 1 m

USEFUL EQUIVALENTS FOR COOKING/OVEN TEMPERATURES

	Fahrenheit	Celsius	Gas Mark
Freeze Water	32° F	0° C	
Room Temperature	68° F	20° C	
Boil Water	212° F	100° C	
Bake	325° F	160° C	3
	350° F	180° C	4
	375° F	190° C	5
	400° F	200° C	6
	425° F	220° C	7
	450° F	230° C	8
Broil			Grill